THE BEAUTIFUL PEOPLE

MARYLIN BENDER

The Beautiful People

Coward-McCann, Inc.

NEW YORK

Grateful acknowledgment is made to the following for copyrighted material:

Excerpts from my own and others' reports in *The New York Times:* copyright 1960–1966 by The New York Times Company. Reprinted by permission.

Excerpts from *Newsweek:* copyright, Newsweek, Inc., June 1962, April 1966, May 1966, August 1966.

Permission was granted by the *World Journal Tribune* to reprint excerpts from Eugenia Sheppard's columns that were originally published in the New York *Herald Tribune.*

Permission was granted to quote from articles in *Women's Wear Daily.*

Excerpts from articles in *Vogue* and *Mademoiselle* are reprinted by permission of Condé Nast Publications, Inc.

Excerpts from the July 1963 and December 1966 issues of *Harper's Bazaar* are reprinted courtesy of *Harper's Bazaar.*

Edmundo Desnoes' article "Suzy Parker and the Third World," which is quoted in Chapter I, was translated and published in the July 1966 issue of *Atlas.*

Library of Congress Catalog

Card Number: 67–23143

To Selig and Jim,
Janet and Mike

CONTENTS

Illustrations will be found
following pages 96 and 192.

ACKNOWLEDGMENTS

THIS book owes its existence to the nearly eight years I have spent at *The New York Times* as a reporter assigned chiefly to fashion. Within the exact framework of that period, something radical happened to fashion and to the attitude of the press toward fashion and so-called fashionable people. This book would never have been written if I had not been a witness to the happening and if I had not had the invaluable assistance of many colleagues at *The New York Times,* as well as access to its excellent research facilities.

Yet this is not at all a *Times* book. The point of view, the opinions, and the conclusions drawn from the evidence are entirely my own.

Although I am grateful to countless friends and acquaintances for information and introductions, I am especially in the debt of Patricia Peterson, fashion editor of *The New York Times,* Mary Ann Crenshaw, Joan Cook, Thomasina Alexander, Shirley Baig, Thomas Hougland, and Gloria Emerson of the Paris bureau. Charlotte Curtis, the women's news editor, rates a vote of thanks.

Away from *The Times,* I was succored by Leila Gicquel in Paris and, on this side of the Atlantic, by Lina Boroznine. Vera Klippel transformed mountains of paper into an impressive-looking manuscript via her typewriter.

Last, but never least, I thank Ellis Amburn of Coward-McCann, Inc., who graciously shepherded this book to publication, and Paul Schoenstein, the incomparable city editor of the New York *Journal-American* (later managing editor of the *World Journal Tribune*), who made me a newspaperwoman once upon a time.

MARYLIN BENDER

May 1, 1967

THE BEAUTIFUL PEOPLE

O TEMPORA, O MORES!

ONCE upon a time—to be specific, it was in the sixth decade of the 20th century—there was a woman who had everything. She was so rich and so powerful that nothing and no one she set her fancy on could elude her grasp. This annoyed a lot of people, of course, so some of them took to muttering, "Who does she think she is, an Empress?" As a matter of fact, she did. And in a 20th-century manner of speaking, she was.

Now this Empress was just crazy about clothes and dressing up. She spent gobs of money on clothes and a great deal of time going places and inviting people to her palace so that she could show off her new clothes. She would never admit that was her purpose, showing off clothes. What she told everyone she was doing was opening art exhibitions, listening to symphonies, reading Urdu fairy tales to her children and standing decoratively in the palace doorway when her husband, the Emperor, came home after a hard day in the empire.

In short she was doing good works. And indeed, all over the empire art galleries opened and symphony halls were built and publishers published Urdu fables for mothers to read to toddlers, when they weren't decorating doorways to look like the palace. And the dressmakers were running around taking orders and shouting how *marvelous* the Empress looked and how *marvelous* everything was because everyone needed new clothes now to keep up with the Empress.

One day the Empress went shopping for a new hat. When she got to the millinery shop, the milliner was not there and the hat racks were empty. Suddenly there appeared a handsome young man attired like a courtier. He whisked up a piece of silk that was lying on a table, threw it on the Empress' head and tied it under her chin. "It's perfectly *marvelous,*" he cried. "You look just like a peasant." The Empress was puzzled but she took his word. The young man then explained that he was a new, double-purpose milliner. "Since it doesn't take me any time to make millinery these days, I also serve as an escort. I can accompany you on your cultural missions when the Emperor is busy with affairs of state."

The next day, the Empress awakened early and went to her favorite shoe store. No one was there to wait on her but loud, jumpy music was pouring out of the floor and down from the ceiling and through the walls. Finally, the Empress got up and started riffling through the piles of shoe boxes on the shelves. Seven-league boots popped out of one box. In the next were a pair of soft baby slippers. She went through 78 boxes until she came at last to a pair of heels attached to a pair of soles. She wiggled her feet into them with difficulty because whatever the upper parts of the shoes were made of (she couldn't see anything) felt stiff and slick. Then she looked down and it was like peering into a fishbowl. There were her feet exposed for all the world to see, large and bony with a bunion on the big right toe of one foot and a corn on the little left toe of the other. Just then, the door opened and the shoe salesman hurried in. "Aren't they perfectly *marvelous?*" he murmured breathlessly, his eyes falling to the Empress' metatarsal. And the Empress replied, "Yes, they are *marvelous.*"

The next morning, the Empress looked in her closet and counted up 176 little-nothing dresses. Mathematics had not been stressed in the finishing school the Empress had attended but by dint of much practice on her fingers, she was able to calculate that a little nothing multiplied 176 times equals a big nothing. So she went to her favorite dress shop to see if the latest styles from Paris had arrived. A crowd was milling around the shop shrieking and pushing. The Empress shoved her way to the center of the furor and found her dressmaker smoking a Danish cigar and doing the Watusi. Before she could say haute couture, eager hands were helping her out of what she had on and leading her up to a great mirror. The dressmaker handed her something that felt lighter than gossamer. It was so easy to slip into. There were no sleeves. They had gone out of style half a dozen years before. No waistline. That was *démodé* long ago. No darts around the bustline because the Empress didn't have one. No seams at all, as a matter of fact. "It's a perfectly *marvelous* design," said the dressmaker. The Empress arched her neck like a swan as she gazed at her reflection in the mirror.

"It's a look," said the milliner who had suddenly materialized behind her. "And I have brought you exactly the right accessory. Isn't it perfectly *marvelous?*" The Empress took the mask that the milliner held out to her and raised it to her face. She preened for a while. "It's perfectly *marvelous,*" she said at last, giving her arm to the milliner, and off they went to show off the Empress' new clothes as the crowd chanted m-a-r-v-e-l-o-u-s and a psychedelic electrician beamed a jumble of colored lights on her face and body.

And there, rather freely adapted from Hans Christian Andersen's fairy tale written more than 100 years ago, is what American fashion has been all about in the Sixties. It is a matter of more and more commotion about less and less dress. "The more minimal the art, the more maximum the explanation," Hilton Kramer, the art critic, has asserted. He might just as well have meant fashion.

Female clothing has been disappearing literally and philosophically. Today, a woman can cut a fashionable swath without owning a hat. Even weddings and funerals can be attended with a kerchief, a bit of lace or a ribbon on the head. Gloves and underwear are vestigial articles. To actually need a brassiere or a girdle is an admission of defeat. The dollies buy nightgowns to dance in. When Sylvia Pedlar, the perfect lady of the lingerie design field, started making nightgowns that looked like toga evening dresses, the die was cast.

Outergarments have been eroding one way or another to the point where James Laver, the British museum curator and fashion scholar, predicted they might recede to tunics. The tunics and tights of 15th-century youth, he suggested at the height of the mini-skirt crisis. Immediately, designers on both sides of the Atlantic began lengthening a few hemlines. They hedged their bets by dropping them on coats that went over short dresses and when women disapproved in 1966, they retreated until the fall of 1967.

Hemlines up, hemlines down. It makes no difference. Women's clothes will never regain what they have lost. Intricate construction, for one thing. The clothes of the future will be made by machines to an even greater degree than they are already, because there won't be any loving hands to sew them except at exorbitant prices and because a dress that is a work of art is a nuisance to a modern woman. The concoctions of the haute couture cannot be navigated without the assistance of a maid or a husband. Maids are practically extinct and the husbands who can afford such luxuries spend a lot of time in airplanes between places like Houston and Rabat. The sympathetic dry cleaner who has not abdicated to a relentless machine is a vanishing species.

The ultimate solution has already been sighted in the paper dress that costs so little it doesn't matter if it disintegrates after a wearing or two. No need to worry that such a democratic dress—one that absolutely anyone can afford—will destroy the fashion elite. The woman of wealth and social contacts can commission an artist to create a special paper dress for a special event, then donate it to a museum, provided the garment hasn't deteriorated on the dance floor.

In Andersen's satire "The Emperor's New Clothes," a monarch was swindled into parading in nonexistent raiment because he and his otherwise honest aides feared being called stupid and unworthy of high position. Only an innocent child could proclaim the obvious, that the Emperor had no clothes. Today, the hoax is staged on a mass level. There isn't much shock value in either nudity or the fact of a leader acting out falsehood to his public. The plotter and the victim conspire for mutual satisfaction. Often it is difficult to discern who is calling the tune.

In the Sixties, mass communications alter mass sensibilities and shape mass culture. At the halfway mark, the decade had been labeled the Pop Decade. *Newsweek,* in its issue of April 25, 1966, asserted that "in five years, pop has grown like The Blob, from a label for what appeared to be a minor phase in art history to a mass psyche."

Starting with 1960, the Pop Decade produced not only an art movement that anyone could understand (what is a painting of a Campbell's soup can but a painting of a Campbell's soup can?), a high society that anyone could enter (certified WASPhood is no longer the only key to the kingdom), superheroes who appeal to the widest possible audience (Batman became the passion of 5-year-old American nonreaders and 30-year-old French intellectuals) and an oracle, Marshall McLuhan, who spoke in aphorisms such as "the medium is the message." Even religion went pop, with frugging in the church aisle, clergymen who preached like advertising copywriters and one who even performed as a nightclub comic.

John F. Kennedy, an intellectual who looked like a movie star, was the first authentic pop politician to be elected President of the United States. The New Frontier that he staked out opened on a desert in which two movie actors, George Murphy and Ronald Reagan, rode off to the United States Senate and the California Governor's Mansion.

Not only candidates and elected officials but their wives were caught in the web of a total, easily merchandisable life style. Particularly on the distaff side, this entails an affirmative interest in fashion. Once Jacqueline Kennedy, the superconsumer of fashion, had reigned in the White House, no politician's wife could afford to be negligent about clothes. Try as she did not to tread in her predecessor's footsteps, Mrs. Lyndon B. Johnson was forced to smarten up. She was hounded by the propaganda organ of the garment industry, *Women's Wear Daily,* to disclose the names of the labels in her clothes. The reward for her cooperation was her nomination to the 1966 International Best-Dressed List, the industry's oldest continuous publicity stunt. Mrs. John V. Lindsay, wife of the Republican mayor of New York, is one of those Anglo-American, eastern-seaboard aristocrats who think that there are more important issues than fashion. She, too, learned to look at the name of the designer on her coat label *before* a reporter asked her. Mrs. Lindsay sometimes attended two fashion shows in one day after her husband declared his intention of doing something to enhance the reputation of Seventh Avenue as a world fashion center. He had no alternative after Jacob K. Javits, the Republican senator from New York (whose wife is a pop fashion celebrity), stage-managed the plot of having fashion included in the list of arts entitled to federal subsidy. Apparel and related fashion products constitute New York City's leading industry in terms of employment and an annual sales volume of more than $2 billion.

Congress supported the proposition that fashion was art just as the critics who dissented from pop art were lamenting "the transformation of art into fashion." Yves Saint Laurent, the aging prodigy of the Paris haute couture, confirmed that fashion had gone pop when he adorned jersey dresses with ruby lips and pink lady torsos and concealed a blinking light in the bouquet of the mannequin who modeled his fall 1966 bridal dress.

The goofiness of pop fashion has led many to compare the Sixties with the Twenties. The go-go girl is a niece of the flapper with her short, shapeless dress (although it is forgotten that auntie didn't really show much more than a flash of dimpled knee or rounded thigh) and her hedonistic emphasis on the present. Even the ideas that pop fashion takes from the underground movement in the arts (a movement fascinated with drugs and perversion) are rooted in dadaism and surrealism. Vulgarity and ostentation are being repeated. This is again the day of prodigals and emancipated women. And yet, those who participated in the fashion hijinks of the Twenties were fairly small segments of the population, the young, the rich and the Bohemian. The jazz age knew neither television nor swinging grandmothers. Fashion was not yet mass-marketed. Today the alienated hippie spits in the eye of the world and then he is invited to help launch a department store promotion.

The incredible fact about fashion in the Sixties is its pervasiveness. In mass culture, it ain't what you do but the way that you do it. Shadow is more real than substance. Fashion is a tool in the frantic effort to prove personal or commercial merit. Advertising agencies sell airplane tickets and dentures by changing what the stewardesses or the models in the television commercial wear. Social acceptance can be won with a wardrobe. Dowdiness can no longer be the ultimate snobbery. After the Mod revolt, *Tailor & Cutter* scored the British Royal Family for being fashion retrogrades. And in Greenwich, Conn., a New York suburb that is one of the last strongholds of the unreconstructed, Anglo-American landed gentry and its beige-faced, tweedy females, a teenager led her mother into the Janet Sloane shop and announced, "I want a horrid coat."

During a period of value adjustment, the dogma of the dressmaker and the fashion editor to the effect that clothes make the woman (and the man) became national faith. In the absence of mass culture, as in a Communist country, the dogma cannot be completely accepted. Take this comment by a young Polish fashion editor who introduced Mod-inspired "baby-baby" dresses and round-toed shoes to the gray Warsaw scene and who subscribed to American fashion magazines. "I don't like people who dress too well," she told Gloria Emerson of *The New York Times*. "I am suspicious that they are thinking of nothing else."

Nevertheless, fashion is a political barometer even under Communism. The teen-age Red Guards who became the harassing troops in the 1966 Chinese purge ordered women to cut off their long hair, straighten their permanent waves, slash their narrow trousers and destroy their pointed shoes. Bourgeois trends, these were called. Barbers were classified as "tools for fostering revisionism," a Peking expression for Soviet-brand Communism. In Prague, the most Western of Communist capitals, on the other hand, girls in mini-skirts and green eyelids attested to an opposite sort of anti-Russian sentiment. Kremlinologists detected in them evidence of the breakdown of Soviet influence in satellite countries. Yevgeny Yevtushenko, the Russian poet who is an international youth idol on the order of Senator Robert F. Kennedy, arrived in New York accompanied by a wife whose fringed hairdo, sashed leather coat and knee-high boots conveyed more than a thousand-word dissertation about how the wind is blowing for poets in general and Yevtushenko in particular in the Soviet Union.

In the United States, the cradle of mass culture, the intellectual no longer scorns fashion. He is free to embrace it. Since the Kennedys, wide-eyed beauties try to sound serious occasionally and Establishment scholars to act silly. Among other things, the party that Truman Capote gave in November 1966 for the 540 he deemed elite indicated that a former Harvard professor like Arthur Schlesinger, Jr., and a dress designer like Oscar de la Renta are now in the same peer group. The professor writes movie reviews for *Vogue*. As for Mr. Capote, he has raised the intellectual sights of at least two members of the Best-Dressed List, Mrs. William S. Paley and Princess Stanislas Radziwill. He introduced Mrs. Paley, the wife of the chairman of the Columbia Broadcasting System, to the writings of Marcel Proust.

Starting with the idols of mass culture, from politicians to millionaire authors and their chic friends, fashion permeates contemporary life, for better and for worse. "The din makes it impossible to differentiate the good from the bad, the worthwhile from the worthless," said Jonathan Miller, the British neurologist, comedian and stage and television director. He was referring to television, the most potent arm of pop culture, but his remark is applicable to fashion as well. Some of the consequences are salutary.

When Roman Catholic nuns asked leading couturiers—Christian Dior of Paris, Sybil Connolly of Dublin, Marguery Burke Bolhagen of Bergdorf Goodman in New York—to redesign their habits, they were complying with the Church's attempt to update itself. The synthetic fabrics, the streamlined silhouettes, the deflated headgear and the hemlines raised a few inches so as not to sweep the floor, did not mean that religious vocations were being abandoned. As nuns get behind the wheels of cars and the controls of medical missionary airplanes, as they march up slum staircases and in civil-rights demonstrations, they will not be impeded by the clothing designed 300 years ago. In the convent, fashion spells renewal.

When Radcliffe College emerges as a fashion fount, as well as a brain factory (boots, textured hosiery, smocked dresses and the manes that middle-aged adolescents and unskilled playgirls were to adopt later were accepted first in Cambridge, Mass.), the cause of female intellectualism is not harmed. One expects to find slim ankles, the scent of perfume and up-to-the-minute silhouettes in the groves of academe these days, even in the dean's office and the chemistry laboratory.

Not only cerebral types, but all kinds of people are more stylish and attractive. The point here is not that fashion is making them more superficial, but that it is erasing regional and social differences. Craig Claiborne, the culinary critic of *The New York Times,* pays no more attention to clothes than the next man and yet, he has mused, "It used to be that when girls came up from Indianola, Mississippi, they looked like hicks. They made their own dresses and did their own hair. Now they look marvelous and I meet them in the Ritz in Paris with the most elegant people and this is their sixth trip abroad." Mr. Claiborne spent his boyhood in Indianola, a tree-lined village as he recalls it. He was educated by the United States Navy, the University of Missouri and a hotel school in Lausanne, Switzerland. Now a constantly journeying resident of Manhattan, he cuts a natty figure in ready-made clothes that identify him as a citizen of the world.

Fashion, of course, is only a secondary cause of the new internationalism. Prime credit belongs to the jet airplane which went into wide-scale service in 1960, bringing Europe closer to New York and Chicago than a train trip from either of those cities to most domestic resorts. As fares have gone steadily down, hordes of ordinary citizens have been skipping over oceans. New York taxi drivers vacation in Rome. Crackerjack refrigerator salesmen from Michigan receive expense-paid trips to Hong Kong and Tokyo with their wives. In the Sixties, French couturiers trooped to America and returned bearing blue jeans, button-down shirts, flowered sheets and barbecue equipment. American designers went to Europe and when they came back to Seventh Avenue they dressed like week-ending Rothschilds in blazers with foulard neckwear. The most photographed mannequin in Europe in mid-1966 was Donyale Luna, a Negro girl from Detroit. The center of fashion has dispersed. Paris is no longer the single capital. On a basic silhouette initiated by Balenciaga in the mid-Fifties, designers work in Dublin with tweeds and knits, in Madrid with leather and beading, in Tokyo with sumptuous brocades. Malcolm Starr, a Seventh Avenue manufacturer operating out of Hong Kong, inundates Europe and the United States with beaded evening dresses. More important than silhouette today are idea and attitude. The two most far-reaching, functional beauty and youthful audacity, came out of Florence through Emilio Pucci and out of London through Mary Quant. The American cowboy with his narrow-hipped jeans and Seventh Avenue with its efficient mass production inspired fashion designers everywhere.

Travel has forged mass fashion, not only by homogenizing taste, but by the necessity for mobile clothes. A woman who travels must have a dress that suffers the crush of a suitcase without wrinkling, that will not bind her as she dozes in an airplane seat. Her coat must be able to deal with a succession of climates.

The descending cost of transportation and ascending affluence have both threatened and stimulated fashion. Once bitten by the travel bug, many would rather invest in a trip than a wardrobe. On the other hand, winter trips, summer trips and week-end trips require special clothing, particularly if sports are part of the junket. Designers and merchants have had to modify their seasonal thinking. The Easter coat is dead. The coat that can travel six months of the year on several continents is alive and kicking. There is no week on the calendar when customers fail to ask for bathing suits.

The makers and sellers of the most innocuous clothes will travel any distance to have them photographed against the most alluring backdrops because they have found that an advertising photograph or store window beckoning to Pago-Pago or Amman will even prompt a purchase from a housewife who is contemplating a visit to her sister in Minneapolis. The word "travel" is the subliminal goad of the Sixties. Unfortunately, the fashion industry exercises little discretion or sensitivity when it tries to whet jaded consumer appetites. In an article entitled "Suzy Parker and the Third World," a Cuban writer, Edmundo

Desnoes, protested the fashion magazines' fondness for using under-developed countries as props for luxury merchandise.

The disdain and ridicule of capitalist countries toward the Third World reached its peak in photographs that appeared in *Harper's Bazaar* using the African continent to launch the latest exotic furs, hats and stockings. In one picture two black faces, sad in their humiliation, are used to show off a red shoe of either crocodile or snake skin. Those solemn Negroes have the moral right to decapitate any white woman who wears those shoes.

There is elegance and exoticism in all these photographs, true, but there is also cruelty. The cruelty that uses men as decorative elements. Here there is no deception, nothing like the humanitarian mask the great colonizing powers wore in Africa; this photo by Gordon Parks expresses the true relation that exists between victimizer and victim; it shows the disdain and exploitation of the colonizer and the humiliation and silent hatred in the guts of the colonized. It is more eloquent than any political pamphlet.

As an avowed *Fidelista,* Mr. Desnoes was predictably dense about fashion's motives which are always politically disengaged. In 1966 and 1967, fashion went on an African safari from the kingdom of Morocco (significant for the burnoose and the caftan) to Johannesburg, which was put on the map regardless of the question of apartheid when Mary McFadden, the society girl who did publicity for Dior-New York, married a diamond executive and moved there. Wild colors, animal jewelry, Congolese hairdos, bush jackets and the pointed breasts of primitive sculptures spread like brushfire in New York and Paris collections. The human props that troubled Mr. Desnoes were a pictorial cliché. Photographers who could not afford Africa found dark-skinned models in the Caribbean.

The urgency of the fashion photographer's quest for novelty is always misunderstood by outsiders, be they Marxists or capitalists. In 1962, many of the latter went into a flap when high-fashion cameramen were taking so-called thalidomide pictures. They were using tricks of distortion that made the mannequins appear to have oversized heads and atrophied limbs just at the time when newspapers and magazines were reporting on an epidemic of deformed babies born to women who had taken a new tranquilizer during pregnancy. The coincidence of photographic style and tragic news event seemed like a terribly sick joke to some. But others reason that women are prepared to accept absurd fashion because they are conditioned by black humor in night-clubs and books, instructed in the absurdity of life by the theater and even by the sight of a lunatic killing a Presidential assassin before a nation-wide television audience. If human existence is a cosmic joke, why endure it in solemn apparel?

One of the key differences between pop fashion of the Sixties and everything that preceded it is the humor. Fashion has always seemed funny in retrospect. Everyone laughed at the hobbleskirts and the chemises, the handlebar moustaches and the laden-down millinery, the bee-stung lips and suits with padded shoulders when they looked at them ten years later in the family photograph album. But the willingness to be laughed at on the spot, to clown while dressing up, used to go against the feminine grain.

Peggy Moffitt, sometime actress and favorite model of America's most experimental designer, Rudi Gernreich, explained the modern attitude in the July 20, 1966, issue of *Queen.* "If you are serious about fashion, you don't take it seriously," said Miss Moffitt, who was photographed in a mini-dress of clashing-colored geometrics and mesh stockings. There was a black triangle under the one eye visible beneath her geometric, Vidal Sassoon hairdo. "I don't think fashion is a joke, but real fashion must have wit. It has to be exaggerated—you can't modify something that's already modified—later it becomes watered down, everybody understands it and finally it's passé."

The purpose of fashion used to be dissimulation, the pretense that women were pretty, had perfect bodies, romantic spirits and that they were essentially helpless. Pop fashion, like pop art, lays the object on the line. Fatty knees, wrinkled elbows, ruthless natures are exposed for all to see. Outrageous fashion externalizes the wearer's anxiety. If a girl is young and properly proportioned, the minimal clothes and eccentric accessories may be vastly becoming. If she's not, like most of the population, she has three choices. She can clutch at the past and be considered a freak. She can follow the counsel of *Vogue,* shrinking her body to fit skimp dresses, taking pills and undergoing cosmetic surgery, painting herself like a cockatoo or a beast of the jungle. Or she can take the constructive accomplishments of modern fashion, the comfort and the ease, and censor the rest.

"We have edited out the vulgar," said Mildred Custin, the president of Bonwit Teller, in the spring of 1966, after viewing the designer showings on both sides of the Atlantic. She admitted that, for the first time, tastelessness was a factor to reckon with in the so-called better fashion houses of Paris and Seventh Avenue. That season was just the beginning. Standards of propriety and intelligence have been plummeting ever since.

In fashion, as in every other phase of the overpermissive pop environment, the challenge of personal censorship is constant. How far should you go? If you're 40, do you shake yourself to pieces in a discothèque? Do you take a trip with LSD or any of the other brands of horizon-wideners that the fashion *cognoscenti* gossip about over the $7.25 luncheon at La Grenouille? Do you buy a silver motorcycle suit with an industrial zipper? Do you walk out on the toilet-bowl sequence in the film that a pop art, fashion and social leader shows at her party? Do you agree with the theory of inevitability stated by Jacqueline Susann, author of *Valley of the Dolls,* the best-selling novel about pill takers? "I'm a realist," she told a *Life* interviewer. "I think we have to accept the fact that one of these days everybody will have their face lifted just like everybody now goes to the beauty parlor. Women can all have bazooms [*sic*] whatever size they want, and wigs, and contact lenses in different colors, and no change of life because of these estrogen injections you can take to keep your uterus from shriveling to the size of a walnut by the time you're 75, the way it does now. What's wrong with that?"

Those are the questions that pop fashion poses. They don't all have to do strictly with clothes. Fashion is less and less body covering and more and more extrinsic matter. Clothes are only a fraction of what makes a female fashionable today. It's her figure, her hairdo, her morality and her philosophy of life. To be in fashion means to try very hard to make the clock stand still. Arrested development is the essential of pop fashion.

In the Sixties, the fashion industry allowed itself to be tyrannized by youth. It was as if the kindergarten teachers had abdicated in favor of the student body. Elegance was mortally wounded because too many fashion editors and merchants lacked the courage and ingenuity to prevent anarchy and because of a mindless and cynical conviction that nonsense would make the cash registers jingle. They and their associates in advertising and public relations who buzzed around the mass culture honeypot were obsessed by the statistic that almost half the population is under 25 years old. The implications of a young nation, reared in prosperity and installment buying, expecting to earn more, spend more and rule the roost, were exaggerated by the pop culturists and anyone who hoped to win votes to make money. If Senator Robert F. Kennedy can brazenly woo the adolescents who will vote in the Presidential election of 1972, it may be too much to expect the fashion industry to argue the virtues of maturity. Yet youngsters were contemptuous of adults who followed their lead. Sane women protested that they were being rejected by the fashion industry. For the most part, they were.

In this decade, fashion disregarded the law of gravity. It ceased to filter down from the top—from the haut couturiers and the women of educated taste whom they dressed—to the masses. It ascended from the populace to the plutocrats. It bubbled up from teenagers, from the underground and outsider culture, from designers never admitted to the fashion Establishment. Economics and the swift pace of modern life call for mass fashion. The Paris couturiers and the American high fashion designers who traditionally set styles might have answered the demand without betraying that other half of the population. Instead, too many of them irresponsibly started producing baby dresses and bloomers. They made fools of their customers and didn't give the kids much to look forward to when they grew up.

Consider what has happened in fashion magazine publishing. When the news of fashion is being made by and for the age group that subscribes to *Mademoiselle, Glamour, Seventeen* and *Elle,* their French equivalent that forcefully promoted the manufacture of ready-to-wear and gloated over the decline of the haute couture, where do *Vogue,* the bible of American elegance, and its rival, *Harper's Bazaar,* go? They raid the territory of their younger sisters. That's where the action is. That's where the money is, they have decided. *Glamour,* which tells more than one million readers between 18 and 30 how to walk in fashion and beauty, has a phenomenal growth record. *Mademoiselle* serves a profitable diet of fashion, beauty and literature to an audience of 18- to 25-year-olds. Both magazines belong to the Condé Nast publishing empire, of which *Vogue* is the flagship.

As soon as Diana Vreeland, generator of pizzaz and unrivaled *doyenne* of the American fashion mystique, took editorial command of the magazine in the spring of 1962, *Vogue* became skittish and ebullient. It shed its air of haughty elegance just as its editor-in-chief cast off the snood and the blue hair rinse that had been her trademark. Bobbed and slightly pompadoured, her hair turned the color of black lacquer. According to *Vogue,* to go gray is to commit venial sin. By coincidence, beauty advertising accounts for one-quarter of the magazine's advertising revenue. The cover of the June 1966 issue summed up the Vreeland policy. It showed Jean Shrimpton, the English Mod model, in a Dynel wig cut like a thatched roof, with enormous colored plastic wedges dangling from her ears. To the left of the photograph was a teaser for an article inside the magazine: CHARTED FOR THE FIRST TIME: WHICH HORMONES TO TAKE WHEN TO BE FEMININE FOR LIFE. TIMETABLE FOR WOMEN AGES 17 TO 85 BY THE FAMOUS DR. ROBERT A. WILSON.

That seems to cover everyone including the readers of *Seventeen,* an ad-packed publication that is the property of the Annenberg publishing network. Asked to identify the composite reader to whom *Vogue* is addressed (since trying to deduce the information from the magazine is impossible), S. I. Newhouse, Jr., *Vogue's* publisher, replied, "She's 33 years old, that's her median age, but that's because there's no great separation between the so-called young woman and the mature woman" (Mr. Newhouse's tiny, blond mother, Mitzi E. Newhouse, a Condé Nast director, looks more like a superchic girl doll than a matriarch whose oldest grandchild is a teenager.)

Harper's Bazaar stirred controversy and vexed some of its advertisers with its issue of April 1965 which purported to show "What's Happening." Along with a glossary of in-most lingo, the magazine ran photographs of the Beatles, underground film-makers, pop artists and girlish astronauts encased in silver tights and plastic helmets or "frugging the fat away" in "tough little jerseys" by Rudi Gernreich. The issue was edited and produced by Richard Avedon, the photographer, as a celebration of his 20th anniversary with the magazine. He subsequently departed to join Mrs. Vreeland, herself a *Bazaar* alumna, at *Vogue.* William M. Fine, publisher of *Harper's Bazaar,* termed the experiment a "creative masterpiece and a commercial compromise." A year later, he promised that the magazine would henceforth serve "the 50 per cent over 25." Evidently, communications broke down between his office and the editorial floor.

Neither *Vogue* nor *Harper's Bazaar* aggressively attempt to increase their circulation, which has hovered around 400,000 for years. Advertising rates are based on circulation and if they went any higher (in 1966 a one-page advertisement in color in *Vogue* cost $6,500), many of their specialty store and manufacturer advertisers could not afford to advertise. The magazines' goal is to sell advertising with costs split among such giants as a fiber producer that wants to keep its name in front of the public and the industry, a movie company, and a manufacturer who is really interested in appealing to store buyers. None of these paying customers is terribly concerned if the woman reading *Vogue* or *Harper's Bazaar* under the hair dryer feels left out of the dizzy editorial message. They see that their advertisements are literal and reasonable. Besides, the store buyers and The Beautiful People will not cancel their subscriptions. There is no other place for them to go for high-fashion information.

Women all over the world complain that fashion is directed to and dictated by the young. But so is the music, and the dancing, the automobiles and the television shows. The "total entertainment" developed by Murray the K, the disc jockey, as if to illustrate the McLuhan message, had teenagers dancing, looking at movies and slides, being assaulted by magnified sounds and flashing lights, and knowing themselves to be the focal point of the universe. Half a year later, the environmental theory had been switched on to sell fashion in stores. It assured the store executives that they were "contemporary" but it didn't make the salesgirls any more helpful than they had been before.

"Youth has become a class," said Roger Vadim, who had been an obscure French film director until he discovered the commercial possibilities of having his first wife, Brigitte Bardot, take her clothes off in front of the camera. "There used to be the young working class, the young middle class; now those who are young recognize each other. Youth is a rallying sign, a secret signal. I have the feeling of being in direct contact with the young generation," said Mr. Vadim, who makes it a rule to marry younger women even as he marches into middle age.

A lot of people want to be in contact, too. Responding to the article on pop culture in *Newsweek,* a reader from Stamford, Conn., Mrs. Diane Funkhouser, sent a letter to the editor:

> A good many devotees of pop culture, myself included, were born during the Depression, our parents fought the second world war, we spent our teen years trussed up in ankle-length skirts and boned waist-cinchers, had our husbands and sweethearts in

Korea and finally emerged to be again bound by setting up housekeeping and raising a family.

Now we are at last free to have fun, risking censure by our children and analysis by the professionals, while in reality we are
only enjoying the childhood we never had. Zowie!

And so youth marches on, the speed and thoroughness of its take-
over varying from country to country. Youth worship and all of
the other ingredients of pop culture are American exports that
were embellished abroad and sent back in more virulent form, sometimes verging on obscenity. Think of Elvis Presley and the Beatles.
Think of blue jeans and Carnaby Street. Think of the youthful American grandmother. She impressed Europeans almost as much as the
skyscraper. But now at the pinnacles of American fashion society,
she is too often seen as a hag in childish clothes designed in Chelsea
and the Rue de Sèvres.

It was England that asserted the primacy of youth in fashion. And
it was there that the fashion explosion was most relevant to what was
happening in the nation as a whole. Bled white in two world wars,
no longer nourished by its colonial empire, Britain was feeling tremors
in its rigid class structure. The left-outs were demanding social and
economic opportunity. The angry young men of the Fifties railed
against the Establishment, whose fallibility was irreparably exposed
in the Suez disaster of 1956. The ebullient young men and women of
the Sixties created their own style and structure. If it seemed primarily
a materialistic, sensual and ephemeral style, it was at least a positive
one.

In the Sixties, talent came out of downcast regions like the provinces and the East End slums of London and channeled itself into
fashion, photography, films and popular entertainment. Other areas
were closed to men and women with the wrong accent and meager
education. These outsiders were joined by Oxford gentlemen and restless aristocrats who appreciated and mastered American techniques of
mass merchandising, advertising and publicity. Together they molded
a pop culture for a hungry, insistent mass market.

A new economic force was exerting pressure. Half of Britain's youth
had been leaving school at the earliest permissible age of 15 and taking jobs. They didn't listen to what Mum said. They didn't aspire to
what Mum had wanted. By 1966, they were spending about $100 mil-

lion a year and establishing identities for themselves with exuberant clothing, records, motorcycles and frenetic dancing. "Decent clothes ... a car, but what's it all about?" asks Michael Caine at the end of the film *Alfie,* in which he portrays a heartless Cockney cad. A jack-of-all-trades and sometime chauffeur, Alfie dresses to the nines. He marches out of his dingy pad in a navy blazer and regimental tie, once the uniform of the gentleman of leisure. His wardrobe is Alfie's instrument of social protest. Others of his station will wrest themselves upward by dint of education and toil as it is becoming possible to do in England now. But there were enough Alfies in the Sixties, over-spending on themselves in order to prove their right to be somebodies. They may have been exploited by merchants who did not give them value, but they caused an amateur, improvised revolution in retailing and a classless fashion.

Mod (meaning modern youth) designers and the cardboard and tinfoil shops with odd names like Countdown, Hung on You and Top Gear on the Kings Road and Carnaby Street made London a women's fashion capital as well as a male center quite apart from the snooty tailors of Savile Row. During a single assault on America, which a group of British manufacturers of effervescent clothes made in the fall of 1965 on the *Queen Elizabeth,* close to $1 million in orders were taken. "The impact of the young gave everybody a shot in the arm. They revitalized all the other phases of fashion," acknowledged Edward Rayne, the British shoe manufacturer (who is part owner of the Delman salons in the United States as well as Queen Elizabeth's shoe-maker) and a ringleader of the London haute couture. The British needed a shock.

The mannerly arrogance of Savile Row and Bond Street had its counterpart in heavy industry. British salesmanship had been a take-it-or-leave-it affair. The look-down-the-nose etiquette of the bespoke tailor, the automobile salesman and the navy-caped nanny was the icing on a stale cake. Effective as supercilious understatement may have been in cowing insecure Americans, it also cloaked inflexibility, antiquated and economically wasteful methods. The striking characteristic of the new young hustlers, whether they speak Cockney or Oxbridge, whether they are selling pop fashion, hairdressing, marketing services, films or other visual arts and crafts, is their genial diligence. They are eager, agreeable and efficient.

In 1966, Mary Quant, the mother of Mod fashion and the mini-skirt, was awarded the Order of the British Empire. A year before, Queen Elizabeth had conferred it on the Beatles. The O.B.E. is a pat on the head for commercial service rendered, a belated mark of respectability and a kick upstairs. It is one of those hollow honors that impresses gullible outsiders like American merchants and mass media. Miss Quant went up to Buckingham Palace to be invested, wearing a mini-skirt that displayed seven inches of thigh and jibing nicely with the "swinging London" delusion of the foreign press. Led off by American weekly news magazines, the reporters and writers from the United States and the European continent had rushed to London to ogle the leggy beauties, to meet the pop aristocracy of fashion designers, models, photographers and publicists and to gambol in the trattorias, the discothèques and the gambling clubs. The pop culture makers of Britain used the American tricks of mass communication they had recently learned to hornswoggle their teachers. The publicity coincided with the austerity measures that the government could no longer postpone and which focused attention on the gravity of Britain's financial plight. The cries of anguish went up from those who preferred that their country be extolled for diplomacy, finance and the art of governing rather than for ostentatious clothes and hirsute narcissists. The mini-skirt was blamed for shrinking England.

But the irate critics had been gulled by publicity, too. England is acutely ill, but Mod fashion is a hopeful symptom of health and self-reliance. The mini-skirt brought hard currency from tourists and buyers into the country, fueled a domestic consumer market and indicated a loosening of lower- and middle-class inhibitions about sex and other sensual delights.

British Mod fashion is sexy as well as democratic just as the folk idols of British pop culture are aggressively heterosexual slum boys. Terence Stamp, who grew up in Cable Street on the East End, and Michael Caine, the son of a Billingsgate fish market porter and a charwoman, embodied the cad hero in British films. The romantic involvements of David Bailey, the Cockney fashion photographer, with Jean Shrimpton, the Mod model, and then with Catherine Deneuve, the French actress whom he married after she bore a son to Roger Vadim, added a dimension that previous practitioners of his craft like Cecil Beaton could not supply. British elegance had been effete (if not noticeably homosexual) and socially discriminating. Not that the Mods are intolerant of homosexuality. Some of the most liberal thinking about sex is endorsed by British fashion and society magazines like *Queen,* which once dressed a male model in girl's clothing and revealed the switch only after several pages of photographs. Yet the essence of the London Look or Mod fashion or whatever one calls the British style of the Sixties is boy-girl. Even when the boy's hair is longer than the girl's and they both are wearing trousers.

In the second half of the Sixties, English films were reassessing the pop aristocracy. Disillusionment lurked underneath the cool. The glorious model girls like Julie Christie's *Darling* were wanton and alienated. Ugly ducklings like Lynn Redgrave's *Georgy Girl* and Rita Tushingham's Nancy in *The Knack* turn out to be the heroines. The photographer in Antonioni's Mod-set film *Blow-Up* searches desperately for reality. Similarly, the Mod fashion designers entered the foyer of middle age and began to concern themselves with quality production and quieter styling. In the long run, they will have set a record of substantial achievement.

In England, repressed youth and the working classes blew the lid off the pressure cooker. In France, the *pot-au-feu* simmered in the kettle. In 1965, half of the population of 49 million was under 33. A market research organization surveyed the incomes and spending habits of the 15- to 24-year-old segment. The majority had jobs (compulsory schooling ended at 14 although that age limit is being extended to 16 as it is in Britain) and, like their English contemporaries, spent most of their earnings on clothes, pop records and releasing their energies on the dance floor. The same was true of the middle-class and rich kids who stayed in school, destined to become France's cultural and economic elite. The teen-age boys affected English dandyism and the teen-age girls pied-pipered their mothers to the boutiques, those cradles of fashion that usurped the authority of the haute couture in the Sixties.

French youth did not have to stage a sensual revolt, however. Sex, gastronomy and fashion had high priority in French culture. Young Frenchmen need to be liberated from hoary economic and political tradition. While President de Gaulle fanned the flames of nationalism and nursed his grandeur complex, they showed signs of thinking as integrated Europeans and supranationalists. The Frenchmen who will lead in the Seventies will be cool, educated, international technocrats. But in the Sixties, France was economically underdeveloped, politically and culturally stagnant. Like the United States in the Fifties, the country was biding its time, recovering from war. Under the benevolent autocracy of de Gaulle, Frenchmen concentrated on materialism and stability. One of the most creative of people was satisfied with imitative mediocrity. French pop culture was borrowed from abroad. The French went on a binge of ketchup and chilled Beaujolais, mock-American drugstores, Humphrey Bogart and Jerry Lewis, the Wild West, Tiffany lamps, Batman, jeans and Scottish kilts. Antoine, the singer with the shoulder-length hair and a degree from L'École Centrale, France's highest engineering school, was an atrocious mutation of the Beatles and Bob Dylan. The mini-jupe never got as far off the ground as the mini-skirt, but French girls instinctively took to shrinking their sweaters.

The state of French fashion has its parallel in the arts. The modern art movement left France and crossed the Atlantic in the Forties. In drama, the ferment of the Fifties subsided. Ionesco, Beckett and Genet had no successors. The movies were the only source of artistic excitement. In fashion, the haute couture underwent the crisis of the fine arts. The big three, Balenciaga, Givenchy and Chanel, rehashed their themes of the previous decade. The three most alert couturiers, Pierre Cardin, Yves Saint Laurent and André Courrèges, looked for survival in mass production. The vitality in French fashion came from young ready-to-wear designers. Chiefly warm-blooded women and men (hitherto unfamiliar types on the high fashion scene), they try to relate clothes to contemporary life rather than to vanishing grandeur. They are preoccupied with using the techniques and materials of industrial technology to create popular fashion rather than costly works of art for a few.

French ready-to-wear manufacturing is growing at a phenomenal rate, but it still produces inefficiently. Like other industries, it is hampered by a lack of capital and sufficient markets, as well as a small-shopkeeper mentality. Pop fashion—in the healthy sense which means the distribution of style at popular levels—is retarded in France. There is more fashion in an Irish village than in a working class district of Paris. Inexpensive French clothes are often as badly made and as out-of-date as the products of the Soviet bloc. As for some of the merchandise in the chic Paris boutiques, it would never pass muster in Omaha. At no level is the workmanship in mass-produced French apparel commensurate with price.

No wonder the French fashion industry flirts with America. It needs the naïve American tourist who loses all perspective when offered a French label and the American manufacturer who will pay the French designer for his idea (original or not) and produce it far more efficiently and profitably than could be done in France.

The United States is the birthplace of democratic fashion, the land where the stenographer and the shopgirl are the style equals of the bosses' wives. What the English have just achieved by rebellion and what the French are moving toward at a slower pace, Americans have had for 30 years or more. The best fashion buys in the world, from the standpoint of a combination of style, quality and price, are still to be found here. American buyers scour the world so that their stores can sell a staggering variety of international merchandise. The technical and financial prowess of the American manufacturer of inexpensive to moderately priced apparel is constantly improving. Jonathan Logan, the largest manufacturer of women's apparel, racked up sales of $200 million in 1966. With 23 divisions, Logan caters to almost everyone from tot to the matron who doesn't care to spend more than $15 to $80 for a dress.

Too many manufacturers lose sight of the fact, however, that Americans don't have to overspend on clothing to prove a point and that they are conditioned to receiving value for their fashion dollar. The merchandise must fit and it must stand up against a certain amount of wear and tear. If it is supposed to be a folly or a gag, then it must be cheap. Jokes do not bear repeating. The most expensive, ready-made American clothes are as well put together as the made-to-order creations of the Paris couturiers and they cost about the same, but they only apply to a sliver of the population. It is in the wide range of middle-class, middlebrow fashion that Seventh Avenue is overpricing itself. Some manufacturers may attribute it to labor costs but the reason is more often psychological. The American fashion industry's continuing and massive inferiority complex works against the consumer. Seventh Avenue has always been filled with people who are ashamed of their origins and their occupation. Their obsessions are making American fashion pretentious and overpriced. A young designer comes out of hicksville with imaginative ideas that are manufactured to sell at reasonable prices. He is acclaimed. His prices soar with his sense of self-importance. He makes store presidents and fashion editors put on black tie and evening dresses to attend the showing of his collection. He prefers to be called an art collector, a country squire, an international playboy, an arbiter of taste, anything but a dress designer or manufacturer. As he gets more pompous, so do his clothes. He competes with other designers and manufacturers for the prestige of a higher price range. The stores have supported the inflation of the designer's image because they think it will help sell clothes. If women learn designers' names and identify with designer-celebrities, they will spend more, the reasoning goes. Up to a point.

Seventh Avenue is bemused by the pronouncements of American affluence. An economics professor estimated the wealth of the United States at $2.2 trillion in 1964. The Internal Revenue Service asserted that 371 taxpayers reported taxable income of more than $1 million a year in 1963. By another reckoning, there were 90,000 millionaires in the country in 1965, and in the preceding decade, 5,000 new millionaires were added every year.

But most new millionaires are no kin to the lavish-handed pirates of yore. They don't live in baronial splendor. Their money is made in intricate financial manipulations and at heart they are just imaginative bookkeepers. Their wives are not likely to show off with flashy clothes either. As for the female Brahmins, they are not about to discard the Puritan ethic at this date. Their status derives from being benefactors, not fashion plates.

Stepping down a level to the managerial class, there is the corporation executive who may end up a millionaire when he cashes in his stock options; even if he doesn't, he has an agreeable standard of living with his salary, expense account and fringe benefits. His wife tends to be trim, youthful, compulsively self-improving and absorbed in her husband, their three or more children and their two or more homes. Despite what *Vogue* preaches, she tends toward subdued hairdos and moderate quantities of rather restrained clothes.

Descend then to lower scales of affluence. One-fourth of the nation's families had earnings of $10,000 or more in 1965 and accounted for about half of the total buying power. The fastest growing age group are the 20- to 24-year-olds. They go to college and to work and get married. Their money is spent on advanced education, automobiles and durable goods to establish new homes. Even with the next older groups, from well-to-do professional to comfortable blue-collar man, it's certain that fashion and clothes are not their chief interest.

Although the United States is the most consumer-oriented nation in the world, there is fierce competition for the affluent American's dollar from other sectors than fashion. Americans spend about $18 billion a year on women's and children's apparel. But they also want better houses, then second houses, two cars in every garage and an endless variety of equipment for their increasing hours of leisure, from motor boats to stereo sets. With a sense of owning property comes the temptation to invest money in the stock market. Twenty million Americans, 9,430,000 of them women, hold shares in public corporations. Travel and art sing siren songs to even the most fashion-conscious. In 1965, Americans spent some $5 billion on travel. Parke-Bernet, the New York auction gallery, grossed $23 million in sales of antiques and paintings in the 1965-66 season, an increase of one-third over the previous season. *Fortune* magazine has estimated the world sales of fine arts and antiques at $10 billion a year.

Education, the most important lever of upward mobility for Americans, takes a bigger bite out of family budgets each year. The average cost of a year's tuition, room and board for a state resident at a public university was $986 in 1966-67, $2,261 at a private men's college.

To counter this competition, the American fashion industry wages an insidious campaign to make fashion first among consumer priorities and national values. The shock troops are drawn from the Seventh Avenue manufacturers, the New York publicists and the press. They, in turn, have seized upon a group of willing exhibitionists from whom they have tried to create the new idols of materialist America.

These negative heroines, the superconsumers of fashion, serve a double purpose. Not only do they set an example of product use, but they give the fashion industry what it has never had but has always yearned for, social acceptability. Hand in hand, the woman who wears the dress and the man who designs it have become fashion celebrities and leaders of the new pop society.

The game is as old as dominoes but in the Sixties it is played at a frantic tempo. The less substance the designers have to offer in clothes and the less need that men and women have for new clothes, the more furiously does the fashion industry create its ersatz personalities and the pseudo-occasions at which their wares can be paraded.

The climate of the Pop Decade made it possible. In Jacqueline Kennedy, fashion had its first superconsuming goddess enthroned in the White House. John Fairchild, the garment trade newspaper publisher whose arrival at the editorial front coincided with Mrs. Kennedy's national elevation in 1960, and Eugenia Sheppard, the syndicated fashion columnist, were the chief propagandists of fashion overconsumption. In the Fifties, the nation had been outraged at a Cabinet member's suggestion that what was good for General Motors was good for the country. Automobiles, however, are the No. 1 industry. Apparel is ninth, but in the Sixties, it demands first claim on public attention.

Curiously, as British and French fashion are sparked by iconoclasts, the American fashion industry scrambles for pedestals. Seventh Avenue and the fashion press are engaged in worshiping the rich and aping the manners and style of the landed gentry. Concurrently, as British and French fashion are infiltrated by he-men and she-women, American fashion turns increasingly homosexual. And the public senses it. "Fashion is being taken over by the pansy boys. We're being made to look like Lolitas and lion tamers. All those boots and helmets," protests Barbara Tuchman, the writer of history. Like other handsome, middle-aged women, she finds shopping for clothes a frustrating experience these days.

Mrs. Tuchman is correct about the homosexual presence but she misinterprets its influence. Now as always, some of the prettiest clothes are designed by homosexuals, some of the worst botches by heterosexuals. Some dress designers (as well as artists and playwrights) bring their homosexuality to their work. Others keep the two apart.

In the case history of most homosexuals, says Dr. Paul Lussheimer, a New York psychiatrist, "there is mother." But not every homosexual designer transposes his anxiety about his mother into a mission of uglifying women. The standard biography of the male homosexual designer contains a reference to a mother who had simply *marvelous* taste, far beyond the appreciation of the Philistines in the dreadful burg in which he grew up. But then, one designer will keep mother at his side and design dresses in the image of her heyday. That may be one reason for the constant revival of the Twenties and Thirties in current fashion. Another designer will put a continent between himself and the mother he refers to as a sot. His forte may be the tarty look. Still other homosexuals are determined to make their customers look like ladies, even if they are not. (The sobriquet "The Ladies" has been applied by *Women's Wear Daily,* the Fairchild publication, and Eugenia Sheppard to a group of bland but rich housewives whom they converted into consumer celebrities.)

There are no statistics to prove that Seventh Avenue has more homosexuals than Wall Street. But clearly, the arts—fine, performing and commercial—are more hospitable to those with unconventional sexual habits than investment banking and heavy industry at the moment. The homosexual doesn't have to camouflage himself on Seventh Avenue. He can flaunt. Desperate manufacturers are known to say, "I'll get myself a fairy designer," but when business perks up, it's more likely to be caused by the designer's talent than his mincing gait.

Still, the word "fag" is being flung about the jealous jungle of Seventh Avenue as irresponsibly as "pink" was in the McCarthy era. To be celibate and even moderately successful in a fashion career means being tagged as a homosexual. The possibility of selfish bachelorhood or spinsterhood from lack of opportunity is cruelly disallowed.

Just as there are latent homosexuals who father several children, so says Dr. Lussheimer, "there are some whom I would call neuter." The neuter woman is part of the folklore of American fashion, publishing and advertising. She invariably douses herself with perfume and smears on the jade eyeshadow before she goes into a conference room with men. Neuter women need neuter men to escort them to the parties that the fashion industry is always giving. If the celebration has anything to do with men's fashion, the blatant homosexuals will descend like pigeons on a sidewalk covered with cracker crumbs. "Trends in men's clothes are set by adolescents and homosexuals because they are the most overtly sexual people," says Robert Riley, design research consultant to the Brooklyn Museum and the Fashion Institute of Technology. He reasons that clothing is devised not primarily to keep people warm or dry but to make them sexually attractive. And indeed, adolescents and homosexuals are in the vanguard of the sexual revolution.

Like fashion, sex is impossible to escape from in pop culture. The gamut runs from explicit though sometimes sensitive treatment in films—notably the imports from Sweden, France and Czechoslovakia —to instruction in elementary schools, to an erotic art exhibition at a flossy gallery, to obscene poetry readings in public parks, to barechested nightclub waitresses. A researchers' document recording the sexual act as performed in a laboratory becomes a best-seller. *Newsweek* magazine reports a trend among university students to set up pre-marital housekeeping. The pregnant bride has become a high-society custom instead of the servant girl problem it used to be.

Next to contraception, homosexuality is the most popular topical allusion in mass diversion. *The Killing of Sister George,* a British comedy about lesbians, was a hit of the 1966-67 Broadway season. Jokes about the chap who prefers guys to dolls are inserted in movies and TV programs, targeted to audiences that include children. *Mademoiselle* makes utterly unself-conscious mention of dikes and faggotry, reports on tolerant attitudes toward homosexuality among college students. *Glamour's* male columnist tells young women what to do if a best beau turns out to be less than a man (ditch him, he advises). The two senior fashion missals do not discuss the subject in text but their photographs disseminate the homosexual point of view. A teenager with a geometric haircut and a pants suit speeding down the avenue on the back of her boy friend's motorcycle can be thrillingly feminine. When *Vogue* puts the same outfit on a horse-faced model and jams a fedora on her head, suddenly it's lesbian. So is a smidgin of a jersey dress when *Harper's Bazaar* sticks it on a visored mannequin and has her stand with her legs spread apart and a gloved hand pointing to her crotch. The laissez-faire policy toward the homosexual is not restricted to collegians, magazine editors and lovers of the arts. Even psychiatrists have revised their diagnoses. "I'm more tolerant now," concedes Dr. Lussheimer, who began his training in Germany in the Twenties. "Then homosexuality was taboo, even for psychiatrists. Now I don't think of it as a vice, certainly, not even an illness. I am inclined to consider it an aberration, just something unusual, a matter of arrested development."

With that view, it is easy to connect the homosexual with the youth-centered phase in current fashion. In this decade, teenagers defied their elders with aggressive hair and clothing and ended up controlling fashion. The homosexuals are defiant, too, and when they add the weight of their considerable influence in fashion to the sheer numerical power of the young, the dice are loaded.

"The fear of aging is more evident in the homosexual person," Dr. Lussheimer asserted. "How frightening it is to normal people and it's getting worse because of our culture. Age means death. In former times, the fear of death was regulated by religion but now there is less conviction of a life hereafter. The real homosexual does something to stay young. He wears a wig, dyes his hair. *The Picture of Dorian Gray* is typical."

Dr. Lussheimer made his observations during the full flush of

Clairol's advertising campaign for men's hair coloring. Shortly after, Revlon introduced Braggi, a line of 17 male beauty products including a bronze powder and a facial pick-up.

If Hans Christian Andersen, through the tale of the Emperor's clothes, has become a contemporary fashion commentator, so has Oscar Wilde. Recall these sentiments from *The Picture of Dorian Gray:*

> For there is only one thing in the world worse than being talked about, and that is not being talked about. . . . Beauty, real beauty, ends where an intellectual expression begins. . . . With an evening coat and a white tie, as you told me once, anybody, even a stock-broker, can gain a reputation for being civilized. . . . Youth is the one thing worth having. . . . And Beauty is a form of Genius—is higher, indeed, than Genius, as it needs no explanation. It is of the great facts of the world, like sunlight, or springtime, or the reflection in dark waters of that silver shell we call the moon. It cannot be questioned. It has its divine right of sovereignty. It makes princes of those who have it. . . . A new Hedonism—that is what our century wants. . . . Youth!! There is absolutely nothing in the world but youth!

Voilà! The manifesto of American fashion in the Sixties as written in 1891 by Oscar Wilde.

Susan Sontag linked Wilde to camp, the third stream of taste, which she dissected and analyzed in an essay in the Fall 1964 issue of *Partisan Review.* By mid-1965, this previously unidentified sensibility, as she called it, had infected fashion. It had already contaminated art with the advent of pop art. Miss Sontag called camp "dandyism in the age of mass culture." Wilde, the dandy, had expressed the democratic spirit of camp, she said, when he asserted the equal importance of a necktie, a boutonniere, a chair, a doorknob and a painting. She also explained the relationship between camp taste and homosexuality. They are not the same, but they have a "peculiar affinity" like that of Jews for liberal causes, she said. While "not all homosexuals have camp taste," she maintained, they are its pioneers.

In fact, camp had been a synonym for homosexual for 40 years in England, for about a decade in New York.

Miss Sontag offered more than 50 definitions of camp. A love of the exaggerated, a spirit of extravagance, "style at the expense of content," and the declaration that there is a good taste of bad taste.

Camp is antiserious, appreciative of the vulgar and the banal. The examples she gave of camp taste—Aubrey Beardsley drawings, Tiffany lamps, Twenties women's clothes including feather boas and beaded dresses, Busby Berkeley musicals like *The Gold Diggers of 1933*—have become canons of faith for fashion display artists, boutique owners and department store merchandisers.

Camp came along when American fashion needed another gimmick to push the clothes that Americans didn't really need. Homosexuals may have sponsored camp but heterosexual businessmen commercialized it.

The homosexual influence on American fashion is subtle and coincidental rather than direct and purposeful. The narcissism, the emphasis on decoration, the immaturity and hostility to natural femininity, the spiteful humor that pervades fashion in the Sixties are typically homosexual. But these traits belong to other deviates from middle-class morality, such as teen-age dropouts in the slums to the grandchildren of tycoons.

The destiny and day-to-day affairs in an industrial superpower like the United States are conducted by corporate organization men, skilled technologists and millionaire politicians. The main channels into the power elite are through education and inherited wealth. The dominant American life style is megalopolitan, competitive, family-centered. The more this is so, the more clamorous the nonqualifiers become. The homosexual in American fashion speaks for large minorities who cannot or will not conform to the preponderant style. His colleagues are the marketers of nonessential goods and services, the social outcasts and the socially advantaged whose wealth is no longer a distinction by itself, the lazy who want the privileges of education without the toil of getting it. He is the lobbyist of taste in an era of hard knowledge and skill. He argues for those who want a knack for personal adornment to be the equal of a master's degree from M.I.T.

Pop art is criticized for debasing artistic standards and for glorifying the banal. But it has also lifted the burden from the viewer of figuring out what the artist meant. If pop art can be construed as a reaction to abstract expressionism, so pop fashion is a rebellion against precious clothes. Anyone can now make a statement with globs of glass and plastic jewelry, strident stockings and a bit of dress. Or by what strikes some as a switch of sexes in clothes. Homosexuals may be the first to champion eccentric styles, but they are not solely responsible for them. All of the designers associated with near-nudity, transparent dresses and postage-stamp bathing suits initially presented their designs as comic relief. They didn't expect them to be bought, much less to be taken seriously, but when the orders tumbled in, they filled them. The editors and the businessmen—mostly heterosexual—who believed money could be made on neovulgarity promoted their gags into fads.

The pants suit for women is a fashion that many see as a sinister, homosexual plot particularly since it comes when men are letting their hair grow longer and showing peacock tendencies.

But if fashion is a historical indicator—like the stock market it may anticipate or follow the condition it reflects—then the pants suit is reporting that the emancipation of women became a fact in the Sixties. The neuter style in fashion may indicate that the differentiation between the respective jobs and roles of the sexes is blurring. In the early Fifties, one out of four married women had a job, in the mid-Sixties more than one out of three. By 1980, 42½ per cent will be at work. The reasons vary. Women work to earn money for children's education, for the extras that make a pleasanter life or, as is largely the case with college-educated women, to reach an amorphous state known as fulfillment.

The tasks allotted to males and females have varied in different societies and at different times. So has the distinction between male and female clothing. There's nothing inherently masculine or feminine about pants, or for that matter, a skirt. Think of a fragile blond equestrienne in English breeches, boots and derby, the tiniest of gold earrings beaded into her pierced ears. Think of the Scottish Highlander with hairy knees exposed between his pleated kilt and coordinated socks.

Well into the Middle Ages, men and women wore essentially the same garment, usually a form of tunic. Not until the middle of the 14th century, in the courts of France and Burgundy, writes James Laver in his book *Costume,* did rapid changes of style become a kind of sexual weaponry. Enter the low-cut dress and the tightly laced bodice. By the Victorian era, women were encumbered with crinolines, buttons, hooks and eyes. Fashion stressed the dependence of women.

In the early 20th century, women left their homes to work in a limited number of occupations, as governesses, typists and salesclerks, wearing clothes that suited their new endeavors. Gabrielle Chanel, a

girl who attracted titled suitors and became one of the cen-
ost successfully emancipated women, made high fashion out
tic working-girl clothes. The working girls could afford them
only when they were mass-produced in cheap copies of the originals
that Chanel made for duchesses and bankers' wives. Unlike other designers, the grand "Coco" reveled in the flattery of imitation.

The painted face, bobbed hair and shortened skirt of the flapper
constituted a further declaration of female independence. Laver considers it a response to social upheaval following World War I. So was
the chemise, which didn't arrive until a decade after World War II.
He considers that Dior's New Look of 1947 was a "back-eddy, a
visible sign of women's unconscious desire to return to the conditions
of a more settled age when servants were plentiful and ladies led a
sheltered life."

Those days are history and some fashion designers realize it. They
are the ones who are trying to restate femininity in contemporary
terms. It's not easy, and meanwhile the sound of the explosion when
fashion went pop drowns out everything including the voice of the
innocent child protesting that the Empress has no clothes.

Unless, of course, there is no innocent child.

II

INSTANT PACKAGED FASHION

FASHION editors call it "a look." Fashion merchants prefer the redundant "total look." Either way, it's the sum of clothing, accessories and hairstyle with which Americans define their own and others' places in the socio-economic structure today. The sociological significance and the caste system of fashion have always existed but in the past they were more narrowly construed. Twenty years ago, in the Seven Sister colleges, shetland sweaters and Norwegian moccasins constituted a prima facie case for belonging. The WASP network recognized each other's diamond circle pins and man-tailored British tweed suits. Mrs. Loel Guinness and the editors of *Vogue* and *Harper's Bazaar* could translate the sign language of a Balenciaga seam or a De Busschère pump.

The *cognoscenti* sneered at plastic shoes, sequins and noisy prints (until suddenly in the Sixties they became high fashion). But the rest of the population neither comprehended nor cared.

In the Sixties, fashion stopped being clothes and became a value, a tool, a way of life, a kind of symbolism. It became human packaging. You don't have to work in an advertising agency to know that packaging sells the product. Any product.

To get elected or promoted, to enroll your 3-year-old in the nursery school that pre-pre-prepares him for Harvard, to be invited to the right parties, to serve notice on the world that one is contemporary, a *Now* person, it is essential to have "a look."

43

The fashion industry's creed, that appearance controls one's destiny, is a tenet of pop culture. Only the very secure dare disbelieve. In the Sixties, the total look is merchandised for mass consumption. It's instant packaged fashion.

Without the connivance of mass media and without easily imitable mass idols, instant packaged fashion would be hard to sell. In 1960, the United States was presented with its first pop fashion goddess. Jacqueline Kennedy, who the Gallup Poll reported to be the most admired woman in the world by Americans for five years running, represents instant packaged fashion. Esteemed for her courage, goggled at for her beauty, she is scrutinized for her clothes and hair. Even her critics cannot afford to disregard her. When Jacqueline Kennedy shortened her skirts to near-mini length in the fall of 1966, she made any woman who did not emulate her seem a downright reactionary. Her effect on the broad spectrum of popular taste is manifold. She not only induced mass conversion to certain styles like the pillbox and the swollen hairdo, but she has unwittingly encouraged the loosening of standards and traditions. She set an example of churchgoing in casual dress with bare legs and arms, sunglasses atop her head and a mantilla clutched in her hand. All the arguments for adjusting one's hemline to one's physical dimensions and taming one's coiffure to the limits of one's age fell apart when Jacqueline Kennedy went girlish in 1966.

Her appeal is unsurpassed. Jacqueline Kennedy is the royal queen Americans never had, more photogenic than any movie star. She is a large woman with a wild, earthy beauty that the camera transforms into fragility. With her incessant coming and going and her colorful playmates, she is a natural gossip-column heroine. Jacqueline Kennedy is a society girl who stepped into the vortex of history. Her debutante frivolity was tempered by marriage and politics. The combination of those ingredients spiced with a professional fashion sense make for a solid, commercial success when appropriated by pop culture.

The tabloid newspapers and the movie magazines have always entertained their readers with the antics and the peculiar moral values of the overprivileged. Their formula was to bring never-never land into the proletariat's living room. Jacqueline Kennedy offered them a continuing fashion education in the bargain.

When John F. Kennedy was elected President, the fashion industry went berserk with joy. Unlike Princess Margaret of Britain, who brought a fashion photographer into the bosom of the Royal Family and then proceeded to dress erratically, Jacqueline Kennedy has never reneged on the promise that her presence in the White House implied. In December 1966, a widely published newspaper photograph showed Princess Margaret looking rather bosomy in a tailored suit, the skirt of which just covered her knees. Her shoes were high-heeled and pointed at the toes. "Look at those gams," a male newspaper editor sighed appreciatively. "Look at those shoes," a fashion editor said with disdain. That month, Mrs. Kennedy was photographed by *Women's Wear Daily* emerging from a New York restaurant. Her skirt was three inches above her knees and her feet were shod in the fashion shoe of the year, the patent leather, low-heeled, silver-buckled pump that Roger Vivier had designed for an Yves Saint Laurent collection.

Jacqueline Kennedy's achievement has been to translate the messages of the fashion industry for a mass audience without ever losing its rapt interest. Even such subtle details as the tucking of a three-strand pearl necklace inside a boat neckline and the carrying of a handbag either over the arm but to the side of the body (never, never to the front and poised over the stomach) or with the fingers grasping the double handles were assimilated by her avid public.

Jacqueline Kennedy has the taste and convictions of a fashion editor, which she might have been, as well as the lean, flat-chested figure that fashion editors extol because it makes the best clothes hanger. In 1951, she won *Vogue*'s Prix de Paris contest for college seniors but did not avail herself of the prize, a year of work in the magazine's Paris office. Her younger sister, Lee, now Princess Stanislas Radziwill, was an assistant to Diana Vreeland when she was fashion editor of *Harper's Bazaar,* and has modeled for *Vogue* since Mrs. Vreeland became its editor-in-chief.

Before Jacqueline Kennedy, the great mass of American women did not understand the esoteric points of high-fashion philosophy. Mrs. Kennedy has a professional attitude toward fashion. In her close circle of friends are *Vogue* editors. She reads fashion magazines, sees *Women's Wear Daily* and does not begrudge the time, effort and money it takes to acquire an extensive wardrobe. Even if her husband had not been elected President, she undoubtedly would have been nominated to the Best-Dressed List.

During the Presidential campaign of 1960 and in her three years in the White House, Mrs. Kennedy tried to deny the size and scope of her clothes closet because it was deemed politically damaging. The Republicans had played up Mrs. Richard Nixon as a cloth coat candidate's wife. When Nan Robertson of *The New York Times* asked Mrs. Kennedy to verify the report in *Women's Wear Daily* that she and her mother-in-law had spent $30,000 a year in the Paris haute couture houses, she replied indignantly, "I couldn't spend that much unless I wore sable underwear." In her book *First Lady,* Charlotte Curtis estimated after considerable research that Mrs. Kennedy had spent more than $50,000 on clothes in the first 16 months after the election.

In any event, the politicians had guessed wrong. No matter how much her clothes cost, however many jet-set playgrounds she frequented, her stock as a pop idol soared. The public does not begrudge their goddesses their extravagances. They enjoy them vicariously. When a nation is consumer-oriented, prosperous and upwardly aspiring, when the idol has such charm that even a chilly autocrat like Charles de Gaulle is visibly spellbound by her, the public revels in her expenditures and eventually imitates them to the best of their ability.

Jacqueline Kennedy, the superconsumer, redeemed fashion from the Puritan ethic of sin. She not only disabused the French of some of their cherished misconceptions about American style-backwardness but she infused the national consciousness with a Gallic appreciation of fashion. Since Jacqueline Kennedy, there is no longer much status in Anglo-American dowdiness.

One of the cardinal principles of fashion-editor taste that the public learned from Jacqueline Kennedy was the importance of accessories. Where a fashion editor would put a $200 alligator bag and a $40 pair of shoes with a $50 dress, the average woman would reverse the ratio. The fashion editor is thinking, in part, of her assignment which is usually to take a nondescript dress and give it impact in a photograph. Accessories help in this direction. But also, fashion editors get their own clothes at wholesale prices and, sometimes, at no cost at all. They can afford to be as snobbish about shoes and handbags as an electrical-appliance sales manager's wife is about her kitchen. And snobs they are. "You can tell a woman by her shoes and bag," is a bit of wisdom that often falls from the lips of fashion editors, many of whom equate personal adornment with art and intellect.

A fashion editor can spot a Gucci morocco leather handbag with a bamboo handle ($89 in the Fifth Avenue branch of the Florence handbag and luggage store) a mile away, and rate the owner with approval. By her sights, the baby crocodile satchel from the Hermès shop on the Faubourg St. Honoré in Paris signifies a member of the international set or an editor or buyer who regularly covers the Paris collections. Early in 1967, the Paris editors sported a handbag that was a miniature of a Vuitton suitcase (the most status-ridden luggage in the world).

From Jacqueline Kennedy, American women absorbed the intelligence about chain handles, which, even before Chanel's quilted-handbag version became a fad, had been appearing in the windows of Henri Bétrix, a Madison Avenue shop of forbidding elegance, or in the collections of Martin Van Schaak, the most exclusive pocketbook salesman in New York. Mr. Van Schaak has no shop. He brings his wares to his gilt-edged clients at their homes.

The clunky shoe is one instance of fashion-editor taste that the masses resisted for nearly a decade. In 1955, Roger Vivier, the most creative and influential shoe designer of the last quarter of a century, inventor of the wedge sole and the modern Louis XV heel, began experimenting with a low-heeled, round-toed pump. He was then designing for Christian Dior in Paris. (In 1963, the shy, blue-eyed designer opened his own salon on the Rue François Premier.) American women were then in the grip of the needle-heeled, pointed-toe shoe. Despite warnings from chiropodists, they felt the silhouette gave their feet a flattering look of aristocratic slenderness. The stiletto heel had originated in France in 1951 and had been refined in Italy and the United States while the sharply pointed toe was a 1956 triumph of Beth Levine, America's most prolific shoe designer.

The two-inch, stacked talon that Vivier liked was associated in the public mind with dowagers and problem feet. With its sturdy and patently comfortable appearance, it contradicted the popular concept of femininity. American men, used to the precipitous grace of the three- to four-inch spike and the illusion of swelling calf and shapely ankle that it provoked, hated the shoe. In 1957, *Harper's Bazaar* put a sequin-embroidered evening edition of the pump with a black, stacked-leather heel on the cover of its Christmas issue. It went over like a lead balloon. The Delman shoe salon in Bergdorf Goodman carried a version of the Vivier style, which it called its marquise pump, in small but steady supply at about $38 a pair. The shoe salesmen were unimpressed with it and seemed surprised when fashion editors and women like the Duchess of Windsor and Jacqueline Kennedy ordered several pairs at a clip. As the Sixties wore on and skirts rose, the lower heel made aesthetic logic but the resistance continued, particularly away from the coastal centers of urban chic. André Courrèges clinched the style with his new fashion proportion which included boots as flat as infants' slippers. Probably no style except the dress without a waistline was a better example of instant fashion identification than the blunt, low-heeled shoe. But it took until 1965 for it to filter into mass acceptance.

By the spring of 1966, high-fashion heels were down to one-half to seven-eighths of an inch. The three-inch heel had slipped into history. "Even two and a half has become a dirty word," acknowledged a shoe buyer for Saks Fifth Avenue, which was selling American-made copies of Roger Vivier's Pilgrim-buckled pump with the one-inch heel by the thousands, at $36 a pair. The buckled shoe was knocked off, as they say in the fashion industry when someone copies without giving credit, at all price levels. By fall, so was the clunkiest shoe of all, Gucci's brown pigskin moccasin with a tiny brass bit, as in a horse's harness.

Jacqueline Kennedy was a powerful propagandist for the low-heeled shoe, but on two other fashion-editor idiosyncrasies she was ambivalent. In the past, fashion editors were rather contemptuous of mink and precious jewelry, implying they were Babbitt habits. They exalted cloth coats and costume jewelry because of their style content, and possibly because, even with a professional discount, mink and gems were beyond their means. Most fashion editors, even though they acquire millionairesses' tastes, work for compelling financial reasons.

Jacqueline Kennedy wore a cloth coat with a collar and muff of Russian sable to her husband's inauguration in January 1961. It was the most photogenic costume she could have chosen, far more than the mink coat a millionaire's wife might have been expected to wear on that bitterly cold day. She managed to avoid being photographed in mink during her White House days. After she moved to New York, her double-breasted black mink coat from Maximilian became one of her uniforms for afternoon errands. By then, the furriers had found a way to bring prices down and to present their merchandise in a context familiar to fashion editors. Jacques Kaplan sold a raft of

Japanese mink coats (a poor relation to Mrs. Kennedy's authentic black-dyed ranch mink) in the same stylishly skimpy silhouette with horizontally worked pelts for about $1,000 apiece.

Among the jewelers, David Webb had become the darling of fashion editors not only because he is an articulate and handsome blond bachelor, but because his flashy animal bracelets and pins made of enamel and semi-precious stones and lightly sprinkled with diamonds reminded them of the showy costume jewelry they were used to. "The ice age is past," said David Webb in 1966. Harry Winston, the iceman of Manhattan jewelers who owns an African diamond mine and sells only precious stones (diamonds, sapphires, emeralds, rubies and here and there a necklace of perfectly matched Oriental pearls), disagreed. "It's a phase, this costume jewelry thing, it'll die," he said. "Women have been looking at the costume jewelry that has been shown with the clothes in the pages of *Vogue* and other magazines for so long that it's affected their thinking."

The fact is that a woman gets infinitely more flash to the dollar from one of Webb's wrap-around bracelets in white and gold enamel with chunky coral knobs for $3,500 and a pair of coral, diamond and gold ear clips for $2,500 than with one of Winston's two-carat, gem-quality diamonds at $3,500 a carat. Middle-class mentality without a fashion education would lean toward the two-carat diamond on the ground that it would be a good investment. At a distress sale or in a pawn shop, the Webb bracelet and earrings would fetch practically nothing. Pawnbrokers don't lend a cent on style.

As a woman of wealth and fashion-editor taste, Jacqueline Kennedy can dabble. With sleeveless linen dresses, she wears one of those colored enamel and gold bangles that Jean Schlumberger designs for Tiffany. Their $1,225 to $3,450 price tags are based on workmanship but they look insignificant in photographs. In the evenings, Mrs. Kennedy wears diamond pendant earrings of a size and shape that Van Cleef & Arpels (whose Fifth Avenue branch she has patronized and where her signed photograph hangs in the private sales chamber) priced in the $50,000 range. In 1966 she honored David Webb by attending an exhibition of his jeweled objects. Mrs. Kennedy advanced upon the jeweler, to whom she had entrusted a piece of coral that her husband had brought back from his naval duty in the Pacific to be made into an *objet d'art*. "Cellini," she addressed him.

The most significant lesson that Jacqueline Kennedy imparted to the public, however, was the simplicity of fashion-editor taste. Within a year after she moved into the White House, women all over the United States had memorized the high-fashion mathematics of multiplying chic by subtraction. Her little-nothing dresses, her unadorned cloth coats, her plain pillboxes and pumps had been upper-crust specialties. They became mass fads. Jacqueline Kennedy is not considered a trailblazer in professional fashion circles. She does not discover or create styles. She espouses them at the point when they are being published in the fashion magazines, but the average consumer has not yet dared them. When Jacqueline Kennedy, the superconsumer, accepts them, the public sees the green light.

The look of pure silhouette emphasized by bright color that she conveyed in 1960 and 1961 was of the Balenciaga and Givenchy school of dressing. Audrey Hepburn was identified with it. Norman Norell and Gustave Tassell, whose designs Mrs. Kennedy also bought, were American practitioners.

Jacqueline Kennedy acquired her Balenciagas and Givenchys in Paris, at Chez Ninon, a New York custom copyist of French clothes, and at Ohrbach's, the bargain store that excels in mass-produced translations. The double-breasted red coat that she wore during the New Hampshire primary campaign and that forced male political reporters to master fashion vocabulary was an Ohrbach's copy of a Givenchy. When Oleg Cassini became her personal designer, he had to forget his predilection for sexy, form-fitting, bosom-baring clothes and think Givenchy.

The pillbox fever that she induced is one of the more amusing footnotes to fashion history. She has a problem head size which accounts in part for her negligence in wearing hats. Jacqueline Kennedy has a larger-than-normal head and a fondness for inflated hairdos which add up to almost 24 inches on the tape measure. Before the Democratic Convention at which John F. Kennedy was nominated for the Presidency, the milliners chided his wife for her hatlessness. She had to mend her ways. During one of her visits to New York, she telephoned the custom-millinery department at Bergdorf Goodman and requested that hats be sent to her suite at the Waldorf-Towers. Marita O'Connor, one of the saleswomen, was dispatched with a selection. Women with oversized heads usually can wear the beret or similarly unobtrusive silhouettes. Mrs. O'Connor tried a black velvet pillbox from Christian Dior with a narrow front and a wider back, but she reversed it with the height to the front because it looked better that way on Mrs. Kennedy. It became a global craze.

"It's amazing how many women ask for the Kennedy hat," an Ohrbach's buyer said in April 1961. "Even older women. They put the hat on the back of their heads, look in the mirror and you can just see what's going through their minds. They're having the time of their lives seeing themselves as Jackie Kennedy. Naturally, we won't do anything to break the spell." In June of that year following her arrival in London, Reuters reported that British milliners were working day and night to fill orders for pillbox hats "just like Jackie."

Since leaving the White House, Jacqueline Kennedy has given the millinery industry small cause to rejoice because she is seldom photographed with a hat on her head. When she went to Runnymede in May 1965, Bergdorf's made a beret to go with the white Courrèges dress she had ordered from the shop's custom salon. After she was photographed a year later on horseback in Andalusian costume at the Seville fiesta, manufacturers rushed into production with black-brimmed hats.

Actually, she buys more millinery than her photographs would indicate. She wore Adolfo's fur hood for skiing. In the fall of 1966, she asked Mrs. O'Connor for a beret "just like the children wear" for excursions to Central Park. She illustrated her note with precise sketches of straight-haired little girls in stem-topped, felt tams, and lamented that she couldn't find one big enough.

As soon as Richard Nixon conceded the election to John F. Kennedy, the fashion industry realized that the Jackie Kennedy look was the most potent merchandising gimmick since Shirley Temple dolls. Mrs. Kennedy's pregnancy was no deterrent. It only boosted the maternity-dress business, particularly the one-piece style that was cut like an ordinary chemise. Lane Bryant, a pioneer in expectant-mother clothes as well as a haven for plump women, used the phrase "First Lady Maternity Fashions" in its advertisements.

Other merchants found it unnecessary to make such direct references. A window mannequin or an advertising sketch of a brunette with a puffed hairdo and widely spaced eyes was sufficient. Before the first of the Kennedy years had ended, the President's wife had restored the sovereignty of the glamorous brunette. She had been in eclipse for decades except for the brief heyday of Brenda Diana Duff Frazier and the pre-World War II debutantes. The empty-headed blonde receded. Suddenly, it was quite all right for a woman to express an opinion on world affairs and cultural matters, provided she did so in vague, breathless, girlish prose and diction.

In the spring of 1962, Jacqueline Kennedy was selling eyeglasses on Madison Avenue. A new fad for horn-rimmed sunglasses with curved lenses that wrap the eyes from the bridge of the nose to the temples was set in motion by newspaper photographs of Mrs. Kennedy wearing them as she rode in a golf cart with the President and an assortment of Kennedy children. Newspaper clippings of the photograph were displayed in the windows of Madison Avenue opticians. One of them added a hand-lettered sign calling attention to "the fabulous 'Jackie' sunglasses." Said another oculist, "It's the hottest style today. It's the style." The one that Mrs. Kennedy was wearing was manufactured in Italy and cost $15. Another rimless version, made in France, sold for $17.50. A cheaper copy was $12.95. The drugstores had a $1.98 edition with plastic rather than ground-glass lenses.

In the same period, Seventh Avenue manufacturers were unveiling their sari fashions following Mrs. Kennedy's fairy-tale trip with her sister to India and Pakistan. During that memorable excursion, a political reporter for the Chicago *Daily News* scooped his colleagues by reporting that Mrs. Kennedy's Italian-made pumps were size 10A. He had peeked when she left them outside during a visit to the Mahatma Gandhi Memorial. The sari fashion, particularly combined with the one-shoulder style of evening dress which she also stimulated, rolled on for nearly half a decade.

Mrs. Kennedy's departure for her Oriental journey in a Somali leopard coat delighted furriers who had cornered the market on spotted pelts. Somali leopard skins, however, are in short supply. That's why coats like the one she bought from Ben Kahn cost $6,000 in 1962. The status of the leopard coat, reinforced by the fact that Elizabeth Taylor and Queen Elizabeth were wearing them too, was utilized for quick turnover by low-margin stores like E. J. Korvette which advertised and sold leopard coats of various origins for $1,700 to $2,500. In the winter of 1966-67, demand for the finest quality skins still exceeded supply and at Ben Kahn, Somali leopard coats were going for $12,000 to $18,000.

While she was First Lady, Jacqueline Kennedy popularized skinny pants (à la Pucci and Jax), the *minaudière* (a small, gold vanity case that she held in the palm of her hand as an evening bag) and English riding clothes. The vogue for riding in an English saddle and the classic tailoring that the sport demands spread to the western states, where once they had been considered effete.

Jacqueline Kennedy's role as instant fashion leader was held in abeyance during the nearly 22 months of her mourning period. When she signaled her return to social activity by throwing a party for former Ambassador to India John Kenneth Galbraith at an East Side restaurant (to which she also invited Killer Joe Piro, the rock 'n' roll dance instructor), her international fan club noticed that Jacqueline Kennedy had changed. Perhaps she had just reverted to being a New York socialite and bona fide member of *Vogue*'s Beautiful People. Certainly, fashion had changed during her absence from the public eye. The Givenchy look of understated, pearl-button-earring and white-glove elegance was passé. Fashion had gone pop and slightly vulgar in more than one sense of either word. Out of the White House fishbowl and freed of political shackles, Jacqueline Kennedy grew younger, bolder and more frivolous, at least as far as her fashion personality was concerned. The cultured housewife gave way to the jet-setter.

She bicycled in Central Park with her hair flowing and her perpetually suntanned complexion devoid of make-up. She shopped in boutiques, shortened her skirts and ordered clothes by mail from Yves Saint Laurent and Valentino, the handsome Roman couturier. On her first skiing expedition to Sun Valley, Idaho, she endorsed bell-bottom ski trousers and poor-boy sweaters. *Women's Wear Daily,* which has become her sycophant, summed up the change when it reported, JACKIE HAS THE KNACK OF LOOKING DARLING.

As a pop idol and mass-fashion instructor, Jacqueline Kennedy alerted the nation to far more than clothes. Fashion included not only coordinated dresses, cosmetics and hairdos but an entire range of attitudes, activities and possessions. It was tantamount to status. Today, fashion is an assortment of items from bilingualism to $25 art books. Fashionable people decorate their houses with literature. They strew French and English publications and readable-looking volumes over their tables and walls. Even for the woman who needs a remedial reading course, a book-lined study has instant fashion cachet in a publicity photograph.

Fashion means greeting casual acquaintances with a continental kiss (a buss on each cheek while the smoocher sizes up the other opportunities in the room) and dining in New York's astronomically expensive French restaurants, where one goes to be seen and not necessarily to gorge on haute cuisine. Many of the luncheon habitués of La Grenouille, Lafayette, Le Mistral and La Côte Basque settle for a plate of hors d'oeuvres. When Jacqueline Kennedy gave a dinner at Le Pavillon (then the finest dining room in the United States) for the Hervé Alphands, who were being recalled to Paris from the French Ambassadorship to Washington, she ordered *navarin d'agneau,* a hearty lamb stew.

American fashion is flower-printed sheets and towels by Porthault, fine French 18th-century furniture, English silver, baby pillows, silver-framed photographs and a clutter of small objects all over the place. Stark, contemporary simplicity is acceptable only for photographers and artists or anyone who is in a position to ask Philip Johnson to help with his interior design.

Ever since Jacqueline Kennedy, a fashion rating cannot be reckoned without flowers. When she abolished them at the White House, stiff and formal arrangements sank to the category of belt loops on dresses. The natural wild look of flowers just brought in from a country garden (preferably by one's gardener) and placed in a bowl is the effect to strive for. Daisies, apple blossoms, freesias and tulips became chic in the Sixties. Anemones, "a sexy flower," according to designer Pauline Trigère and one that many people cannot pronounce, are instant fashion. Gladiolas, on the other hand, are instant disaster. Better send paper flowers.

To be in fashion means to be on the go. Jacqueline Kennedy's restlessness is difficult to emulate unless one is awfully rich or married to an airline executive, but the important thing is to keep moving, to arrive after everyone has heard of the place but before everyone has been there. Acapulco, Antigua, Gstaad, Hawaii, the Greek islands have all had their moments of glory. Repeat visits are worthwhile to Rome, Paris, London and one's house in the country (meaning the North Shore or the Hamptons of Long Island, northern New Jersey if one goes there for the fox hunting). Fairfield County in Connecticut may be the New York industrialists' bedroom, but Mrs. Kennedy has never given it the seal of approval, possibly because it's Anglo-American drab country, as far as fashion goes.

The Jackie Kennedy look settled into status quo during her period of mourning. The next helping of instant packaged fashion was ladled out by André Courrèges. Unfortunately, many women did not digest it properly. They wore the little white boots or the cowboy hats with voluminous, below-the-knee coats. Piecemeal Courrèges was a catastrophe. The total look of Courrèges, however, was a synonym for contemporary. The woman who adopted it, becoming or not, served notice that she had cut her ties with the past. The short, boxy silhouette rendered in stark white, pastel or checked fabrics resembled the concrete, steel and glass architecture of modern cities more than traditional dresses, coats and suits. The white boots, the zombie glasses and the astronaut baby bonnets were the cartoonist's approximation of the moonbound maiden.

But Courrèges provided more than contrast piping or pants with V-shaped cuts at the bottom. He heralded the new ideal of femininity. Courrèges' woman had a boy's cropped hair and angular body. Courrèges, the pelota player, didn't believe in brassieres any more than he did in shoes with heels.

The woman who accepted Courrèges was also assenting to the new humor in fashion. Total Courrèges was the decade's first fashion put-on. After Courrèges, it was clear sailing for all pop fashion, from motorcycle suits to bikini dresses that glowed in the dark and the whip as a fashion show accessory.

Like it or loathe it, the total Courrèges look had meaning. By exposing a longer span of leg, the abbreviated skirt required a new proportion. The boots were intended for aesthetic adjustment. They were, incidentally, supposed to be spanking white, a point that many wearers overlooked. The headgear was not designed to fasten under slackening chins.

After Courrèges, it was obvious that fashion could broadcast a far more inclusive message than merely the duty to consume clothes. Big business discovered the selling power of pop fashion. Advertising agencies concluded that avant-garde designers spoke more eloquently than the glibbest copywriters when it came to marketing food, kitchen appliances, soaps, whiskey, steamship travel and a host of other products and services otherwise unrelated to clothes. Even banks and stockbrokers, traditionally reluctant to employ showmanship, used high fashion as bait.

"Fashion is the quickest way of identifying things today," said F. William Free, president of the Marschalk Company which prepared the advertising campaigns for Tab, a low-calorie soda, and Pillsbury baking products. "There's a new kind of person we want to reach. This person is younger, better educated, richer, more sophisticated and certainly more knowledgeable. We try to get a quick identification with this group by the way in which the woman in the ad is dressed."

Mr. Free retained China Machado, a fashion editor of *Harper's Bazaar,* to style the Tab ads. She procured the gaudiest rhinestone chandelier earrings as the magnet of the advertising illustration which showed the lower half of a woman's face (parted lips and giant ear baubles) and a well-manicured hand pouring the contents of a Tab bottle into a glass. THE NOW TASTE OF TAB was the printed message.

Mr. Free quoted, of course, ad alley's favorite statistic. Half the population is 25 years or younger. *Ergo,* one must think young to sell young. Madison Avenue is absolutely convinced that everyone from 25 to the grave wants to look, act and buy young, too. In 1965, this inexorable logic led to Courrèges boots. Dancer-Fitzgerald-Sample injected white boots into an advertising campaign for the Frigidaire refrigerator-freezer which had been christened the Gemini 19. The agency's task was to glorify the machine's compressor, which the client called a power capsule. In the advertisements, the refrigerator was flanked by models garbed in bi-colored mini-dresses by John Kloss, Courrèges-y sunglasses, Courrèges-y white boots. One model's head was encased in a transparent plastic bubble, another's in a purple Courrèges-y helmet.

Another combination of youth and fashion was used by Grey Advertising for its client Dentu-Creme. A model in her 20's was outfitted with a sleeveless, low-backed shift in orange crepe. "So that the audience will identify youth with dentures," explained Benjamin Alcock, executive vice president of the agency.

Given a British bank as a client, J. Walter Thompson forged the link between fashion consumption and checking accounts. Young male and female Mod models were attired in the newest exuberant shirts, hipster pants, peaked caps, mini-skirts, lacy stockings and vinyl pants suits. The text of the advertisements listed the designers and the prices of the clothing, then gave a sales pitch for opening an account with the bank.

Probably the most theatrical fashion tie-in was that of Emilio Pucci, the Italian designer, and Braniff International. When Harding Lawrence, president of the Dallas-based airline, asked for a new image as a world carrier for his company, Mary Wells, the brown-eyed blond bombshell of Madison Avenue, hit on the creator of the statusful stretch silk jersey dress. Mrs. Wells asked Pucci to restyle the uniforms of the stewardesses and the flight crew. Pucci devised the stewardesses' "air strip" to dramatize the airline's flights from cities in the northern United States to the heart of South America, a schedule that involves radical temperature changes. Printed leotards to match above-the-knee shifts, derby hats and plastic wind bubbles or rain hoods shaped like space helmets, hooded fur coats and clear plastic boots by Herbert Levine gave the passengers something to talk about. Together with the pastel paint jobs that Mrs. Wells recommended for the jet aircraft, they created a "new look" and instant identification for Braniff.

The financial community, as one might expect, latched onto more conservative names in American fashion. Merrill Lynch, Pierce, Fenner & Smith, Inc., the stock-brokerage house with branch offices throughout the nation, affiliated with Adele Simpson in a joint promotion involving 50 stores. Women were invited to see an Adele Simpson fashion show (and to meet the designer or her daughter, Joan Raines) and then listen to a lecture on securities investments. Adele Simpson is a 4-foot 9-inch designer of timely clothes that sell from $100 to $300. One of Seventh Avenue's landed gentry, she dwells in a Manhattan town house and on an estate in Greenwich, Conn., that has a swimming pool, a lake and an exotic vegetable garden. There is no such thing as a readily identifiable Simpson style since the forte of her $5 million-a-year wholesale business is to reflect the current mood without jarring middle-aged nerves. Nevertheless, the name of Adele Simpson offers instant fashion identification to women who want to keep up with fashion but never march ahead of the parade. Mrs. Lyndon B. Johnson is a Simpson fan.

Another designer with instant fashion recognition, particularly outside New York, is Oleg Cassini. The fashion editors of the magazines and of the New York newspapers, as well as the buyers for the more elegant Manhattan specialty stores, have snubbed him ever since he opened his wholesale house in 1950. Cassini was known as a creator of "sexy" clothes, anathema to the priestesses of the fashion mystique. After Jacqueline Kennedy named him her personal designer, their scorn deepened because Cassini's collections tacked to the Givenchy side of the First Lady's taste and then reverted, in a mild manner, to outlining female anatomical characteristics. When Mrs.

Kennedy left the White House, Cassini's position as court dressmaker went up in smoke, but the thousand days of service has been converted into a lifetime annuity. Oleg Cassini has become an international celebrity everywhere but in the bosom of the fashion industry. In March 1966, the Mellon Bank of Pittsburgh, a tower of financial prestige, imported him to stimulate its credit card business. Eleven thousand women who could prove recent purchases of at least $10 charged to the Mellon Bank Credit Card, streamed into Pittsburgh's Civic Arena to watch a fashion show of Cassini clothes and accessories with commentary by the gray-haired, black-moustached six-footer, still slim-hipped and broad-shouldered at 52.

A bank spokesman explained why Cassini. Three years before, in order "to show women that we liked them," the bank sponsored a fashion show with Cassini, Hedda Hopper, the Hollywood columnist, and Josephine Lowman, the newspaper beauty columnist, as stellar attractions. After one announcement of the show in local newspapers, lines of women formed at 8 A.M. for the tickets which were to be distributed at 3 P.M. Thirteen thousand women attended. When the bank found itself in a competitive situation with another institution that was also offering a credit card, the name of Cassini leaped to the executive mind. "We checked Norell and Mr. John and were led to the inescapable conclusion that Cassini was the man for us," the spokesman said. "He is glib, distinctive and masculine. The brass wanted assurance of his masculinity which I was able to provide." Oleg Cassini has been twice married and divorced. His first wife was Merry Fahrney, a cough-medicine heiress. His second marriage to Gene Tierney, the actress, whom he also served as dress designer, lasted a decade. They had two daughters.

As a fashion show impresario, Cassini is a better than mediocre, stand-up nightclub comic. He is noted for his double-entendre, sometimes off-color quips and uncomplicated sense of humor. The staleness of his material doesn't seem to bother his audiences, possibly because they are free-associating about his cosmopolitan charm and the luscious models who accompany his road shows. As Cassini has often said of himself, he is an amateur of beauty. In January 1966, at an informal showing of dresses and bathing suits presented on a strip of territory between the pari-mutuel windows and the clubhouse restaurant at Roosevelt Raceway on Long Island (to which he had been coaxed by the fashion innocents in the track's public relations department who hoped his presence would shed chic and publicity on the opening of the harness racing season), Cassini did not hesitate to pull out 10-year-old chestnuts. "Missionary's Downfall," he mumbled as a mannequin appeared in a version of a Courrèges dress that Cassini took credit for designing. "Chief of Navel Operations," he called out as Greta Chi, a Swiss mannequin of Chinese and German ancestry, ambled out of the ladies' room into a circle of leering trot fans. "She was gold mining," he added, brandishing his microphone as though it were an electric shaver.

But during the Kennedy years, he made a valiant effort at dignity, at least when the press was within earshot. "If you trip me in one thing of bad taste today, which is customary with me, I'll give you a dress free," he told an audience of buyers and reporters who were packed as caviar into a jar in his showroom at 498 Seventh Avenue to see his first showing after the Kennedys had moved into the White House in 1961. "This is my philosophy," he told them. "It's very easy to be a nice guy when you are a success. The trick is to be arrogant when you're a flop." As a certified member of the White Russian exile branch of international café society, Cassini had mastered the trick in childhood.

His mother, the late Countess Marguerite Cassini, was the daughter of one of Czar Nicholas II's Ambassadors to the United States. His father was Alexander Loiewski, a Russian diplomatic attaché.

Oleg Loiewski-Cassini was born in Paris in 1913 and raised in Florence where his mother ran a dress salon after the Russian Revolution. He studied law and art and would have preferred to have been a diplomat or a professional soldier. Instead he opened a dressmaking salon in Rome in 1933. "In those days, to be a designer was almost as bad as being a tailor. I thought it was the end," he admitted more than 30 years later.

"I always tried to redesign the job of designer to suit a man. Fashion shows are distasteful to me. They're exhibitionism and I'm really conservative. People look at you one-dimensionally. With a mixed audience, men don't like you."

In 1937, he and his younger brother, Igor (nicknamed Ghighi), emigrated to New York. Their mother advised them to use her maiden name for its celebrity value. Fiercely loyal to each other and to their parents in good times and bad, the brothers chose different means of raising income that did not interfere with their main occupations as society playboys. After unsatisfying stints in the New York garment center, Oleg gravitated to Hollywood as a movie costume designer, served in the United States Cavalry during World War II and eventually drifted back to Seventh Avenue. Igor became a society columnist for the Hearst newspapers under the pseudonym of Cholly Knickerbocker. He coined the phrase "jet set." Two of his three marriages ended in divorce. His first wife, Austine "Bootsie" McDonnell, subsequently married William Randolph Hearst, Jr. His third wife, Charlene Wrightsman, daughter of an oil magnate who is a friend of the Kennedys, died of an apparent overdose of barbiturates in 1963. That year, Igor's fortunes collapsed. He was indicted for failing to register as a foreign agent for the Dominican Republic. He pleaded *nolo contendere* which meant he declined to fight the case, was fined $10,000 and put on probation for six months. The episode was embarrassing to President and Mrs. Kennedy, who had been receiving the brothers at White House parties. In the fall of 1961, Oleg Cassini had introduced the twist at a dinner dance for Princess Radziwill. In 1965, Igor Cassini founded *Status* magazine, the title of which precluded further definition. A year later, it merged with *Diplomat,* another society publication.

The fashion industry had been appalled and baffled by Mrs. Kennedy's choice of Oleg Cassini as her personal designer. She was, after all, a disciple of the French haute couture and a devotee of the chemise. Cassini had waged unremitting battle against the hegemony of Paris and the sack silhouette. He once sent a model down a runway attired in a hooded dress made of burlap. When the mannequin pulled the hood over her head, potatoes rolled out. "That emphasizes my opinion of the sack. It's a cruel and floppy thing that deprives woman of her most glorious attribute—her shape."

Cassini never had any illusions about why he was selected by Jacqueline Kennedy. The most clothes-conscious First Lady of the century needed a professional fashion coordinator, as well as workroom facilities, for her considerable wardrobe. The paths of the Kennedys and the Cassinis had crossed on the New York and Palm Beach society circuit. As Cholly Knickerbocker, Igor Cassini had nominated Jacqueline Bouvier the top debutante of 1948.

Wounded by the slings and arrows that Seventh Avenue shot against his appointment, Cassini rationalized that it would benefit the entire fashion industry. "It raises fashion to the status it enjoys in Europe," he maintained. "When I go to the White House, I go as a guest, not through the back door. Up to now, the President has named no Italian to a position of consequence in the administration," said Cassini, who had become an American citizen in 1942. "My position is not the same as a Cabinet post. But still, the Italians can now say, 'We, too, are in the White House.'"

While the fashion industry sneered, Cassini enjoyed the manna from heaven. Orders for his summer 1961 collection surpassed the previous year's by 25 per cent, he reported. As a model filed into his showroom, he commented with his customary candor, "This dress can look like $275 or $2.75. I guess it's who you buy it from. Will you please buy it from me? This is my year."

But it was only the beginning. The Kennedy association gave Cassini instant fashion appeal the world over and enabled him to found a licensing empire. "The hottest name in mass-class fashion," said a member of the staff of the House of Cassini, which was established in 1964 in a Renaissance-style mansion on East 19th Street. Although he was still manufacturing upper-medium-priced dresses on Seventh Avenue, Oleg Cassini was concentrating his energies on franchise agreements with manufacturers of women's hosiery, hats, shoes, gloves, girdles, jewelry, furs, swimsuits, sportswear, sunglasses, men's slacks, neckties, belts, and sweaters, as well as bed and bath linens and a child's doll. Seventeen manufacturers had been signed up by the middle of 1964 to produce merchandise attributed to Oleg Cassini. He expected gross volumes, on which he received royalties, to reach $20 million by the end of that year. Cassini was supposed to supply the licensees with ideas and sketches which they were to "refine," as his aide put it, and submit for his approval.

Prospective licensees and the press were invited to the House of Cassini and permitted to wallow in Cassini-Romanov-Kennedy memorabilia. The two-story wood-paneled living room was hung with feudal-looking crested banners. "From his family," the aide murmured. A collection of 6,000 lead soldiers was displayed in glass cases in the hall. The dining room curtains were red brocade with a gold and blue motif. "The crest of his mother and father," the aide whispered. Upstairs in Oleg Cassini's bedroom, there were photographs on the tables flanking what was said to be a 15th-century bed from a Florentine palace. One of them showing Mrs. Kennedy and Princess Radziwill on their Indian trip was inscribed, "For Oleg, au revoir Givenchy, bonjour Cassini, Lee" and "Who made us the two best-dressed women in Asia, Jackie." The other photograph was of Mrs. Kennedy at an audience in the Vatican. When it comes to clinching a deal with a prospective licensee, Cassini once conceded, "the house will do it for me."

In January of 1966, he had raised his estimate of sales of Cassini merchandise to $30 million a year. "Even if I die, I hope my name will be as powerful as Dior's," he said, referring to a poll of newspaper readers which indicated that American women knew two fashion names, his and the deceased Paris couturier's.

He was still grateful to his former benefactor. "Mrs. Kennedy was the greatest thing that could have happened to me," he admitted. "Because the whole world had to take notice of me." Licensees were selling Cassini sportswear in Italy, bathing suits in Mexico. "That's where Mrs. Kennedy was irreplaceable, in the eyes of foreigners who think that Mrs. Kennedy would pick the best designer."

"I'm the only one who hasn't written a book on the White House," he said proudly. "Everybody has, even people I never saw there."

The parlaying of a pop idol's name into a commercial fashion windfall was not the exclusive accomplishment of Oleg Cassini. Others attempted to squeeze dollars out of tie-ins with movie stars or the titles of their films. The pretense of creating style was usually minimal. *Doctor Zhivago* prompted a rash of promotions such as the "Caviar Collection" by Abe Schrader. The clothes had a tenuous link to the film by way of frog closings on jackets and overblouses that buttoned at the shoulders like a Russian man's shirt. But they bore fruit in seven pages of advertising in the March 1, 1966, issue of *Vogue,* the cost of which was shared by Mr. Schrader, Metro-Goldwyn-Mayer and the Celanese Corporation (whose fibers were in the fabric of which the clothes were made). The willingness of American men to break out in fur hats may have been stimulated slightly by the film, but that trend had been growing for a decade, ever since the Soviet Union encouraged the admission of tourists from the United States. Geraldine Chaplin wore a coat with frog fastenings and a circlet of fur at the neck in the picture and such a coat was one of the fords of the 1966-67 winter season. But the style had been a status symbol since 1964 when stores started buying it from Cortefiel, a Madrid manufacturer who called it the Anna Karenina coat. Even Marc Bohan, of Christian Dior, pricked the balloon when he announced that he was thinking of Napoleon III's army officers and not of Russia when he designed his mid-calf-length military coat that year.

The owner of the tie-in rights to *Viva Maria* exuberantly predicted sales of $20 to $40 million of merchandise associated with the film including $1.5 million on facsimiles of the bomb bag, so called because it was carried by Brigitte Bardot playing the part of a revolutionary. During the following year, there was a ripple of granny dresses and thrift shop clothes among the young, but there was scant evidence to ascribe it to the circa 1907 costumes in the movie.

American women can no longer look to Hollywood for fashion instruction as they did when devastating elegantes like Joan Crawford, Marlene Dietrich and Carole Lombard dominated the screen. Except for the admitted habit of Seventh Avenue designers to devour old movies from their television sets (which might be one reason they persist in trying to revive the Thirties), American movies do not provide much fashion education.

Foreign films do. British productions like *Morgan, The Knack, Darling* and *Blow-Up* (in which the Mod characters spend a great deal of time wriggling out of clothes and revealing the Mod-ish dismissal of underwear) explain the total London look better than any store display or magazine article. The French film *Jules et Jim* tempted millinery designers to tackle the cap. Delphine Seyrig's Chanel wardrobe and shingle hairdo by Alexandre in *Last Year in Marienbad* thrilled fashion addicts, even though they couldn't agree on the merits of the movie. On a less sublime note, the unmade-bed style of hairdressing was certainly aided and abetted by actresses like Miss Bardot and Julie Christie. *Cleopatra* had a deplorable effect. Ever since the $40 million epic, some women refuse to take their morning coffee before they ring their eyes with kohl.

An instant fashion identification of a snobbish caliber can be used to upgrade an entertainer's image. After Barbra Streisand hit her stride, earning $5,000 a week as the 22-year-old star of *Funny Girl* on Broadway and signing a $5 million television contract, she decided to drop her thrift shop, kooky-kid-from-Brooklyn affiliation. In her one-woman TV spectacular in March 1965, Miss Streisand incorporated a nine-minute segment of fantasy at Bergdorf Goodman. She sang and flitted about the street floor of the Fifth Avenue specialty shop in the most opulent, throwaway chic by Emeric Partos, the custom fur designer, and Halston, the custom milliner. Partos, the diminutive Hungarian who got his start designing in cloth for Christian Dior, is the most nonchalant handler of luxury furs in America. The author of the now classic, bone-buttoned Autumn Haze mink polo coat, Partos once put a snap-out lining of white mink in a shocking pink terry cloth peignoir. "Nobody realizes how many poor little rich girls there are living in town houses in the East 60's and 70's and Murray Hill," he explained. "The heating in those houses is terrible. Why, those girls just freeze."

For Miss Streisand's entrance, he provided a $15,000 full-length Somali leopard coat sashed as casually as though it were a bathrobe in black leather. He gave her white mink knickers to play newsgirl in. She sashayed about in a long evening suit of white broadtail and cavorted in a printed velvet jump suit with a matching robe lined in the finest Canadian wild mink. The TV audience watched her stamp on the mink.

"I used to hate mink," the evolving Barbra Streisand said during a fitting for the show. She had arrived in what she called her slob clothes, beige corduroy jeans, a maroon suede coat, poor-boy sweater, wool socks and gray suede ankle boots. "But now I appreciate it for its solidity."

The blue-eyed, copper-haired singer gave assurance that she really belonged in Bergdorf's. "I really didn't like boa scarves as much as they say I did. I like simple elegance, neat. I'd rather change my jewelry and have a few things and wear them all the time. A person is more important than clothes. A dress should fade out of sight but greatly."

For her next television show, she landed Chemstrand as a sponsor. They arranged for her to attend the Paris haute couture showings in a whirlwind of publicity to select clothes for the television program. Richard Avedon photographed her there for *Vogue* in designs by Dior and Grès. Miss Streisand never went back to feather boas.

The television association with Barbra Streisand was part of Bergdorf Goodman's continuing effort to prove that it had changed, too. For a decade, Andrew Goodman, the affable son of the store's founder, and Leonard Hankin, his forceful executive vice president, had been trying to overcome the snooty, *grande dame* image that intimidated many potential customers. They realized that snob appeal can be a cogent sales factor, as long as it does not scare away the younger, not necessarily rich but intensely consumer-oriented segment of the population. The Miss Bergdorf department with middle-class price tags on clothes that seem to suit every kind of woman from 19-year-old secretaries to trim dowagers had been set up in 1958. It became the store's most profitable operation. If Bergdorf's were to grow (and vigorously enough to launch a public offering of its stock one day), it had to attract what Leonard Hankin called "the new generation of money spenders." For them, some of that yeasty, pop fashion had to be swept into the bastion of formidable elegance. In the spring of 1966, rock 'n' roll was piping loud and clear in its Bigi department for teenagers. Bergdorf's next broke out the motorcycles in its windows. The Hondas were not for sale. They were punctuation for a group of grown-up dresses in vinyl and flower print such as had previously not borne Bergdorf Goodman labels. One was gouged out to the top of the mannequin's posterior. Another dress was a risky exercise in anterior décolletage. A flower decal reposed on the bare expanse of the dummy's bosom. Pinned to the dresses were buttons emblazoned with one word, "Tigermorse."

In the semaphore of fashion, Tigermorse spelled instant avant-garde chic of the new, rebellious, nonserious kind. Tiger Morse was a sometime boutique owner, designer, partygiver and La Pasionaria of the dropout subculture of pop. In the early Sixties, she answered to the name of Joan and ran a boutique called A La Carte in an Upper East Side mansion from which she sold little-nothing dresses and costumes in sumptuous fabrics she collected on her world travels. Jacqueline Kennedy and a number of proper society matrons paid many hundreds to several thousands of dollars for these morsels.

Tall, skinny and a bottled blonde, Tiger Morse is a mistress of the put-on, that pop cultural affectation of the outrageous fib. Her flexible autobiography contains references to graduation from a Brooklyn high school, three marriages, a teen-age son and a string of universities from Syracuse to the Sorbonne at which she variously claims to have studied. The salons she has furnished and dismantled are chock-full of treasures and trivia. Oriental art objects nestle with camp atrocities. An energetic kook, she is never too tired to dream up new shocks for jaded playmates. Those who prefer death to being considered not "with it" follow Tiger Morse. They include the press, which in the Sixties could be gulled into publicizing anything as long as it was extravagantly packaged and attended by a few of the celebrities they had manufactured.

Joan Morse closed A La Carte, took a sabbatical in England, and returned in 1965 to open new headquarters. As Tiger Morse, she christened her showroom on East 58th Street Kaleidoscope, decorated it as a flea market and used it as a base for her custom-made, wholesale and other activities, chief of which was the inflation of her pop personality. She gave mob parties in unexpected settings like artists' lofts or gymnasiums to which she invited store presidents and their French perfumed wives, along with wild-haired youths whose seedy clothing reeked of an unmistakable, bittersweet smell. The fashion Establishment came to see and to be seen and because the press had reported that Tiger Morse had genuine intuition about style. Didn't she do marvelous things with vinyl, such as printing HATE on the sitting part of a plastic dress and LOVE on the front? Didn't she concoct a dress with light bulbs so that she could turn herself on and off in a murky discothèque? This Mrs. Morse talked of psychedelics and electronic environment rather than elegance. By putting Tiger in the windows, Bergdorf Goodman was swearing it wasn't square. At those prices ($150 to $495), it must be hip, not hep.

The following autumn, Tiger Morse opened her Teeny-Weeny boutique at Madison Avenue and 73rd Street and brought paper dresses, silver boots, motorcycle suits and buttons inscribed GO NAKED, I LIKE BOYS, and STONED to a neighborhood of residences, churches and nursery schools. Soon, she had enough instant fashion recognition to lure a mass manufacturer. Weldon, Inc., a company previously identified in the trade as makers of sleepwear for the whole family, commissioned "the design pet of the jet set" (which someone had convinced the president that Tiger Morse was) to create a nightie and pajama collection. The colorfully printed sleepwear she designed was inoffensive enough but Mrs. Morse persuaded the manufacturer that it should be introduced at a nocturnal gathering in a West Side health club. Buyers, press, pop society sachems like Andy Warhol and Mrs. Robert Scull and a passel of sketchers and hairdressers' assistants milled around a swimming pool in a steamy basement. A plump brunette in a cashmere cardigan, see-through tights and a bandanna tied around her hips to simulate the front half of a bikini, executed bumps and grinds on the diving board. She was spelled by the hostess, a gaunt figure in silver striped jeans and shirt. A dead, black butterfly was pasted to her left cheek. Mortician's *maquillage* and mammoth, hexagonal sunglasses completed the vision that was Tiger Morse. She tumbled into the pool followed by a man in a transparent plastic shirt and mink chaps that disclosed considerable portions of his anatomy. The excuse for the brawl? Classic pajamas were a declining share of the market. How could a company like Weldon persuade the buyers that it was capable of salable excitement unless they "blasted" them with a Tiger in the boudoir, the executives asked defensively a week later. After all, as the sales promotion brochure pointed out, didn't her clients include Fords, Vanderbilts and Kennedys? Didn't she once study for a Ph.D. in art history? At least that's what Tiger said.

A Tiger Morse collection had, in fact, once been presented in an art gallery. "A Kaleidoscope of extravagant fashions and accessories" was how the Greenross Gallery on East 57th Street had dignified her bikinis, harem pants and tapestry dresses in April 1965. It was one of many events that confirmed the worst fears of serious art lovers and critics. Not only were painting and sculpture being manipulated as stylish commodities, but galleries and museums were being converted into fashion show arenas. All through the Sixties, the art exhibition preview had rivaled the charity ball as an occasion for social climbing and identity-seeking. It was obvious that many of those in attendance spent more time beforehand choosing what they would wear to catch the press photographers' attention than in looking at the works of art when they arrived.

One of the most eclectic fashion shows of the decade was the opening of the Whitney Museum in its new ziggurat building at Madison Avenue and 73rd Street on September 28, 1966. It drew Jacqueline Kennedy in white satin and long gloves, girls in mini-dresses that plunged recklessly fore and aft and, of course, Andy Warhol with a leather jacket slung over his dinner suit and Mrs. Robert Scull in an Ohrbach's copy of Balenciaga's dress of feathers over nude net.

Mrs. Scull and her husband, whose income derives mainly from his fleet of taxis and a taxi-insurance business, are the decade's pop success story. Taxis may have transported them from the financial doldrums to a Fifth Avenue apartment and a house in East Hampton, L.I., but it was Mr. Scull's *chutzpah* in buying Jasper Johns' beer cans and flag paintings and such, and insisting that they were works of art back in 1959 and 1960, that gave the Sculls social standing. By 1962, the year in which pop art was recognized, Robert Scull surfaced as *the* pop-art collector. New York society, which had been lowering its barriers for amateurs of art, didn't seem to mind that he had been born on the Lower East Side and hadn't gone to college.

But it was Ethel Scull's fashion tie-up and her movie starlet's flair for publicity that pushed them over the border into pop celebrity-land. As a starter, Mrs. Scull, before her marriage a bourgeoise from West 86th Street, could announce that she had attended the Parsons School of Design. When Courrèges shot into the fashion firmament, Mrs. Scull was one of the first New Yorkers to appear in public in the Courrèges look. She was immortalized in it when George Segal, the pop-art sculptor, cast the Sculls in plaster. The Segal sculpture occupies the foyer of their apartment. Plaster Ethel sits on a settee in her Courrèges dress and boots, sunglasses perched on her dead-white nose. When Saint Laurent designed his see-through dress as a publicity gag, Ethel Scull bought a copy at Ohrbach's. The purchase was duly noted in newspaper fashion columns. Mrs. Scull is very cozy with the press. She kisses Eugenia Sheppard, the syndicated fashion columnist, when they meet and responds warmly to less important members of the fourth estate. Ethel Scull endeared herself to the mass media not just with her hospitality, but because she makes good copy. The names of the swingier but most expensive French, Italian and American designers trip knowledgeably off her tongue (she refers to Saint Laurent as Yves) and their clothes (in the original or in translation, Mrs. Scull never makes clear which she is wearing) look photogenic on her slender figure. Kenneth does her hair in the tawny, restless-savage style that is the instant fashion badge of the international socialite.

A conspicuous consumer of fashion, Mrs. Scull is also a verifiable link with art, the three-letter cure that the American garment industry takes for its inferiority complex. In the Sixties, fashion and art mingled on a spectrum ranging from the unhealthiest fringe of the new Bohemia to the solemn side of philanthropy.

In the fall of 1966, Abraham & Straus, Brooklyn merchants to the family trade, invited Andy Warhol to demonstrate how to paint paper dresses in its notions department. The inscrutable, pasty-faced and silver-haired guru of pop art and underground films never goes anywhere without his dark glasses and a team of displaced disciples. He brought Nico, a blond German model, and two male assistants from his "Plastic Inevitable" traveling psychedelic nightclub. A 4-year-old, identified as Nico's son, Ari, accompanied the troupe. Nico reclined on a desk attired in a white paper shift, lacy stockings and shoes.

Warhol poured purplish paint through a silk screen frame that an assistant held over her body while Ari sprayed green paint on her hosiery. Nico, a pop-age Marlene Dietrich whom Warhol has called the first psychedelic singer, changed her dress several times. FRAGILE was stenciled on one, paper bananas glued on another. Whether they realized it or not, the audience of housewives, art students and diversified males who are at leisure to wander in department stores at mid-afternoon, received a liberal education in more than paper-dress decoration, courtesy of one division of the nationwide Federated Department Stores chain. Sales of $2 paper dress and paint kits were brisk, a store executive reported with satisfaction.

Andy Warhol entered the fashion picture through a legitimately prosaic door. The son of a construction worker from McKeesport, Pa., he came to New York in the Fifties and eked out a living as a fashion sketcher. Shoes were his specialty. His work appeared in advertisements for I. Miller & Co. and the women's pages of *The New York Times*. When art popped in 1962, his clients realized that Warhol was not just an alienated beatnik but an *outstanding American artist,* an apostle of tasteless trivia whose literal paintings of Campbell's soup cans and Brillo boxes were commanding prices in the four figures. Success did not affect Warhol's detachment or his sense of propriety. In April 1965, he was invited to a preview of an exhibition of American painting at the Metropolitan Museum of Art. Two hundred and sixty titans of the art world and the *Social Register* dined with Mrs. Lyndon B. Johnson in the museum restaurant. After dinner, a second string of art authorities was asked in for coffee and to join the panjandrums on a tour of the galleries. Among them were Andy Warhol in paint-splattered work pants, dinner jacket and sunglasses and, on his arm, Edie Sedgwick, a fragile creature with cropped, silver-rinsed hair. She wore a lilac jersey jump suit and furry shoulder bag.

Andy Warhol had already descended from pop painting to underground films where he intended to stay. (In a full-page advertisement in *The New York Times* on January 29, 1967, taken by a group of artists protesting the war in Vietnam, he listed himself as a film-maker rather than a painter.)

Warhol, the cinematographer, is a starmaker. His first vedette was Baby Jane Holzer, a lion-maned Park Avenue housewife. Edie Sedgwick, a blue-blooded twig from a Boston Brahmin tree, was his next superstar. Pop society anointed this mixed-up heartbreaker, who resembles a skinny Marilyn Monroe, Girl of the Year 1965. *Vogue* called her a "youthquaker." She was superseded by a series of over- and underprivileged runaways from middle-class morality, some of whom were united in *The Chelsea Girls*. This 1966 Warhol epic of homosexuality, dope and LSD addiction and blasphemy was the first underground movie to be booked into a commercial theater. The movie critics, not unlike the fashion industry, couldn't agree on whether Warhol was a menace or a genius.

Not all of fashion's involvements with art are as seamy as the Warhol connection. Paris designers like Yves Saint Laurent and Janine de Poorter and Americans like Betsey Johnson put pop symbols and word messages on clothes. Op art was also "prostituted by the dress and fabric industry," as John Canaday, art critic of *The New York Times,* said. Earlier, John Kloss believed that abstract expressionism could be worn as well as hung on a wall.

In 1963, Jacques Kaplan, the Franco-American Fifth Avenue furrier, commissioned five avant-garde artists to paint fur coats. Richard Anuszkiewicz did an op-art arrangement on calfskin, Marisol a pink nude. Kaplan, an art hobbyist who had been bartering fur coats for paintings, later staged fun fur shows in art galleries. A graduate of St. Cyr, the French military school, and holder of the Croix de Guerre for his exploits with the Free French Army during World War II, Kaplan may be the most candid character in American fashion. He drives to work on a Honda and he admits that arty antics help to sell profitable $4,500 ranch mink coats. He also talks freely about his psychoanalysis and his coming to terms with the fashion business.

"One of the few means of self-expression left today is fashion, if you are not talented as a writer, artist, etc.," he told Grace Glueck, the art columnist of *The New York Times*. "*Liberté, Fraternité, Personalité*—that's the new motto. I really like fashion, for that matter. Twenty years ago, I used to hate to be a furrier. I thought it was the lowest degree, socially. Now I'm very pleased to be one. It's a sort of fulfillment."

Seventh Avenue had been using art as psychiatric therapy for several decades. In the easy-money period of the Forties, several manufacturers, craving the cachet that the needle industry could not give them, started art collections. One of them actually succeeded in becoming a connoisseur and patron. In 1963, Larry Aldrich, a taciturn dress manufacturer who plainly longed to be a scholar, sold 57 of his paintings by modern masters like Monet, Gauguin, Picasso and Matisse for $1,121,300. After disposing of his impressionist and post-impressionist classics, Aldrich turned to the avant-garde. In the fall of 1964, he commissioned Julian Tomchin, a textile designer, to work out fabric designs based on paintings in his collection by artists like Anuszkiewicz and Bridget Riley. It inflated the op-art bubble in fashion. In 1965, he acquired a 182-year-old house in Ridgefield, Conn., near his week-end estate, and converted it into a museum for the exhibition of contemporary art. Aldrich, whose $2.5 million-a-year dress business was in the safe design hands of Marie McCarthy, served as his own curator.

The fashion industry likes romping in museums. Twice a year, it gets a chance at the Metropolitan Museum. One occasion is the Party of the Year, a $100-a-ticket dinner to benefit the Costume Institute, a valuable repository of pictures, clothing and other sources of historical research and inspiration for designers, under the direction of Polaire Weissman.

The Coty American Fashion Critics' Award presentation affords another opportunity for dressing up and feeling respectable within the museum's hallowed halls.

The Edward C. Blum Design Laboratory at the Brooklyn Museum is another stronghold of fashion lore. Established by contributions from Abraham & Straus and other members of the Federated chain, it is supported by membership fees and is rarely publicized despite the excellent services it offers.

Eleanor Lambert, American fashion's most powerful press agent, has been intimately involved with the Coty Award and the Costume Institute during the past 25 years. She is a tireless matchmaker between fashion and art.

Whether fashion should presume to call itself art is moot. It is not farfetched to apply the term "artists" to jewelry designers like Jeanne Toussaint of Cartier in Paris, Jean Schlumberger of Tiffany, Fulco di Verdura (a Sicilian duke transplanted to Fifth Avenue), and Marc Koven, an Americanized Frenchman who is also a sculptor. But in the case of garment makers, even the designers themselves disagree.

Norman Norell once termed it a commercial art form. "It's important from the standpoint of history because fashion reflects an era.

If, 2,000 years from now, people want to know about us, they'll look at our clothes."

Applied art, perhaps, thought Antonio del Castillo, the Spanish grandee's son who became a Paris couturier. "My old friend from Spain, Picasso, used to put his arm on my shoulder and preface his remarks by saying 'between us fellow artists' but I always protested because I knew I was a poor relative."

Nevertheless, Eleanor Lambert kept insisting that fashion was art and, with the help of Senator Jacob K. Javits of New York, got Congress to agree. Fashion was inserted into section 211 of the bill to establish a National Council on the Arts and a National Arts Foundation which went before the Senate Labor and Public Welfare Committee in the spring of 1963. In that section, the arts were defined as "the major art fields including music (instrumental and vocal), drama, dance, folk art, literature, architecture and allied fields, painting, sculpture, photography, graphic and craft arts, costume and fashion design, motion pictures, television and radio." The measure was enacted in 1965.

Early in 1963, Miss Lambert had formed the Council of Fashion Designers of America, an organization of supposedly "creative" individuals rather than manufacturers with business mentalities. She became CFDA's public relations adviser. "CFDA is an honorary society, nonprofit, and except for seeking recognition of American fashion as a creative force, all its activities are to aid the other arts," she explained later. Fashion didn't want money from the government, just the prestige. After all, she acknowledged, "Fashion is one of the few arts that makes a living."

In December 1963, Seventh Avenue entered the gates of heaven via "The American Pageant of Fashion and the Arts" (produced by Miss Lambert). By paying $100 a ticket, fashion moguls like Andrew Goodman of Bergdorf's, David Evins, the shoe manufacturer, and Seventh Avenue designers and manufacturers like Bill Blass, Donald Brooks, Sydney Wragge, Ben Zuckerman, Ceil Chapman, Jo Copeland and Mollie Parnis could sit down in the same Waldorf-Astoria Grand Ballroom as Joseph Verner Reed, the financier, Eugene R. Black, the international banker, Thomas S. Gates, Jr., and Robert A. Lovett, the former Secretaries of Defense, Amory Houghton, the former Ambassador to France and others of the American Establishment pantheon. Proceeds of the event went to the John F. Kennedy

Center for the Performing Arts in Washington and the American Shakespeare Festival, Mr. Reed's pet hobby in Stratford, Conn. Miss Lambert has always known that the gods will bend down from their pedestals and smile for money. To help the causes they deem worthy, that is.

On September 25, 1966, the American Ballet Theater was the beneficiary of a choreographed fashion show presented in a Broadway theater. The ballet group and the CFDA were co-producers. Sales of the $75 tickets were boosted by the honorary chairmanship of Mrs. John F. Kennedy, a coup that Miss Lambert managed through Oliver Smith, the co-director of the American Ballet Theater, and Mrs. Kennedy's personal art teacher. The rumor that the former First Lady would attend was kept aloft until her secretary, Pamela Turnure, shot it down a few days before the performance. Mrs. Kennedy, it seemed, planned to be in Boston that evening. "A Fashion Show in Dance" turned out to be a gathering of the Seventh Avenue clan rather than the kick-off of the New York social season that had been promised But it raised $75,000 for the Ballet Theater Foundation, and by showing clothes on nondancing fashion models and nonmodeling ballerinas, it swung the pendulum toward the action-packed presentation of fashion. From then on, it behooved any young woman who wanted to earn a living as a mannequin to learn to dance.

In November, Seventh Avenue designers moved on Washington with a fashion show to benefit the costume wing of the Smithsonian Institution. Mrs. Lyndon B. Johnson sent her regrets, but her press and social secretaries and a sprinkling of Washington socialites attended the show in the Smithsonian's auditorium. In 1967, CFDA donated $25,000 to match the grant of the National Council on the Arts to the Costume Institute for an exhibit of contemporary and historic fashions.

Art and fashion were getting to be a habit.

III

THE POWER OF THE PRESS

"Send a man out to kill somebody—we must have news."
—*Command attributed to James Gordon Bennett,
founder of the New York* Herald, *in 1835.*

GENUINE fashion news comes in rare spurts such as Christian Dior's New Look (1947), the hot summer of the chemise (1958) and Courrèges' brave attempt to conquer the space age (1964-5). The rest of the time it has to be manufactured.

In the Sixties, the fashion press carried Bennett's dictum to such lengths as would have astounded the canny editor. They not only connived with the merchants of fashion to make news out of their insignificant wares but they created idols to quicken the national appetite to consume and overconsume apparel, accessories and beauty products and to spend and overspend energy and money on events at which they could be worn. Then they committed the capital sin of journalism by swallowing their own hokum.

A game that had been played before on a small, exclusive basis was picked up by the mass media and enlarged. Baby Jane Holzer, a young matron with a knack for clothes and publicity, passed from the pages of *Vogue* and *Women's Wear Daily* into the American idiom. Her name was recognized in Chicago, Phoenix, Savannah and, yes, London. Lawrie Bowes, a Chicago post-debutante, was rechristened Baby Lawrie by the Second City's press because she also had a golden mane and wore Mod-ish baby dresses and white stockings in September 1965 when the only white stockings in Chicago came from nurses' uniform stores. (A friend in New York sent her the chic kind.)

There had always been fashion leaders but their secrets had been confined to the pages of *Vogue* and *Harper's Bazaar,* publications that promise to deliver to their advertisers a small, snobbishly select audience. Besides, the allure of a Mrs. Harrison Williams or a Millicent Rogers was limited to a handful of true fashion believers. Such women were impossibly rich, cool and remote. The mass appeal of a Duchess of Windsor, a stiff personage whose magic charm eludes the camera, was in her feat of capturing a king at the age of 40.

Fashion influence on a broad scale had been wielded by movie stars and the costume designers who dressed them. But in the Sixties, Hollywood was a wasteland and actresses whom American women (increasingly sophisticated through travel and the communications media) would want to emulate in fashion were lacking. Audrey Hepburn, the only actress with reliable taste and high-fashion sense, operated as an international figure on a distant plane. Until 1966, she was almost totally identified with Hubert de Givenchy, the aloof and aristocratic Paris couturier. Furthermore, the Hepburn-Givenchy little-nothing look had been oversold to the public by a far more engaging goddess, Jacqueline Kennedy.

To whip up desire for something that people don't really need, at least not in endless quantity, glamorous idols are essential. If desire begets need, then envy begets desire. The stimulation of envy or a longing to imitate is the function of the idol. The fashion industry, through its press agents and an eagerly cooperative, self-serving press, had to manufacture new goddesses. They had rather meager material to work with, it would seem. The new celebrities were relatively unintriguing women. As a rule, they had money of varying amounts and origin, a place in what passes for society and a willingness to ally themselves with the makers and purveyors of fashion. Lacking intellectual purpose or equipment, special talents or visions, they were delighted, once shown the way, to establish identities through the labels in their clothes. Although it was never spelled out that way, they serve as bait in a consumer-oriented economy.

The press collaborated with the publicists, their traditional sparring partners, for various reasons. Fashion and other consumer news is a form of editorial support for the advertiser. The less obvious the support (as in a news account of Mrs. William S. Paley wearing a coat she bought at Ohrbach's to a fashion show at Bergdorf Goodman rather than an outright plug for merchandise at either store), the happier the writer. Editorial employees cherish the illusion of independence as one of the compensations for being underpaid. Compared to the reporting of hard news, be it simple tragedies like tenement fires or layered complexities like public-housing scandals or civil-rights skirmishes, the writing of manufactured fashion news is easy fun—especially when the manufacturers provide clowns, tightrope walkers and dancing girls.

Except in the newer electronic forms of journalism like television, reporters gratify their egos not so much through financial reward as through the space allotted their stories, the frequency with which their by-lines appear and the feelings of power they acquire, even subconsciously, over their subjects. Diplomatic correspondents invariably confuse themselves with prime ministers and presidents, financial reporters with industrial wizards. Fashion editors can't help regarding themselves as taste molders, who could, if they half tried, make or break a designer. Society reporters become hooked on the social opiate they peddle. They take no pride in the inverse cachet of the fourth estate. They would rather sit with the nobles.

In the Sixties, journalistic consciences were noticeably feeble. In 1966, a former newspaperman named W. H. Ferry lumped newspapers, radio, television and magazines together under the epithet "masscomm." In a report prepared for the Fund for the Republic's Center for the Study of Democratic Institutions, he charged that "masscomm's delight in the shoddy, the tasteless, the mind-dulling, the useless, is well established. . . . It is a direct consequence of masscomm's allegiance to organized rapacity. Ethical qualms about the effects of dishonest commercials disappear like morning mist in the glow of a comfortable advertising contract. . . . Masscomm does not portray what is there. It does not stand apart. It has signed up with the Yankees, so to speak—with the rich and powerful, with the government, with the successful."

Mr. Ferry was directing himself to what he considered a failure of the mass media to instruct the public on such crucial issues as Negro rights, Vietnam and poverty. He could have added that some of the space which the mass media might have used to fulfill their educational mission had been pre-empted by the fashion idols and their antics.

Eugenia Sheppard of the New York *Herald Tribune* and John Fairchild of *Women's Wear Daily* had created a new kind of celebrity, the fashion socialite. They instigated a merger of fashion and social gossip that spread like an epidemic through the press, even to supposedly liberal or middle-highbrow publications. The editors of those journals called it sociology but it was really backstairs-maid mentality. Even the tabloid New York *Post,* which drew its advertising strength from such sources as the borscht-belt resorts and its editorial distinction from left-of-center cerebral columnists like James Wechsler and Max Lerner, started beating the bushes for a society columnist, preferably white, Anglo-Saxon and Protestant. Doris Lilly, who once wrote a book called *How to Marry a Millionaire* (but didn't heed her own advice), was finally engaged to sprinkle chitchat about countesses and *principessas* and magnates on the same page with the solid, gracefully written prose of Ruth Preston, the *Post*'s fashion editor, who never mentioned her Phi Beta Kappa key and her bachelor's and master of arts degrees.

"I think the only thing people are interested in is people. I think it's a starstruck nation," said Diana Vreeland, in defense of idolatry. Mrs. Vreeland christened her goddesses The Beautiful People and she lowered their pedestals slightly. She made them jump for her photographers, confess their beauty secrets to her editors. Technically, the title The Beautiful People was a copyreader's brainchild, Mrs. Vreeland insists. "I hate to see it misused," she has said. "We mean people who are beautiful to look at. It's been taken up to mean people who are rich. We mean the charmers but there is no harm to be rich." That *was* Mrs. Charles Engelhard, wife of the precious metals nabob, in leotard and tights, standing on her head in one of her backyards, wasn't it? That *was* her daughter, Mrs. Samuel P. Reed, whose husband's heritage includes mining and armaments, showing off her false hairpieces.

Unlike American newspapers which are supposed to enlighten the citizenry of a democratic nation, special-interest magazines like *Vogue* were founded to deliver customers to their advertisers. In *Vogue,* the implausible Sybarite serves a purpose. She sells luxury. Nor do the ethics of the strictly commercial magazine forbid familial back-scratching. Countess Rodolfo Crespi (who was Consuelo O'Connor, a New York model, before her marriage) is not only *Vogue*'s Rome editor but the wife of a public relations man for the Roman designers. Count Crespi's half sister, Princess Luciana Pignatelli, is a Beautiful Person as well as a sportswear designer.

Diana Vreeland is the conduit between The Beautiful People and the *petite bourgeoisie* of the United States. She does not rub elbows with the masses. By birth and marriage to the late T. Reed Vreeland, a banker, she belongs to oldish New York society. She travels in chauffeured limousines, and except for the difference that she works extremely hard and with exceptional professional skill, she communes with The Beautiful People and lives like a Beautiful Person amid Porthault linens and scented candles. She is The Beautiful People's Sherlock Holmes. It was she who detected the star quality in Jane Holzer in the summer of 1964 and asked her to pose for *Vogue*. In due course, Mrs. Holzer appeared in *Women's Wear Daily*, Eugenia Sheppard's column, a profile by Tom Wolfe that was reprinted in his book, then in *The New York Times, Life* and other newspapers and national magazines. It is more than coincidence that *Vogue* and the newspapers most responsible for creating the new idols share the same enthusiasms for Mesdames Samuel P. Peabody, Henry Ford II, S. Carter Burden, Jr., and Wyatt Cooper, now known to multitudes as Judy, Cristina, Amanda and Gloria. Mrs. Freeland sniffs them out and the grubbier journalists magnify them into pop culture.

This worshiping at the shrine of the moneyed clotheshorse by the American press is a curious aberration of the Sixties. The French press is still serving a diet of movie stars and pop singers like Sylvie Vartan for fashion and moral inspiration. The British added a new set of idols to their chinless giants and ladies-in-waiting. Among the pop aristocrats like the models, photographers, film-makers and actors, the snobbish edge is held by the Cockneys and other formerly disadvantaged. But the point is that all of them are doers and workers.

No matter how many imitators have tried to appropriate her formula, Eugenia Sheppard remains the Boswell of pop fashion society. Yew-JAYNYA, as she is called by some of her chums like Geraldine Stutz, the Chicago-reared president of Henri Bendel, is also its Louella Parsons. But there is no hint of sexual escapade in her columns, although she was the first to mention the pregnancy of one goddess eight months before delivery date. Generally, Miss Sheppard's heroines concentrate on clothes buying and partygoing.

In 1956, Eugenia Sheppard had mated that specialty of the yellow press, the gossip column, to fashion reporting in the pages of the literate eastern Republican's favorite but ailing newspaper, the New York *Herald Tribune*. She thus conceived a new hybrid, the fashion-society celebrity. In the process, she won for Seventh Avenue the social position it craved but that money, heretofore, had been unable to buy.

"Eugenia has gotten the designer into the vernacular," said Bill Blass, executive vice president of Maurice Rentner Ltd. and one of Seventh Avenue's most socially desirable bachelors. "There used to be a stigma about designers. I didn't used to like to say what I did. When someone asked me at a dinner party what I did, I would say something vague, like manufacturing. But now people know that designers are a substantial part of the community and interested in other things."

Miss Sheppard put in a long apprenticeship for fame. Twenty years before she started her column, she had come to New York from Columbus, Ohio, an ambitious divorcée, former Junior Leaguer and society editor of the Columbus *Dispatch.* She had attended Bryn Mawr College.

"It's either for students or girl athletes and I wasn't either one," she once told a reporter for *Editor & Publisher,* the trade journal of the newspaper industry. The unscholarly bent she ascribed to herself was one of her chief assets. Miss Sheppard had a sharp, well-schooled intelligence which, combined with Everywoman's way of looking at clothes and a writing style that went down as smoothly as banana ice cream, made addicts out of readers of both sexes.

In New York, she worked on *Women's Wear Daily,* then joined the *Herald Tribune* in 1940 to cover home furnishings. Later, she added beauty to her beat, then fashion. She married Walter Millis, assistant chief editorial writer for the newspaper and an erudite military historian. Mr. Millis does not mingle with fashion society. His wife makes her evening rounds alone, accompanied by bachelor designers or her widowed friend Eleanor Lambert.

The Millises live at the Dakota, a grimy fortress at 72nd Street and Central Park West that fashion society acknowledges as the only socially acceptable address on Manhattan's West Side. Residence in that apartment house, which had such cooperative owners as the Carter Burdens, Lauren Bacall and Jason Robards, Susan Stein and her sister, Mrs. William vanden Heuvel (who had the power to attract Kennedys to her living room), gave Miss Sheppard a front-row seat on the action she was covering.

Miss Sheppard is an aggressive reporter who works in the moribund tradition of *The Front Page.* Nothing escapes her narrowed blue eyes. During the decade after she started her column "Inside Fashion,"

Eugenia Sheppard became a celebrity in her own right, one of fashion's go-go girls. Despite the tongue-lashings she administered, the industry adored her because she surrendered herself completely to it. Even in her 60's, after a full day of news gathering and writing a succinct, lively column, she had enough strength for party-hopping. On the dance floor, at fashion shindigs, she swung like a quivering blond dumpling to the new music.

The first column of "Inside Fashion" arose from an overflow of news about Grace Kelly's marriage to Prince Rainier of Monaco in the spring of 1956. Almost all of the American press was manic over that event. Miss Kelly had everything—a snooty kind of beauty, chic, money and a second-generation, Irish-American aristocracy which Americans were soon to be nourished on via the Kennedys. She was also a movie star who had won a prince, albeit of a kingdom the size of Central Park. In retrospect, she becomes the forerunner of "The Ladies," but with one difference. Miss Kelly could act.

"But really, I just wrote the first column to see what would happen," Miss Sheppard told a reporter for *Newsweek* in 1962 when she was already rating a profile in their press section. "It was when there was so much stuff coming in about Grace Kelly's wedding and I thought, 'Isn't this amusing stuff and nobody's reading it.' So I put it into a column. The management didn't show any sign that there was a new column for six months. Then the managing editor said: 'I like it. Would you keep on?' It was utterly casual. I hope it still is." Eventually, it was syndicated to more than 80 newspapers throughout the United States.

Actually, Miss Sheppard wrote about another bride-to-be in her first columns. Margaret Truman, the only child of former President Harry S. Truman, had become engaged at 32, to Elbert Clifton Daniel, Jr., son of a pharmacist in Zebulon, N.C., and a rather dashing foreign correspondent. He had been summoned back from the Soviet Union because of a severe case of ulcers, to be assistant to the foreign editor of *The New York Times*.

At the press conference held at the Carlyle Hotel in New York following the announcement of the engagement, Mr. Daniel dazzled the general-assignment reporters with his fine head of prematurely silver hair, his Southern accent that bore the inevitable gloss of 10 years' residence in London and his British tailoring. One reporter, more accustomed to gangland funerals than high fashion, was overcome by his double-breasted vest. Margaret Truman and Clifton Daniel had a quiet wedding in Independence, Mo., and took up residence in New York. He became assistant managing editor of *The Times,* then managing editor in 1964.

Although he and his wife did not really swing with any of the branches of society, he had an insatiable appetite for the kind of information dispensed in society columns. A prolific memo writer, he once carried on an international correspondence for more than half a year over the spelling of Prince Stanislas Radziwill's nickname. Charlotte Curtis, after checking with the White House, had used "Stash." Mr. Daniel insisted on "Stas."

Clifton Daniel first tasted fashion fame, even though indirect, through Miss Sheppard's column. On March 16, 1956, she wrote:

> Unlike Grace Kelly, Margaret Truman is the prepared type of bride. She had bought most of her trousseau before she announced her engagement. The trousseau will probably be international and will probably include one or two costumes from the Fontana sisters in Rome. Margaret became good friends with the likeable Fontanas in Italy and gave a luncheon for Micol Fontana when she was here recently.

In the beginning, when she was underbudgeted, understaffed and unrecognized either by society or her own newspaper, Miss Sheppard had no alternative but to rely on Miss Lambert, Jo Hughes, a saleswoman with a society following, and others who could lead her to the news of fashion or make it to order. On December 18, 1956, she gave up part of her space to Jo Hughes who did a "Dear Eugenia" column on the Bachelor's Ball. "Three of my fashion favorites and favorite customers, Mrs. C. V. Whitney (Eleanor Searle), Mrs. Raymond 'Tucky' Guest and Mrs. John Fell, wore dresses by Galanos and Philip Hulitar," Miss Hughes reported.

After the Whitneys were divorced, the sportsman's next and fourth wife, the former Marie Louise Schroeder Hosford, became one of "Jo's Girls," as Miss Sheppard also called the Hughes' clientele, and acquiesced heartily in her publicity build-up.

It didn't take long for society women to become intoxicated by the sight of their names and faces in print. Eugenia Sheppard was invited everywhere. The late Elsa Maxwell, the international set's partygiver, pronounced her "indispensable" to New York party guest lists. But

Miss Sheppard is loyal. She never fails to report a ball or fashion show with which Jo Hughes is connected as though it were a beatification. With Miss Hughes' customers as a nucleus of pawns, the saleswoman and the fashion writer enlarged their power concurrently through the Sixties.

Once Eugenia Sheppard had trained them, women in the so-called highest reaches of American society acted like starving movie starlets. The *rara avis* was the one who turned down a fashion interview, even with Miss Sheppard's imitators. For Eugenia, though, they would jump through hoops. In 1966 not only did Mrs. Anne McDonnell Ford and her two daughters agree to pose for her in Mrs. Ford's 18th-century French palace of an apartment on Fifth Avenue, but the motor magnate's first wife obliged Bill Sauro, the photographer, by swinging her coltish legs over the arms of a Louis XV chair. Mr. Sauro had been stymied by the aesthetic problem of posing two pregnant brides and their doll-sized mother. The photograph was reprinted in national news magazines to the horror of the sensitive public relations officers of the Ford Motor Company. As a result, when the incumbent Mrs. Henry Ford II was asked to pose for a photograph in the showrooms of the Puritan Dress Corporation, where she had gone to pick out something to wear at a Ford Thunderbird-Puritan promotion party, she demurred. Henry would be upset, she said. But she told the photographer to wait in the street and snap her picture when she left the building.

In the first few years after she began her column, Eugenia Sheppard was refreshingly candid. She did not hesitate to write that Paris lacked gutsy ideas one season or that many rich women were wearing mink coats like bathrobes.

> It's funny how seldom you meet a woman who really loves clothes [she wrote on October 2, 1959]. Fashion has become increasingly important but in a much more calculated and commercial way. Lots of sheer, unadulterated love of clothes went out of the picture along with the little dressmaker and the long hours of co-designing and collusion at home. . . .

Five years later, Miss Sheppard seemed convinced that clothes, and parties to wear them to, were as important to a woman as oxygen. Even the few surviving little dressmakers had been banished from her consciousness. Next to the name of her husband, the American woman most needed the names of Bill (Blass), Ben (Zuckerman), Donald (Brooks) and Mollie (Parnis). Such was Miss Sheppard's subliminal message.

Sometimes she shot a cruel arrow, as in a column of January 6, 1961, headlined WAR ON SMOCKS DECLARED:

> This department has declared war on the maternity smock. Probably no more unbecoming garment than the maternity smock has ever been taken to its heart by the clothes-buying public. Unless it's the smock's partner in crime, the straight skirt with the ghoulish round hole cut out in the center.

Although no names were mentioned, the last sentence drew blood from Elsie Frankfurt, the brown- and blond-haired president of the Page Boy Company of Dallas. Twenty years before, she had scissored a hole in her pregnant sister's dress and revolutionized the maternity fashion business with the kangaroo or expansion-front skirt. But Miss Frankfurt had kept in step with the times and was already turning out one-piece dresses when the column appeared. (Two years later, seeing the handwriting on the wall that the shift had written for the maternity manufacturer, Miss Frankfurt started a new venture called Lotus, Inc., makers of culotte-type designs for active, not pregnant women.)

> A few celebrated characters have proved that pregnancy can be sustained without the wearing of the smock [Miss Sheppard went on]. Take Jacqueline Kennedy, who swept to the head of the best-dressed list in her maternity clothes. Never caught napping in a smock, she wore nothing but one-piece dresses, slim at the sides. . . .

Miss Sheppard, who never lost her own girlish, Midwestern tones, noticed that young women were imitating Mrs. Kennedy in other ways, as, for example, her voice, which sounded like "a dear little girl who has been running and doesn't want to be late." This was in 1962 and the whole little girl business was due to get worse.

In February 1965, after reviewing the haute couture collections in Europe, she decided:

> America may soon have to turn in the championship blue ribbon for the best-looking legs. Not that American girls' legs are physically any less perfect than they used to be. It's just that they are a little out of style. The American, long greyhound look with the

slightly swelling calf has been the ideal for a long time, since Florenz Ziegfeld put it on a pedestal, in fact. Stacked up against the legs of some of the European girls, though, it's beginning to look dated. . . . Whatever country it comes from, the new leg is a little girl leg. It looks as undeveloped and unsexy as the Gay Nineties-type leg now looks too full-blown and overripe. This isn't a skinny leg. It's delicately round, but with absolutely no calf. To be stuck with legs and calves is just too crass for words, according to Paris. The new ideal leg is a round little pole. Actually, it looks as much like a forearm as a leg. Legs and arms seem to match, as they do with a child. The look is 100-proof Lolita.

"Inside Fashion" had made its debut on a twice weekly basis. When the management of her sick newspaper decided that it was a drawing card for readers and potential advertisers, they coaxed Miss Sheppard to write it six times a week and to provide several pages of fashion-society coverage on Sundays. Like the trooper she was, Miss Sheppard did not protest. Filling a column is like feeding a tapeworm and she needed her friends more than ever. But something had to go. What went was objectivity, perspective and the news of fashion beyond the narrow boundaries within which her Galateas moved.

The sharp, level-headed analysis of fashion was proportionately reduced. The ersatz celebrities she had created dominated the column. Foremost among them was Mollie Parnis, the Seventh Avenue dress manufacturer who is a client of Miss Lambert's and a major supplier for Miss Hughes. Miss Sheppard had introduced Mollie Parnis in her first column along with Margaret Truman's trousseau. The manufacturer was already known to the American public but was nowhere near the celebrity that Eugenia Sheppard was to make her.

Mollie Parnis will surely be represented in the trousseau, too [she wrote]. Margaret Truman has been wearing her clothes since White House days. In fact, when Mollie Parnis (in private life Mrs. Leonard [sic] Livingston) first appeared at the White House as designer to Mrs. Eisenhower, a shocked doorman greeted her with "well you certainly do get around Mrs. Livingston."

During the Kennedy Administration, Miss Parnis suffered a weakening of her White House affiliation but when Mrs. Lyndon B. Johnson became First Lady, she edged back into the limelight. In the meantime, however, Eugenia Sheppard had humanized her and broadened her social personality as she did for other manufacturers. At first it was with tidbits such as this one of October 9, 1956: "Mollie Parnis' new broadtail cape from Maximilian has three snap-on collars—ermine, sable and chinchilla." Miss Parnis cooperated to the fullest extent by residing in a Park Avenue duplex decorated by Billy Baldwin, the society interior designer. She had a Matisse painting over her living-room sofa, wore David Webb jewelry and gave parties. On November 4, 1965, Miss Sheppard wrote:

> Mollie Parnis' party to hear the election returns ended with all the girls upstairs and around a mirror swapping techniques on false eyelashes. Lots of little black dresses, again. Joan Muss in black point d'esprit, Marilyn Evins and ex-model Nan Reese (wife of the plastic surgeon) in black crepe.

When Miss Parnis' friends, Mrs. Stanley Donen of London and Mrs. Kirk Douglas of Los Angeles (wives of a movie director and an actor), came to visit, Miss Sheppard devoted a few lines to a major segment of her column to their arrival and their views on fashion. Miss Parnis also cultivated people in government and other newspapers such as *The New York Times*. When she felt slighted by *The Times'* fashion reporters, she discussed her pique with *Times'* editors over the dinner table. Afterwards, her showings were properly covered. It can be argued that Miss Parnis is entitled to behave like a prima donna. Isn't she, after all, a celebrity?

If Eugenia Sheppard is the fashion industry's Pygmalion, then Eleanor Lambert is its master puppeteer. She began her career in Manhattan in 1925, coming from Crawfordsville, Ind., the cutely blond daughter of a circus advance agent. She had studied sculpture, "but I wasn't good enough," she admits in the flat, whiny voice that can rise to an angry crescendo when the performances of others fail to meet her expectations. She stepped off the train with $100 and an installment-credit coat that fell apart within a few weeks, she recollected for a reporter. At the time of the interview, she was dwelling in a Fifth Avenue apartment furnished with French antiques and modern painting, and had a substantial week-end retreat in Port Jefferson, L.I. Miss Lambert likes to talk poor mouth à la Rockefeller.

A fortune-teller at the Paris Flea Market had said to her, "You're not really rich, you just look it," she confided to another scribe one morning in her office on East 57th Street. There she was, amid the beige carpeting, French furniture, modern paintings and a signed photograph of President Eisenhower and her husband on the wall— a 60-ish, trim blonde with sleepy brown eyes, attired in a taupe linen dress with three strands of pearls slipped under its neckline, a diamond and ruby starfish pin on its left shoulder, on her fingers a ruby ring paved with diamonds and a gold wedding band, on her wrists a wide gold watchband and a David Webb enamel, gold and diamond jungle bracelet. Pearl and diamond circlets glittered softly at her ears.

Miss Lambert started off in New York doing publicity for art galleries. While she was the press attaché for the newly established Whitney Museum, she met Seymour Berkson, a handsome and brilliant newspaperman whose ambition matched her own. They were married and their careers soared on swift, parallel lines. Seymour Berkson was, at his death in 1959, publisher of the New York *Journal-American*. No one ran a close second to his wife as a fashion publicist and promoter. The Berksons were an unbeatable team. They knew exactly what they wanted and usually managed to get it by a combination of shrewdness, flexible charm and single-mindedness. They were attractive hosts whose guests were assured of being wined, dined, pampered and presented to other fascinating people. Miss Lambert accepts credit for introducing Sloan Simpson to the late Mayor William O'Dwyer, and Geraldine Stutz to David Gibbs, the English painter whom she married.

Eleanor Lambert has always known how to capitalize on opportunity. She has a knack for sensing and exploiting others' needs. Her accomplishments are all the more impressive because they arise out of seemingly total confusion. She is chronically tardy and affects a vague, helplessly feminine manner at times but always manages to pull her chestnuts out of the fire.

Miss Lambert has garnered as much publicity for distinguished nonclients like Norman Norell, Rudi Gernreich and John Weitz as for paying accounts like Samuel Winston, Anne Klein, Ship 'n' Shore Blouse and Kimberly Knits. She is as much a drumbeater for the institution of American fashion as for individual manufacturers and designers. She may be feared and disliked for her temper and her steamroller tactics but she cannot be disregarded.

She has been doing publicity for dress designers since 1932. In the early days, it was with the help of the late Dorothy Shaver, who became president of Lord & Taylor and the first retailer to advertise and promote American designers. First, Miss Lambert succeeded in making the names of American designers as familiar to American women as the elite couturiers of Paris. On the next plateau, as she explains it, "I tried to make people seem as interesting as opera singers, make them personalities and give them rounded appearances."

In 1943, she inaugurated twice-yearly press weeks sponsored by 30 manufacturers whom she had welded into the New York Couture Group, the prestige arm of the New York Dress Institute. The latter was an organization established by the International Ladies' Garment Workers Union and the city's dress manufacturers to stimulate clothes buying. Fashion editors from the 150 largest cities in the country were invited to attend a week of continuous fashion showings. The number later rose to 200. Their newspapers were offered a refund on the editors' round-trip transportation, an offer that half of them accepted.

In its heyday, each session of press week was estimated to earn 10 million lines of newspaper space for Seventh Avenue fashion. The editors worked hard but they were also cosseted. They were wined, dined, taken to the theater and permitted to rub noses with designers. Their publishers gave lip service to the interest of their women readers in fashion but they did not go as far as to allow budgets for photography or travel or any of the expenses that are necessary for independent reporting. Fashion reporting had been held in low esteem by the newspaper profession anyhow. The women's page was considered a dumping ground for sob sisters with failing health or wits, as well as an adjunct of the advertising department. With press week, Miss Lambert was only giving the newspapers what they wanted, a free and easy supply of copy for their women's pages.

In 1955, Elizabeth Penrose Howkins was appointed women's news editor of *The New York Times*. She persuaded Arthur Hays Sulzberger, then the publisher, that the so-called women's interest subjects warranted as competent and critical handling as Broadway and the arts. In Craig Claiborne, she found a food editor of unassailable integrity and knowledge. Patricia Peterson loved fashion but formed no entangling alliances within the industry. She was one of the first fashion editors to grasp the portent of Courrèges.

Mrs. Howkins asserted the right to report Seventh Avenue collections when they were news, *i.e.*, when the store buyers first saw them about a month before Miss Lambert's spoon-feedings. There ensued a comic war on Manhattan's West Side with some obedient manufacturers barring *The Times'* fashion reporters and the latter, like a pack of Nellie Blys, taking back door information when they were refused admittance at the front. Finally, the manufacturers backed down. *The Times* and other newspapers that could afford independence covered the collections from the outset. In October 1962, Miss Lambert resigned as press director of the New York Couture Group. Kittie Campbell was her successor.

The dependent press was then confronted with rival press weeks. With a nucleus of her clients, Miss Lambert launched the American Designer Series of semi-annual showings. She also rallied a new organization, the Council of Fashion Designers of America, which nominated her as its public relations adviser and established its headquarters in her office. The CFDA was the organization with cachet, membership being limited "strictly to individuals known for their creative force within a fashion firm." Just plain manufacturers, as opposed to creative designers, belonged to the Couture Group. Some designer-manufacturers belonged to both.

Miss Lambert had turned disaster into triumph. With the CFDA as a platform, she was ready to take the fashion industry where she thought it should go next. She managed recognition for fashion as one of the arts entitled to federal government support. Miss Lambert appreciates the value of the laurel wreath, which confers as much on the donor as it does on the wearer. Lift the curtain on most of fashion's major accolades and one finds the hand of Eleanor Lambert. She promotes the Cotton Fashion Award, she is chairman of the American Committee of the International Fashion Awards sponsored by the London *Sunday Times,* whose powerful fashion editor, Ernestine Carter, is a British Eugenia Sheppard (minus the latter's writing skill). But all of these pale in significance next to the Coty American Fashion Critics' Award and the Best-Dressed List, which were Miss Lambert's babies and which are still firmly tied to her apron strings.

The Coty Award purports to honor the best creative American fashion design. Newspaper and magazine editors who cover fashion vote to confer a "Winnie" (a nude bronze statuette, clutching a bit of drapery, that was designed by Malvina Hoffman) on the best designers of the year. Coty, the fragrance company, picks up the tab, in the neighborhood of $23,000, for the presentation and fashion show at the Metropolitan Museum of Art. The industry turns out in full regalia.

Fashion editors maintain that the Coty Award is the only irreproachable award in the business. But in June 1963, Norman Norell, a member of the Coty Hall of Fame, where three-time winners are installed, sent back his "Winnie" because he said the voting was not fair and would never be until every member of the jury saw every designer's collection. That year, there were 72 jurors. Some of the fashion magazines sent half a dozen or more representatives who formed voting blocs. At a subsequent meeting of the executive committee, publications were asked to cut their teams down to four. Partly because of the death toll among newspapers, places were offered to editors from previously excluded magazines like *Seventeen.* And the Coty Award, "coordinated" by Eleanor Lambert, marched on. She also continued to coordinate the International Best-Dressed List. "The French who had been getting out a list of best-dressed women since 1924 were interrupted by the war so I thought it would be a good idea to take it over," she told *The New York Times* in 1965. She sends about 2,000 ballots to fashion editors throughout the country and to "every designer I have ever heard of in every capital, every woman ever mentioned, society editors, columnists, every socialite, man and woman I think should have an opinion, restaurant owners."

The ballots, which contain 12 write-in spaces, are accompanied by a handy reference list of 101 names compiled by a committee of fashion editors whose identities are not made public (so the editors won't be pressured, of course). They also compile the nominees to the Hall of Fame, where perennial winners like the Duchess of Windsor, Mrs. Winston Guest, Mrs. William S. Paley and Mrs. Norman K. Winston (wife of the international builder and real estate investor and one of Miss Lambert's closest friends) are considerably kicked upstairs to make room for younger achievers.

About 600 ballots are returned. Among those who purposely refrain from responding have been Olive Dickason, women's editor of the Toronto *Globe and Mail* who said she didn't fill out her ballot "because it would be useless at best, dishonest at worst." In an article on the Ten Best-Dressed List in the January 5, 1963, issue of the *Saturday Evening Post,* Miss Sheppard explained that the secret committee supplemented the vote and "toned down" misguided public enthusiasm by substituting its own choices. It was quite clear that she is present at these luncheon meetings. She also disclosed how the "limelight" around Mrs. John F. Kennedy, who jumped to the head of the list in 1961 (the committee tastefully refrained from nominating her at the end of 1963), drew attention to her sister, Princess Radziwill, and her friend, Mrs. Wrightsman. The latter was yanked into tenth place in 1962. On November 22, 1966, Eugenia Sheppard devoted a column to hints about who would make the list for that year. Mrs. Lyndon B. Johnson and Mrs. Henry Ford II were among those touted. Lo and behold, they made it on December 30. The committee never anoints any of the countless women of taste and means who live in Chicago, San Francisco, Detroit and Montreal for an obvious reason. Those women don't associate with the New York fashion editors and publicists.

Miss Lambert's connection with the Best-Dressed List won her an exclusive interview with Queen Sirikit of Thailand after Miss Lambert started her syndicated newspaper column "She" in 1964. A colored photograph of the Queen in a silver frame adorns a marble-topped *bombé* chest in the publicist's office. "I called up the paper in Bangkok when I was there and said I have some connection with the Best-Dressed List. She had made the list. And they arranged the interview," Miss Lambert reminisced.

Some 40 newspapers around the country took her thrice-weekly column when it was first distributed by the Hall Syndicate. "I started the column with trepidation," she said. When the syndicate first approached her, she recalled, "I said, 'I can't do that because I have a publicity office.' But they said, 'We need a column to tell women how to dress. We understand you're a small-town girl and still think like one.' "

Miss Lambert didn't argue the last point with them although she had, by then, become an international operator. She had added Fabiani of Rome, Molyneux and Castillo of Paris to her client roster and she had done stints for Pierre Cardin. A national magazine had photographed her in what it identified as her Paris *pied-à-terre*. "It wasn't. I don't have an apartment in Paris. It was Gloria Guinness' apartment where I was staying. I can imagine what Gloria thought when she saw that," Miss Lambert said with a small smile.

At first, she discounted the syndicate's proposition. "But then I was in Paris sick, with something frozen in my hip. The doctor said it was nervous exhaustion, and I thought maybe I should do something else.

Well, now I'm up to 60 papers. It's not going to make me rich. I'm ashamed of the style but I'm trying to do the thing that will be down to earth and informative. I don't want to be New Yorkish. I would like to get my sister-in-law in Lafayette, Indiana, informed. Why, out there they can tell you the names of 20 American designers but they don't know Schiaparelli isn't working any more."

Occasionally, a newspaper editor far from New York complained about the names Miss Lambert drops in her column. Not the names of clients like Malcolm Starr or Ben Zuckerman or Helen Lee, but names like Mrs. Palmer Dixon and Mrs. Brooks Howe, the same names that Eugenia Sheppard's readers have been raised on.

Miss Lambert didn't just write about clothes. She did a column on LSD, "but the syndicate didn't send it out. I said we're facing a time when our grandchildren will feel it's a social habit like smoking or drinking," she said. Her son, Bill, was then 27 and a bachelor. "I have a friend who said she's tried it. She was a friend who said she'd never have her face lifted. She said she wouldn't touch her body but would try anything to enlarge her mind. I felt I didn't mind tampering with my body but not my mind and my soul."

She also told her readers about Acapulco, which was so publicized in the mid-Sixties that Palm Beach regulars began to vacate the chilly Florida island in February for the Mexican resort. "I bought a house in Acapulco because I'm mad about it there," she explained. "The Mexican Tourist Council are such nice men that I helped them but never for money. I went down with June Weir (of *Women's Wear Daily*) and Jo Zill (of *Sports Illustrated*) and Eugenia but just for fun."

The fun paid a dividend in torrents of print.

No one understood the psychology of the press better than Miss Lambert. It had always been a tradition to keep an eye peeled on one's competitor, and failing to scoop him, to copy him. In the Sixties, the fashion press became such cutthroat competitors that they were going around in circles, and the nonfashion publications, stepping up their coverage of pop culture, accepted the expertise of the fashion specialists and joined the chase.

If Eugenia or *Women's Wear* or *The Times* had something, *Time* and *Newsweek* might pick it up. Sally Kirkland, *Life*'s fashion editor, belonged to what *Newsweek* called "The Mouse Pack," a foursome consisting of herself and the Misses Lambert, Sheppard and Stutz.

Miss Kirkland usually delivered the message packaged for world-wide mass consumption. The wire services and the women's service magazines stepped up and orchestrated the same themes. Even if individual fashion editors didn't want to imitate, their superiors were reading Eugenia and demanding to know why they didn't follow her gospel.

Starting in the early Sixties, many of those senior editors were also taking *Women's Wear Daily* with their morning coffee. When Clifton Daniel, then an assistant managing editor, was contemplating the revitalization of the good, gray *New York Times,* he consumed *Women's Wear* before the women's editor reached her desk at 11 A.M. Clippings and memos awaited her. After he succeeded Turner Catledge as managing editor, the task of reading *Women's Wear* (as well as Eugenia Sheppard) was delegated to Harrison E. Salisbury who filled his shoes. The dour, scholarly, Pulitzer-Prize-winning correspondent, who had coped calmly with Stalin and Khrushchev, was clearly flustered by the assignment. He was unable to evaluate the relative significance of the No-Bra Bra, "The Ladies" in Zuckerman suits or a blouse trend that *Women's Wear* was puffing up in its back pages. Part of the problem was that Mr. Salisbury, whose round, steel-framed spectacles suddenly made him a camp leader, had no grasp of pop culture.

Mr. Daniel arranged for special tutoring by sending him and his wife for a night on the town with Charlotte Curtis and Sydney Gruson, then the foreign editor (who counted among his wide circle of acquaintances not only prime ministers, premiers and chancellors but Mollie Parnis and Jacqueline Kennedy). They took in the British film *The Knack* and advanced to Arthur, the discothèque. It didn't help much. Eventually, Mr. Salisbury escaped to a three-month tour of Asia and the Soviet Union. When he returned, however, he was assigned to a summit luncheon with Mr. Daniel and Norman Norell, who, egged on by *Women's Wear,* had barred *The New York Times* from his showroom. After Mr. Salisbury's historic trip to North Vietnam early in 1967, he was relieved of fashion chores.

The Norell-*Times* confrontation delighted John Fairchild, who craved the role of power broker. He was an heir to the Fairchild empire of nine solid but dull trade newspapers, of which *Women's Wear* was the leader. He shook up his dominions, unnerved his neighbors and made some of them dance to his tune. It was as if Britain's Prince Charles had come home from Australia and started acting like

Charles de Gaulle. His mission of grandeur succeeded. The circulation of *Women's Wear Daily,* the garment industry's only newspaper, rose from 51,498 in mid-1962 to 60,591 in mid-1966, the highest in its history. Among those subscribers who paid $20 a year to receive their copies by mail were not only the corset manufacturers and the suit buyers whom the newspaper had originally been supposed to inform, but Mrs. C. V. Whitney and a doctor's wife in Chicago who didn't know a soul in the business but liked the gossip columns and the pretty pictures.

Starting in 1960, when his father, Louis W. Fairchild, then chairman of the board of Fairchild Publications, Inc., brought him back from France where he had headed the chain's Paris bureau to run *Women's Wear Daily,* John Fairchild acted in informal concert with Eugenia Sheppard. He fortified the new genre of fashion reporting she had devised—aggressive, gossipy, personal and habit-forming—as well as the new set of fashion celebrities and the new garment center aristocracy. Miss Sheppard was harmless and uncomplicated and did nothing to make Bryn Mawr disown her. Mr. Fairchild deepened the hue of yellow journalism.

Tall, brown-haired and blue-eyed with slightly protruding teeth and a dimple scooped out of the center of his chin, John Burr Fairchild is the great-great-grandson of two Protestant ministers, one Dutch Reformed, the other Presbyterian. "I wonder why I'm an Episcopalian," he once mused during an interview. His grandfather, Edgar W. Fairchild, founded the string of apparel industry newspapers in Chicago in 1890. Fairchild was educated at Kent School and Princeton University from which he graduated in 1949. His wife, Jill, is half English and half Russian, was raised in South America, educated at Vassar, wears Chanel and Norell (enthusiasms that are reflected in *Women's Wear* pages), is highly intelligent, attractive and multilingual. It was by listening to her order groceries on the telephone during the five years they lived in Paris that her husband says he learned French.

There is no reason to doubt him. *Women's Wear* is larded with language that can easily be mastered by dropouts from freshman French who are confident because the stewardesses on Air France, the hall porter at the Plaza Athénée and Yvonne de Peyerimhoff, *directrice* of the house of Yves Saint Laurent, understand them perfectly. *Women's Wear* has coined such franglicisms as haute camp, fashion brut, Les Hotsies (manufacturers like Jerry Silverman and Hannah Troy whose collections pleased Mr. Fairchild one season) and the Sportive Look. "Sportive meant any girl who is interesting and just might be a little dangerous, not sporty, but very attractively dangerous and maybe a little sexy," Mr. Fairchild protested after the sportive tune he piped in the spring of 1963 prompted an epidemic of knee high boots, walking sticks and even sportive girdles. It had started as a typical Fairchild joke.

The headlines day after day, week after week, month after month, drove the edgy, humorless manufacturers into ludicrous, outdoorsy binges: BRIDES SHOULD BE SPORTIVE, TOO; SEVENTH AVENUE GENTLEMAN TAILOR SEYMOUR FOX GOES MORE SPORTIVE THAN EVER; SCHOOL SPORTIVE (sizes 7 to 14); SPORTIVE BY AIR (the arrival of 143 friends of Charles Aznavour for a Carnegie Hall concert); and SAINT LAURENT NOW THE SAVIOUR OF THE PARIS COUTURE, SAINT LAURENT SPORTIVE.

"When the corset manufacturers came out with sportive girdles, I couldn't believe it," he said later, claiming as usual that he had been misunderstood. He wondered whether the public perceived that "Her Elegance," his title for Jacqueline Kennedy, was really a take-off on "Her Royal Highness." When she was in the White House, *Women's Wear Daily* campaigned against the lengths to which she went to hide the extent and origin (often French) of her fashion purchases. An attack on an idol that is a skillful mixture of righteous indignation and fawning is an effective way for a pygmy of the press to call attention to itself. And anyway, the newspaper soon reverted to outright flattery. In 1966 and after, its photographers and reporters relentlessly pursued Mrs. Kennedy, lying in wait for her outside her New York apartment house, the restaurants she frequented and the parties she attended. "Jacqueline Kennedy is ahead of events," it reported on July 22, 1966. "That Hawaiian bikini-shift [*WWD*, page 1, July 20] . . . her bikinis . . . her shorter skirts . . . and that long heavy hair . . . SHE'S A REALGIRL."

JACQUELINE FORMIDABLE was the headline on a double spread of photographs taken outside the Lafayette Restaurant on December 4, 1966. The pictures proved that Mrs. Kennedy had shortened her skirts several inches above the knee. They were reprinted in newspapers and magazines throughout the world and recharged the mini-skirt movement just when it was thought to be expiring.

Jacqueline Kennedy and Gian-Carlo Menotti enjoy THE LONGEST
LUNCH at Quo Vadis Thursday [*Women's Wear* reported on
March 3, 1967, next to a full-page photograph]. Jackie arrives
at 1:15 P.M. in her little leopard coat . . . looking terrific with a
white turtleneck and beige jumper underneath. She and the com-
poser leave at 4:30 P.M. as the chauffeured car drives up on cue.
The lunches are getting longer . . . and the leopard coats shorter.

Under John Fairchild's direction, *Women's Wear Daily* outstripped
Eugenia Sheppard in toadying to the socially established while purposefully fusing them with the fashion industry. THEY'RE BACK! headlined the daily feature on pages 4 and 5 of Thursday, September
8, 1966:

'Tis not yet Autumn . . . 'tis not even Indian Summer . . . 'tis not
even yet the end of Real Summer. . . . But . . . The Ladies . . . Are
. . . BACK: To the endless rounds . . . the forever decisions:
Where to shop, what to buy, what to wear, where to wear what,
when to go, how to go, why to be there . . . and—Who With?
BACK: To the favored noontime spas . . . the Midtown Man-
hattan Muncheries . . . the Colony . . . La Côte Basque . . . La
Caravelle . . . La Grenouille (it reopens for the season today).

Accompanying photographs were of Truman Capote, Eugenia Sheppard, Elieth Roux of Bergdorf Goodman, Norman Norell, Mrs. Anne
McDonnell Ford, Mrs. W. Palmer Dixon, Mrs. Winston F. C. Guest,
Mrs. S. Carter Burden, Jr., Mrs. Stephen Smith and Minnie Cushing.
Mr. Fairchild appreciated the value of belonging. Before he took
charge of *Women's Wear Daily,* its reporters had been the untouch-
ables of the fashion caste system. Bergdorf Goodman put them in the
back row at showings if it invited them at all. *Vogue* and *Harper's
Bazaar* were always seated on facing, upholstered French settees
flanked by Eugenia Sheppard and Patricia Peterson on opposite,
upholstered bergères while everyone else rated hard folding chairs to
the side and behind. Similar treatment was accorded *Women's Wear*
on Seventh Avenue.
In less than three years, Mr. Fairchild transformed a stodgy, un-
selective journal into a zesty, irreverent, opinionated, controversial,
heartless, and superbly illustrated tabloid. Its columnists were in the
front row at Bergdorf's. In the spring of 1966, Mrs. Samuel P. Pea-

body of the *Social Register* was kissing June Weir of *Women's Wear* hello in Chester Weinberg's showroom.

Although John Fairchild would seem to have the requisites for personal tranquillity, he suffers from a galloping case of social malaise. "I really am afraid of lots of people," he has said. "I suffer going to parties." The Fairchilds live without fanfare in New Canaan, Conn., to which he likes to repair on the 5:09 P.M. out of Grand Central. The relatively few invitations he accepts are those which guarantee the presence of friends like the Frederick Eberstadts. He went to college with Mr. Eberstadt, a fashion photographer and son of a Wall Street investment banker. Isabel Eberstadt is one of *Women's Wear's* earliest heroines. "Mrs. Frederick Eberstadt, leader of the New Social Wave in America . . . young, perky, very much alive to Everything and Everyone . . . an individual . . . a young Arrogant Elegant all the way," it said of her in a two-page photographic essay on August 24, 1962, which was merely the prelude to her elevation to the pantheon. Mrs. Eberstadt repaid this and other tributes by writing a laudatory article on Mr. Fairchild for the New York *Herald-Tribune.*

The term "Arrogant Elegant" was coined by William J. Cunningham, a Boston-born milliner whom Mr. Fairchild persuaded to serve as one of his columnists for nine months. Mr. Cunningham recalled that Arrogant Elegance originated at a ball he attended:

> Elsa Maxwell and her elderly crowd were there dripping charm and dripping phoniness in their dripping cool dresses. Everyone was eating dinner but there were these three empty tables. Then the elevator opened and the Eberstadts and their friends came in. They were so marvelously chic and above it all. They came in as if they were the only ones and their clothes the only clothes.

Being arrogant was also a characteristic of clothes, circa 1962-63:

> Those stiff, cutout little Givenchy coats didn't give a damn. The coat was so sharp and brittle and so positive it was right. Not that the women were arrogant. The clothes made them arrogant. People thought the people were arrogant. I didn't mean that, although some of the people only needed a slight push.

Mr. Cunningham wrote a perceptive column and then became fashion correspondent for the Chicago *Tribune.* After his departure, his thrice-weekly spot was taken by Carol Bjorkman, a brunette with a

Veruschka in stenciled body make-up. Photograph by Franco Rubartelli, courtesy of *Vogue:* copyright © 1966 by The Condé Nast Publications Inc.

Jacqueline Kennedy, January 20, 1961. Wide World Photos

Jacqueline Kennedy, Caroline and John, Jr., January, 1966. Wide World Photos

Oleg Cassini
at Roosevelt
Raceway,
January, 1966.
*The New York
Times* (by
Robert Walker)

Dress by Gernreich, hairdo by Sassoon. 1966. Reprinted courtesy of *Queen*

Photograph by Art Kane, courtesy of *Vogue:* copyright © 1962, by The Condé Nast Publications Inc.

IT'S SUPER-FASHION!

Stalking her prey—or is she being stalked?—the Fashion Mover (left) in the ear-splitting sound of color, ultrasonic violet-striped knit. Shape: clean, taut, uncompromising. About $40. From Paraphernalia. A Wakmann-Breitling watch for those with sporting blood. Boots by Golo.

On guard, lifeguards! No-baby's romper suit (opposite), diaper-tied over the strongest, sparest body. Swimsuit by Edie Gladstone, in Helanca stretch nylon knit. About $36. At Bonwit Teller; Jordan Marsh, Florida. Rolex watch. Both pages: huntress masks by Emme. Viola Weinberger gloves. Opposite: On the body, John Robert Powers' Bare Beauty, a translucent, moisturizing head-to-toe make-up that covers what it touches with a seaside tan, splashes happily in the water all day without disappearing (for that, only a handy bar of soap will do).

Photograph by Hiro, May, 1966, courtesy of *Harper's Bazaar*

Things to make the scene in

Suit by Foale & Tuffin : 19½ gns. **Sweat** Rosalind Yehuda : 6 gns. **Stockings** by Aristoc : 15/11. **Shoes** by Terry de Hav 4 gns. **Cheque Book** by District Bank : you get one when you open an account (which you can do with less than the pr the shoes). A District Bank account ma it easier to save up for things—and whe you see the suit you just *must* have but you haven't enough money on you, the you know how convenient your cheque book is. You just write a cheque !

Find out more by walking into your n est branch of District Bank. (You can look up the address in the phone book.) Any member of the staff will be happy to help you.

DISTRICT
BANK

Courtesy of *Vogue:* Copyright © 1966 by The Condé Nast Publications Inc.

Diana Vreeland, editor-in-chief of *Vogue,* with Nicolas de Gunzburg, a fashion editor (left), and S. I. Newhouse, Jr., the publisher, 1966. *The New York Times* (by Barton Silverman)

1967. Eugenia Sheppard covering a story. Her coat is Ohrbach's copy of a Balenciaga. *The New York Times* (by Larry Morris)

Barbra Streisand and Halston during a fitting at Bergdorf Goodman, 1965. *The New York Times* (by Jack Manning)

Jane Holzer in Chanel from head to toe. 1964. *The New York Times* (by Arthur Brower)

Bill Blass with Louise Savitt and her dummy. 1964. *The New York Times* (by Neal Boenzi)

Right: Mrs. Samuel P. Peabody at the ballet in a dress by Bob Bugnand. 1965. *The New York Times* (by Larry Morris) *Above:* Mr. and Mrs. Wyatt Cooper at a Broadway theater opening. Her dress is by Mainbocher. 1965. *The New York Times* (by Larry Morris)

Susan Stein (in a jump suit by Linda Hackett) with Paul Young at a *Mademoiselle* party at the Cheetah. 1966. *The New York Times* (by Larry Morris)

flawless bone structure—and extensive social contacts. She would arrive at fashion shows, usually a little late, sweeping in with her white poodle, Sheba, daintily throwing back her coat so that the Balenciaga label was clearly visible and making the press photographers forget to focus on the models.

Miss Bjorkman had grown up in Pittsburgh, acted in a Hollywood movie (*Letter From an Unknown Woman* in 1948) and worked in New York as assistant to Valentina, the dressmaker to Greta Garbo among others. There she met such stars as Mrs. William S. Paley, Queen Soraya and Rosalind Russell. Later, she was a dress buyer for Saks Fifth Avenue (among her customers: Mrs. Charles Wrightsman and Mrs. John F. Kennedy). Then for a year and a half in Paris, she took charge of American customers for the fledgling house of Yves Saint Laurent. There, Mr. Fairchild met her and induced her to write a column. At first, it was illustrated with a photograph of her mouth, later by constantly changing photographs of her head, shoulders and torso, and sometimes of her exceptional bosom popping out of a décolleté evening dress.

Miss Bjorkman brought a spontaneous, feminine point of view of fashion. Her presence assured *Women's Wear* of a seasonal scoop on the collection of Saint Laurent, who makes the rest of the press wait until a few days after he has shown to buyers, lest adverse criticism scare the merchants away. Miss Bjorkman can be trusted.

"The buyers . . . must clean up on this collection," she wrote on August 1, 1966, in a column describing a mythical chase to sleuth out the news of his designs.

> YVES WENT BACK TO HIS APARTMENT on the Place Vauban and we went inside and chatted. "I started my collection with another feeling—it is true, but now I find what I have done plus amusant than the dame trop chic. It is like my bride, she is a conventional bride, but she wears a plastic flower that is lit from within the dress and will light up and make a noise." I don't know about anybody else but send me my checkbook.

Buyers read this account before they saw the collection. When they did, reactions were mixed, although not according to Miss Bjorkman's account. The next day, she cabled:

> Yves Saint Laurent put the juice back into the couture with his fabulously successful collection Monday. You must have heard

the applause over there. By 12 o'clock every red-blooded journalist was in front of his 30 Bis Rue Spontini to hear the buyers and private client report. "I am absolutely ravi," said top private client of the house as she was still going strong after ordering 12 things so far. "It is the most fabulous collection I have seen," she said. This is just a soupçon compared to the raves soaring all over Paris. Some buyers gulped down their lunch so they could go right back to the house and place their orders first.

Carol Bjorkman is meticulous about her work. She never writes about a party unless she has attended it. Parties are a recurring theme in her column, which is studded with the names of fashion consumer celebrities like the Eberstadts and Judy Peabody, the Denniston Slaters and the Joe Tankooses and the Carter Burdens. She has made the scene with a variety of escorts from a coat manufacturer to a television executive to Halston, Bergdorf Goodman's custom milliner. She has attended the Metropolitan Opera, sitting in a box with Mrs. Bruno Pagliai (Merle Oberon) and Mrs. Henry Ford II. The Duke and Duchess of Windsor invite her for lunch and dinner when she is in Paris.

Miss Bjorkman, however, would like to be more than a gadabout. She is acutely interested in art and literature and started writing a novel in 1966. That year, her column took a more serious tone. She followed Senator Robert F. Kennedy on a speechmaking trip to upstate New York. ("When he got up to walk around, his pants—while they weren't hipsters—fell down on his hips almost like a cowboy's," she disclosed.) She interviewed David Rockefeller, president of the Chase Manhattan Bank.

> At first, it is hard to keep your mind on business—there are so many things to look at [she wrote, and then proceeded to describe what Mr. Rockefeller was wearing]. . . . He is charming and polite, but he doesn't like interviews, I say to myself. I have a feeling he is saying to himself: "What does *WWD* want to know about me?" I try to put him at ease by saying the photographer is the same one who photographed Miss Garbo. He smiles, but somehow I don't think it made a dent. . . .

In print as everywhere else, Miss Bjorkman is good-natured, generous and kind. It is in the rest of the columns and features of *Women's Wear Daily* that the malice shows. "Jean vanden Heuvel needs a new hairdresser." That remark was part of the "reporting" of the opening of the new Metropolitan Opera House. "That little old dressmaker is at it again," was the caption under a photograph of Mrs. Hubert H. Humphrey arriving at the Capitol in January 1967 for the State of the Union Message, which *Women's Wear Daily* covers as a fashion event and finds disappointing. "Another one of those 'dumb' costumes," was the comment under the photograph of Mrs. Stuart Symington, who looked fetching in a simple dress and jacket. Bitchiness is the industry's word for the mood and operating style of the Paris haute couture. John Fairchild brought it back to Seventh Avenue. "If they don't get rid of some of those people, I'm going to quit," *Women's Wear* reported Jacques Tiffeau, the designing partner of Tiffeau-Busch, as saying on October 10, 1966. He was talking about membership in the Council of Fashion Designers of America. "Non-creators like Mollie Parnis and Vincent Monte-Sano should get out. They weaken the prestige and authority of a group which should just include this country's top creative designers. . . . I am not trying to be bitchy," the French-born designer said. A few months before, he had resigned from Mr. Monte-Sano's firm. Three years before, Mr. Fairchild had moved up to direct the editorial course of all of the Fairchild empire. He is now president of Fairchild Publications, Inc. He passed the job of *Women's Wear* publisher to James W. Brady, a handsome and aggressive newspaperman.

But key designers still hear from John Fairchild and he has drawn a very precise blueprint for his staff. He had started by inviting designers and manufacturers to lunch, one at a time, shortly after he arrived from Paris, unsought and unknown. He preferred the Oak Room of the St. Regis. ("The last time I had the shrimp curry here with Mr. Norell, there was glass in it," he chirped to the maître d'hôtel during one interview.) His luncheon companions were pumped, cajoled and enlightened as to what was expected of them. Exclusive news. Advance sketches of designs before the collections. Feuds. *Women's Wear* rushes into print on what responsible journalists would consider insufficient grounds. A cruel rumor is hatched. The principals are called; they deny the rumor because it is completely false. *Women's Wear* prints it as a "rumor squelched," which nevertheless attains the objective of circulating the canard.

Mr. Fairchild had behind him a record of victory in Paris. Only Balenciaga and Givenchy had resisted, but Balenciaga had a staff that was willing to betray the master just a little bit. He met with little opposition in America. There were a few stout-hearted types like George Stavropoulos, who refused to leak sketches of the dresses that Mrs. Johnson ordered from him. But the rest realized that John Fairchild would pay well for service rendered. Although he gave the industry a chronic case of nervous stomach with his abrupt shifts and feints, he reciprocated its cooperation by raising the self-esteem of what had formerly been called the rag trade, even as he taunted and titillated it.

Norman Norell could be counted on. Before each collection, *Women's Wear* (and then Eugenia Sheppard) published an interview in which the designer discoursed on his plans. Venting his displeasure at *The New York Times'* less than adoring treatment of him, Norell sent a letter to Charlotte Curtis, advising her that she and her staff were no longer welcome in his showroom. A few hours before the missive was received by Miss Curtis, *Women's Wear's* subscribers were reading about it. Norell was rewarded with the sobriquet "Fashion Great," usually in capital letters. But in November 1966, James W. Brady flew across the continent to pay court to James Galanos, the Los Angeles-based designer who shares the pinnacle of American fashion with Norell. Galanos had been barring *Women's Wear* from his collections for several years because he said that he had been quoted out of context. Brady wrote a glowing report about Galanos and was rewarded by being admitted to the designer's next showing. By then, *Women's Wear* was whittling the 66-year-old Norell down with a new title, "Old Master."

Those who cross John Fairchild are punished. One victim was Priscilla Kidder, whom Luci Johnson chose to design her wedding dress. When Mrs. Kidder steadfastly refused to divulge anything about the dress, *Women's Wear* published an inaccurate sketch obtained from another source. As a consequence, the newspaper was barred by the White House, thereby reaping national publicity for itself. As part of its second-hand coverage of the wedding, it reported:

> There was Priscilla in front of the President . . . in front of Lady Bird . . . in front of Pat—and at one point her backside completely blocks the camera's view of Luci. All of this effort—just to carry the three-yard lace train. . . . A keen-eyed Washington observer, very close to the White House, comments, "I was interested to see how Priscilla was fawning over Lynda all during the reception."

Except for a brief cease-fire, John Fairchild kept trying to provoke a battle with *The New York Times*. Somehow he had persuaded himself that the newspaper with more than ten times the circulation of his, and a reputation in many quarters for being the greatest newspaper in the United States, was his competitor. He fought the enemy by sniping at it and by allying himself with Eugenia Sheppard. *Women's Wear Daily* christened her Miss Fashion Right. On May 25, 1963, this item appeared in the "Eye," *Women's Wear's* principal gossip column:

> FASHION FAMINE: Some of *The New York Times'* big advertisers —meaning the New York stores—are complaining about the way *The Times'* fashion pages are looking. . . . Too much devoted to fingernail hygiene—cooking—home furnishings—emotional problems, etc.—and no fashion.

It just so happens that reader mail and telephone calls indicate that Craig Claiborne's food columns are the strongest attraction of the women's pages. The average woman reader is also interested in decorating information, family problems and, to some degree, what to wear when. She seldom puts pen to paper about fashion coverage except to protest that the models look bizarre and the fashions unreal. The fashion industry and the new fashion celebrities are more vocal. The more often they find their names in a newspaper, the more complimentary they are about the publication.

A survey of *Times* readership had shown that 43 per cent of the readers on weekdays and 48 per cent on Sundays were women. Only 52 per cent of them had attended college and not all of those had graduated. Fifty-six per cent of the readers of the *Herald Tribune,* which was dying at the time of the survey, had gone to college. In 1964, 60 per cent of *Times* readers had family incomes below $10,000.

Figures and surveys can be used to mount any offensive, defend any position. One might have concluded that such a body of readers would not be interested in massive injections of high fashion and the foibles of the jet set. A survey by an independent, retailing consultant in the fall of 1959 showed that executives in leading department and specialty stores throughout the United States read the Sunday editions of *The New York Times* intensively and thoroughly to obtain fashion information from both its abundant advertising columns and its editorial features. The merchants not only studied the visually exciting, double-page fashion reports in *The New York Times Magazine,* but they gleaned the trends of fashion, merchandising and promotion from the advertisements of the major New York stores.

Stores within a 300-mile radius of New York City said that many of the social and style leaders in their communities asked for merchandise they had seen advertised in the Sunday *Times.* The survey concluded that the newspaper "exerts an influence much greater than any other single medium, and quite possibly greater than the combined effect of all other printed media, apart from local newspapers." Even without a survey, one could lift the Sunday *Times* and often discover it weighed as much as a lusty, newborn baby.

The surveyors learned also that the foundation of *The Times'* acceptance as an advertising medium was in its standing as a general newspaper. People believed what they read in the news columns of *The Times,* even though it may have been heavy going for some, and their faith carried over to the advertisements. Not only did *The Times* contain "all the news that's fit to print," the motto adopted by Adolph Ochs when he bought the paper in 1896, but the best merchandise was displayed in its advertisements, they assumed. Ochs' heirs, through his daughter Iphigene's marriage to Arthur Hays Sulzberger, publisher from 1935 to 1961, carried on that tradition of responsibility. While sparing no expense to gather and disseminate the news, they also waged intensive drives to boost circulation and advertising. *Times* advertising men are formidable adversaries. They beat the bushes for the small, suburban shop's advertisements no less energetically than for the billion-dollar corporation's. And they keep them both happy with sales. Even the most obscure notices in *The New York Times* yield impressive results.

The power of *The New York Times* as a fashion medium comes, primarily, from its Sunday magazine section, which contains more advertising than any magazine, even the fashion bibles like *Vogue* and *Glamour.* The advertising strength of *The New York Times Magazine* derives from the mammoth producers of apparel fibers like nylon and rayon, and fabric finishes like Ze Pel and Scotchgard, as well as from the giant manufacturers of moderately priced clothing. The butt of jokes for many years was the juxtaposition of the lively brassiere advertisements with the egghead articles on politics and international affairs by experts like Barbara Ward and Adlai Stevenson.

The business titans want their advertisements to reach store buyers and merchandise managers. They don't give a hoot about editorial support inflating the importance of Ferdinando "Nando" Sarmi and Mollie Parnis, among the exhibitionists of the new society. The New York *Herald Tribune,* which *The Times* considered its only competitor in the morning newspaper field, gave that kind of support. Nevertheless, in the year just before it lost its rival, *The New York Times* carried 1,751,203 lines of wearing apparel advertising—41,959 lines of it on weekdays, the rest on Sundays. This figure included fiber and clothing manufacturers but not department stores. The New York *Herald Tribune*'s total in the same category was 195,474 lines, of which 30,874 were on weekdays.

The *Herald Tribune,* it would seem, campaigned to capture the fashion consumer through Eugenia Sheppard's chronicles of the super-consumers. *The Times,* meanwhile, went after the big corporate spenders. The consumer campaign thrilled the retail merchants as well as the Seventh Avenue designers and manufacturers, whom Miss Sheppard and Mr. Fairchild had lifted to new heights of dignity. Unfortunately, Norman and Bill and Mollie, grand though their style of living may be, are small tycoons with annual sales volumes in the very low millions. They do not and cannot show their affection with significant advertising budgets.

When the retailers were polled by *The New York Times,* they replied that although they found *The Times* indispensable, they couldn't take their morning coffee without reading Eugenia Sheppard first. Nonetheless, when the *Herald Tribune* expired in 1966, Media Records revealed that it had run 3,750,000 lines of retail advertising in its daily issues in 1965, and 4,800,000 lines on Sunday. *The New York Times'* daily retail score was 12,400,000 lines, with 14,000,000 lines on Sunday.

As for circulation, which is a key factor in advertising decisions, the New York *Herald Tribune* had 352,490 weekday readers in the spring of 1960, as again *The Times'* 686,246. On Sundays, the line-up was 521,568 versus 1,371,939. Six years later, the *Herald Tribune* had 331,341 daily readers, *The Times* 725,480. On Sundays, it was 415,850 versus 1,441,913.

In the six-year period, both newspapers had undergone the 114-day strike of 1962-63. The *Herald Tribune,* which had raised its daily readership to more than 400,000 before the shutdown, found it had lost 22 per cent of it when it resumed publication. It never won it all back.

Eugenia Sheppard is a plucky fighter. She could not have been expected to save the *Herald Tribune* all by herself. The fact is, however, that as her personal stock rose, her newspaper's fortunes declined. She did manage to scare its mighty opponent, though.

The editors of *The New York Times* pride themselves on their independence of the business side of the newspaper. But the psalms that Seventh Avenue and the retailers sang to the advertising legions of *The Times* about Eugenia Sheppard happened to strike a familiar chord when they were relayed to the editorial side. The editors were seeking ways and means of updating the paper. They were using less news space than before the second world war and being more ruthlessly selective about what they did give the reader. Livelier writing and a greater variety of subjects were being offered. *"The Times* should be needed by people who want to be informed. . . . We want *The Times* not only to be needed; we want *The Times* to be wanted," was the way Turner Catledge, managing editor (later executive editor), put it.

Clifton Daniel, Mr. Catledge's heir-apparent, who had also been pondering the revitalization of *The Times,* felt that society news was necessary for cultural enlightenment. Defending intensive reportage on that one socio-economic group, he said to some of the reporters, "They're more interesting than most people. They have more variety. More money. I think rich people are fascinating." A number of *Times*-men disagreed with him, but Mr. Daniel won out. In 1963, he gave Charlotte Curtis carte blanche to develop a society beat. *"The Times* has never been interested in social chitchat," he told *Time* magazine, "but in applying good journalistic standards to an area of news, society, that is important to all of us."

Like Miss Sheppard, red-haired Charlotte Curtis was tiny, tireless and came from an eminent background in Columbus, Ohio. The daughter of a surgeon and of one of the first women to distinguish herself in the United States Foreign Service, Miss Curtis was a Vassar graduate. She warmed to her assignment as though she were a doctoral candidate. She preferred to think of herself as a social historian rather than a society reporter. She trailed the Brahmins and the climbers to Newport, Southampton, Palm Beach, Boston, New Orleans, San Francisco and even London and Paris and detailed their

doings with tongue in cheek and piles of genealogical and other perti-
nent and impertinent data. She was aware of what her characters wore.
In Palm Beach, she computed the carats they changed with each meal
and noted that hairdressers were being invited to parties. Although
she made her own discoveries, like Mrs. Alfons Landa, who dwelt in
French 18th-century splendor decked out in Puccis and Sarmis, and
Mrs. Stephen "Laddie" Sanford, the gregarious wife of the carpet heir,
inevitably she wrote about Mrs. C. V. Whitney and other Sheppard-
Hughes-Lambert idols.

Pretty soon, Miss Sheppard's admirers were talking about *The
Times* and dropping the name of Charlotte Curtis. She was profiled
by *Newsweek* and *Time*. *Women's Wear Daily* printed her perceptive
observations on fashion on May 18, 1965. A little later, it had a
flattering interview with Mrs. Clifton Daniel.

As Elizabeth Penrose Howkins, *The Times'* women's news editor,
announced her retirement in the spring of 1965, Mr. Daniel begged
the fashion makers and merchants for suggestions as to her successor.
Some of them like Pauline Trigère, the dress designer, mentioned
Charlotte Curtis. As soon as *The Times* was ready to announce her
appointment in June, Clifton Daniel wrote Miss Trigère thanking her
for her advice.

Charlotte Curtis banished the fingernail hygiene and emotional
problems that had distressed *Women's Wear Daily*. She, too, merged
fashion with society and refused to tell readers how to rearrange the
living-room furniture or how to survive a child's passage through the
age of terrible two. The superconsumers and the new idols romped
through the women's pages of *The New York Times,* with the reporters carefully counting the source and quantity of their fortunes.

Letters of outrage from readers who objected to having Amanda
and Judy and Susan, as well as Mollie and Bill and Ben, with every
breakfast were politely answered, filed and forgotten.

Soon after she took command, Charlotte Curtis was invited to
lunch by John Fairchild. He indicated that he was ready for new
alliances. When she didn't repay his invitation, he renewed his guerrilla
attacks on *The Times:*

> BOMBS AWAY: Norman Norell is steaming. He's escalating his
> war with *The New York Times* [*Women's Wear* reported on
> July 14, 1966]. No privileged sanctuaries this time, vows em-
> battled Norell. The cause célèbre this time is not that *The Times*

(banned by the house) sketched from buyer descriptions (no one worries about that anymore) but that they didn't say so, gave the impression they actually saw the collection. "We expected this of Miss Curtis . . . but not of *The New York Times*," says a communiqué from Norell.

Women's Wear was incorrect again. The sketches were based on information from a far more reliable source than Mr. Fairchild guessed. But *Women's Wear* was correct when it reported a month later that Miss Curtis and Mr. Daniel had lunched with Miss Sheppard at Barbetta's. The *Herald Tribune* had just withdrawn from its proposed fusion with two of the city's evening newspapers after a four-month strike halted publication. The possibility of Eugenia Sheppard's writing her column for *The Times* was broached at the luncheon. Miss Sheppard decided, however, to carry her winning formula over to the new evening newspaper, the *World Journal Tribune*. *Women's Wear Daily* gave her a rousing send-off. They quoted Eleanor Lambert as saying, "Thank heavens, Eugenia is spared to the public via the newly merged newspaper. . . . Finally, I hope the advertisers have learned a lesson and that they will support Eugenia by advertising."

After that, it was impossible to escape from the new idols. They were in *The Times* in the morning, and the *World Journal Tribune* in the evening and in almost every type of mass media. Suzy Knickerbocker (the pen name for Aileen Mehle, a Hearst gossip columnist), whom one could formerly rely on for tart revelations about society's romantic involvements, started relaying whose dresses they were wearing. The *World Journal Tribune* lasted eight months. It expired in May 1967.

Meanwhile, *Women's Wear Daily* took another step away from its captive blouse buyers and corset salesmen. John Fairchild had admitted years ago that he considered himself a "fashion intellectual," a phrase he developed for one who dared to say what he thinks. Now his newspaper was doing features on lexicography, the birth-control pill and Red China, plastering Dame Rebecca West on the front page and interviewing foreign directors of new-wave films.

The readers be damned as long as the editors are happy.

IV

BY DESIGN:
THE HIGH SOCIETY WAY

BILL BLASS, the boy from Fort Wayne, Ind., who grew up to become a Seventh Avenue peer, as well as a national celebrity sought after by hostesses of the new society, put it this way. "I've found that ladies who spend a lot for clothes like to relate to the designer." Mr. Blass, who likes London tailored suits and mannequins with Anglo-Saxon looks, was indulging in a bit of British understatement. In the Sixties, the separate and unequal worlds of American fashion and American society not only became related but they were united in a blissful marriage of convenience.

The pedigreed woman was ardently wooed. To the surprise of some, she succumbed easily. She opened her heart as well as her pocketbook to members of a tough, honest business that had lacked social standing. People in the rag trade, as Seventh Avenue used to call itself (the term is still used in England but in America it's now spelled f-a-s-h-i-o-n), had been rated higher than butchers and bookmakers but not half as acceptable as bucket-shop operators. The snobbish inequity lay in the East European and Southern Italian origins of the industry, its lack of education and polish. In France, the dressmaker often studied art or architecture before he turned to pins and needles.

The romance between fashion and society wasn't a sudden, strange passion. It had ample precedent. In England, there had been the haughty dressmaker, usually homosexual, but with connections to the

107

nobility. In France, the couturiers have always appreciated the value of having their designs displayed by the *haut monde*. The Duchess of Windsor and Jacqueline de Ribes, a banker's wife, are examples of distinguished models who don't shrink from divulging their couturiers' names. (Actresses like Melina Mercouri and Brigitte Bardot are equally considerate.) The haute couture can be flexible about payment of bills.

Paris couturiers have also employed society belles for tasks that come under the heading of public relations. Carmen Rodriguez, the ebullient daughter of a Venezuelan diplomat, speaks for shy Marc Bohan of Christian Dior and accompanies him on business journeys. Robin Butler serves in a similar capacity for Christian Dior-New York; the divorced wife of Michael Butler, the polo-playing heir to a Chicago paper fortune, is a product of the Philadelphia Main Line, Miss Porter's and Vassar. Nicole Alphand, wife of the French Ambassador to the United States during the Kennedy Administration and the capital's No. 1 hostess then, became Pierre Cardin's secret weapon after her husband was recalled to Paris.

French designers and hairdressers are accredited to *le tout Paris* as the jet set calls itself. The band of hedonists is crazy about clothes and costume parties. When Regine, owner of New Jimmy's, one of their beloved Left Bank discothèques, told the women to come as Jean Harlows to one of her gatherings, some of the men showed up in blond wigs and satin dresses, too.

The Italian fashion industry, which mushroomed after World War II, is dominated by titled impresarios. The most famous is Emilio Pucci, a Florentine marchese who assisted Benito Mussolini's daughter, Edda Ciano, to escape from war-torn Italy into Switzerland in 1944.

Princess Irene Galitzine of Rome is a Russian-born specialist in evening and at-home clothes and lingerie. She has cruised with Jacqueline Kennedy on Aristotle Onassis' yacht in the Mediterranean. The Henry Fords gave a party for her in Grosse Pointe. Italian fashion is loaded with princesses. Princess Orsetta Caracciolo Torlonia directed the Rome salon of Valentino, the dashing Milanese, who is also approved of by Mesdames Kennedy and Ford, until she transferred to Federico Forquet. Princess Luciana Pignatelli, a leggy, blue-eyed, streaked blonde, introduced her first collection of hostess and play clothes to buyers in the living room of her apartment in the Palazzo Taverna in Rome in 1966.

In the United States, almost every prosperous suburb has had a dress shop whose owner was financed by her affluent friends when her own fortune declined. Other impoverished gentlewomen who didn't want to be ensnared by business problems simply steered their friends to Seventh Avenue manufacturers, Madison Avenue shops and wholesale furriers. They received commissions in cash or merchandise.

On a loftier scale, Mainbocher has played the subtlest variations on the social theme. The only American who had ever penetrated the Paris haute couture—he made the bland blue dress in which Wallis Simpson was married to the former King of England—practices the art of haughty dressmaking in a salon in the KLM Building on Fifth Avenue. He charges more than the Paris couturiers (a Mainbocher suit and blouse can come to as much as a year's tuition and board at Harvard) and is far more selective of his customers. Women with Mainbocher labels in their clothes tend to be WASP-y and possessors of well-seasoned money unless they are too temptingly rich, like the daughters and wives of Greek shipowners. A few talented wage-earners like Anita Loos, the writer, or Mary Martin, the actress, are admitted, too. Mainbocher (born Main Rousseau Bocher in Chicago shortly after the 19th century entered its last decade) employs gentlewomen to serve them. Rebekah Harkness, the balletomane, was one of his salesladies before her marriage to William Hale Harkness, the philanthropist. Mrs. Winston F. C. Guest ("Cee-zee") and Mrs. Wyatt Cooper (the former Gloria Vanderbilt de Cicco Stokowski Lumet) can be relied on to murmur his name in reverent tones when asked to identify their dresses.

Impoverished noblemen have always found berths with the jewelers. Prince Filiberto de Bourbon and his daughter, Maria, work for Van Cleef & Arpels in New York. Harry Winston has had the Vicomte de Rosière and Count Vassili "Vava" Adlerberg, a pillar of White-Russian-society-in-exile-in-Manhattan, on his payroll.

The fashion magazines, particularly *Vogue* and *Harper's Bazaar,* traditionally put post-debutantes on their mastheads. They were alleged to have the taste and contacts necessary for creating an elegant ambience besides being able to afford the slight wages those publications prefer to pay. One of Diana Vreeland's fortes is discovering "those attractive, greedy little monsters who are up and about." Caterine Milinaire, the stepdaughter of the Duke of Bedford; Aline Romanones, an American married to a Spanish count; and Topsy Taylor, who is listed in the *Social Register* under the wing of her mother, Mrs. John Crawford, are Vreeland finds.

Not all fashion magazine contributors are poorly paid. When Gloria Guinness, wife of one of the world's wealthiest men, agreed to write articles for *Harper's Bazaar,* she drove a bargain that would have pleased any professional author. But then, from the magazine's point of view, her words were priceless. In her first article on elegance in the July 1963 issue, she said, "Elegance is in the brain just as well as in the body and in the soul. Jesus Christ is the only example we have of any one human having possessed all three at the same time. Shakespeare's elegance of brain remains unsurpassed." Mrs. Guinness put Antonio del Castillo, one of the Spanish-born Paris couturiers she likes (the other is Cristobal Balenciaga), in touch with the sources of capital to finance the couture house he established after he left Lanvin.

Currying favor with affluent bluebloods, then, wasn't a new stratagem for those who had to earn their bread in fashion. But in the Sixties, it was enlarged in and beyond the industry. Eventually, it enabled social ciphers to climb into the same ring with some of the Old Guard, provided the newcomers had enough money and stamina, wore the right clothes to the right places and were willing to talk about them to the press.

At every level of the fashion industry, social sponsorship was sought. Unsuspected talents as models and even designers were unearthed in young women of good family. For some, the courtship of society was more rewarding than for others. The most effective Cupid was Mark Klauser, advertising director of Ohrbach's, who developed the concept of getting classy dames to promote cut-rate merchandise for free.

Jerry Ohrbach, son of Nathan Ohrbach, who had founded the store on East 14th Street seventeen years before, discovered Mark Klauser in 1940. Ohrbach's neighbors then were the soapbox orators of Union Square and S. Klein, a cash-and-carry competitor. Women flocked to both stores in search of anonymous merchandise from leading manufacturers at bargain prices. Chic it wasn't at Ohrbach's and Klein's.

Mr. Klauser was then an ex-varsity tennis and soccer player, a sportswriter and publicist. He had worked his way through Brooklyn

College and St. John's Law School during the Depression covering sports for *The New York Times*. He was a basketball scout and press agent for the team of his Brooklyn synagogue. This was the era before professional teams and television had taken over sports. Ohrbach's major source of publicity was its basketball and swimming teams, for which it recruited college athletes and pitted them in city and nation-wide competitions. Some of them went on to careers in merchandising. Jerry Ohrbach asked Mark Klauser to take on a temporary assign-ment publicizing the store's basketball team. It grew into the post of director of advertising and public relations. "Our basketball team played in Madison Square Garden two years in a row. That's over 16,000 capacity," Mr. Klauser says with pride. His brown hair is thin-ning; his bright brown eyes require glasses for reading. He controls a million-dollar advertising budget and Henry Ford's daughter calls him regretfully when she can't attend his fashion show. But Mark Klauser's perspective hasn't changed. "You see a showmanship at these events," he said, his mind drifting back to the Garden. "By osmosis, I got it," he concedes modestly. After the hurly-burly of the sports arena, fash-ion editors were a pushover.

Ohrbach's had been selling solid fashion in a grubby environment and attracting glamorous customers. In 1947, its buyers started going to the Paris collections. In August 1954, at a cost of about $2.5 million, Ohrbach's moved uptown to 34th Street near Fifth Avenue. The neighborhood still wasn't chichi but it was just around the bend from Fifth Avenue stores that had the carriage trade. Sydney Gittler, a coat and suit buyer whom *Women's Wear Daily* was to crown "The King," joined the company. He refined the formula for buying models in the European haute couture, having them copied exactly by the best Seventh Avenue manufacturers, like Ben Zuckerman, and putting the translations out at prices that aren't cheap but are still excellent value. His bailiwick is the Grey Room. Margaret Kennedy did the same thing with dresses until she left for Best & Company, and Irene Satz, the fashion director, backs the promotion with the newest Euro-pean accessories. Ohrbach's does a fantastic job of bringing Paris to New York and Los Angeles. "If we didn't have the merchandise, all of my efforts wouldn't mean a damn thing," Mark Klauser says. But Paris is important to Ohrbach's because it's the only handle they have for promotion. Ohrbach's is a low-margin store. If other retailers take about a 44 per cent mark-up on women's apparel, then Ohrbach's takes about 10 per cent less. The same dress or coat costs less at Ohrbach's than it would at a traditional store. But if it is the same dress, the manufacturer won't let Ohrbach's boast about it. He won't let Ohrbach's use his label or advertise his name. Many manufacturers refuse to do business at all with the store lest they lose their more prestigious accounts. Or they sell Ohrbach's special merchandise that the comparison shoppers of other stores won't recognize.

Among American stores, Ohrbach's has been the largest single purchaser in the failing Paris haute couture because the French designers permit it to use their names. Only Dior has enforced the transparent trick of labeling copies below a certain price level as the handiwork of Monsieur X. Twice a year, Paris gives Ohrbach's a chance to shout about its merchandise. These promotions may result in one-third to one-quarter of their annual business in better coats, suits, and dresses. "When we moved uptown, it was my idea to keep building the Paris fashion program up, to make it a happening," Mr. Klauser has admitted. "A lot of celebrities come to be seen, and to be seen in the papers. Everybody wants to be associated with the top names in society, the diplomatic world, entertainment. Now we've reached the top, the absolute cream in every walk of life. There used to be a time when society wouldn't mingle with the entertainment world. But now it's not a matter of social prestige or money, it's more a matter of accomplishment. There's respect for the fashion designer or artist and top society is more than happy to associate with them.

"I was just putting that idea to use," he said, enunciating slowly and in the accent of his native borough. "It was the newspapers even more than anybody else who helped me." Like most master puppeteers, Mr. Klauser is somewhat uncomfortable when drawn into the spotlight.

In March and September, as soon as it can produce its copies of the imported designs, Ohrbach's puts on two fashion shows. The public is invited through newspaper advertisements to the one at 5:45 P.M., but earlier in the day, at 12:45 P.M., the "happening" is staged. It is not advertised but 1,500 guests are invited. The color of their tickets of admission denotes their status. Every year the colors are changed. One year, the wives of United Nations ambassadors waved lavender tickets. Theatrical personalities like Eva Gabor and Lauren Bacall were assigned green. White tickets with mauve lettering were for the press; navy tickets with white lettering were for general admission, *i.e.,* good but not famous customers, manufacturers and some competitors. White tickets with navy printing were for "private friends" or that increasingly important group of social prominent women like Mrs. Lowell Weicker and Mrs. Gary Cooper (who subsequently married Dr. John Converse) whom Mr. Klauser arranged as decoys for the New York press.

The invitation list is Klauser's masterpiece. He works on it all year round and from year to year. "It's a continuous effort, like Macy's Thanksgiving Day Parade. I read. I cut out things where the name didn't mean anything to me before. Like Mrs. Richard Harris didn't mean anything to me until I read in *The Times* that she was Mrs. Anne Ford's sister. If she'd been on the Grey Room List, she'd wind up in general admission but when I saw who she was, I decided I'll seat her and her sister together," says Mr. Klauser, whose wife is a technical writer for the New York Telephone Company. The Klausers live in Peter Cooper Village, a middle-income housing development in Manhattan, and make no attempt to socialize with the celebrities he has helped to create.

There are lists within his master list. Mrs. Lyndon B. Johnson, Mrs. Robert F. Kennedy and Mrs. John F. Kennedy are on the special list to which personalized invitations are sent. The last time Jacqueline Kennedy attended she was a Senator's wife. Mr. Klauser doesn't expect her to accept his invitations anymore. "There's a big difference between being a Senator's wife and who she is now," he says. Mrs. William S. Paley doesn't come to the shows either but word leaks out about her purchases. Special customers arrive the day of the show before the store is open, slipping in through the employees' entrance at 8 A.M., and the press is informed of their purchases, too. Mrs. Paley is granted a preview a few days ahead as befits someone who has been called America's most elegant woman. The wife of the chairman of the Columbia Broadcasting System neither seeks nor discourages publicity but she can be very helpful. At a Bergdorf Goodman showing, she told reporters that the coat she was wearing came from Ohrbach's.

About a week before the customer show, the press is granted a preview. Mr. Klauser has built that into a happening, too. Invitations have to be rationed. As many as eight reporters and editors from a single publication will attend in order to submit early bids for those relatively few copies of the imports that are made in the original fabrics. The newspapers report on that showing as well as on the customer presentation.

It was because Irene Satz was nervous that season and felt she needed some extra insurance that Ohrbach's invited a few celebrities like Mrs. S. Carter Burden, Jr., Mrs. Michel Legendre, wife of the French consul, and Mrs. Jacob Javits, wife of the New York Senator. Mrs. Javits brought her friend Mrs. Lewis Schott. The photograph of the women, seated together, was widely published. It showed, left to right, Mesdames Javits, Schott, Legendre and Burden, who had arrived late. The latter was led ostentatiously to her place. She switched her Alice in Wonderland mane as she sat down and the photographers, like a pack of Pavlov's dogs, started clicking. "The seating arrangement is very important. I set it up from the picture standpoint," Mr. Klauser said. "I put certain names that will make good pictures together. You work through the night before a show with the seating and one woman knocks one thing out of line and she knocks the whole chain out."

He said he "almost killed the usher" for seating Mrs. Schott next to Mrs. Javits. "I wanted Mrs. Javits next to Mrs. Legendre." But it turned out to be a happy accident. The newspapers used a big picture of them all. They even used it in Milwaukee.

Despite the success of introducing a social celebrity at what had been a strictly working press affair, Mr. Klauser had to retreat the next season. The Burden appearance put some noses out of joint. Other celebrities like Susan Stein and Mrs. Robert Scull demanded previews, too. Because he wants the eyes of the nation, not just New York, on Ohrbach's, Mr. Klauser tries to serve something for every journalistic appetite. The names he produces "depend on the media."

"For *The New York Times,* society is better. The New York *Herald Tribune* will mix, they even tend to mix entertainment and society," he said as he was planning his fall 1966 triumph. "TV doesn't give a damn about society. The names and faces have to be immediately recognizable. Radio is the same. The names must be national in recognition. For those media, it's the entertainment and the diplomatic names that count. Paley you don't consider strictly society anymore. She has been so intricately tied in with so many events that she's not strictly society. The name William Paley means something and she has world-wide fashion recognition. We practically live in one world now. Amanda is going along the same path."

What are national faces? "A Hope Hampton, a Carol Channing, the girls on the panel shows like Kitty Carlisle. Buffalo took Amanda, Kitty Carlisle and Celeste Holm, Henry Fonda and his wife, Mrs. Jacob Javits and her friend Mrs. Lewis Schott. Milwaukee took Mrs. Anne Ford and Mrs. John Converse. AP serviced Ford and Converse." The Associated Press had sent out photographs of the first wife of the motor magnate and Gary Cooper's widow seated together at the show. The Pittsburgh *Press* also picked it up.

In the fall of 1965, Mrs. Ford's daughter, Anne, had come to the show along with Mrs. Samuel P. Peabody and Mrs. Frederick Eberstadt. Another season she couldn't make it, but she telephoned her regrets, Mr. Klauser said. "Even the biggest and the wealthiest have no qualms about throwing Ohrbach's name around. Only the ones who are insecure and climbers do," he added.

He was right. But his joy was tempered by the presence of a challenger. On March 21, 1966, he had reserved the date of September 26 at 12:45 P.M. for his fall show. He staked out his claim with Ruth Finley, publisher of the *Fashion Calendar,* a catalogue of upcoming dates mimeographed weekly on pink paper. Miss Finley acts as a clearing house for fashion-show events. On May 3, Alexander's filed notice of its decision to show at 11 A.M. and 3 P.M. on September 26.

Alexander's had become Ohrbach's closest rival for the hand of the fashionable socialite in the Paris import copy sweepstakes. Like Ohrbach's, Alexander's operates on the principle of high turnover and low mark-up. Unlike Ohrbach's, Alexander's is a department store. It carries appliances, lures customers to its suburban branches with yoga lessons, stock-market investing sessions and auto rentals. It has struggled to secure a high-fashion reputation. For it, too, Paris offers the best chance, twice a year, to drop designer names.

Alexander's first became a threat to Ohrbach's in the fall of 1965. George Farkas, the chairman of the board, had founded his chain in 1928 with a store on Third Avenue in the Bronx. He then spread out with branches in the Bronx, Long Island, Paramus, N.J., and Milford, Conn. Good, well-populated, lower-middle- to middle-middle-class communities but not within screaming distance of the upper crust.

Late in the summer of 1965, Mr. Farkas moved down to Manhattan. He established his flagship in a glass and marble palace at 59th Street and Lexington Avenue, next door to Bloomingdale's, the neighborhood store of Manhattan's fashionable Upper East Side. Bloomie's, as its loyal patrons call it, does a superior job in both high fashion and home furnishings. Its executives do not talk about their customers. Bloomingdale's management was concerned about the newcomer but before long, it was clear that if anyone had a problem about Alexander's, it was Ohrbach's, 30-odd blocks away. Ownership of that store had passed from the Ohrbachs to the Brenninkmeyers, a Dutch family with a chain of European department stores. They had the sagacity to leave Ohrbach's successful buying, advertising, and promotion team intact.

George Farkas spent $20 million on his nine-story Manhattan headquarters, said to be the costliest retail store ever built in New York. Long before the Hanoverian glass chandeliers and the candy pink and green plastic display decorations were in place, he had taken on Serge Obolensky Associates as public relations consultants. Obolensky was the 75-year-old darling of New York society. Even an Iowa farm girl had only to gaze upon him, six feet three inches tall, lean and graceful as he clicked his heels and bent to kiss an aristocratic hand, to realize that blue (nay, purple) blood coursed through his veins. Specifically, it was the blood of Rurik, the Varangian whom the Slavs invited to found a Russian dynasty in the 9th century. Serge was the son of Prince Platon Obolensky, a landed gentleman and former aide-de-camp to the brother of Czar Alexander III. The prince had his son educated by a Scottish nanny, at the University of St. Petersburg, and Christ College, Oxford. When World War I broke out, the younger prince served with the First Cavalry Regiment of the Imperial Guard and was wounded. He was nursed back to health in a Crimean hospital by Princess Catherine Alexandrovna Yourievska Bariatinska, the daughter of Alexander II. They were married and, during the Revolution, fled to England. After their divorce, the princess came into the late czar's fortune.

In London, Serge Obolensky met another heiress, Alice Astor, descendant of John Jacob Astor, the fur trader, and daughter of the fourth John Jacob Astor, who went down with the *Titanic*. They were married in 1924, had two children, and were divorced in 1933.

Princess Alice remarried several times. Prince Serge remained a grass widower, not, though, for lack of trying on the part of New York society women. He remained on excellent terms with his second wife's brother. "Vincent is one of my best friends," he was quoted as saying as he was being divorced.

In *Who's Who in America,* Serge Obolensky identifies himself as a hotel executive and lists the top positions he held with Vincent Astor's real estate company and the hotel interests that grew out of it. He doesn't mention his title of president of Serge Obolensky Associates, Inc., which has its headquarters in the office of Rogers & Cowan, theatrical press agents. Colonel Obolensky holds the Bronze Star for his activities in World War II on behalf of the Office of Strategic Services and as a paratrooper who jumped behind enemy lines. A colonel in the Air Force Reserve, a title he now prefers to prince, he can do the flaming dagger dance at the Russian New Year's Eve celebrations without singeing his moustache.

Serge Obolensky is a formidable opponent on the social battlefield. "He's been dancing with those women for sixty years. Why shouldn't they come when he calls?" Mark Klauser consoled himself as Colonel Obolensky called out the female regiments of New York's Old Guard society. For Mr. Farkas' debut as a Manhattan merchant, he arranged a luncheon fashion show to benefit one of society's favorite charities, the New York division of the American Cancer Society. He imported five European princesses to model the European fashions the store had bought. Princess Charles D'Arenberg, the former Peggy Bedford Bancroft, a Standard Oil heiress and international partygiver and guest, strode down the pink felt-covered runway in a Balenciaga copy priced at $69. Baroness Fiona Thyssen, who had been married to a Krupp steel heir, was in tweed by Galitzine. Princess Luciana Pignatelli wore at-home pants by Valentino. Princess Ira Furstenberg, whose former husbands included a Spanish Hohenlohe and a Brazilian Pignatari, plumped for Saint Laurent, Monsieur X and Balenciaga, while the Marquesa Pimpinela de Belvis, a Spanish Hohenlohe in her own right, advanced the cause of Rodriguez of Madrid. The society troops, 1,500 strong and encircled by racks of misses' coats and dresses on the third floor of the store, sat at round tables sipping champagne and partaking of the contents of picnic lunch baskets.

For the spring 1966 extravaganza, Colonel Obolensky dropped the princesses but kept the picnic. He persuaded the Duchess of Windsor to be honorary chairman of the luncheon show. Alexander's underwrote the expenses and the proceeds went to the Boys Club of New

York, an eminent charity. Colonel Obolensky stood near the escalator greeting the throng, almost all of whom had pastel coats, chain-handled pocketbooks, calf pumps, pale faces and the hot-potato accents of the eastern-seaboard aristocracy. Until the very last, reporters expected to see Amanda Burden, whom the colonel had invited. She had just graced the Ohrbach's press show. Mrs. Burden did not appear, but the reporters were informed later that she had ordered the red, white and blue sequin suit copied from a Saint Laurent design at $750.

By the fall of 1966, pressure had mounted to the boiling point. Alexander's put the socialites on the griddle by scheduling its two shows so that they bracketed Ohrbach's on the same day. Colonel Obolensky had selected the Soldiers', Sailors' and Airmen's Club, of which he was then president, to benefit from the $5 admission fees to the shows. (He had given up food altogether.) "We thought we should have a military charity, this time. With Vietnam, people are more apt to come," said Alexander Tarsaidze, vice president of Serge Obolensky Associates, Inc., and an untitled member of White Russian exile society.

Colonel Obolensky induced Mrs. William Woodward, the grandest of *grandes dames,* and Mrs. James H. Van Alen, wife of a publisher and tennis enthusiast of Newport, R.I., and Madrid, to be co-chairmen. Mrs. Van Alen had been a perennial on Ohrbach's celebrity list. "Yes, I've been going to Ohrbach's and they are marvelous. I'm a good customer there," Mrs. Van Alen admitted. The straw that practically broke Ohrbach's back was an Alexander's publicity photograph published in the New York *Daily News* in which she was wearing a Saint Laurent design that the 34th Street store's buyers were positive had been bought from them.

"But my heart belongs to Alexander's now. They've been so generous and so kind. I wish Ohrbach's would tie in with us, too," she said. But Ohrbach's didn't mess around with charity. It didn't charge admission or do anything to distract from the main object of the exercise, selling the clothes before and after the happening.

Alexander's snatched other Ohrbach's faithfuls for its patroness committee, like Maggi McNellis Newhouse, who used to commentate the show on 34th Street before she was replaced by Carol Bjorkman (Alexander's asked Eugenia Sheppard to do its commentary); Mrs. Gerald F. Warburg; Mrs. Nicholas R. DuPont; and Mrs. Henry

Berger, who, before her reincarnation as a fashion celebrity, had been Anita Louise of the movies. Colonel Obolensky also reinstated the princesses. He "personally selected" (as Mr. Tarsaidze put it) Princess Sophie Troubetzkoy and Countess Cristine de Caraman-Theodoracopulos of Paris, Lady Sarah Chrichton-Stuart of London, Countess Gioconda Cicogna Mozzoni of Rome and Princess Caroline Windisch-Graetz of New York and *Harper's Bazaar* to "donate their services as models." Mrs. John V. Lindsay, wife of the mayor of New York, attended both stores' showings. So did Mesdames Berger and DuPont and Mrs. T. Suffern Tailer, also an Alexander's patroness.

Alexander's outpointed Ohrbach's socially. In the usual, eclectic, Klauser style, Ohrbach's offered actresses Greta Thyssen and Joan Fontaine, Lisa Kirk of the nightclub circuit and Peggy Cass, a TV panelist, as well as a quartet of socialites whom *The New York Times* presented in a four-column picture, or roughly the same amount of space it might allot to a photograph of the President of the United States addressing the United Nations. But "when it came to the jingle of the cash register, the 34th Street store won hands down," *The Times* reported.

Although Colonel Obolensky took his master plan from his client's closest competitor, he borrowed another leaf from the notebook of Bergdorf Goodman, the Fifth Avenue specialty store. He advised Alexander's to nominate Mrs. J. Averell Clark, Jr., wife of a scion of a Long Island polo-playing family, as fashion consultant. This meant that she would invite her friends to shop at Alexander's. To ease their journey into terra incognita, they would be permitted to do their buying in her private office and dressing room. Mrs. Clark was thus to be pitted against Jo Hughes, society's supersaleswoman and another of fashion society's marriage brokers. Encouraged by Eugenia Sheppard, Miss Hughes had taught her customers to proclaim less that their ancestors had arrived on the *Mayflower* than that their dresses had come from Seventh Avenue.

Josephine Blair Hughes is a tall spinster with coppery hair and a highly combustible temper. Dallas-born, educated at Madeira and Smith (class of 1931), Miss Hughes received her professional training as a Hearst fashion-society writer and as Girl Friday to the late Hattie Carnegie. From 1948 to 1954, she ran her own dress shop, Jo Hughes, Inc., on East 56th Street.

Later, her customers followed her to a tiny, unmarked office behind the better dress, suit and coat department at De Pinna, a Fifth Avenue store that belongs to the same corporate family as Brooks Brothers, the Ivy League men's store, and Garfinckel's, the Washington, D.C., specialty store. When she moved uptown to Bergdorf Goodman in 1966, she hoped to better her De Pinna sales record of $300,000 a year by introducing her clientele to the boundless luxuries of Bergdorf's. Since Miss Hughes is only a saleswoman (and proud of the job, too), she can only offer her customers what the buyers of her store have ordered. In theory, at least. At De Pinna, she had developed a "bonus" for "The Ladies." She led them to Seventh Avenue to attend the showings of those designers and wholesalers with whom she had achieved her warmest relationships. Among them were Ferdinando Sarmi, a former count and Roman lawyer, whom Miss Sheppard and "The Ladies" took to calling Nando. He rushed to Saratoga, N.Y., once to fix the dress that Mrs. Cornelius Vanderbilt Whitney was going to wear to a ball. There was Mollie Parnis, Bill Blass, Oscar de la Renta and Ben Zuckerman, "the greatest perfectionist since Hattie Carnegie," who never failed to come through on time with a special order. "The Ladies" loved making the trip over from Fifth Avenue and in from Oyster Bay, L.I., to the cement canyons of Seventh Avenue between 36th and 39th Streets. It gave them the chance, just as they would have in Paris, to see complete collections including the make-up and the accessories that made up the designer's "total look." With rare exceptions, stores never buy all of the styles from a collection.

Furthermore, as fashion editors, designers, saleswomen like Jo Hughes and her clients complain, most buyers avoid the avant-garde or really significant designs and stick to what they think they are sure to sell. The manufacturers and designers who cooperated with Miss Hughes found it instructive, at first, to see the distant creatures who bought their clothes and whom they never could have met under their own steam. It helped them with the designing, they said. And they and "The Ladies" liked seeing their names and photographs in the papers. After a while, Miss Sheppard and then the other papers got in the habit of stressing the collections that were attended by social celebrities.

There was only one fly in the ointment. Store buyers and presidents, like Andrew Goodman of Bergdorf's, were annoyed. They didn't want customers knowing the wholesale prices of clothes or, worse still, buying them wholesale. The manufacturers swore up and down they'd never sell to private customers. But a few wealthy women managed to save money by taxiing down to Seventh Avenue. A few manufacturers, like Bill Blass of Maurice Rentner, stood their ground. They said they invited only the ladies who were their friends to special press showings at which the prices were not quoted. Some stores retaliated by giving little customer parties at which designers were invited to present their entire collections.

When Bergdorf Goodman decided it couldn't do without Jo Hughes and her followers, Andrew Goodman, who had been so emphatically displeased by retail customers trespassing in wholesale paradise, issued a tactful statement: "We buy collections in great depth. In the event occasionally where a customer has a warm, personal relationship with a designer and prefers to have him fit her, we have no strong feeling about continuing it in a limited way and only in circumstances where it is warranted."

Her clientele of old rich and newly celebrated had done a lot for Jo Hughes. But then she did a lot for them. Mrs. Cornelius Vanderbilt Whitney explained it:

> I don't have time to go shopping at five or six different stores. Jo answers the whole thing. I'm going to Rome. I want clothes. I'll go in for the day and get everything from top to bottom. You could have a favorite clerk in some store but they don't know what you should wear to the White House. Jo Hughes goes to the same places we do, she goes with the people we all know and she knows what we wear. It's understated in certain resorts. A regular shop clerk wouldn't know that.

Mrs. Whitney is a blue-eyed, pale blonde with porcelain skin and an inexhaustible supply of good humor. Upon seeing a reporter whom she hasn't encountered for a month or two, she is likely to advance, hand outstretched, and say, "Hello, I'm Mary Lou Whitney." Mrs. Whitney was photographed at an art exhibition in Palm Beach in a raspberry costume by Cosmo Sirchio, the young custom designer. But she soon stopped mentioning non-Hughes designers when she was interviewed. Miss Hughes does not like wanderers. "People have got to take me seriously," said Miss Hughes, who sometimes tells her customers whose dress they should wear when. "I take this profession as seriously as doctors do theirs. The fashion business is as much an art or a profession as any serious thing. Despite all the publicity, I'm probably the most underpressured salesperson. I've never let anyone go out and buy anything they shouldn't be seen in. It's sort of like being a doctor. Some women need to be led. I'm firm but I'm underpressured. I live my business 16 hours a day. When I go to a party, I quickly look them over to see do they look all right. The wrong shoes ruin everything.

"My whole business is personal. I have the great advantage of knowing my customers as friends. I lead the life they lead, week-ends in Long Island. In England, I stay in castles. My life is their life." In Paris, Miss Hughes used the apartment of a friend, Baroness Hubert von Pantz, to give a party honoring her employer, Andrew Goodman. Other customer-friends are Mrs. Averell Harriman, wife of the former governor of New York and once a wife of C. V. Whitney (Miss Hughes has dressed at least three out of four of the sportsman's wives), Mrs. John R. Drexel III, Mrs. Marion Oates Leiter, and Mrs. David K. E. Bruce, wife of the Ambassador to Great Britain. Most of her customers never used to have their name in the papers except when they were born, made their debuts, married, divorced or died. But then, Eugenia Sheppard created the fashion-society gossip column and "Jo's Girls" became national celebrities. Even *Life* photographed them in color.

Not that Jo Hughes made it easy for the press to exploit her "Girls." In the beginning, she wouldn't admit *Women's Wear Daily* to her twice-a-year luncheon fashion shows. In a column headlined THE TWO HUNDRED in the garment trade newspaper on October 12, 1962, an unidentified columnist, whose name was William J. Cunningham, wrote:

> Yesterday the smartest little group of real society met for the annual Jo Hughes De Pinna luncheon. You haven't seen what exclusive means till you've seen this little group meet each fall and spring—real rarefied perfume. They wore brilliantly colored tweed suits, four of the same Zuckermans Jo was wearing. Everyone had the diamond or gold pin on either shoulder and I'm sorry to say I counted only 25 hats, usually of the matching fabric. [Mr. Cunningham had just retired from the millinery business.] The hair was NATURAL. . . . Last year watching from behind a potted palm and this season from under the rug. This is the most "in" place to be. . . .

For a few years, Miss Hughes barred *The New York Times* from those luncheons. It meant that Eugenia Sheppard had a clear beat on the event in the morning newspapers. When the Duchess of Windsor came to buy some clothes from Jo Hughes, Eugenia Sheppard was there with a photographer and devoted a column to the encounter. She mentioned it again in a round-up of the leading fashion events of 1965.

Some of Miss Hughes' customers graduated into fashion jobs of their own. Mrs. Herbert Scheftel, the Dublin-born blond wife of a prominent investor in Wall Street and television, was hired by Seymour Fox, a patent-haired coat and suit wholesaler. "Strictly on her ability and not on the basis of her socialism," Mr. Fox maintained. "I think what he wanted me to do as I never worked before was to do the public relations," Mrs. Scheftel said on the eve of his fall fashion show, for which she was to act as commentator. "It's ghastly. I'm frightened. I'll probably pass out," she added. She also defined her work as wearing her Balenciaga and Chanel originals in the showroom and assisting Mr. Fox on buying trips to Paris and Milan. "My friends think it's marvelous. They think they should go to work, too," she said.

If Miss Hughes was responsible for adding a new dimension to the lives of the sheltered rich, she certainly performed also for the ambitious moguls of Seventh Avenue. She brought them not only business but the heightened social esteem they longed for.

"Seventh Avenue is as glamorous as the magazine business," she said. "I'm intimate friends with all of them. They're stimulating people, as is anyone who does something successful."

The pink-and-red invitation to her first fall-winter fashion luncheon after she joined Bergdorf Goodman was an example of her achievements in integrating fashion and society. It was held October 5, 1966, at Delmonico's, for the benefit of Music Therapy for Children in Hospitals, a division of the Musicians Emergency Fund, Inc. Mrs. Lytle Hull, once the wife of Vincent Astor, was honorary chairman. The chairmen were Mrs. John R. Drexel III, an Anglo-American pillar of Newport society, and Mrs. Walter S. Gubelmann, wife of a Long Island yachtsman.

The list of patrons was woven with other platinum-society names, such as Mrs. John F. C. Bryce, the A & P grocery heiress; Mrs. Wiley T. Buchanan, Jr., wife of President Eisenhower's protocol chief; Mrs.

Thomas H. Choate, an investment banker's wife, who had been photographed the previous week at the Ohrbach's import show; Mrs. Nicholas R. DuPont; Mrs. Charles W. Engelhard, wife of the precious-metals industrialist; Mrs. Edward F. Hutton; Mrs. John A. Morris (the former Edna Brokaw, a Mainbocher admirer); Mrs. Stanley Rumbough, daughter of a Post-Toasties heiress and known theatrically as Dina Merrill; along with one representative each of the Warburgs, Whitneys, Phippses, Pells, Schiffs, and Fords.

Also on the list, which had been alphabetically arranged, were Mrs. Nat Bader, whose husband runs a wholesale coat and suit house named Originala; Mrs. Vincent Draddy, whose husband was in dresses; Mrs. Andrew Goodman and her friend, Mrs. Sol Kann, whose husband owned Hutzler's, a Baltimore store; Mrs. Leon Livingston, who was also listed as Mollie Parnis elsewhere in the program; Mrs. Joseph A. Neff, one of the socially aspiring daughters of the late Moses Annenberg, the racing-publishing czar; Mrs. Charles Revson, wife of the man who makes Revlon tick.

The junior committee was headed by Topsy Taylor and included a Baker, a Guest, THE Amanda Burden, two Cushings, a Drexel, Mrs. David Muss, a realty investor's wife and an up-and-coming fashion socialite, and the two married daughters and one daughter-in-law of Andrew Goodman. Last but not least was a committee of fashion patrons that included Miss Hughes' trusted manufacturers and friendly press representatives from *Women's Wear Daily, Vogue* and the *World Journal Tribune.* Also on that list were several bachelors whom society women had come to appreciate not only for their designs but for their qualities as escorts and extra men at parties. Foremost among them is Bill Blass, the prototype of the new breed of Seventh Avenue gentleman. Blue-eyed and perpetually tan, he has light brown hair that is just beginning to be flecked with gray. Jerry, the Madison Avenue hair stylist, keeps it growing into his collar and slightly puffy at the sideburns.

Although he went from high school in Fort Wayne ("my father was in hardware") to the back rooms of Seventh Avenue without tarrying in college or even the Parsons School of Design, the fashion industry's École des Beaux-Arts, Bill Blass acts as though he were to the manor born. Executive vice president of Maurice Rentner Ltd., a $3.5-million-a-year wholesale firm, designer of bathing suits, furs, raincoats, children's wear, men's wear, stockings and paper patterns as well as of dresses, coats and suits that retail from $200 to $2,000, Mr. Blass has the relaxed posture of a man whose major activity is clipping coupons.

When his admirers surge into the models' room to kiss and congratulate him after his seasonal showings, they find him clad in a dashing suit tailored by the London firm of Kilgour, French and Stanbury, with appropriately natty shirt and tie. The costume befits someone who abides in a penthouse tended by a manservant, week-ends in Palm Beach and Southampton and vacations in Marrakesh, "where Winston Churchill used to spend his winters." Bill Blass is secure enough not to own a Rolls-Royce, Jaguar or other Seventh Avenue automobile. When he is escorting someone to the theater or a ball, they go by chauffeured limousine service.

Twenty-five years after he started as a sketcher for David Crystal, Bill Blass was adjudged a national celebrity. An advertising agency selected him for a snob appeal campaign for Haig & Haig Scotch whisky. He was photographed surrounded by merrymakers in his model's room but in no way was he identified. The assumption of the ad men was that "in" people would recognize him and those who didn't should worry and ask for Haig & Haig Pinch. Among others used in the campaign were Benny Goodman and David Merrick.

"It's amazing to me that anybody would know who I am," Mr. Blass remarked right after the advertisement appeared. A men's fashion magazine had just asked him to pose in clothes from his personal wardrobe. Another advertising agency was using his photograph to promote the sale of wall-to-wall carpeting.

"A celebrity? I suppose I am though it's hard to evaluate. In the Fifties, Ceil Chapman was the best known American designer because her clothes were worn on television so much. But there is such a thing as overexposure. You have to be discriminating."

Mr. Blass traveled a long, straight road to glory. His next step after lowly sketcher took him into the United States Army. He was a sergeant in the Engineers Corps when he was discharged after three years of service in the European Theater during World War II. "That's when I had my first glimpse of Paris," he said.

He exited from the military into the workrooms of another Seventh Avenue dress house, named Anna Miller. Mrs. Miller was the sister of Maurice Rentner. When he died, the two firms merged under the Rentner name. Mr. Blass rose from sketcher to second designer to top banana and, finally, to an officer of the corporation.

"I have a business sense," he said with some pride. "I'm a designer who can be talked with and worked with. If three-quarters of the country lives in tropical climate, why should I insist on heavy fabrics? The little black dress is dead, everybody knows, but it isn't. I must have a handful in every collection. If I'm successful, it's because of my contact with the customer. Literally, women are my inspiration. I find out what they need."

Occasionally, he goes off on tangents. He fell for the "sportive" joke played by John Fairchild of *Women's Wear Daily,* and muffled and booted his ladies in 1963. He even handed them walking sticks as though they were inhabiting the English moors. At the height of the nymphet phase, he whipped up baby dresses frilled with white lace and introduced them on an 18-year-old innocent-looking model named Helene Sullivan whom he rechristened Amanda (as in Burden). "Amanda was an accessory," he confessed the next season, after he had gone back to Kit Gill, a size eight, five-foot nine-inch, brown-eyed blonde who looks and comports herself as a young Lauren Bacall. Miss Gill treats her master with the faintest degree of insolence.

"Kit represents the prototype of the lady I dress," said Mr. Blass. "She's in the current image of the Anglo-Saxon tawny blonde, messy-haired but very attractive and sporty. She dances all night, swims and skis. The sporty look has always been popular in America. I think Cristina Ford and Happy Rockefeller have it." (The wife of the governor of New York had become a regular at Rentner press showings.) "Being clean and healthy, that's what I like," Mr. Blass went on. "It appeals to me to dance with a woman whose hair is freshly clean.

"The ideal kind of lady I design for is not obsessed with fashion. She cares about clothes but about her family and home, too. I can't bear a woman who spends all of her time in the fitting room. Girls like Judy Peabody are working on charity from 9 to 5. Isabel Eberstadt is a writer on the side. They don't have time to stand for fittings all day long or to spend it at the hairdresser. Missy Bancroft is not obsessed with clothes. Louise Savitt is very natural about them."

Mrs. Thomas Bancroft, Jr., is the former Melissa Weston, a good-natured, blond post-debutante who modeled on Seventh Avenue.

Before her marriage she was frequently escorted by Mr. Blass. Those were the days when Eugenia Sheppard was beginning to recognize his social celebrity potential. Later, Mr. Blass started being seen with Mrs. Savitt, who was separated from her husband, Richard, a tennis player. She is the daughter of Mrs. Ruth Adler Liberman Lehrer Tankoos, wife of a real estate investor who owns Delmonico's in New York and the Colony in Palm Beach. The latter is considered the resort's only socially acceptable inn. Mrs. Tankoos owns 550 Seventh Avenue, the garment industry's most prestigious loft building. Maurice Rentner Ltd. moved there from 498 Seventh Avenue as soon as space was available. Mrs. Savitt wore a dress by Ferdinando Sarmi when Mr. Blass took her to the Belmont Ball one spring. "She told me she was dying to wear it. I don't treat it as personal effrontery," he said. "The best-dressed woman in the world is Babe Paley. You are never conscious of what she is wearing but only that she looks better than anyone else. She dominates the clothes instead of the other way around."

Mr. Blass does not confine his studies of women to New York. He has lectured on fashion in other cities and makes personal appearances in stores all over the United States. Invariably, "the Judy Peabody of Lake Forest" or some other posh enclave gives a party for him. "Dayton's made Minneapolis really have a fashion image. Houston is very fashion-conscious," according to the Blass analysis. "Beverly Hills? There the old-time snobbery of California still exists more than anywhere else. Four times a week the same people see each other and so they need more clothes there. Chicago, curiously, is very conservative although there's a hell of an attractive young group with one or two swingers. Atlanta? Here again, because of Rich's, they are on to fashion. Palm Beach is interesting because it's a composite. People come there from every city. Women who are conservative in Detroit will break out in Palm Beach. In a resort, women will let themselves be bizarre. The big difference between New York and out-of-town is that, literally, there is no luncheon place out-of-town. In New York, women wear clothes to go to lunch. Fashion needs things to do and places to go. Neiman-Marcus has always created occasions to dress up and wear clothes in Dallas."

Mr. Blass also does research abroad. In 1963, when he was making twice a year journeys to London, he observed the youthquake. "It

began at Ad Lib and Annabel's where I was seeing youngsters looking divine. And then I went to Paris and saw old bags. It influenced
me. Suddenly, clothes had to be made snappy and young." His vacations in Morocco propelled him, as it did others who followed, toward
the djellabah, the loose-fitting robe worn by North African men. It
became the basis of an American women's evening dress fad.

In February 1964, Kenneth Jay Lane accompanied Mr. Blass to
Morocco. "I don't mean that I do things just to be in with *Vogue*
but I knew that when Diana Vreeland had gone to see her son who
was stationed there [the *Vogue* editor's son, Frederick, is with the
U.S. Foreign Service], Morocco was going to be big," Mr. Lane
recalled two and a half years later. He was then 34, dark-haired, lean
and glowingly suntanned, the king of the counterfeit jewelers and pet
of the fashion socialites on both sides of the Atlantic. It was late
summer and he had reported for work in his office-showroom in a
converted brownstone on lower Park Avenue in beige chinos, a blue
bateau-necked jersey, brown loafers and no socks. He looked every
inch the Southampton croquet player. The month before, Tzaims
Luksus, the bearded fabric designer from Bennington, Vt., had
invited the press and socialites who might be willing to invest in his
new dress manufacturing business to a midnight showing of his collection in a restaurant. Mr. Lane attended that soiree in black pants
and a white shirt opened to the base of his chest. His bare feet were
shod in patent leather evening slippers.

He had come a long way from his boyhood in Detroit where his
father was an auto parts dealer. "I was born in the same hospital as
Marion Javits," he said. Mr. Lane is a graduate of the Rhode Island
School of Design and the merchandising department of *Vogue,* where
he took his first job. The professional and social contacts he made
during that year have endured. Next he went to Delman as assistant
to Roger Vivier. Delman, as well as the American company licensed
to manufacture shoes under the name of Christian Dior, were absorbed by Genesco, the giant corporation that manufactures and sells
everything women and men wear and scent themselves with.

"At Delman, which was one of the last of the great shoe factories,"
Mr. Lane said, "I learned an embroidery technique I still use. They
made a satin shoe and then they decorated it by pasting on rhinestones. The rhinestones didn't fall off the shoe so I said to myself

why not put them on plastic or cork for jewelry?" He started in September 1962.

"I had an office near Maxey Jarman [chairman of Genesco] and his secretary. But I was moonlighting jewelry. I used my initials, K.J.L., to keep it quiet. I had a studio two blocks away and I ducked out of my office whenever a customer was on his way to the studio." Mr. Lane perceived that a radical change in taste was in the making. Affluence was so rife in America that parody was in order. In the Twenties, Chanel had invented costume jewelry, using mock pearls and colored stones to copy her own fabulous jewelry. Now, in the Sixties, the cycle of taste was swinging back to the same sort of razzle-dazzle. Women who could afford moderate quantities of genuine jewelry were willing to imitate their wealthier sisters whose jewel boxes were filled like maharajahs' coffers—but with blatant fakes made of glass and cheap metals. The nothingness of clothing seemed to demand a big splash about the ears and neck and wrists. And the spirit of camp was sanctifying the previously vulgar.

In 1960, a fashion editor, who used to emulate the old rich by having her dressmaker run her up those desperately quiet, little dresses that innocents might mistake for Mainbochers, completed her image by investing in a discreet ring made of steel and chips of clear, dark blue glass. Worn on the third finger of her left hand and viewed from afar, it could have been mistaken for one of those engagement rings that turn up in bulk, paired to platinum or gold wedding bands on the fingers of alumnae at Smith College class reunions. Five years later, the same editor, having changed her "look," had five-carat glass diamonds at her earlobes and wrist. And her editor-in-chief was wearing Kenny Lane's enamel leopard bracelet right next to her David Webb enamel zebra bracelet. One cost roughly a hundredth of the price of the other.

David Webb, the precious jeweler of the new fashion society, didn't mind too much. He found, with some bafflement, that even after the Kenny Lane copies of his beastly bracelets had become a fad, women who owned one of the earliest Webb designs in enamel and gold, for which they had paid from $2,500 to $5,000, were willing to pay $35,000 to $50,000 for the same idea paved with diamonds and studded with emeralds. The Lane knock-off, as they call a copy in the trade, only enhanced the value of the Webb original.

And anyway, Kenny Lane never failed to give credit where credit was due. "Take this necklace," he said, pointing to four strands of mock pearls, pink rubies and emeralds. "It was inspired by Eleanor Lambert's Indian necklace. Seventy dollars retail and I've sold enough to buy her necklace. This one," he said, holding up a strand of pearls and carved rubies, "was inspired by Jo Bryce's necklace from Van Cleef & Arpels. Only hers was pearls and rondelles of diamonds. Jo Hughes sold more of my necklace than anyone else and Jo Bryce is her best customer. Babe Paley was at the Truman Capote reading wearing a marvelous necklace. She didn't want me to see it but I saw enough to get the idea of gold beads and rondelles.

"The first woman to recognize me was D. D. Ryan," said Mr. Lane gratefully. Mrs. John Barry Ryan III is a former fashion editor who is married to a descendant of Otto Kahn, the banker. "She invented a new style, one black earring and one white earring. With a big store, you figure they can sell anything you make. There's always someone who has bad enough taste to buy it. But when you get a friend who has the good taste to wear it, that's something. Now, I'm slowly breaking through to the few last girls who held on to real jewelry, girls like Judy Peabody and Louise Savitt. They wear my stuff when they feel secure," he said with a mischievous gleam in his brown eyes.

By the summer of 1966, Mr. Lane had established a beachhead in Europe. Givenchy was selling Kenny Lane jewelry in the boutique of his Paris haute couture house. So were the Carita sisters in their salon on the Faubourg St. Honoré. "A friend of mine, Didi Abreu [Mme. Jean-Claude Abreu], is a customer of theirs and she said, 'You should have them.' "

British *Vogue* had depicted his gewgaws on their covers. "I'm negotiating for the right boutique in London. Through Jo Hughes, Kitty Miller [Mrs. Gilbert Miller, daughter of Jules Bache, the financier] was wearing something of mine and Evangeline Bruce said, 'My God, Kenny Lane's, where can I get it here?'

"Eleanor Lambert says I'm the best-known American designer in Europe. I was invited to a dinner in Rome. All older people. I arrived late wearing a black shirt. They thought I was a gigolo," Mr. Lane said, pronouncing the word ZHEE-go-lo. "Until they were told who I was. Some of the women were wearing my jewelry. I became respectable. I have a triumvirate of *principessas* as my agents in Europe.

Elizabeth Oxenberg [a former Yugoslav princess who had been married to a New York maternity manufacturer] is my agent in England. Allegra Caracciolo [a princess who worked for Federico Forquet, the Roman couturier] is my agent in Rome. In Madrid, I have Princess Pimpinela Hohenlohe. The whole thing started with friends," Mr. Lane concluded.

Another bachelor designer whom society has taken to its bosom is Oscar de la Renta, a slender Dominican who lived in Spain for 15 years and could pass for a Spanish grandee. He assisted Antonio del Castillo when the latter was with the House of Lanvin in Paris. Then de la Renta moved to New York to fill the spot Castillo previously held as custom designer to the demanding cosmetic empress, Elizabeth Arden. In 1965, at the age of 31, De la Renta became designer and part owner of the Seventh Avenue house of Jane Derby. His backer was Ben Shaw, who also supplied capital for other designers like Ferdinando Sarmi, Geoffrey Beene and Donald Brooks.

"Socializing helps," Mr. de la Renta said. "When a woman buys an expensive dress, she wants to know whose dress she's buying, just for the sake of vanity. It helps me to know people. I know that when my friends go to shop, they will ask for my clothes first."

But Mr. de la Renta doesn't mind if they don't. Among the women he has escorted about town are Mrs. Winston F. C. Guest, the platinum-blond wife of an heir to the Phipps steel fortune who is a cousin of Winston Churchill. Mrs. Guest is mistress of Templeton, an estate on the North Shore of Long Island, an admirer of horses, Barry Goldwater, Spain and Mainbocher. "I adore Cee-zee and, of course, she is completely identified with Main's clothes," Mr. de la Renta said sympathetically.

While visiting in Newport, R.I., an Old Guard watering place, Mr. de la Renta met Mary "Minnie" Cushing, daughter of the Howard G. Cushings. She was 22, and a graduate of Foxcroft. She liked to draw and she told the designer that she was interested in a fashion job in New York. He hired her to be his "extra pair of eyes," which encompasses coordinating his fashion shows and dealing with the press. *Vogue* considers her one of The Beautiful People. A rangy athletic brunette with a friendly manner and a sweet expression, Miss Cushing reported for work on Seventh Avenue on a motorbike. Her hours were supposed to be from 10 until 5 with plenty of leeway for her social life. She circulated widely, usually in De la Renta dresses, which sell in stores from $125 to $2,000. "My parents thought that Seventh Avenue was a rough and strange place but my friends are jealous," she said.

Moving swiftly along the trail blazed by Bill Blass is Chester Weinberg. At age 35, he became a one-third owner of a wholesale dress firm bearing his name.

"Basically, I really love women," said the bachelor designer on the eve of his first showing in May 1966. A short, compactly built man with thinning, jet black hair that is tended by Eddie, the Madison Avenue hair stylist ("he's terribly chic"), coffee-colored eyes and a wide, pearly-toothed smile, Mr. Weinberg was attired in a double-breasted gray flannel suit from Kilgour, French and Stanbury of London, a blue and white striped shirt from Turnbull & Asser, also of London, and brown suede shoes from Rome. "I have my evening shirts laundered in Paris," he added.

Mr. Weinberg expounded on his affection for the fair sex. "As much as I might try to do something in the wind or that will create a stir, something stops me from becoming overpowering. I'm interested in making women desirable, not freakish. Women will feel young, contemporary and loved in my clothes. They'll know I care," he said. He made good his promise at his premiere which was attended by Mesdames Peabody and Eberstadt and a sprinkling of other fashion socialites. His clothes sell in stores "from about ninety to under four." Four hundred dollars, that is.

"Women want to wear names. They want to see this person in flesh and blood," Mr. Weinberg said with conviction. It took him about a dozen years of plucky maneuvering and determination to gratify their wishes. He was born in Manhattan. "My father was in the restaurant business," he said vaguely. He made his first design at the age of two. "It was an absolute scribble but now I'm told it was a wedding dress, and by the time I was in kindergarten, I was the leader in our art world."

He won a scholarship from the High School of Music and Art to the Parsons School of Design and graduated from there to sketching for Leonard Arkin on Seventh Avenue. He progressed through the design rooms of Jo Copeland-Pattullo, Herbert Sondheim, Harvey Berin and Teal Traina. Chester Weinberg describes those years as an ordeal in which his taste and creativity were continuously being throttled.

His rendezvous with history came when Eugenia Sheppard had Jane Holzer photographed in a brown lace dress that he had designed for Teal Traina. Mrs. Holzer liked the dress enough to pay a visit to his showroom where, according to Mr. Weinberg's recollection, she cried something like, "My God, my friends would love your clothes." She invited him to dinner a few times. "And I took it from there," he said. Mr. Weinberg asked Mrs. Holzer to model one of the first "nude" dresses, which he presented in his next show. It was a black chiffon with nothing underneath the bodice except strategic banding.

Mrs. Holzer's parties were the launching pad from which Chester Weinberg could blast off into the elegant regions where he felt he properly belonged. "I'm not interested in the Third Avenue movie crowd," he said. Through Mrs. Holzer he met Mrs. Samuel P. Peabody and her mother, Mrs. Taylor Dunnington.

In the spring of 1965, Mrs. S. Carter Burden, Jr., was photographed at the ballet in another dress he had designed for Teal Traina. It was white voile with a ruffled hem. Mrs. Burden bought the dress at Henri Bendel. "Gerry Stutz said there is romance about my clothes, she said there's romance about my feeling for women," Mr. Weinberg said, referring to the president of the store. "When Amanda Burden bought that dress, she was reaching for something romantic. She represents the thing I love. It's directly opposed to everything that has to do with vinyl. I'm romancing the idea of meeting her," he said later. But the confrontation did not occur until June 13, 1966, at a supper dance to benefit the New York Shakespeare Festival, of which Judy Peabody is a trustee.

By then, Mr. Weinberg had his own business and was making his mark as a man about town. Six weeks before, *Women's Wear Daily* had reported on "the charming little dinner party for Federico Forquet and eighteen other guests" that he gave in his apartment just around the corner from Sutton Place. Mesdames Holzer and Peabody were there as well as Susan Stein and Mrs. William Rayner and Princess Allegra Caracciolo.

Chester Weinberg doesn't want to be mistaken as a designer for just the glittery handful at the top. His aim is much broader than that.

"There's a whole marvelous world of gals who have two kids in private school, a house on the Island, who read all the fashion columns. They want to be loved. They don't want to look ridiculous. They want to look contemporary. This is the group I want to dress."

Take, for example, Anne Weinberg, who's married to Chester's brother, Sidney, a textile executive. "They live at 91st and Park. She's a very good ten, very contemporary. She knows who's dancing at the Bolshoi, what's going on at the Met. She has two kids in private schools. She can talk about private schools to Sam Peabody [who heads the lower grades in a suburban day school]. She represents an entire segment of gals across the country. I have two worlds going for me, Anne and Judy. They give me the true balance. Where Judy might need ten important dresses, Anne would need two."

Still smaller in stature, but grander in taste, than Chester Weinberg, is Arnold Scaasi, who started spelling his last name backwards when he came to New York from Montreal.

Scaasi is a gracious liver. His apartment overlooking Central Park South was decorated by Valerian Rybar, the society interior decorator who was once married to an Irish Guinness. John Rieck, a former assistant to Rybar, helped him furnish his Victorian summer house in Quogue, L.I. According to an early press release, he owes his taste to his Aunt Ida, with whom he went to live in Melbourne, Australia, in the mid-Forties. Aunt Ida was used to Paris clothes and other perfections. "My aunt was a great influence," says the blue-eyed, brown-haired designer in the drawl with which some Seventh Avenue gentlemen approximate Groton and Yale.

Scaasi studied design in Montreal, at the House of Paquin in Paris and with Charles James, the mercurial genius of American fashion, with whom he worked when he first came to New York. Although the fashion editors admired his flamboyant clothes and conferred the Coty Award upon him, Scaasi had his trials as a wholesale designer. After he received financial backing late in 1963 from Mrs. Cortwright Wetherill, the former Ella "Tootie" Widener of Philadelphia, he sailed into the quieter waters of custom dressmaking on East 56th Street. He keeps in touch with the masses by designing men's neckties, as well as children's clothes for Montgomery Ward.

Among his publicized customers are Mrs. Guy Burgos, daughter of the Duke of Marlborough, Arlene Francis, Sharman Douglas, Mrs. Samuel P. Reed, Mrs. Anne McDonnell Ford and her two daughters. He made Charlotte Ford Niarchos' maternity wardrobe. Mrs. Burgos' daughter, Serena, worked for him before she turned to managing a little boutique at Bergdorf Goodman.

The publicity generated by the peacocks assures him the patronage of many wealthy wrens. His least expensive dress is about $550, or about the same as a lesser Paris couturier, and about $300 less than a made-to-order dress at Bergdorf's. His own clothes are custom-tailored by Chipp's in New York and Cardin in Paris. The jackets are made without buttons or breast pocket. "I don't carry a handkerchief," he said.

At least one designer has managed to captivate fashion society despite the fact that he is forever hurrying home after work to be with his pretty wife and three young children. Cosmo Sirchio is a tall, dark and lean gentleman from New Jersey, a graduate of Lafayette College who gave up a budding career as a Philadelphia stockbroker for dress designing. He was employed by Teal Traina concurrently with Chester Weinberg but left the jungle of Seventh Avenue for the deserted prairies of custom dressmaking.

Fortunately, he was taken under the wing of Lewis B. Calisch, one of the most effective promoters in American fashion. An advertising and sales promotion executive of Genesco, Mr. Calisch, whom everyone calls Budd, publicizes Delman shoes, the New York Shakespeare Festival and Orsini's, one of the few non-French restaurants on the high-fashion luncheon circuit. Tall, blond, blue-eyed and almost too handsome to be believed, Mr. Calisch never sells anything. He barely suggests. He is just so agreeable, so helpful and so informed that editors would break their necks to oblige him. He is one of the ubiquitous bachelors of fashion society.

It was at a small showing of Sirchio designs arranged by Mr. Calisch at the Delman salon that Mrs. Denniston Slater ordered a white satin jump suit with feathered cuffs. She wore it to an Election Night party in November 1964. As a Goldwater adherent, Mrs. Slater needed something to pep up that affair. Mrs. Slater is the blond wife of the big-game hunter and chairman of the Fanny Farmer Candy Shops, an inveterate partygiver and goer who will stop at nothing to amuse her husband and friends even if it means having a live bear stand in the receiving line at her Fifth Avenue apartment. Her fashion philosophy is succinctly expressed. "I enjoy being a girl." Mrs. Slater has the wherewithal, including an alabaster skin, a small waist and an excellent bosom. Cosmo Sirchio gratefully acknowledges that she has given his designs "the social stamp of approval."

The morning after the Election Night party, Mr. Sirchio received an order for the jump suit from one of the guests, a wealthy visitor from Los Angeles. Mrs. Henry Kaiser of Honolulu, wife of the retired industrialist, ordered it in six versions. A third guest paid him the compliment of having her little dressmaker copy it. Mr. Sirchio's prices start around $400.

Jump suits had been in fashion but more in theory than in practice. Mrs. Slater's endorsement gave others courage. Cosmo Sirchio made a jump suit that was just a mass of lace ruffles for Barbra Streisand's manager's wife. That focused the eyes of the theatrical crowd on Sirchio.

Meanwhile, he was making more jump suits for Mrs. Slater, who managed to wear them when the press was watching. Lisa Hammel, a reporter for *The New York Times,* described the one Mrs. Slater modeled at the "Night in St. Moritz" Ball as looking "like skin with ruffles." As Mrs. Slater waxed more enthusiastic—"My husband likes Cosmo's things enormously. He doesn't do any mud colors, just flattering ones"—her friends, like Mrs. Cornelius Vanderbilt Whitney, started streaming over to Sirchio's barren atelier on East 58th Street. A photograph of Mrs. Whitney in a yellow lace dress by Cosmo Sirchio in a Palm Beach newspaper brought new customers immediately. The ultimate accolade came when Lady Sarah Consuelo Spencer-Churchill Russell asked him to make the dress for her wedding to Mr. Burgos.

The flood of press notices generated by Mrs. Slater and Mr. Calisch had several consequences. They reassured Sirchio's faithful clients, who never get into the fashion columns but read them. The stories in *The New York Times* mollified his father-in-law, a conservative businessman who takes a dim view of the dress business. And it brought him a new offer from one of the gaudiest exhibitionists in New York, another fashion socialite who is not averse to being photographed in a knock-out dress or jewelry at a ball, then returning it to the store the next morning. "I'd like to wear your clothes because I get lots of publicity," she told Mr. Sirchio.

It was not the first time that the suggestion had been made to a designer who hobnobs with fashion society.

V

LADIES, GO-GO GIRLS AND
OTHER FASHION LEADERS

So you want to be a fashion leader. Or a member of the new society?

They're really one and the same these days and they're not impossible for anyone to achieve. After all, don't the social critics—that's a mass-media euphemism for society columnist—say that American society today is a society of achievement? You don't have to be born into it.

"There is no class any more. Everybody is equal," is the way Mrs. Leonard Holzer sized it up late in 1964. Baby Jane Holzer belonged to at least two minority groups. She was Jewish and said so to Tom Wolfe, the dandy biographer of pop culture. And, as she told James W. Brady of *Women's Wear Daily,* who characterized her as "switched on" in a paean published that year, "I was thrown out of college, actually I wanted to quit so I made them throw me out because it was a very exclusive college and I wasn't learning anything. So I'm uneducated, because I didn't graduate from college."

But these handicaps didn't keep her from a vital role in the new society. Some of her best friends, like the Samuel P. Peabodys and the Frederick Eberstadts, were in the New York *Social Register* although some of the others, like Andy Warhol and the Rolling Stones, were not.

The common denominators for these disparate types were hedonism and fashion. In the Sixties, they unlocked the gilded cages in which some of the aristocrats had felt confined and gave the former outcasts a chance to have a whirl inside. From this new union of pleasure-seekers, the publicists and the press created a new set of American idols, the fashion-society celebrities. There is another crucial attribute, however. If you have it, you can succeed despite a lack of one or two of the other important assets, such as money, taste, beauty and lineage. Fashion has become a Barnum-and-Bailey world and it takes more than any of those to stand out from the noise, the glare, and the action. It requires star quality. An apt essential, since one reason the American press was so anxious for new idols was the dearth of female American movie stars.

Now star quality means you have to project. You can't be a shrinking violet. "When they hear that photos are being taken, they show up faster than Polaroid," said Philip Leff, an editor of the New York *World Journal Tribune,* of the new fashion society.

Star quality means making people look at you even when there are a thousand other persons and stimuli competing for their attention. It means going to the premiere of the film *My Fair Lady* and upstaging Audrey Hepburn, Joan Crawford and Mrs. Cornelius Vanderbilt Whitney by arriving in a black, chiffony dress that makes the photographers suspect there is nothing between it and your bare bosom. Caterine Milinaire did that and henceforth the press learned how to spell her name. Miss Milinaire is a French girl who was hired by Diana Vreeland of *Vogue* to keep the magazine in rapport with the international young swingers. Her mother is married to the Duke of Bedford, a democratic peer who gets plenty of publicity in England by letting tourists see his ancestral digs. But Miss Milinaire would have got lost in the fast shuffle of the new society if she hadn't had star quality.

The *My Fair Lady* premiere was in October 1964, and being a fashion editor, Miss Milinaire was anticipating a trend. Strictly speaking, Countess Christina Paolozzi, whose mother is a Spaulding of Boston, had preceded her. Richard Avedon photographed her nude from the waist up for *Harper's Bazaar* in January 1962. Mr. Avedon isn't afraid to repeat himself. In the October 15, 1966, issue of *Vogue,* to which he had then switched allegiance, he arranged Veruschka, the German model who loves to caper in the buff, in a similar pose.

It was after Miss Milinaire's coup, though, that even the women with the most genteel upbringings started becoming exhibitionists. In the name of sweet charity, they walked down runways before hundreds of spectators. At the luncheon fashion show that benefited the National Society of Interior Designers' scholarship fund, Mrs. Denniston Slater, a platinum blonde who would never be caught without her blue-tinted spectacles and a diamond engagement ring the size of a headlight, primly strode forth in bare-midriffed pajamas that Cosmo Sirchio had whipped up out of a few towels.

It was at the same show, in the spring of 1965, that Mrs. S. Carter Burden, Jr., first heard the roar of the crowd. "I'm just terrified," she whispered backstage as Mr. Rodney of Kenneth's glued green glitter down the middle of her exquisite nose. But when she marched out, smiling shyly in a brocade costume by Sarmi, the decorators went wild.

By the spring of 1966, smart designers had sensed something and come up with the nude look. Mrs. Burden bought Ohrbach's copy of Saint Laurent's transparent dress, a flesh-colored marquisette shift with sequins arranged in strategic places. So did Mrs. Robert Scull.

Star quality is what Charlotte and Anne, the blond daughters of Henry Ford II, were demonstrating when they denied a request from *The New York Times* to sit for a photograph. But they told the reporter and photographer that they would be arriving at 21 at 7:45 P.M. on a certain evening and would not object to being photographed as they swept through the door. After her wedding to Giancarlo Uzielli a year later, Anne Ford held a press conference in the lobby of her mother's apartment house. It was just like the great old days with Marilyn Monroe. She used to like to deal with the press on the outside, too. Then, shortly before the birth of her first child, Mrs. Uzielli went to the premiere of the movie *Hawaii* in a filmy mini-dress.

It couldn't have been anything but the instinct of a star that made Gloria Steinem, the brunet writer, give an interview to *Women's Wear Daily* in which she discussed the men in her life as well as the famous people she knows. Although she sounded offhand about the labels in her dresses, Miss Steinem is knowledgeable about fashion. She dropped two of the right names, Pucci and Bendel's.

In the fall of 1964, she had the wit to turn up at the LBJ Discothèque—a temporary dance hall improvised by Democratic fashion society on the premises of El Morocco to raise money for the campaign—in a clingy, jersey dress that revealed her long-legged curviness, even in the nearly total darkness. It was just an old Gernreich, she said as the photographer took her picture.

Miss Steinem swings with the new society despite the fact that she is what used to be called whistle-bait. (As a rule, overt sexiness and fashion leadership are incompatible.) She also earns her own living, has a Phi Beta Kappa key and has evidenced more than casual interest in politics and civil rights. But then, after all, the New Frontier made intellectualism fashionable.

Miss Steinem is one of several working girls with whom the leisured classes mingle in the new society. Generally, they labor in the arts, communications and modeling. Marisa Berenson, granddaughter of Schiaparelli, and Benedetta Barzini, daughter of the Italian author Luigi Barzini, are mannequins with entrée to the circle. Physicists, teachers and social workers haven't qualified yet. But they may, provided they dress right and emote properly.

There is even a small group of Negro girls on the threshold of the new society. Their credentials are the same as the others who come without quantities of money or a listing in the *Social Register,* namely, a small-boned beauty, a certain élan and the current fashion packaging. The latter can be bought, not for a song but for less than the rich girls spend, if one is astute, at certain shops like Jax, Splendiferous and Henri Bendel. Incidentally, it's necessary to refer to Henri Bendel as BEN-del. Pronouncing the name Henry BenDEL indicates immediately that you're not with it. Pronouncing it Ahr-ree BahnDEL tells that you haven't bought there since Geraldine Stutz became president of the store.

It was in the custom workrooms that Bendel's still had in 1962 that Donald Brooks executed the clothes that he designed for Diahann Carroll, the Negro actress, when she played a model in the Broadway musical *No Strings.* He packaged her in the Stutz-Bendel's ladylike look of 1962, which consisted of low-heeled lizard shoes, an alligator bag with chain handles, white gloves, pearls and a scoop-necked evening dress with a sash at the waist that was pure Mainbocher.

As long as you package yourself correctly and remember to keep enunciating your fashion credits, there is no reason to face discrimination from the new society by reason of race, religion, geography, finances or mental equipment. Fashion society craves new faces constantly, but it wants them to look familiar. They're not lying when they say theirs is an open society. It's just that they are hopeless conformists.

Nevertheless, what counts is not who you are inside or who your ancestors were but who your current playmates are and where your clothes come from. The last detail is something they haven't grasped too well yet outside New York and Los Angeles. Ask a well-dressed woman in Phoenix whose dress she has on. She'll probably answer something like "It's by Rose somebody" or "Nobody's. I just like it." But that's beginning to change. Even Arizona has a few educated fashion plates like Mrs. Newton Rosenzweig, wife of a jeweler, real estate developer and supporter of Barry Goldwater. When a *New York Times* reporter put the question to her at a tea in Phoenix, she replied instantly, "My suit is a Zuckerman, my shoes are by Charles Jourdan, my ostrich bag is a Koret. I bought everything at Magnin's."

Of course, it's essential to cultivate friends among designers and the press. Then you won't have to hire a press agent as some of the middle-aged, very rich and socially insecure women do. If the press agent is run-of-the-mill, he will just telephone the fashion reporters to be on the lookout for his client, who will be wearing so-and-so's dress at the ball or museum preview. Or he tells a fashion society columnist that the client is visiting her brother at his vast estate in California or that she flew over to Paris for fittings at Saint Laurent. But if his social wires are strong enough, the press agent will also arrange for the client to be invited to the right parties or to be nominated to the right charity-benefit committees. She'll have to make an awfully big contribution, in time and money, but then she'll have the unspoken gratitude of all those French orphans and distressed musicians.

Finally, you must be choosy about the men in your life. They must be gregarious and broad-minded. The kind of man who likes to woo a girl with tête-à-têtes in little Italian restaurants or holding hands in the movies or gets edgy when she's the first with a new style or when he notices that he doesn't have to be jealous about all the "boys" she knows—that kind of man won't do. Nor will a husband who is stingy about clothes, hates to see his wife's picture in the newspapers and can't find anything to chat about with the other men in fashion society. A spouse who travels a lot on business and acquiesces to his wife's gadding about with her dress designer while he's gone is a splendid choice.

The new fashion society has its stars and its extras and many who play supporting parts. There never was a shred of doubt that Mr. and Mrs. S. Carter Burden, Jr., were destined for top billing. To the fashion press and publicists, they are the greatest pair of starring sweethearts since Mary Pickford and Douglas Fairbanks, to whom Mr. Burden is related on his mother's side. They're naturals, an authoritative observer ascertained less than two years after their marriage in June 1964. The analyst was Jacques Kaplan, who made a white ermine jacket for Mrs. Burden and promptly saw a trend develop. For a long time, the white fur had been mink. "The two little Burdens are the sort people like to look up to. They're young, pretty, of good family, with a lot of money. And they're involved with modern art. Why, the Larry Rivers' have been to their apartment," he said. "The Burdens have the whole formula. They touch all the bells. It's as if the Queen of England were a yé-yé girl."

In more contemporary terms, the Burdens might be the new Jack and Jackie Kennedy. The tall and blondish Mr. Burden is interested in politics. In 1966, he became an aide to Senator Robert F. Kennedy. Even without making a speech, Mr. Burden has the garment manufacturers' vote sewed up. Some, who see fashion as the axis upon which the world turns, think that nothing can prevent the Burdens from sweeping into the White House one day. They have everything in their family closets, including all kinds of money, two party affiliations, three religions and a shrineful of American heroes and entrepreneurs as ancestors and relatives.

Shirley Carter Burden, Jr., dropped the Shirley and the Jr. as soon as he was listed in the Manhattan telephone directory. He is the great-great-great-grandson of Commodore Cornelius Vanderbilt. His uncle, William A. M. Burden, has made an impact on aviation and modern art. A Republican, William A. M. Burden served as Assistant Secretary of Commerce for Air under Presidents Roosevelt and Truman. President Eisenhower appointed him Ambassador to Belgium. A former president of the Museum of Modern Art, he has a pond in the foyer of his Fifth Avenue apartment which Philip

Johnson designed. In 1949, he and his brother Shirley, Carter's father, established William A. M. Burden & Co., a private-venture investing company. One of the things that set Carter apart from his classmates at the Columbia Law School was the office and secretary he maintained at Burden & Co.

Like Cornelius V. Whitney, another multimillionaire to whom the fashion industry feels warmly disposed, Shirley Burden saw opportunities in Hollywood in the Thirties. Mr. Whitney invested in *Gone With the Wind*. While he was connected with motion pictures, Mr. Burden met and married Flobelle Fairbanks, the niece of Douglas Fairbanks. She once starred for 42 weeks on the stage of the Flatbush Theater in Brooklyn. In 1966, when Britain's Prince Philip was visiting New York, the Douglas Fairbanks, Jr., entertained him in the apartment of their cousin, Carter Burden.

Young Carter was educated at Portsmouth Priory, a pedigreed Catholic boarding school in Rhode Island, and at Harvard, from which he graduated in 1963 with honors. He had finished his first year at the Columbia Law School when he married Amanda Jay Mortimer, the 20-year-old daughter of Stanley Grafton Mortimer, Jr., a grandson of Henry Morgan Tilford, who was in on the beginning of the Standard Oil Company. John Jay, the first Chief Justice of the United States, was another of her ancestors. Mr. Mortimer's second wife is the former Kathleen Harriman, daughter of Averell Harriman, the railroad financier's son who became a Democratic governor of New York.

Amanda's mother is the former Barbara Cushing, the youngest and most beautiful of three extraordinary successful daughters of the late Harvey Cushing, the Boston brain surgeon. Betsey Cushing married James Roosevelt, eldest son of the President of the United States. Her second husband is John Hay Whitney, the Republican venture capitalist, art collector, newspaper publisher and sportsman. He adopted her daughters, Sara Roosevelt, now the wife of Anthony di Bonaventura, a pianist whose father was a barber, and Kate Roosevelt, who married William Haddad, a newspaperman and Kennedy Democrat. Mary "Minnie" Cushing married Vincent Astor and, after him, James Fosburgh, an art scholar.

After her divorce from Mr. Mortimer, Barbara Cushing married William S. Paley, the son of a Chicago cigar manufacturer who had surpassed his father's achievements by becoming chairman of the Columbia Broadcasting System. In 1945, when she was still Mrs. Mortimer, she emerged as a dark horse to head the list of America's Ten Best-Dressed Women. In 1948, she repeated the feat as Mrs. Paley.

The fashion industry is ga-ga over Mrs. Paley, whom it calls by her nickname, Babe. Her flawless bone structure, her long, aristocratic nose and lofty cheekbones, her graying black hair springing back from a rounded forehead, her luminous eyes and her swan's head and neck spell perfection. Furthermore, Mrs. Paley has a professional regard for clothes. Between marriages, she was an editor of *Vogue*. She respects fashion and she doesn't despise publicity. She appears at the haute couture showings in Paris and in New York at Bergdorf Goodman and Chez Ninon, the custom salon run by two society women who copy Paris clothes. She lunches at La Grenouille, the garment industry's noontime hangout, and she is never rude when photographers start clicking. Her secretary politely refuses interviews with newspapers like *The New York Times*. But in July of 1963, she submitted to an interview with *Women's Wear Daily*. It christened her "America's Most Elegant . . . one of the Greatest American Beauties of all time."

In the interview, she declared that her consuming interests were her four children, and her homes, particularly Kiluna Farm in Manhasset, L.I., and the place in the New Hampshire woods. But she did confer a few blessings on Givenchy, Norell, Mainbocher and Lord & Taylor. In conclusion she was quoted as saying, "MY GIRLS? Neither of them are too conventional. Thank goodness, they don't attach too much importance to fashion." A year later, Mrs. Paley's older daughter, Amanda, was married and the fashion industry proceeded to worship a new idol.

At first, she stood in her mother's shadow. "It's been a burden to be the daughter of Mrs. Paley," said an industry press agent, shaking his head in mournful sympathy. "She's the most beautiful girl going," said Halston, Bergdorf Goodman's custom milliner, who hadn't sold her a hat yet although her mother was one of his best customers. *Vogue,* which carried a rhapsody in color photographs and text of the young Burdens in February 1965, quoted an anonymous friend's description of the hazel-eyed beauty: "She looks like a gazelle whose mother was a flower, don't you think?"

Her mother, even 25 years ago, had a worldly air, but Amanda Burden seems bent on perpetual innocence, what with her chestnut hair worn in Alice-in-Wonderland style, her nickname, Ba (her brother's pronunciation of "baby" when they were children), her finishing schoolgirl manners (polished at Westover and not diluted at Wellesley, which she left in the middle of her sophomore year to prepare for her marriage the following June), her choice of storybook heroine clothes and her guileless responses to the press.

"Carter wouldn't like it," she murmured when reporters asked her to pose for photographs in Saint Laurent's see-through dress. She had gone backstage to try it on and order it after a press show at Ohrbach's, to which she had been invited as a kind of sugarplum for the press.

"It has been decided that I should seek anonymity for a while," she said meekly when a reporter sought an interview soon after that episode. It was already bruited about in fashion society that Amanda Burden was in danger of being overexposed. Four months later, she went to Paris to see the collections on the very week when the American fashion industry and the reporters were assembled there. It had been just two years since her first encounter with an ardent press.

They had turned out for her wedding. *Vogue* assigned Cecil Beaton to do its photographs. It was the society scribes' dream assignment. There was the flock of millionaires arriving at St. Mary's R.C. Church in Roslyn, on Long Island's North Shore, the 20-year-old bride in her white organza dress by Mainbocher, who gave the couple a Grandma Moses landscape for a wedding gift, the 23-year-old groom, who whisked the fair princess off to a summer-long honeymoon abroad. On the yacht cruising in the Greek islands, their friend, Henry Koehler, did their portrait.

Five months of silence and then the young couple granted their first interview, to *Women's Wear Daily*. IT'S RIGHT TO BE PROPER, the story was headlined on page 1 of the November 10, 1964, edition, dominating other stories on the same page headlined HEAT'S ON— AND SALES GET SINGED, 5% YULE GAIN IN SOCK FINISH, OVER-COUNTER BETTER FABRICS FLAWS MOUNT.

> WWD THINKS IT'S RIGHT TO BE PROPER . . . back to good manners, neat grooming and feminine charm . . . back to reading a

book, to small gatherings with friends and quiet family week-
ends . . . back to contributing to your community with a Personal touch . . . doing what they want but not trying to be with
it—not forcing it.

WWD THINKS SWITCHED-ON HAS HAD IT. Amanda and Carter
Burden epitomize the New Spirit—It's Right To Be Proper.

Ermina Stimson, then the newspaper's fashion editor, and June
Weir, a reporter who later succeeded to that post, ecstasized further
on pages 4 and 5:

WWD THINKS AMANDA AND CARTER TYPIFY NEW YORK'S FRESH-
EST NEW FACES WITH A WELL BRED APPROACH TO MODERN
LIVING. MARRIED IN JUNE, JUST SETTLING IN THEIR NEW HOME
IN THE OLD DAKOTA ON CENTRAL PARK WEST—MR. AND MRS.
S. CARTER BURDEN, JR., REPRESENT THE BEST OF EVERYTHING.

Such as her collection of bells and pugs, his of soldiers and bulls,
and their joint venture in Staffordshire, and modern art. She was
bicycling and bird-watching while he was keeping fit running in
Central Park.

CARTER IS INTRIGUED BY ANYTHING FAR-OUT IN THE ARTS—
"even if I don't understand it." Experimental films are his latest
interest. "Andy Warhol, at a party the other night, wanted to
do a movie of my arm in this sling." (A navy and red polka
dotted scarf protects his arm, broken while he was riding down
a hill on a skate board.)

. . . AT THE MOMENT, AMANDA FINDS BEING A WIFE A FULL-
TIME JOB. Every day she's still arranging and rearranging their
apartment . . . writing thank-you notes . . . taking piano lessons
(on her Steinway grand—Carter's wedding gift to her) . . . learning how to cook.

Last night the Burdens had their first dinner party, starting with
pâté en croute, saddle of lamb and ending with orange ice. It
grew to 16 and Amanda supervised each detail.

It was a birthday party for Carter's sister, Mrs. Daniel Childs—
and guests included member of the family . . . the Fosburghs,
the Burdens (his parents), the Eberstadts, Truman Capote,
Mainbocher and others.

Women's Wear's reporters finally got the Burdens to talk about clothes. Amanda Burden disclosed that Bendel's was her favorite New York store, that Marie Martine was the boutique she liked in Paris, that she adored Sarmi for evening and that her father-in-law was giving her Mainbochers.

> Growing up, with her mother continually on the Best-Dressed List, Amanda has a sound attitude towards it. . . . "I thought it was ridiculous until I heard my mother's ideas about it— that it wasn't the most important thing in life by any means."
>
> Her husband agrees that there is some good in the BDL—"It's not like the *Social Register* which is the greatest anachronism, because there you're just put on."

In January 1966, when she was just 22, Mrs. Burden was awarded top place in the International Best-Dressed List.

The Burdens had developed new interests. Mr. Burden had decided not to perform in Warhol films. While her husband was in his last year at law school, Mrs. Burden was taking a history course at Columbia. She was still buying at Bendel's, but she had moved off the staid and rarefied Mainbocher track into more democratic emporiums. Orhbach's rated her among its top celebrity customers (the other was her mother). She had also made an appearance at Macy's when it imported a batch of society women to publicize its copies of Paris clothes.

At Splendiferous, the Third Avenue boutique, William, a young salesman who had waited on the Burdens, could hardly contain himself. Mrs. Burden had worn a T-shirt dress by Rudi Gernreich that he had sold her to the premiere of the movie *The Group*.

"They're fantastic," he gushed. "They must work as a team in everything. He tells what he likes and she tells what she likes and they go through the whole thing together. Usually husbands who come in here just sit back and grunt. But he takes a real interest. I'm sure she is dressing for him. It's wonderful."

But someone in the family circle of advisers was becoming concerned, it seemed. In June, at the supper dance for the New York Shakespeare Festival, Mrs. Burden, the co-chairman, reneged on previously publicized plans to wear "the nude look." Among 24 members of the new fashion society who had consented to wear revealing, Shakespeare-inspired dresses by leading designers, Amanda Burden was the only one who borrowed a high-necked, crinolined costume for Rosalind in *Love's Labour's Lost* from the Festival's wardrobe. At the party, she looked like Beth of *Little Women* misplaced in a harem.

The Burdens were obviously preparing to ascend to their next plateau. They were to move out of the Dakota and into vast acreage atop the River House, Manhattan's most exclusive apartment house, overlooking the East River. But they didn't let the fashion industry down.

In the August 1 issue of *Vogue,* this tidbit appeared: "Beauty Checkout: Mrs. Samuel P. Reed and Mrs. S. Carter Burden overheard in New York restaurant greeting each other, 'gotcherbandaidon?' " They were spilling their secret for keeping hair back in a perfect ponytail. The men's fashion feature in the same issue of *Vogue* disclosed that "the new evening ties that Carter Burden, Jr., bought are of silk velvet— one black, another purple."

Vogue, of course, had been among the first to tell the world about the Burdens. In the February 1, 1965, issue, three months after the *Women's Wear* scoop, *Vogue* came out with eight pages of color photographs by Horst entitled "The Young Joyous Life of Mr. and Mrs. S. Carter Burden, Jr." The photographer had been permitted to roam through the honeymoon nest in the Dakota. He caught them holding hands on their balcony looking out over Central Park and being otherwise occupied amid their Giacometti sculpture, Renaissance bronze, their Francis Bacon painting and 18th-century English furniture. She reclined against a chair in her flower-papered bedroom. In his dressing room, his slippers were arrayed on a rug woven to look like a $10 bill. The slippers looked like those navy velvet ones with the gold embroidered monograms that Lobb, the London shoemaker, makes to order at $75 a pair plus $3 for each monogram letter.

Even if they hadn't been so intensely rich and beautiful, the Burdens would have captivated the industry because they are such proficient superconsumers. "Mrs. Paley and her daughter can do their hair as well as any hairdresser and because they want to," Kenneth once said. "Most people say they don't want to be bothered." Mrs. Burden goes to America's No. 1 hairdresser for very special occasions or to buy the falls, switches and hairpieces of which she has a number.

Women's Wear Daily reported some of her beauty tricks. "I wear more make-up than you think I do," they quoted her as saying. "Three eyeshadows and lots of pink rouge below the cheekbones . . . but I don't wear false eyelashes. I can't get away with it . . . the point is to look as if you don't wear any make-up."

At one of those Ohrbach's showings, Mrs. Burden told a fashion editor that she was going to have to do knee exercises. There was just one thing that the angels—and the press—overlooked when they created Amanda Burden: a heavenly pair of gams.

They apportioned those to Judy Peabody, the dimpled blond patrician who has been a prime catalyst in the integration of fashion with society. "Nothing gives me greater pleasure than bringing friends together. The fact that they are in different fields is less important than their personality. Nothing is duller than the same old faces at a party. I like a mixture of people," said Mrs. Peabody, who has seated dress designers and Wall Street scions at the same table without suffering a casualty. "I like A for this reason and B for this reason and I'm sure they would like each other if they met," she said, blushing as she denied that she had been a purposeful matchmaker.

By her own antecedents, as well as through marriage to a certified Boston Brahmin, Mrs. Peabody is listed in the *Social Register*. The former Judith Anne Dunnington of New York, she was educated at Miss Hewitt's Classes and the Ethel Walker School in Simsbury, Conn. She made her debut in 1947 at the Piping Rock Club in Locust Valley, L.I. She left Bryn Mawr after two years. Back in New York, she worked five afternoons and one evening a week, "playing the piano, making pot holders and organizing amateur theatricals" in a home for delinquent boys.

Then she met Samuel Parkman Peabody, son of an Episcopal bishop, grandson of the founder of the Groton School and brother of a reform Democratic governor of Massachusetts. They were married in 1951. Mr. Peabody became a teacher, first at St. Bernard's, New York's most English-accented private school for boys, then the head of the lower school at Rye Country Day School in suburban Westchester County. Their daughter, Elizabeth, was born in 1956. "Sam gets up at 6:15 A.M. to go to work and so we can't stay out late," his wife said. "We go home after the ballet or the opera instead of going on for a drink with someone afterwards."

In 1965, Mr. Peabody's mother, then 73, was jailed in St. Augustine, Fla., for participating in a civil rights demonstration. His older sister, Marietta Tree, is the wife of an Anglo-American multimillionaire. In the Fifties, Mrs. Tree, a friend and political disciple of the late Adlai Stevenson, was considered the reigning goddess and salon-keeper of the intellectual wing of the Democratic party. Regal, curvy and golden-haired, with topaz eyes, Mrs. Tree steadfastly refuses the blandishments of the new fashion society. "How can you know who designed your dress when you got it at Lord & Taylor?" she once remarked, with a tart edge to her velvety voice.

Mrs. Samuel Peabody always knows. Tall, slender, blue-eyed and fragile-looking, she has carried the message of several designer friends by wearing their clothes and seldom failing to be photographed in them at parties and premieres.

Although she "adores" Bill (Blass) and Ron (Amey) and Donald (Brooks), Mrs. Peabody has been most identified with Bob Bugnand, a designer who used to have a salon in Paris and then established himself in Manhattan doing custom work for a wealthy clientele. In 1962, he started designing clothes for the wholesale house of Sam Friedlander, to sell in stores from about $90 to $345. The Peabodys and Bugnand met at the Hotel Gritti in Venice. They exchanged Christmas cards and when the designer presented his first collection in New York in 1957, Mrs. Peabody was one of his most eloquent admirers;

> I thought his clothes were simply beautiful. I wasn't nearly as involved in fashion as I am now, but I tried to introduce him to people, to the girls working on the magazines. He makes my evening dresses for me and also makes very beautiful dressy suits. When one spends that amount of money, one can't get a whole wardrobe.
>
> He designs beautifully in a specific way. He knows Isabel [Mrs. Frederick Eberstadt] likes to look one way and I another. It's fun to work with someone like that. They know that one person needs things for one kind of life and another person for another kind of life. We can help them because they see how we live and they help us with very specific things. I was talking to Bob and I said, "I wish you could come up and pack for me." I'm going to London in three weeks and I'll be in Italy for the summer. [This was in June 1965. Mr. Bugnand had given a dinner

party for 38 at his apartment in honor of her birthday a month before.]

And Bob said, "Take this and this and this."

Why should designers be treated differently than anyone else?

They're talented and charming. I never have a disassociation of those two things. The talent and the personality go together. Why shouldn't fashion be considered just as important as anything, as any other art?

Mrs. Peabody is devoted to music, ballet and drama. She has been involved in theater, first as a production assistant to Sidney Lumet, later as an Off-Broadway producer of plays by Eugene Ionesco and other contemporary playwrights. In the fall of 1964, she was elected to the board of trustees of the New York Shakespeare Festival, which gives top-flight productions of the Bard's plays in Central Park without charging admission. Through the fiery zeal of its producer, Joseph Papp, a Brooklyn boy who reincarnates the rough charm of a John Garfield, the Festival had managed to stave off annual bankruptcy. In 1966, the Festival acquired a building for a permanent home and projected plans for experimental theater, chamber music concerts and art exhibits.

Until this point, the Festival had been rescued from its crises by philanthropists like George T. Delacorte, the publisher, and Mrs. Louis K. Anspacher, a self-effacing dowager. Mrs. Peabody, who had backed up her verbal enthusiasm with important financial support, encouraged the other trustees to interest a younger segment of New York society through a fund-raising supper dance. She recruited "two young, glamorous, marvelous, hard-working people, both so creative and involved in the life of New York," to be co-chairmen. They were Mrs. Burden and Susan Stein, one of the go-go girls of the new fashion society.

"I adore Judy, I adore Amanda, I adore Shakespeare," cried Miss Stein, the dark-eyed, raven-haired daughter of Jules C. Stein, chairman of the Music Corporation of America. Her father registered his approval by becoming a Festival donor (one who gives between $1,000 and $5,000). "I majored in drama and philosophy at Vassar. I love *Henry V* and *King Lear*. *The Tempest* I did at college. I wrote the

music," said Miss Stein. It was her idea to have designers create special dresses based on the new, nude look. "It seemed the newest
thing," she said.

Donald Brooks, the first designer she approached, suggested tying
the dresses in with Shakespearean characters. He and Miss Stein
jointly decided to miscast the energetic, talkative and strong-minded
co-chairman as Ophelia. Mr. Brooks provided her with what she described as "a cute dress that makes me look like I just came out of
the water dripping flowers." And her bosom overflowed the neckline.

Miss Stein drew up a list of Shakespeare's feminine characters and
let the designers and fashion socialites have their pick. She served as
arbitrator. Most of the designers researched their assignments. Most
of the models, with the exception of Miss Stein and Gloria Steinem,
who knew that Lady Macbeth "was at least an intelligent, interesting
woman even if she came to a bad end," had the vaguest notions about
whom they were impersonating.

"I know Othello tried to kill her," said Minnie Cushing of Desde-
mona, whom she was impersonating. The tall brunette from Newport,
R.I., was substituting for Anne Ford Uzielli, who was originally supposed to wear the dress of sheer net latticed with gold that Miss
Cushing's employer, Oscar de la Renta, had concocted. Mrs. Uzielli
had bowed out, pleading pregnancy as an excuse.

"Hermione's husband thought she was unfaithful but my husband
and I don't like that interpretation," said Mrs. Montague H. Hackett,
Jr., a spirited brunet lawyer's wife and *Social Register*-ite who had
just taken up designing pants and hostess clothes for Saks Fifth Avenue. "I'm sticking to the fact that she turned into a white statue."
For her character from *Winter's Tale,* Emilio Pucci had designed a
jump suit out of gossamer white jersey, with harem pants and a halter
neckline that plummeted to the waist. He had arranged for Harry
Winston to lend Mrs. Hackett $300,000 worth of diamonds to
relieve the stark simplicity of the outfit. The jeweler sent a body-
guard who hovered doggedly at Mrs. Hackett's elbow.

Plans had called for the models to attend the performance of *All's
Well That Ends Well* at the Delacorte Theater and then proceed to
the supper dance at the Plaza Hotel. The threat of inclement weather
forced the cancellation of the performance in the open-air theater and
the gala event was reduced to just the party. It was enjoyed on two

levels. The fashion socialites and their designers reveled in posing for the press photographers and marching in a procession around the dance floor.

Seated apart from the birds of brilliant plumage were the loyal Festival supporters. They quietly supped on chicken tetrazzini and rosé, danced and regretted that the play had been scratched. They observed the pretty show-offs politely but not avidly. Some of them looked a little puzzled. "This is the first time we've ever done anything like this and I think we'd better assess it," said an industrialist from the board of trustees.

"The real true Shakespeare lovers gave a hundred dollars and stayed home," a Festival employee said.

But when the smoke cleared, it was seen that the gala had netted about $57,000, and that about 27 per cent of it had come from new sources. "From people who will rally to Judy's and Susan's side," the Festival's fund raiser admitted. "Now giving to Shakespeare becomes associated with having a good time." A farce can serve a serious purpose. And it had garnered national publicity for free Shakespeare in New York.

No one had worked harder than Miss Stein. She had typed letters, importuned friends to buy tickets and take advertisements in the program and she had attended to sudden problems like the arrival at the airport during the weekend of the dress that Federico Forquet had designed in Rome for Mrs. Henry Fonda to wear as Virgilia. "When this is over, I'm going ballooning in Holland," Miss Stein announced. And she did.

Susan Stein throws herself completely into whatever her current interest is. A capable linguist, she is fluent in French and Spanish and "can communicate vaguely in Chinese and sing in 10 languages." She studied Chinese at Columbia after she graduated from Vassar. She has made a record, acted in summer stock and in one Broadway play. In 1964, she and four socialite friends decided to capitalize on their vast travel experiences and personal contacts by opening a travel agency. Ports of Call arranges trips for people who have already been everywhere and provides them with special services, such as the name of the best tailor in Bombay. As a travel agent, Miss Stein has an excuse—not that she needs one—for gallivanting around the globe. She almost killed herself on a trip to Bermuda when her motorbike flew off the road and into a stone wall. But Miss Stein recuperated quickly and was soon back on the telephone and on the discothèque dance floor with customary verve.

"Please don't make me sound like a butterfly because I'm not really," she had asked a reporter a few months before. Miss Stein functions as a playgirl activist in the new fashion society. She led it to the Dom, a neighborhood bar in a Polish meeting hall on the Lower East side, and thereby paved the way for the slum area's elevation to a certain beatnik chic. Like her older sister, Jean vanden Heuvel, Susan Stein is a celebrated hostess. She resides in a rambling, high-ceilinged apartment at the Dakota, overlooking Central Park. Her back door neighbors are the Jason Robards. The apartment is decorated with a mixture of English furniture and Oriental art. A silk rug, embroidered with rows of shahs, was a gift from the late Aly Khan to her father. One room is dominated by a billiard table. Miss Stein is a competitive player and will give a billiard party at the drop of a hint.

Equally bold with clothes, Miss Stein has been among the first to espouse styles as English Mod dresses, caftans, clingy jump suits, mini-dresses and anything that makes a thousand onlookers swear she doesn't have a thing on underneath. (She usually does, although it's only a nude-colored slip or body stocking.)

> I have a passion for costumes. I love collecting them, remaking them and using them. I bought a very old coat that an Indian nobleman used to wear. It's called a sherwani and it was gold and silver and lined in red. I had a dress made to match the red and wore it to an opening once. Krishna Menon and Nehru were there and they stared me down. Everybody in New York thought it was a Mainbocher. And then Yves Saint Laurent put the rajah coat in his collection [she said with a smile].

> I have a Moroccan caftan of embroidered velvet that I wear around the house with a gold belt or unbuttoned and over an evening gown to the theater. I have a Turkish harem coat that I found in the bazaar in Istanbul. It's orangey red silk and bound with gold and silver cord. I found some pale orange chiffon and had a dress made out of it to go with the coat.

> I had this old costume in garnet velvet and gold that was what Moroccan Jewish girls used to wear the night before their marriage. It had a wide, envelope skirt. I had a new velvet skirt made, tube-shaped, with the gold down the side. And I wear it

with a sleeveless, low-cut top. I had the blouse cut into a bolero. And I wear it with my Moroccan jewelry.

I had a beautiful piece of French lamé. I sent it to a dressmaker in Fez with a pale blue and gold sari I bought in India. She made me a caftan out of the lamé and a transparent coat with gold borders out of the sari.

I have all this gold and silver cord from the souks in Fez and Tangier. I used some of it to bind a black velvet Chanel suit. The rest I bound some velvet cushions with.

Fashion is where I find it. I'm a frustrated designer. I'll wear anything that appeals to me. I splurged once at Chanel, but I'm more likely to buy a sample at Dior or Simonetta. I won't buy anything from the couture that can be copied, but I've gone to town at Ohrbach's.

In American, I like De la Renta, Tiffeau, and Brooks. I've had a sealskin coat for ten years. I have a tiny mink jacket. I had a mink border and cuffs put on a silk and lamb's wool lining so that I can button it on to several different coats.

I wear my clothes over the years and I change them. I will adapt a designer's dress to myself. I'm not afraid to buy fabrics or costumes and put them away. I have closets of things I've bought over the years. I believe in the old trunk method.

Even more restless than Susan Stein is fashion society's most far-ranging narcissist, Jane Holzer. One can imagine what Miss Stein might have done with her first-rate education and skills if her father had stuck to his first profession, ophthalmology, instead of organizing the General Motors of theatrical talent. One suspects that Mrs. Holzer would have blazed the same moth-like trail whether or not her father had been successful in Florida real estate.

Susan Stein is perfectly capable of coherence. She adjusts her intellectual thermostat to her audience. Jane Holzer's communications are appreciated most by pop culturati and high campers. Her specialty is the put-on (the pop equivalent of kidding, but with hallucinogenic overtones) which leaves the rest of the citizenry baffled or bored.

Where Miss Stein throws a smokescreen around her intelligence, Mrs. Holzer attempts to be profound. "My generation was born slightly before the atom bomb was exploded," she said when she was

24. "We have an insecurity and supersecurity. Not too many of us are afraid to die."

That was in 1964, in retrospect the vintage year of pop fashion. London had become a Mod world. Courrèges was relating to the space age in Paris. And in New York, Tom Wolfe crowned Baby Jane Holzer the Girl of the Year. It was an ephemeral title, of course, but just then the new fashion society was crystallizing and the quest for idols was intense. Like Barbra Streisand, who refused to bob her Semitic nose, Jane Holzer had lots of the wrong things right with her. Her maiden name was Brookenfeld and as she informed Sidney Fields, the columnist for the New York *Daily News,* "I was born in Palm Beach, which is practically impossible. I mean everyone sort of goes there. No one is really born there, are they?" Unlike Miss Streisand, however, "I have this horrible voice problem," she also said. Because of it, Mrs. Holzer was taking voice lessons as well as acting lessons. She had done some modeling and lots of shopping for clothes before she was married at 22 to Leonard Holzer, who had gone to Princeton and then joined his father in building apartment houses. They had a conventional wedding in a Manhattan hotel with the bride wearing a white evening dress and a fat, round diamond solitaire.

"I learned a sad lesson doing my trousseau," she said later. "I spent a lot of money here and I was uncomfortable. Then I went to Paris and had my clothes made and now I'm comfortable."

Chanel, Givenchy (whom she calls Hubert, pronouncing it You-BARE), Balenciaga, Saint Laurent, Dior, Courrèges—Mrs. Holzer had been to them all. She was one of the first to buy the Courrèges pants. "That sari dress Balenciaga did. I didn't buy it because everyone in town bought it. It was the most beautiful dress in Paris," she sighed.

Mrs. Holzer was playing the young classic elegante that day. It was in December 1964. Tom Wolfe's story had appeared in the New York *Herald Tribune* a few days before and the telephone was ringing constantly in the gloomy Park Avenue apartment with the dark green brocade walls and the Flemish paintings where the young Holzers lived with his father. The only clue that a pop idol dwelled there was the chinchilla pillow on the green velvet chair, and the fox and zebra pillows on the yellow brocade sofa. But on that day, she was a little jittery about sudden fame. And so she kept a reporter and a photographer from a rival newspaper waiting while she wandered around in mid-afternoon in a wrapper and bare feet, ejaculating Anglo-Saxonisms and shouting to the maid to bring her lunch. Finally she emerged in a soiled white wool Chanel coat, lined in Mongolian lamb, a matching skirt attached to a navy blouse, a Maltese cross on a chain, beige and black Chanel sling-back pumps, a quilted Chanel bag slung over her shoulder.

"My closet is a Chanel suit," she announced. "I'm completely dressed in Paris but when I want to wear cheap clothes, I go to England." She was one of the first to know about Foale and Tuffin.

She wanted the record set straight. Tom Wolfe had written at length about the Mod Ball that had been given a couple of weeks before in the studio of Jerry Schatzberg, the photographer, in honor of the Rolling Stones. They were then the newest British rock 'n' roll phenomenon and Mrs. Holzer's passion of that moment. At the party, there had been a cake for Baby Jane, whose 24th birthday happened to coincide with the soiree. There had been lots of electrified noise and dancing and broken glass until 5 A.M.

Although Jane Holzer comprehended the meaning of the social revolution in Britain, and was very close to David Bailey, the photographer, and all the other pop aristocrats from the East End, she wanted it made clear that day that she herself was not a Mod. "The Mod Ball was just a kicky thing. People in New York were slightly bored. One day I went to lunch in dungarees and a sweater, you know, and someone decided I'm a Mod. Mods are 14 to 17 years old. If you're over 17, you're too old to be a Mod. Everyone missed the point about that," she said.

It was at a Paris showing that Diana Vreeland, editor-in-chief of *Vogue,* had discovered her, five months before. "Marvelous, glorious," Mrs. Vreeland confirmed the encounter later. "She just happened to have the greatest head of hair. And a tiny face like a narcissus. Lovely bones. She just looked great. That's all anyone's supposed to look. She just looked super. I saw her at the Chanel collection. I remember someone murmuring, 'You ought to cut your hair.' "

Mrs. Vreeland has never been keen about cropped locks and in 1964, the couturiers and coiffeurs were all decreeing the small-head look achieved by short, straight hair. When the editor spotted Jane Holzer's lion's mane, she asked her to model for *Vogue.* The first photographs appeared in the October 1, 1964, issue. They helped to generate a trend. Other society girls, like Anne Ford, had refused to forfeit their swollen heads, even though everyone was saying that bouffant hairdos were passé. Quantities of hair overcompensate for insignificant features. Marc Sinclaire had been giving Miss Ford a puffed coiffure flipped up at the ends.

Take away Jane Holzer's blond hair and you have a plain face with a long, straight nose. Her coiffure is actually of the same un-made-bed school as Brigitte Bardot's. But Holzer is no Bardot. She is fashionable skin and bones, except for her legs, which are on the solid side. Nor is she a Marilyn Monroe, despite her baby-blue-eyed stare; with Monroe, there was a touching innocence that shone through all the tawdriness of her life. Nevertheless, Jane Holzer, whose friends nicknamed her after the movie *What Ever Happened to Baby Jane?*, longs for cinema stardom. She was Andy Warhol's first underground superstar. The pop artist had immersed himself in producing 16-millimeter films that were called underground movies not only because of the infinitesimal budgets and haphazard schedules under which they were created, but because their flavor was too gamy for standard audiences. Archer Winsten, reviewing a Warhol film in the New York *Post,* defined its components as "perversion, degradation, seeming influence of narcotics, suggestion of a depraved gathering . . . whips, sadism, masochism and acres of sheer unintelligibility." Baby Jane Holzer performed without salary in about half a dozen Warhol films with names like *Dracula* and *Camp.* In *Soap Opera,* she told Sidney Fields, "I'm this girl who keeps getting all these boy friends and I don't know where they come from. Honestly, I've never kissed more men in my life."

To the inevitable question, she replied, "No, I don't know if my husband objects to my working. I don't see too much of him, which is a problem, isn't it? We've been married for two years and the thing is like he likes to play cards or when he gets home from the office he's tired and goes to sleep. I'm tired too, but I can't go to sleep at 8 o'clock. I have to prepare for the next day and read scripts or I go out."

Five months later, Carol Bjorkman interviewed Mrs. Holzer. She found her at home of a morning with her dogs, Scoupidou and Chou-Chou, being served breakfast by Johnny. Miss Bjorkman identified him as a combination secretary-cook-valet and sleep-in maid. And since he was the same size as Mrs. Holzer, he also went for try-ons of her clothes.

Once, her friends in the press had mentioned the possibility of a part for Baby Jane in *Who's Afraid of Virginia Woolf?* but the Burtons managed without her. She did get on NBC-TV's *Hullabaloo,* wearing Victor Joris' transparent plastic pants suit, and into the New York segment of the filming of *Jack of Diamonds,* with George Hamilton. The society columnists reported that she was at a party for Michael Caine and that she was testing for a part in *Valley of the Dolls.* During one of several visits to Hollywood, she said to an interviewer, "I really don't need to work. But I like to perform." It may have been her most significant statement.

Some women in the new society are esteemed not only because they are committed to fashion, but because they contribute ideas that may inspire designers or incite a trend. They view clothes through the lens of the professional. It doesn't make for normal vision by ordinary women's standards.

"Probably eighty per cent of women choose clothes to make themselves look pretty," Isabel Eberstadt reflected. "I think there are a few women for whom looking pretty is not so important as creating a mood." Mrs. Eberstadt generally creates her moods with the most avant-garde designs of the Paris haute couture and the fantasies of Adolfo, the Cuban-reared milliner, who believes that women should bedeck themselves for evening in feathered headdresses and jeweled masks. "I guess I don't mind being laughed at," she added. Fully two years before most American women were aware of Courrèges and three years before his little white boots and squared-off dresses had become a summer uniform, Mrs. Eberstadt was singing his praises and buying his designs.

Isabel Eberstadt is a willowy brunette with a pale complexion, a retroussé nose with deep nostrils, and extraordinarily expressive hands. The wife of a fashion photographer, she knows how to strike a dramatic pose.

Her father is Ogden Nash, the poet-humorist. She was educated at Miss Porter's School in Farmington, Conn., and made her debut in New York and at the Bachelors' Cotillion in Baltimore. In 1954, she left Bryn Mawr during her sophomore year to marry Mr. Eberstadt, the son of Ferdinand Eberstadt, a Wall Street investment banker. The young Eberstadts are in the *Social Register,* but their parties are a *paella* of society, fashion designers and editors and the visual arts. They made their mark when Jacqueline Kennedy came to one of their bashes during her White House days. Mrs. Eberstadt is the mother of two children and the author of a novel and several magazine articles. She and her husband co-authored a couple of children's books. Mr. Eberstadt is a pioneer of the longer hairdo for men and the shaped, Cardin suit. Mrs. Eberstadt didn't have to push to be noticed by the fashion press. John Fairchild of *Women's Wear Daily* was a classmate of her husband's at Princeton. He is enchanted with Mrs. Eberstadt. All through 1962 and 1963, his newspaper starred her as a "Locomotive," a "Young Individualist," a "Young Arrogant Elegant" and "Marvelously Brainy." She made the Best-Dressed List in January 1963.

Many of the *cognoscenti* rate Chessy (pronounced Chezzy) Rayner the most prolific fashion idea woman of all. The former Chesbrough Hall, a 1949 debutante in New York and Boston, thinks like a pro, acts like a pro and gives other pros lots of ammunition. She retired at just past 30 after working for nine years as a fashion editor at *Vogue* and *Glamour*. Her blond mother, also a Chessy, is married to Iva S. V. Patcévitch, the president of Condé Nast Publications. Chessy Rayner's husband, William, is his assistant. The Rayners have written two books on gourmet cookery.

They live in a Park Avenue apartment, the living room and dining room of which were decorated by Billy Baldwin. They are lively, cozy rooms with pure yellow walls, paisley-covered footstools, collections of shells and crystal, a scented fire in the grate, masses of paper flowers in vases and modern paintings. In 1966, Mrs. Rayner embarked on a career as an interior decorator.

She is a tall woman whose distinctive looks are compounded of a square jaw, high cheekbones, dark brown eyes and hair. She keeps slender and fit with exercise classes. "I loathe short hair and little heads. It's a luxury to have a lot of hair," she has asserted. There is always something eyecatching about her head, be it flowers wound in abundant hair (implemented by the wiglets and switches *Vogue* advocates) or a headdress concoction. She was one of the first to go dancing in a little black dress, like a Gustave Tassell brocade, and a float of white ostrich feathers attached to her hair with a comb. "In a sea of black dresses, how can anyone tell who you are?" she asked. At the Shakespeare Festival dance, on the other hand, Mrs. Rayner stood out by being the least sensational. She simply looked strikingly pretty and ladylike as Titania from *A Midsummer Night's Dream,* in a dress by Bill Blass, one of her favorite designers.

She was an early admirer of Micia, the knit house owned by two American fashion photographers, Jack Bodi and Joseph Leombruno, who live and work in Italy (Jack's hobby of knitting put them in the manufacturing business as a profitable sideline). In 1964, she was already wearing clothes from Foale and Tuffin of London and Michèle Rosier of Paris. She also liked Venet, a small Paris couturier, for coats and suits. She ordered by mail from Venet and from Alix Grès, from whom she bought one or two evening dresses a year. Mrs. Rayner was shopping for $3.50 chino and $6 corduroy trousers and other sporting clothes in the Army-Navy surplus stores on West 42nd Street before the newspapers and magazines wrote about them and before Yves Saint Laurent visited them and went back to Paris and put the pea jacket in his collection. "With day clothes, I'm strictly the cheap department," she said. After dark, she bursts into splendor. The mink coat she got at 19 hung unused in her closet for a dozen years. Feeling the need of an evening wrap one season, she decided on a French turkey feather jacket that Anne Rubin made to sell for $700.

She preferred Kenneth Lane's fakes to real jewelry because, she reasoned, she could have a picture or a set of chairs or a trip for the price of the latter. "A diamond pin is not very interesting or fun," she said. In 1966, Altman's had mannequins made up that looked like Chessy Rayner and put them in their windows at Fifth Avenue and 34th Street, wearing clothes that she had selected to go with her style of life.

Louise Savitt had been put into Saks Fifth Avenue's windows two years before. "It's a little frightening to walk by and listen to the comments of people who are looking at your mannequin. 'Oh, that hair,' they say and then they punch each other," she sighed. Like Jacqueline Kennedy, Mrs. Savitt kindles violent reactions with her hair. It is auburn and teased into a bouffant coiffure. "Most people dislike my hair," she said. "I don't have the kind of hair that I can wear flat. Unless you're one of those models with the wonderful cheekbones, you don't look good with a little, flat head. I wouldn't let Kenneth cut my hair. I'm very bad with hair. So I have it teased so it lasts for two or three days. Then I run in and have it combed."

In her mid-20's, small-boned and thin but not scrawny, a divorcée with a young son, Mrs. Savitt exemplifies the ladylike, rich-girl school of dressing. She is the daughter of Herman M. Liberman, Jr., a Wall Streeter, and Mrs. S. Joseph Tankoos, Jr. Her maternal grandfather was a real estate investor whose holdings included choice properties on Seventh Avenue. She was educated at the Spence School in New York and Briarcliff College. She made her debut in New York and married Richard Savitt, the tennis champion. She has worked at various times for *Vogue*.

Mrs. Savitt is modest but direct about being considered a fashion molder. There are two ways you might be influential, she said:

> Somebody gets on to you. They see you five or seven times and realize that you know what you're doing. Not necessarily right or wrong but it's a look. They do something about you. They latch on to you. *Women's Wear* and Eugenia Sheppard are two big influences. People read them and swear by them. *Vogue,* too, in a more glamorous way. They say you wore ostrich feathers [Mrs. Savitt wore an ostrich hat to an art gallery opening] and suddenly everyone is wearing ostrich feathers.

> Then you can influence a designer as someone he knows. Bill Blass doesn't ever do a collection without me in mind. He can always tell which dresses are going to be for me. Often, I'll say a color is great or "Do my neckline one quarter of an inch higher." It's a matter of being a little different rather than being well-dressed.

Most women don't have the knack, she said. They either don't try or they accept as gospel whatever the fashion magazines say at the moment:

> Some women believe because they read it that this year the color is blue and their eyes should be brown. I've seen little, fat women wearing those Adolfo headdresses right out of *Vogue* magazine. Nobody means that everything should be taken exactly as they show it in the magazine.

> I had no background in fashion. I just got a job at *Vogue*. I always sort of knew how to dress. I always had innate taste. *Vogue* changes your ideas a bit. It helps give you more scope. I was a little bit more conservative before I worked there. My mother has good classic taste. She wears expensive clothes. She can go to Paris and pick the five best dresses. I can pick, perhaps,

the five best for me. [Her mother, Mrs. Tankoos, invariably turns up where society gathers, looking like a fragile doll, in an exquisite Balenciaga with coordinated jewels]. Neither of us is a believer in kooky clothes. Where I wear sweaters and skirts in the daytime, she will wear Norell.

For daytime, Bill makes me skirts in a few fabrics and I wear them with Jax tops. I own four little jersey dresses to go out to lunch in. I don't spend much money in the daytime.

Evening is the big thing. I buy, say two very expensive evening dresses a year. To a certain extent, it depends on whether you're used to wearing expensive clothes. Once you've had a good dress, you can't go backwards. Once you've had a Norell, you don't feel right in a Junior Sophisticates. I'm a bug for things that people never see. Good underwear. The way Chanel's jackets are lined.

Jewelry? If I were really rich, I'd rather have an amusing bracelet than a big diamond. [She likes to flank a gold bangle with David Webb's coral and lapis lazuli bracelets].

I always thought a mink coat was chic besides being very useful for those cold, rough nights. I have a brown one. Something I love more than anything is Bill's sleeveless black mink pullover with a long evening dress.

I never understood English Mod clothes. I'm so against crazy stockings I could scream. I believe things have a use, like you wear boots in the park. I went through a big thing of looking flat-chested and all that. But you can't forget you must look pretty and occasionally, look sexy. Some women forget that.

Summing up fashion leadership, Louise Savitt said, "If you spend a certain amount of time and money on fashion, it's nice to be recognized. But the publicity can be embarrassing. People think of you as a clothes horse. There are 105 things more important than fashion. When every day you are in some publication, it's a bore. And then you will be dropped. My own father asked me, 'Do you have a publicity agent?' "

Mrs. Savitt doesn't need one.

One major fashion trend that started in high society is the Lilly. The tropical-colored print cotton shift owes its existence to the fact that the daughter of Mrs. Ogden Phipps and wife of the grandson of a famous publisher doesn't look good in pants. Mrs. Herbert Pulitzer of Palm Beach, Fla., confided that fact to her dressmaker in the late Fifties and the two of them worked out a garment that was nothing more than an exuberant housedress.

"The great thing about the Lilly," said Lilly Pulitzer, a tall, substantially built brunette and mother of three, "is that you wear practically nothing underneath." Although Mrs. Pulitzer, whose great-grandfather, Jabez Bostwick, helped John D. Rockefeller put the Standard Oil Company together, likes the casual, barefoot life, she has the genes of an entrepreneur. So does her husband, who goes by the name of Pete.

He works hard growing orange and grapefruit along the Indian River. But raising children and running a house overlooking Lake Worth didn't begin to use up Mrs. Pulitzer's energy, so in October 1959 she opened an orange juice stand with citrus donated by her husband.

She did a thriving business. One day, she brought a dozen of her shift dresses to the stand. Her partner, Laura Robbins, who used to work on *Harper's Bazaar,* hung them on plain hangers from a pipe rack and concocted a dressing room with a mirror and a screen. Thirsty customers plucked the hangers clean and suddenly Mrs. Pulitzer was in the dress business. The fact that Jacqueline, Ethel and Joan Kennedy were Lilly-fans didn't hurt at all.

After some amateurish fits and starts, the Lilly became big business. Its snob appeal emanates from a shoe box of a shop in the Via Mizner, an alley sliced into Worth Avenue, Palm Beach's elegant shopping thoroughfare. The orange juice stand is just across the way. The salesgirls are pretty young socialites, who don't have to exert themselves too much with a pre-sold item.

By 1965, more than $1 million worth of Lillys were being manufactured in a factory in Miami and sold in nine retail shops from South to North for around $30 to $75. Lord & Taylor introduced them to the corporate wives and suburbanites who don't happen to vacation in the resorts where most of the Lilly shops are situated. They like the Lilly because it's such a nothing of a dress but so cheerful and so comfortable. The basic design is changed three times a year but as subtly as a Mainbocher creation. Mrs. Pulitzer elaborated on the original theme with ruffles and scallops. She added floppy pajamas, sunbonnets and bikinis that are not acceptable everywhere. "They won't let you show your belly button at the Bath and Tennis Club," she said without animus.

There are little-girl Lillys, called Minnies after her middle child. Caroline Kennedy has worn them. And "Sneaky Pete" batiste nightshirts for men. Early in 1967, printed Lilly pants were introduced because Laura Robbins, the partner, had liked pants all along.

The Pulitzers avoid the frenzied social pace set by the winter visitors and the aspiring newer millionaires in Palm Beach. "I can't remember attending a charity ball but I must have been to one once," Lilly Pulitzer once said in her laconic manner.

It takes all kinds to make fashion leaders.

VI

THE CREATORS

IN the Sixties, fashion designers have reached new heights of esteem. They are lionized by hostesses, ennobled by the press, admitted to the ranks of pop celebrities. Yet this fashion-drenched decade has produced only a handful of creators. Those few —on both sides of the Atlantic and at opposite ends of the American continent—have initiated the new dialogue of fashion, which no longer takes place between the haughty dressmaker and his elegant client but between the mass designer and the adventurous hordes. Such creative designers have affected the way women look not so much by sketches or specific garments as by the ideas behind them. It is their perceptiveness about current history, economics, sociology and psychology—often an intuitive rather a reasoned understanding —that has made fashion in the Sixties so different from what preceded it.

There is no nostalgia in their attitude. The language they speak has a clipped, modern vocabulary that startles those who cherish older concepts of prettiness and feminine fragility. When they fantasize, as fashion designers always do, the fantasies often strike an abrasive note that accurately reflects the contemporary environment. Many wish it were not so.

After these creators inscribe the handwriting on the wall, other designers transmit the message for the majority of women who are always discomfited by strenuous novelty. Fashion is nothing more than aesthetic judgment, a case of the eye's getting used to new arrangements of color, shape and proportion. Although the pace has accelerated in the last decade, fashion is still a filtering process.

Some of the decade's most distinctive philosophy—the themes of the body beautiful and the streamlined, functional apparel as well as the pattern for the fashion designer as a far-ranging thinker-activist —had been anticipated in the Fifties by the Marchese Emilio Pucci di Barsento. One of the most enduring Sixties status symbols in the fickle world of fashion is a dress of silk jersey with his signature, "Emilio," chicken-scratched into its tropical geometric print. A figure-skimming dress that weighs four ounces and can be crumpled into a handbag without danger of wrinkling, it costs $150 or more in the original. Far less expensive copies in synthetic fabrics are the world traveler's uniform, steadfastly overshadowing any temporary design fireworks out of Paris or other fashion centers.

When it was introduced in 1957 at the Italian fashion showings in Florence, buyers said that no American woman would be caught dead wearing it. The same erroneous prediction had been made about Pucci's skinny trousers, known as Capri pants, which unmistakably outlined the lower half of a woman's body and was thought to violate the American Puritan tradition. The Sixties have seen the crumbling of that tradition and the acceptance by women that they must shape up and shrink down, via diet and exercise, to fit their clothes.

Pucci is a nobleman whose family fought the Medicis 500 years ago. He is also a sportsman and an art collector, a former pilot who served in the Italian Air Force during World War II and a current member of the Italian Parliament, a scholar with degrees from the Universities of Milan and Florence and Reed College in Portland, Ore. Above all, he is a shrewd businessman. To his office in the medieval Palazzo Pucci in Florence come 200 letters a month asking him to design furniture, shoes, toothbrushes, watchbands, book jackets and packages for soap and medicine. He has assented to many of these assignments, to say nothing of yachts and stewardesses' uniforms, the sleek and action-geared ski clothes that provided his entrée into fashion in 1947, a natural fanny girdle and a sexy perfume that smells of sea and sand rather than sable and drawing rooms.

Pucci is the foremost of the 20th-century renaissance men of fashion. In the Sixties, many are trying to be the same.

American designers come in infinite varieties, addressing themselves to different audiences. There are the one of a kinds, like George Stavropoulos, a fiercely independent Greek émigré married to a lively brunette from New Jersey, who adapts the ancient chiton or tunic in Sixties terms, and Pauline Trigère, a fine French dressmaker who has become an all-American after a quarter of a century on Seventh Avenue. There is the Southern contingent like John Moore of Texas, who is infatuated with the Thirties, and Geoffrey Beene, a medical school dropout from Haynesville, La., whose penchant for stark simplicity conveys the immediate present. Among the crew of breezy youngsters is Deanna Littell, whose zaniness is curbed by unerring taste.

Two of the most provocative inventors of fashion do not create in the cement canyons of Seventh Avenue. James Galanos and Rudi Gernreich (the two most respected by European designers who would prefer to preserve their illusion that American design is watered-down French) are based in California. They live and work in Los Angeles, but explicitly disassociate themselves from the nation's second largest garment industry. Gernreich commutes between the coasts and sees most of the store buyers in his Seventh Avenue showrooms. Galanos goes to New York twice a year, in January and June, to present his collection in a single, dramatic showing at the Plaza. His airy, two-story factory, in an industrial area near Santa Monica, lacks a showroom. It does have a fitting room, though, for the use of the best customers of Amelia Gray, the Beverly Hills specialty shop owner who buys everything Galanos makes, including his austere millinery. Galanos fans fly to Los Angeles from as far away as New York and Mexico City to acquire their wardrobes from Mrs. Gray.

An haut couturier of ready-made clothes, Galanos maintains the great dressmakers' tradition of opulent fabric and painstaking workmanship, but he avoids contact with the women who buy his clothes. "I hate the idea of personalities and society ladies going to showrooms," said Galanos, whose name does not appear in gossip columns. "It gets out of hand." One price a designer pays for improving his social standing by dining and dancing with women who wear his designs is their inevitable desire to save the retail mark-up. Galanos says:

> I am in the wholesale business. I'm not interested in selling individuals. Otherwise, I'd be in custom-made. I'd like that very much in a way, because I'd know that my clothes were properly worn. Too often they are sold to stores where the salespeople, unfortunately, don't know what's right.

Galanos exudes indignation in a well-modulated voice that rises no higher than a loud whisper. His tiny face, with its sharply pointed nose and crowning mop of tight, brown curls, breaks into a bashful smile. "I'm out every night," he says, denying that he is anti-social. His German housekeeper, who used to work for Charles Boyer, is a wonderful cook, but Galanos likes to dine late and so he eats in restaurants.

"The Daisy is my hangout," he says, referring to the Beverly Hills bistro that Jack and Sally Hanson, the owners of the Jax boutiques, opened in 1964. "You eat and sit and get up and dance a little. I love to dance—everything," says Galanos, a bachelor of medium height with the frame of an undernourished fifth-grader.

"I used to be shy in a way," he says, hanging his head, "but mostly I shied away from customers."

James Galanos has always marched to the sound of his own music, and it has brought him to the summit of American fashion in the Sixties. Born in September 1924, he is a quarter of a century younger than Norman Norell, the dean of Seventh Avenue, with whom he has always been compared. Galanos finds it tiresome to be coupled, like Laurel with Hardy, with Norell, whom he says he admires for his taste.

The comparison is valid in terms of price and quality. The two designers make the most expensive ready-made clothes in America and their standards are equal to the best in the declining Paris haute couture. A coat by Galanos or Norell is like armor. It has authority on a hanger and when a woman puts it on, no matter how lacking in confidence she may have been, she picks up power.

Norell has been kinder to women over the years, what with his mouth-watering colors and his sequined sheaths that make the wearer look and feel like a worldly mermaid. Galanos makes no flattering compromises, although he is sympathetic if a buyer from a store in the Southwest says that he cannot sell a coat in heavy fleece. Norell makes the merchants dance to his tune. For years, he summoned the potentates in retailing and the press to attend his collections at 9 P.M. in black tie and evening dress.

"It's a business," says Galanos, who invites them for mid-afternoon and serves them champagne and Scotch at the end. "We're not here to entertain," he says. "If you've got the talent, you don't need the trimmings."

Norell, who started his career in 1922 as a costume designer for silent screen stars like Mae Murray and Gloria Swanson, has occasional jazz-age lapses. Galanos never looks back.

Norell panicked in the height of the youth madness. He castigated Seventh Avenue for not being original enough and creating in the shadow of Paris, and promised to deliver "a new proportion" for fall 1965. He served up vintage Chanel. *The New York Times* illustrated its report of the collection by running a sketch of three Chanels from the 1926 issue of *Vogue* alongside its sketches and photographs of Norell's hip-belted chemises, sequined cardigans and boxy suits that he punctuated, lest someone miss the point, with bushy-tailed fox scarves, gardenia boutonnieres, Reboux cloches and feathered headache bands. The models had even rouged their knees.

Norell's jazz-age fling followed on a similar wave by designers of teen-age and college fashions. There was a real question whether Norell's middle-aged Zeldas could make the transition from the Charleston to the frug.

Galanos, a man who chooses his words carefully, has had little to say about youth. "I never talked too much about youth because I always made young-looking clothes for older women. That's why I cannot show my clothes on teen-age models because the people who buy my clothes are in their thirties and up."

Galanos fits his designs, as he creates them, on Pat Jones, a doe-eyed brunette with lofty cheekbones, flaring nostrils and a body shaped like a needle.

"She has subtlety and quality," the designer has said. "She is able to put my clothes across. Even a bad dress may come through because of her. I rely heavily on her taste. She doesn't say anything. She just looks." Hearing this estimate of her ability, Miss Jones arched her neck like a swan and just looked. "Eventually a design she doesn't like is thrown out. One needs an outsider who is just a little bit aware that maybe you aren't quite as good as you think you are," he said appreciatively.

Miss Jones travels with Galanos to New York, where four other models, who have the rare distinction of being able to accommodate themselves to the Jones-structured samples, are recruited for the showing. They are Claire Eggleston, a tight-lipped brunette who models for Norell; Audrey Sedor, a Jackie Kennedy type; Pud Gadiot of the cinnamon-colored hair; and Ursula Arnold, who once explained her qualifications thus:

> I'm five foot seven and a half inches, 110 pounds. My build is identical to Pat's. I'm boneless. I'm almost built like a snake. You might say I have no shape, more or less. Absolutely no hips, no midriff, a little bit of bust though [she added regretfully]. That's my flaw.
>
> Oh, yes, I'm taupe-colored. It's marvelous. I go with everything. I have slightly golden skin, really dirty blond hair and gray eyes. I'm perfect for Mr. Galanos but not perfect for many other people.

Mr. Galanos expounded further on his criteria. "When you're making clothes that are so-called elegant and sophisticated, you need the haughty old kind of look that represents that unattainable kind of thing. I look for a model that looks as though she could be a rich woman."

He is the only one of the creators who works primarily for the affluent. Only they can afford Galanos prices, which range from about $500 to several thousands. A pair of striped, at-home pajamas, one of the hotcakes of 1966, sold for $1,055.

Among the most ardent wearers of his clothes are Mrs. David Evins, wife of the shoe magnate (she calls out the numbers in a sepulchral voice at his shows); Mrs. Charles Revson, wife of the chairman of Revlon; Mrs. Alfred Bloomingdale, wife of the president of the Diners' Club; Rosalind Russell; and Mrs. Hilaros Theodoracopulos, the former Betsy Pickering, who modeled for him before she married into a shipowning family. Galanos designed the dress that Mrs. Ronald Reagan wore to the ball to celebrate her husband's inauguration as governor of California in January 1967.

"My favorite look," Galanos confided, "is Gloria Guinness. I don't know if she's bought my clothes. But I like the dark certain thing. I like a European quality or something that European women have." Mrs. Loel Guinness, the Mexican-born wife of one of the wealthiest Britons, has most of her clothes made to order in Paris at Balenciaga, Givenchy and Castillo.

Galanos' roots are in Greece. He speaks the language fluently. His father emigrated from there and opened a restaurant in Philadelphia. Jimmy, as the fashion industry now calls him, and his three sisters helped out. At the age of 17, Galanos sold his first sketch for $2. He held a series of apprenticeships on Seventh Avenue, in Hollywood (where he was assistant to Jean Louis, then the designer for Columbia Pictures), and in Paris in the house of Robert Piguet. Unable to find a job when he returned to New York, he migrated to Los Angeles and, in 1951, founded Galanos Originals, with a bankroll of $200 and a staff of two.

It was an uphill journey until some fabric manufacturers extended him enough credit so that he could bring an important collection to New York. The orders from that showing came to nearly $400,000 and have mounted steadily into a business of more than $1 million a year. Galanos clothes are sold in 35 shops in the United States.

Galanos' designs do not make instant fashion. They do not immediately appear on secretaries' backs, because they are too difficult to copy directly. But his arcane ideas infiltrate fashion through other designers' collections. Galanos' refusal to let the chemise succumb to the opposition of American husbands encouraged others to keep it going until women could appreciate its meaning. His jeweled robes heralded the covered-up ball dress. On the heels of that, he pointed the direction of a new nakedness for evening, first with bead-encrusted, brassiere-topped dresses, then with décolletages that bared the bosom at the sides. The importance of prints for evening owes much to Galanos.

"I try to do something different," he acknowledged. "I have no patience with designers who say they change seven-eighths of an inch. Courrèges tried something but it fell flat. It was still old Balenciaga but he had something with his boot and short hem. The others chopped off the hem and went on making the same old dress."

Galanos gives his followers a hard time when it comes to color. "I'd rather be subtle although the buyers and the women don't like it.

I put a mossy green and an I-don't-know-what kind of eggplant together."

He is also impelled toward widow's weeds. Invariably, a Galanos collection contains a series of unadorned, black wools and dull silk crepe dresses that industrialists' wives might wear to their husbands' funerals under strict black mink or Russian broadtail coats. Afterwards, they can return to their symphony board meetings or the management of their inherited enterprises in Galanos' sad-sack jersey dresses or broad-shouldered, narrow-hipped suits with matching helmets that obscure the hair. Galanos' women may be rich, but they didn't get that way by being cuddly, soft or careless. Or if so, it was a long time ago. Now they are hard and run the show.

After dark, they cheer up considerably. Galanos' evening clothes, of which there may be as many as 70 in a collection of 165 designs, are devastating. Brilliantly colored and magnificently cut, they are sometimes even sexy, although in a cold, bitchy way. They have just one drawback. They require a backdrop. The average woman couldn't rustle around in a three-room apartment in a Galanos hostess dress without intimidating her guests. A Galanos requires a mansion overlooking the Pacific or a penthouse on Fifth Avenue with a museum in the foyer.

There's nothing casual about Galanos except possibly the meticulous pullovers and slacks in contrasting colors that he wears at home. He lives in a brick Regency house furnished with Louis XV and other French and contemporary furniture, a collection of crystal and piles of books. The house has a courtyard and a lily pond. Characteristically, James Galanos has no swimming pool although he does have a two-car garage for his black Rolls-Royce and his black Jaguar sedan. He drives the Rolls himself.

"In California, we drive our own Rolls. It's pretentious to have a chauffeur," explained his friend, designer Gustave Tassell, who has one too.

Although they are friends and respectful of each other's professional caliber, Galanos and Rudi Gernreich, his fellow Californian, are otherwise poles apart. "The minute a dress is too high-priced, it gets too serious," Gernreich has remarked. Most of his dresses sell well below $100. "People are finally waking up to the idea that clothes are not that important. It's bad taste to be expensively dressed." Gernreich once made that remark during a showing at Bonwit Teller, a store that consistently puts the most expensive clothes in America—Galanos, Norells, Zuckermans *et al.*—in its Fifth Avenue windows. Gernreich wasn't teasing. He is a thoughtful, sensitive man, this extremist of American fashion whose predictions usually come to pass. Like many prophets, he has been reviled as well as revered. The publicity over the one design he would like to forget, the topless bathing suit, brought him recognition and the opportunities for more constructive accomplishments.

Television interviewers and total strangers are forever accusing him of trying to make women ugly. It disturbs Gernreich to engender such animosity and misunderstanding. His attackers have never sat through a Gernreich collection like the one for fall 1966 in which he introduced the notion of being totally coordinated from the skin out. He used the timeless striptease to put his point across. The models—impudent girls with Vidal Sassoon haircuts and moth eyes—stalked into the showroom in tiger- and cheetah-printed outfits that revealed nothing but their eyes through the slits in their hoods. Then, with catlike grace, they proceeded to peel. Off with the hoods, off with the printed calf jackets and matching skirts, off with the matching Banlon jersey dresses, through which the swell of rosebud bosoms and nipples were perceived. Down to matching bras and tights.

"One more," the press photographers cried. And the middle-aged buyers in the audience indulged in the kind of fantasies for which they seldom have time in the afternoon. As for Rudi Gernreich, he stood in conspicuous silence near the door to the models' dressing room, a bantam in sausage-tight gray jersey trousers, double-breasted navy blazer, blue-and-white striped shirt, red paisley tie and black boots. A lock of brown hair fell asymmetrically across his suntanned brow. He smiled like a seven-year-old who has just merited a gold star for spelling.

"Clothes are disappearing," Rudi Gernreich said a few days later. He enunciated his words in perfect American English. Only the cadence and the round *ooh* in words like shoe gave a clue that German was the language he spoke first. Gernreich was born in Vienna into a prosperous family that knew Hedy Lamarr when her name was Hedwig Kiesler. His father was a hosiery manufacturer. The Gernreichs fled to the United States in 1938 and settled in Los Angeles.

Rudolf Gernreich Americanized the pronunciation of his name to

"Gernrick" (which many of his followers still use) because he wanted to put his past behind him. He was 16 when he arrived and in short order he became "the most American teenager that ever was. I remember the style of wearing one trouser leg rolled up to here." He pointed to the middle of his calf. "Well, I rolled mine up to here." He hacked at the middle of his thigh and laughed.

Nowadays, Iris, his Seventh Avenue showroom girl, answers the telephone, "Rudi Gernreich," pronouncing it in the German way, with the *sh* whistling through the throat. And so do many of his customers, because Americans are much better about foreign languages since the war, Rudi Gernreich observes. When he talks about women's clothes, however, he uses the international code of modern fashion thinking:

> There's an absolute fusion about what's on the outside and what the person has inside [he said]. Since this era has not changed the silhouette, what there is from here to here [he points to the neck and then to the knee] is an accessory to what happens around it. This totality, therefore, involves the attitude of the person. I can't make a statement with a dress. It's the ring, the fingernail, the eye, everything.

> The antagonism against people like me is coming from those who used to get security from clothes, from those who used to buy something that was hanging like a body on a rack, waiting for them.

Different kinds of women worship Gernreich. Rene Carpenter, the blond astronaut's wife, wears his clothes. So does Mrs. Jacob K. Javits, Betty Furness, who also likes Galanos, and innumerable young unknowns like the girl from Alabama transplanted to an editorial job in New York who said, "My whole life changed when I started wearing Rudi's clothes and got a haircut from Vidal. Why, a friend said the other day, 'You used to be such a drudge.' And I was. I didn't used to do the dances either. Rudi's clothes and Vidal's haircut changed my whole life."

Rudi Gernreich isn't a socializing designer so he can only hazard a description of his ultimate customer:

> I think she's a woman who doesn't think clothes are the most important thing. That's the difference between her and the older

generation who spent the major part of their days at the dressmaker. The younger ones are much too busy even if what they're busy with is not important. They are women who come to terms with fashion. How they look is important, but only as part of an active life. Clothes are just clothes, after all.

Rudi Gernreich studied art at Los Angeles City College, spent 10 years as a modern dancer with the Lester Horton Company, started designing swimsuits and has finally got around to everything else— dresses, coats, suits, stockings, underwear, children's clothes and costumes for a musical comedy. Fame has enabled Rudi Gernreich to try them all.

"If a girl is not pretty, it doesn't matter. With my clothes, her personality sticks out. My really simplest clothes are the best. Too much idea gets into conflict with the personality. The women who resent me, they hate what I challenge them to be," said Rudi Gernreich, lighting up a cigarillo and looking like a timid Napoleon.

Gernreich posed the first challenge in the early Fifties when he came forth with the knitted tank suit. In the era when women went down to the water bolstered by Lastex and inner construction, this flimsy garment that resembled a gym uniform required a small, unfleshy body that few women then possessed. Gernreich commented:

> When I showed the first suits to a small group in California, silence greeted them. It was unbelievable. The audience didn't know how to react. Good or bad. They were embarrassed. They were used to corseted bodies and with those cones nobody knew what kind of breasts a woman had. Oh, sure, the models adored my suits.

> I knew there was a need because well-dressed women had said to me, "God, I can't find a swimsuit that doesn't have those things in it." That's when it's good. When you formalize a need and make a statement. It becomes authoritative design. I don't initiate. My design is just an interpretation of what people want.

> The way young women are throwing things together today. A boy's sweater and a skirt from the little girls' department. There's a need and they find it. Then when I take it and design past it, it becomes high fashion. But it must come from the girls. Now it's happening with men. Boys are seeking to identify with what they want to wear.

It took half a dozen years at least before the public caught up to the need that Gernreich formalized with his tank suit. In the Sixties, diet and exercise to achieve a lithe, fit body at any age became a mass preoccupation.

From knitted swimwear, he branched out into knitted clothes and then into a variety of fashions that the industry tidily classified as sportswear even though some of them were chiffon dresses that women wore to dinner parties. By the mid-Sixties, such categories for clothes had become meaningless because manufacturers were crossing into one another's territory, and most clothing, except for gussied-up evening dresses, had become casual anyway.

Gernreich was one of the first designers to hike hemlines, but he was also one of the first to decorate legs with patterned hosiery. A pioneer in concealing everything about a woman's body in hoods, boots and murky, printed, chemisey evening dresses, he was the first to undrape.

The topless bathing suit was the bombshell of 1964. Rudi Gernreich winces when it is mentioned. Early in June of that year, he showed buyers and the press a pair of knitted trunks that were held up by a pair of stringy straps. The suit was shown in the hand. *Look* had published a photograph of it on a model taken from the back. When the television cameramen and the newspaper reporters crowded into his showroom for a closer inspection, they were offered photographs of Peggy Moffitt, his favorite mannequin, who had posed in the suit for her husband, a photographer named William Claxton. Miss Moffitt epitomizes the Gernreich girl. A brunet space-age flapper, she has a piquant face, a small, high-rising bosom and a gift for mimicry. The press had to use her husband's pictures, if they dared. After much ado about nothing, *The New York Times'* editors dropped the photographs into a wastebasket. *Women's Wear Daily* ran a front view reducing it to the smallest possible size. Within a week, a television network reproduced the *Women's Wear* photograph. The walls of prudery were coming down.

By mid-July, policemen in Chicago and Los Angeles were dutifully arresting females who were charging bare-breasted onto the beaches. And the French Minister of the Interior, Roger Frey, responded by officially banning the monokini. He called it a "public outrage." In Moscow, *Izvestia* did what was expected of it. "The

American way of life is on the side of everything that gives the possibility of trampling on morals and interests of society for the sake of ego . . . so the decay of the moneybag society continues," it said in its report on Gernreich's design. Next came the topless waitresses in California and New York, who managed to keep in print by being hauled regularly into court.

Even more to Gernreich's dismay were the orders he received for the suit. He had shown it only as a prophecy, and also because he was afraid that Emilio Pucci would do it first. "Fashion was at an awful standstill," he conceded much later. "It was timely to get it out of the rut."

As a Southern Californian (he has a bachelor abode in the Hollywood hills), Gernreich knew that sunbathers were dropping the upper portions of their suits when they were alone on their patios and yachts. He also sensed that a change in sexual attitudes was occurring. But he didn't think nudism was imminent. He wasn't even sure that the topless bathing suit should be produced at all.

The first order was placed by Hess Brothers, the promotion-minded store in Allentown, Pa. Then came orders from Dayton's in Minneapolis, Magnin's in San Francisco, the May Company in Denver, Neiman-Marcus in Dallas. In New York, Altman's and Lord & Taylor were among the intrepid. But said the buyer for one large store, "We will not promote it or display it. If a customer asks for it, we will take her into a fitting room and show it to her. Please don't quote me." Later, the buyer had a change of heart and sold the 21 suits he owned to Splendiferous, which had no trouble disposing of them.

The furor about the topless bathing suit—"I hate to talk about it," Gernreich says—was responsible for his next significant contribution. Irwin Roseman, executive vice president of Exquisite Form, telephoned Gernreich in Norway, where he happened to be a couple of months later, and asked him if he had any thoughts about brassieres. Gernreich did. The man who had taken the armor out of the swim suit thought it was time to do the same for the brassiere. His No-Bra Bra, an arrangement of pale jersey without a single steel bone or piece of elastic, made its debut that fall. At the same time, Warner's, another corset manufacturer, emerged with the Body Stocking, a flesh-colored, stretch nylon maillot that molded the body and obviated the brassiere for the girl who didn't need one anyway. The Body Stocking gave the green light to designers to step up production of transparent dresses. The reactions to the No-Bra Bra surprised Gernreich further:

> The buyers heard about it and, regardless of their age or shape, they all asked to see it when they came to my California show-room. I had a few pieces there. One day, a middle-aged lady, a very nice lady, a buyer, asked to see it. She went into the dressing room and soon she called out for me to come and look at her. I'm sure this woman had never exposed her breasts before. She seemed to want to show me. The jersey is completely transparent, you know, although the bra does give good support.
>
> This desire to reveal, but in a completely proper way, was an interesting reaction. At the same time, it's very healthy. Why should you be ashamed to show your breast? There's nothing to be ashamed about. Exhibitionism, though, is wrong.

Gernreich said he had wanted no part of such "forced" nudity as the New York Shakespeare Festival Gala in which leading designers were asked to create dresses in the "new, nude look" for socialites to parade about in.

> Of course, it's always the context in which something is done. I felt all of a sudden that there was a whole new attitude. Certain things were not offensive any longer. Certain things are possible that were not possible two years ago. There is a changing attitude toward prudery, toward sex. Clothes are no longer just a stupid dress. They are symbolic of what is going on.
>
> The idea of the bikini, very brief, revealing instead of hiding the body, sort of happens because people want it, need it and are feeling it.

One afternoon in 1960, he recalled, friends came over to his swimming pool:

> In California, it's the way people live, everyone has a swimming pool [he said, half apologizing]. I had these French friends, a couple, visiting me. The wife wore the tiniest bikini. She was the oldest woman there, in the briefest bikini. The younger, American women were in high-necked maillots. I could see what was happening.
>
> The Frenchwoman had the body of a 50-year-old lady, but a good one. She was totally free. She wanted as much sun and

comfort as she could get. The Americans were shocked a little. But they also felt all wrong covered up.

It's not that standards are different. It's that the more we are used to seeing the natural body, the more that differences of bodies become acceptable. Certain faults can make them more attractive.

And if not? Gernreich was equally irritated by the commotion over skirt lengths and knees:

This concern with length of skirts is nonsense. It's the whole thing that's important. Everybody is talking about three inches, five inches above the knee and that knees are ugly. O.K. So knees are ugly. But skirts are short.

Shortly after this discourse, Gernreich went on to make stick-on, vinyl patches with which the wearer of a bikini could decorate her body. The following season, he applied the idea of adhesive patches to hosiery. Fashion design, he insists, is not premeditated:

If you intellectualize too much, it doesn't come off. My most successful designs have been unconscious evolvements. Those are then timely and correct. Somehow one was in tune. That's part of talent. I don't want to be pretentious. I'm not saying I'm a great designer. It's just part of your talent, if you are on the higher level, and I think I am there.

The best ideas come when I'm uncluttered and not bugged by a thousand details, and have put myself in a state of half sleep. Basically, the idea has to be thought out, but the sort of magic part is unpremeditated. The whole underwear-innerwear thing was not planned to make a commercial success. But it happened to be right for our time. The way of presenting it, the striptease, is thought out.

In the fall of 1964, Gernreich and Jacques Tiffeau raised daytime hemlines to three inches above the knee. Despite the advancing miniskirt in London, the baring of the knee and some of the thigh did not catch on in America until the summer of 1966. By then, Jacques Tiffeau was thinking of descent. In his fall collection, shown on Seventh Avenue at the end of May, he introduced a brown suit, the hemline of which fell a few inches below the knee where it was met by matching gaiters. Only Bergdorf Goodman and Neiman-Marcus ordered it as he designed it. The other stores asked for the hemline to be shortened just as, two years before, they had asked him to lengthen his short skirts. "But American women have beautiful legs and beautiful knees," he protested then.

In July 1966, two months after Tiffeau lowered the skirt, Marc Bohan of Christian Dior and Yves Saint Laurent essayed coats with mid-calf lengths.

Jacques Tiffeau is used to being ahead of the Paris haute couture. In 1960, he declined an offer to replace Yves Saint Laurent at the house of Christian Dior. Tiffeau had been a friend of Dior's whom he met when the author of the New Look visited New York. Marc Bohan finally accepted the job.

"Paris is dead. They cleaned it up, but it's dead," says Tiffeau, the cigarette dangling from the edge of his lower lip, in French, old-wave movie style. He could take the part of the cynical detective. A medium-sized, swarthy man with thinning brown hair, hazel eyes and a tiny mole on each cheek, he disdains the role of the Seventh Avenue gentleman. He prefers the image of the chic peasant. Tiffeau is, in fact, a farmer's son. His father is the mayor of Chevenelles, a village near the Loire Valley. He visits the farm twice a year, when he escapes to France after presenting his collections, checks with pride and intense interest to see how the lambs and calves are doing. He also has a house at Mougins, where Picasso lives in the south of France, and an apartment on the Rue du Bac on the Left Bank in Paris.

Jacques Tiffeau was a provincial tailor before he emigrated to the United States in 1951 at the age of 23, not knowing more than a phrase or two in English. He now speaks fluent American slang, embroidered with profanity, in a fine French accent. When he appears in his showroom, after his collections, to accept the kisses and congratulations of buyers and editors, he wears the white jacket of a laboratory technician.

Tailoring was the trade he had learned in school. "I was not very good in school. I was stupid," says Tiffeau. "It was during the war, World War II, that war, and they asked me what I wanted to study and I said tailoring."

Upon his arrival in New York, Tiffeau was hired by Monte Sano &

Pruzan, one of the higher-priced coat and suit manufacturers. "I made some toiles and they were lousy," he recalls. Instead of being fired as he expected, he was sent to the Art Students League to learn sketching. In 1958, Max Pruzan, one of the partners in the firm, offered as a sideline to put him in business with his daughter, Beverly Busch.

In Tiffeau & Busch, the young Frenchman was able to meld his superb cut and tailoring to vigorous, young ideas. Retail prices for these clothes start at about $150, just half of what they were in the more conservative collection he did for Monte Sano & Pruzan.

"The higher price bracket is passé," he declared after he submitted his resignation to the older firm in the summer of 1966. Max Pruzan had just retired. "At Monte Sano, they are always talking about their customers as 'our lady.' Lady is dead, passé. Give me a girl," grunted bachelor Tiffeau.

Girl quality is what he looks for in a model. "I am bored with nothing here and here," he said, gesturing toward the chest and the hips. He is in favor of bosoms, but he doesn't think girls should wear undergarments. He tells his models to forget about being ladies and to go out into the showroom and project what they feel. They do, to the strains of "Engine Number Nine," "Heartache," "Swing Low Sweet Chariot" and various rock 'n' roll or player piano selections that he has chosen to be piped from a record player into his shoe box of a showroom. The buyers and press are crammed there, cheek by jowl, attentively watching a show that is almost as good as the latest British or French film playing in the East Side art theaters uptown. It is an educational experience, too, one of the few presentations on Seventh Avenue that is relevant to the contemporary spirit blowing through London and the ready-to-wear fashion market of Paris.

In case any of the audience are dense, they are aided by a mimeographed sheet placed on their folding chairs. NEW YORK—MY CITY, one such résumé began:

> The most stimulating place I know in the world today is New York. Fifteen years ago I discovered the "New World."
>
> I never realized it would give me so much. Thank you one and all.
>
> I have not designed a collection for tea at the Palm Court, the Plaza Hotel.

Nor Suits for the "Orient Express,"
Nor the Furs for the Mississippi River,
I have not designed Coats for the nights at Monte Carlo,
Nor Evening Gowns for the Debutant [sic] Ball,
Nor Hats for the "April in Paris" Ball,
Nor Shoes for the Strip-teasers at Minskys,
Nor Hairdos for Shirley Temple,

But clothes that are Modern, Easy and Comfortable for the Women of 1966.

And then the ideas came spilling forth on Ellen Harth, the carbon-haired German model with the Sassoon cut whom Rudi Gernreich uses for his showings, on a blond Julie Christie girl, on a creature with bobbing, chestnut hair who might be swinging down the Rue de Sèvres. They are pulsing with life and health and they love Tiffeau's brisk coats, the neat pants suits he had been suggesting for two years before they hit the sidewalks of New York, the spare dresses cut out to show glowing shoulders and firm, round, girlish arms, or sashed above the waist and unseamed below the armhole so that their breasts spill out at the sides. They roll their eyes and undulate their hips and muffle themselves to the eyeballs in red fox stoles. They slink about in shock-colored, chiffon smockdresses.

In the fall of 1965, Tiffeau sent his models out with paneless spectacles pushed down on their insolent little noses while Al Jolson whined "Ain't I the Fool" from the record player. Three years before, he had equipped them with sunglasses and goggles, stimulating the trend to nearsightedness as a fashion asset. Glasses, he said, "make a girl look mysterious and dangerous. Maybe hearing aids will be fashionable next."

Tiffeau puts in all the punctuation marks when he presents a collection. It is, as they say in the fashion business, a look and the look is of now. Jacques Tiffeau doesn't acquire it by asking society women what they need. "I don't socialize, I have my life, it's my own," he said. It consists of an apartment on the Upper East Side, furnished in clean, modern style and housing a growing collection of contemporary art. A passionate cook, he shops for his cheeses on Lexington Avenue and 85th Street, for fruits and vegetables in the open-air markets on Ninth Avenue and the upper 30's. But he refuses to cook for those American friends who take too many Martinis before dinner. He takes them to restaurants. Some weekends, he unplugs the telephone, walks in Central Park and goes to bed early.

"I don't believe in socializing or dressing up the way Bill Blass does," Tiffeau said. For lunch at La Grenouille, where he holds court on a red velvet plush banquette up front, he might wear brown suede boots, beige trousers, a deep blue shirt, green checked tie and a gray flannel jacket. He opens the jacket to show the label, BAKER CLOTHES. "I only believe in *prêt-à-porter*," he said with a roguish grin.

He would never design men's clothes, he insisted. Cardin's men's clothes: "They are for faggot. Women dress to attract. Men should be quiet and have something else, like personality. They should dress in gray and navy blue. They don't need jazzy clothes."

Ideas either come to him or they don't. When they don't, he goes off for a swim at the New York Athletic Club.

"Fashion," said Jacques Tiffeau, "is a love affair."

Betsey Johnson was caught up in fashion by the time she was 21. The youngest and rashest of America's creative designers, she started as a moonlighting dressmaker for the editors of *Mademoiselle*. She had been a guest editor of the magazine's college issue in 1964. After graduation from Syracuse University, she was offered one of those glorified slave-girl jobs that were supposed to entice bright youngsters into the so-called glamour of magazine publishing.

While doing odd chores, Betsey was doodling clever little sketches on pads and accepting assignments for home sewing from the fashion editors. Two of them, Nonnie Eilers Moore and Sandra Horvitz, showed her sketches to Paul Young, the Englishman who had forsaken architecture for mass-produced American fashion. Mr. Young is a vice president of the Puritan Fashion Corporation, charged with developing the youngest, most avant-garde merchandise for its budding network of licensed Paraphernalia boutiques throughout the country. The pilot Paraphernalia boutique on Madison Avenue, a few doors from the Vidal Sassoon hair salon, looks more like an art gallery than a dress shop.

Paul Young signed Betsey Johnson to a contract and turned her loose in a workroom on West 36th Street. Within a year, she was the hottest property off Seventh Avenue and a one-woman rival to the Kings Road and Carnaby Street. Julie Christie and all the visiting

English Mod firemen signed up for her fan club along with those American sprites who are on Betsey's kinetic wave length.

Betsey Johnson looks like anything but a fashion person. She is short and chubby with dark blond hair and the well-scrubbed demeanor of a 4-H girl who decided to become a beatnik. Nothing is too mad or Mod for her to design or wear. Sometimes she tacks thrift shop items, like a pair of Ruby Keeler dancing shoes, onto her own designs. The most famous of these is the Basic Betsey, a skimpy garment, with long, narrow sleeves, that snuggles over the chest, pays no attention to the waist, skims over the hips down to the middle of the thigh where it ends in a flip.

She put plastic grommets on the hem of a bare-backed halter and called it the noise dress, a necessary fashion for total environments like the Cheetah nightclubs or Murray the K's. Then she produced the do-it-yourself dress, a shell of clear plastic that cost about $30 and came with a $5 kit of adhesive squiggles, numbers and letters with which the purchaser could decorate according to whim. Canned panties and silver motorcycle suits are other inventions.

She churned out chalk-striped gangster pants suits for girls and satin and velvet evening clothes for men. Antoine, the French protest singer, modeled the latter when they were introduced. "This is only the beginning," said Betsey as the entertainer with the shoulder-length, curly hair appeared in a black velvet shirt studded with nail-heads on the collar and cuffs, flaring pants of navy velvet, a silver belt and a flowered vest.

Clearly, Betsey is the most prolific designer of radical pop fashion, as well as the spokesman for a generation that demands something totally different from what their mothers asked of clothes. They want it cheap (Betsey's designs sell for $50 and under) and they don't care if it falls apart tomorrow (Paraphernalia's merchandise carries no warranty). And if they scare the settled citizenry half to death, *tant pis.*

In an interview in the August 1966 issue of *Mademoiselle,* Betsey Johnson said it very plainly:

> I like people to make the shape of the garment, so I don't believe in darts and frills and all that junk. No two people look alike in the same dress, anyway. I really design for myself since I don't like what is around. I believe in the shape of the dress, the importance of the cut, having clothes that move when people do.

This is the reason that the only kind of fabric I use is jersey. . . . My clothes are really unconstructed: they don't confine or shape you. People just want movable clothes.

Everyone wants to be looked at, to be creative about wearing clothes, and you have to exaggerate what you're doing if you're going to have any effect at all. It's a phase that fashion must go through; the same thing is happening in music, literature, art. It's a good time for young people with open minds. My clothes are for young people who are saying, "Look at me—I'm alive!" . . . Dressing is becoming a way of self-expression; it's artistic and should be as uninhibited as possible.

Talented as she is, Betsey Johnson might not have become the Manhattan fashion wunderkind if another madcap had not paved the way for youth a decade before. When Queen Elizabeth conferred the Order of the British Empire upon Mary Quant in 1966, the designer said that the award belonged as much to the whole group of designers who had made London a capital of modestly priced, ready-made, exuberant fashion. She meant designers like Roger Nelson, tailor of the swinging classics; Sally Tuffin and Marion Foale, diviners of meltingly feminine clothes for girls who go to parties on the backs of motorcycles; Jean Muir, the timid soul with the marionette's face who authored the smocked dress, among other little girl clothes; James Wedge, the milliner with the space-agey boutiques called Countdown and Top Gear; and Gerald McCann, the irrepressible jokester.

But it was Mary Quant who threw the first stone through the stained glass windows of British fashion, and the crash eventually resounded throughout the world. In 1955, Mary Quant, Alexander Plunket Greene and their friend, Archie McNair, an ex-lawyer and owner of a photography studio, started Bazaar, a boutique on the Kings Road in Chelsea, the Bohemian quarter of London. Mary Quant is the brown-eyed, russet-haired daughter of Welsh schoolteachers. Alexander Plunket Greene is one of those pale, blue-eyed giants of the British aristocracy, last of a long line of decadents and eccentrics. On his maternal side, he is a distant cousin of Bertrand Russell, the philosopher, and the Duke of Bedford, who turned his Woburn Abbey into a sightseers' haunt.

Mary and Alexander were incipient rebels who met and joined forces as students at Goldsmith's College in Southeast London.

After leaving art school, they gravitated to Chelsea where an unplanned rally of creative talent, mostly artists, photographers, writers and actors, was to challenge the Establishment.

At Bazaar, the new fashion coalesced. It wasn't only the clothes that Mary Quant slipped into designing because manufacturers didn't make what she liked, but the whole manner of displaying and selling them. The teenagers of Britain, like their generation in other industrialized countries, were exerting a new influence through their buying power. They didn't want to be looked down upon, preached to or ignored by snobbish salesclerks. Bazaar was like a youth club where the customer could find friendly advice, a congenial atmosphere as well as realistic clothes at cheap prices. Sometimes even alcoholic refreshment was included.

"The young are terrified of salespeople," Alexander Plunket Greene has said. "Our selling people must never sell. They must be in sympathy with the young and show them things always aiming toward self-service but never to pressure them. Fashion is part entertainment and should be fun."

When Mary Quant took her clothes to exhibit abroad, she underscored the new attitude by showing them on beautiful girls who pranced, danced and clowned on the runway to the speedy beat of jazz. Initially, Mary Quant was responding to the Mods, who sought positive expression and gratification in dressing up. Because they were "modern youth," they had to break with the past. Mary Quant was their Chanel. And like the French peasant girl who brought fashion into step with the first half of the 20th century, Mary Quant and her colleagues forced the older generation to catch up, too.

> My mother is always taking me to task about clothes [she said once]. She is so worried when she goes away on holiday, so worried about what to take. She and her friends go shopping five times without buying anything. The young girls are not obsessed that way. They enjoy the things they acquire. They make them feel happy. They're not dabbing their noses and asking how do I look. The older generation was twitching all the time.

Nevertheless, she said during a visit to New York in the spring of 1966 when two continents were in a dither over the mini-skirt and the pants suit, "I didn't ever think I was designing for a particular age. I just didn't agree with clothes. But if one is 40, 60, 70, 80, I don't see why the clothes of the past are any better," she added in her soft, classless voice.

"It's true, many of the items shouldn't be worn by people over 28," boomed Mr. Greene in his upper-class diction. Mary and Alexander are a husband and wife team who not only live and work together but talk together. To converse with them is like playing a piano, with her responses coming from the treble, his from the bass.

"But many teen-age girls have great fat arms and shouldn't wear them either," said she.

"It's the shape and attitude of a woman that count," said he.

"But legs stay throughout a woman's life," said she. Mary has excellent gams.

Skirts were shorter in London than in Paris, he noted.

"The French have good bosoms and we have good legs," she observed. That's a moot point.

"We started shortening skirts in 1955 and finally Courrèges made it respectable," said Alexander. "But fashion always looks best on women with the best-shaped bodies."

"And they're not necessarily 17," said Mary.

"It's very much a young time now but people can go on being youthful indefinitely," said Alexander, who was born in 1932.

"I always found crinkles attractive. What's unattractive about age is stolidness, complaining, giving upness," said Mary, who was born in 1933.

"It used to be that a girl was attractive until she caught a husband. Then she let go," said Alexander. "In England now, girls choose husbands because they like them. And they don't give up so soon."

Mary Quant gave her definition of a fashionable woman. "She is sexy, witty and dry-cleaned."

As a fashion designer, she added, "I am trying to find a modern way of being feminine."

"Before the war," said Alexander, "there was this great, gracious living bit. I used to loathe things like *Vogue* with their titled boredom in a 40-room house."

Mary put in, "It must have pleased six people and made the others feel low."

"Fashion leaders were duchesses. Fashion was not democratic," her husband went on. "Now it has become realistic and available.

None of the really rich girls, the millionairesses in their own right, and you'd be surprised how many millionairesses our poor little country has, would be caught dead in a mink coat. They'd rather buy $20 dresses. It's smart to be holding a job at a really good salary."

"I feel most pleased when I design something I can wear to work because that's where one is most of the time," Mary said.

"The young here think a display of wealth has an aging effect," said Alexander, an elder statesman of the Mod movement who drives an E-type Jaguar not because it costs a bit but because it is very fast. "We don't own valuable pictures," he said. Their eclectic home does boast an all-plastic dining room, though. "We spend money more on traveling, spending weekends in the obscure places of the world."

His wife agrees with his sentiments, which are not shared by those Americans who winter in Palm Beach and attend the April in Paris Ball in New York in October. "Too much jewelry," Mary Quant said, "makes you look old, as if you were rejected by lots of rich, old men who paid you off."

She wears her wide, gold wedding band on the middle finger of her left hand because it is too big for the third. She discovered that when Mr. Greene produced the ring at their wedding ceremony at the Chelsea Registry Office, years and years after they had been joined as students, business partners and lovers. Mary Quant made a point of disclosing that fact in her autobiography, *Quant by Quant,* a book that lacked dates and chapters but contained other such peripheral intelligence about Mod mores.

Mary Quant will go down in history as the mother of the miniskirt. "In the beginning I had to be arrogant, to get something across. I felt desperate. I couldn't convince people skirts ought to be short," she said. Whether she was really the first with raincoats that looked as though they were made of oilcloth, high boots, shoulder bags, the crocheted look, the little-girl look and the poor-boy sweater (Mary said she bought a 7-year-old boy's sweater at Harrod's and got the idea from that) or whether they originated across the Channel is debatable. In an age of jet-sped internationalism, it's not too important.

Her feeling about color changed after she visited the United States in 1959. "I liked things beige and brown and faded but when I saw your bright colors I liked them and now the English are coming around," she said, admitting also her debt to America for mix-and-match coordinates.

In April 1961, *Seventeen* introduced Mary Quant to America. Rosemary McMurtry, the magazine's fashion director, persuaded Juniorite to manufacture a group of her designs, 35,000 pieces of which were subsequently sold. That fashion promotion started the kooky look for teenagers.

In 1962, Paul Young, then with J. C. Penney, prescribed Mary Quant designs as a potion to rejuvenate the chain's image. She still does two collections a year for Penney's. When Mr. Young went over to the Puritan Fashion Corporation as a youth medicine man, he arranged for Mary Quant to design four collections a year for them. Contracts to design stockings for Bonnie Doon and patterns for Butterick followed.

The Mary Quant Company in London now grosses $12 million a year as a design source for 16 licensed manufacturers all over the world. It employs 35 people to turn out some 28 collections a year. The three Bazaar boutiques in London sell clothes by rival English designers and Rudi Gernreich as well. "We'll always keep them because they are successful and profitable and because they keep us in touch with real people," Alexander said. "When you're working for the mass market, you can't be arrogant and apart."

The company does not manufacture although it does own half of the Ginger Group, a marketing company for Mary Quant designs in the United Kingdom and Europe. "We never will do men's or children's clothes or airplane interiors, only what women jolly themselves up with because that's where Mary's talent lies," Alexander has promised. "It would be arrogant for Mary to tell men how to dress. Her success has come from the fact she's a woman and has the experience of wearing clothes. I don't see how men, no matter how creative, can do this because they always have this minus. Unless they are very queer indeed, it's unlikely that they wear dresses."

Mary Quant also designed a line of cosmetics packaged in modern, stainless steel containers that concisely present the contents of a model's tote bag. The nail polish comes in shades like white, camel's hair, and gray that relate to clothes rather than to matching lipsticks. "Your hands are down more than up so why match your lipstick?" Mary asked, raising her childish hands with squared fingernails to her iridescent pink lips. The freckles across the bridge of her nose came from the brown eyeshadow box.

Her next project is perfume. "It must smell absolutely new. All the great French perfumes are relating to the past. The most famous came out 15 or 20 years ago and were related to women when they were 25."

"We feel the basis of scent is nostalgia," Alexander said. "You must remember something."

"I remember when I was 14 or 15 and thought I was in love," asserted his wife, wrinkling her nose. "The perfume will probably smell of surf or haystacks. Seaweed is terribly erotic to me. The smell of wooden bath houses at the beach, m-m-m."

Now that they are rich and nearly middle-aged, Mary Quant and Alexander Plunket Greene are concentrating on quality. They admit that their clothes were shoddily made in the past.

"We don't kid ourselves anymore," said Mary. "In mass production, a designer is as good as what comes off the conveyor belt. If it's turned out in millions, it's got to be good design. I want to make clothes like motor cars. I'm lazy. I don't like working. I don't like overconstructed overseamed clothes. I like clothes that don't look as if human hands ever touched them. I want clothes that are made by beautiful machines."

In the beginning, they called Emmanuelle Khanh the Mary Quant of France. There are similarities. Emmanuelle is a free-lance designer with prolific ideas, another of Chanel's altar-girls who charges herself with carrying Coco's work into the 21st century. Like Mary Quant, she is the most publicized member of a rebellious fashion movement. She is also a married woman whose creativity has been brilliantly merchandised by her husband.

Born in 1937, married at 18 to a Vietnamese engineering student two years her senior, Emmanuelle Khanh is a shy creature with frail, birdlike bones. Her brown eyes were luminous behind giant, round spectacles with interchangeable lenses, clear for ordinary use, dark for the sun, yellow for the snow. They became her trademark and the impetus for a fad. Later, she changed to bullet-proof hunting glasses with transparent, plastic sides.

Her walnut-colored hair is long at the sides, short enough in back to bare the neck. Vidal Sassoon cut it in 1963. Now she has it

James Galanos and Pat Jones. February, 1967. *The New York Times* (by Larry Morris)

Rudi Gernreich. 1965.
The New York Times
(by Edward Hausner)

The topless bathing suit by **Rudi Gern-reich**. 1964. Photograph by William Claxton

Mary Quant and
Alexander Plunket
Greene. 1966.
*The New York
Times* (by
Arthur Brower)

Betsey Johnson
(in striped suit)
with Antoine at
Paraphernalia.
1966. *The New
York Times* (by
Edward Hausner)

Above: Emmanuelle Khanh. Courtesy of *Mademoiselle:* Copyright ©1964 by The Condé Nast Publications Inc. *Below:* Christiane Bailly. By Édouard Boubat

Paco Rabanne adjusting one of his plastic disk dresses with pliers. 1966. *The New York Times* (by Neal Boenzi)

Emilio Pucci's niece, Idanna, wearing a Pucci in the Pucci boutique at Saks Fifth Avenue. 1967. *The New York Times* (by Meyer Liebowitz)

The poor boy sweater from Paris. Courtesy of *Mademoiselle:* Copyright © 1964 by The Condé Nast Publications Inc.

Elie and Jacqueline Jacobson of Dorothée Bis. 1966. *The New York Times* (by Larry Morris)

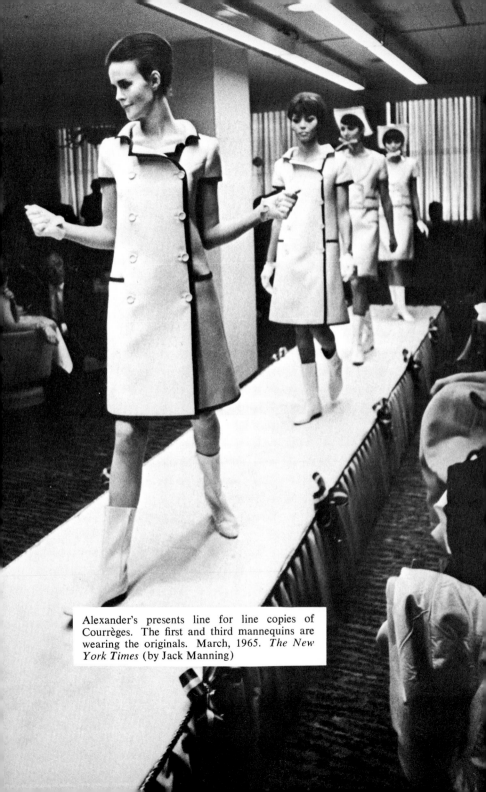

Alexander's presents line for line copies of Courrèges. The first and third mannequins are wearing the originals. March, 1965. *The New York Times* (by Jack Manning)

André Courrèges. February, 1967. Photograph by Martine Franck

Pierre Cardin and Hiroko. 1963. City News Bureau of Washington, D.C.

Yves Saint Laurent and Yvonne de Peyerimhoff in New York. 1965. *The New York Times* (by Jack Manning)

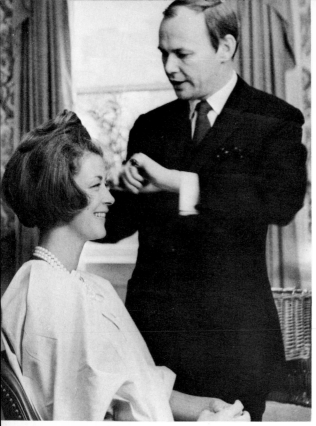

Left: Kenneth and Mrs. Thomas Bancroft, Jr. 1963. The New York Times Studio (by Bill Aller)
Below: Vidal Sassoon.

Alexandre. 1961. Pierre Boulat, *Life* Magazine © Time Inc.

Mr. and Mrs.
John Weitz at
the New York
Shakespeare
Festival benefit,
June, 1966. She is
costumed as
Hamlet. *The
New York Times*
(by Barton
Silverman)

modified by Elrhodes, the Paris brothers who style hair in the Sassoon vein.

"I like long hair for girls. It's more sexy," says Nguyen Khanh, her moustached husband. Beyond a shadow of a doubt, he is the head of the house of Khanh. They live with his mother and his aunt, his sister and her husband, who has a doctorate in chemistry, in a house on the Left Bank in Paris between Montparnasse and St.-Germain-des-Prés.

Emmanuelle Khanh was a model for Balenciaga and then for Givenchy. She made her own clothes. They caught the attention of the editors of *Elle,* the magazine that is the fairy godmother of French ready-made fashion, who asked to photograph them and have them manufactured. Her first collection was assembled in 1961. The next year, the fabric manufacturer Lalonde sponsored a collection under the label "Emmachristie" of the designs of Emmanuelle Khanh and Christiane Bailly, another alumna of the model's *cabine* at Balenciaga.

It was still the era of hard chic as promulgated by Balenciaga, the sovereign of Paris, and Givenchy, his crown prince. The Emmachristie collection was the blueprint for the yé-yé revolution.

The influence of English sporting clothes (the riding habit, the raincoat, the shooting costume) was unmistakable as well as that of the military uniform stripped of addenda and decorations. Gone was the stiffness and the false pride, the sculptured look of a work of art.

These designers intended their clothes not for the grand salon but for the street. By this they meant that they would be worn by active young women whose plane of existence was the office and the walk-up apartment, the Métro and the bistro.

During the next few years, a loosely affiliated team of such designers would challenge the Paris haute couture already grown arid but still perpetuated as a myth. The rebels, called yé-yé designers after the French pronunciation of the Beatles' sound, worked for the *prêt-à-porter* (ready-to-wear) manufacturers who constituted a scattered, inefficient industry totally lacking in authority and prestige. Soon the couturiers were appropriating their ideas and following their lead.

Emmanuelle Khanh's clothes had a singular charm based on a limp but decisive cut, the high armholes of the English tailor, low-slung skirts and long collars that drooped like hounds' ears.

"I like suits you can wear like an old raincoat," she said. "The couture is concave in the front with a loose back. I see it the other way around. My clothes hang forward."

"It was very good for her to be a model," her husband said. "It made her lose her complex. I can do better, she said. People used to put high fashion on a pedestal. One must remember that it is only the creation of a human. It's just a question of talent. The haute couture is like going to church."

"The older houses create an idea of beauty and it is an artificial one," said Emmanuelle Khanh. "It's for very rich people and you can't move in it. Chanel is great. She remembers that clothes are worn by women. I want to create new classics for a new era."

The yé-yés sold their designs to manufacturers who either paid them outright or granted them royalties on sales. This free-lance method, in contrast to the traditional custom of working for one house, enabled them to range far and wide.

The most diversified talent belongs to Emmanuelle Khanh, who designs coats, suits and dresses, ski clothes and furs, shoes, pocketbooks and luggage, men's and women's knitted underwear, bathing suits and gloves. Besides the droopy dog collar, her most copied ideas are the patchworks of color and pattern for luggage as well as clothes, the handbag made of strips of leather around a mesh frame, perforated gloves and the vivid, crinkled cotton button-down shirt that was a fresh twist on a staid American style.

Americans fell in love with Emmanuelle Khanh largely through the efforts of Shanna Simon and Paul Young. Early in 1964, Miss Simon put her designs into the Macy's Little Shop, an oasis of high fashion for which she was then the buyer. Mr. Young signed her up with J. C. Penney and, later, for the Paraphernalia boutiques.

After completing an assignment on the Manicouagan Dam in Canada, Nguyen Khanh gave up engineering in 1964 to manage his wife's business affairs. He designed some furniture and in the summer of 1966 presented his own collection of dresses under the name of Quasar, a celestial body. The key feature of the dresses were their metal breastplates. Most observers regarded the collection as an exercise in egocentricity.

By then, it was obvious that the think-as-one Khanhs had become fascinated with industrial environment and pop culture. On a visit to New York, they begged to see the Broadway musical *Superman*.

They bought a size four Batman sweatshirt for their son, Othello.

"Batman and Superman are symptomatic of our civilization," said Nguyen Khanh. "It is popular among French intellectuals to read comics."

The main motif in Emmanuelle Khanh's collection that season was a metal collar from which brightly colored shifts could be interchangeably suspended.

> We are impressed by the Indianapolis speed races [her husband said]. By the cars which are like tubes suspended toward four wheels. And your suspension bridges. Your Buick Riviera is one of the most beautiful designs. In Paris, we can appreciate it. Here, it's lost in the crowd. Everything is spoiled; it disappears. You don't even notice it; that's the problem. Here, everything looks cheap. It's terrible. On Seventh Avenue, all those Lincoln Continentals. [He shuddered.] In Paris, everything looks expensive.

> What's the difference today between designing a dress, a bridge, a dam or a luxury car that is functional and beautiful at the same time? Whatever it is you are making, the process of creation is the same. You must analyze the need, define it, encompass it and then satisfy it.

Having made the world sit up and take notice of them, the rebels developed a certain ambivalence. Some of them like Emmanuelle and Nguyen Khanh began to fantasize about the modern woman of 2000 A.D. They could hardly wait for the year to arrive. Although Emmanuelle was still concerned with the wearability of a design, and the ease of producing it, considerations which she had to heed since she works for mass manufacturers, she was increasingly experimenting with a kind of outer-space elegance.

Dresses made of aluminum or plastic are not any more realistic or comfortable than the boned and intricately snapped concoctions of the old haute couture. They do, however, enliven fashion shows, make sensational photographs and delight fashion editors. A satiric film on that tendency, *Qui Êtes-Vous Polly Magoo?*, by an American fashion photographer, William Klein, tickled Paris in the fall of 1966.

Christiane Bailly seldom lets her imagination run to abstraction. Of all the creative yé-yés, she is the least known in America, although her work is highly esteemed in Europe. Five months before

Saint Laurent put nailheads into his fall 1966 collection, Christiane Bailly was strewing them over her gentle crepe dresses and suits. A photograph of one of her suits in orange puckered leather studded with nailheads appeared on the cover of the July 6 issue of British *Queen,* almost a month before Saint Laurent's showing. She also preceded the haute couture with a mid-calf-length coat and a long belted jacket.

> The object of the clothes I design is to be worn. To give protection, ease of movement, poise to a woman, and within those technical limits, as much imagination as possible. My clothes are not designed for photographs. They elicit the maximum effect by being worn. Movement fulfills their true purpose.

It's a very difficult feat but Christiane Bailly accomplishes it regularly. Take one of her coats that she did in a textured plastic that could pass for leather, rimmed with matching rabbit. It clung lightly to the body and endowed the wearer with the haunting grace of a modern Anna Karenina. But this was a coat for a young woman who goes to work in the morning not knowing what the day will bring in the way of weather or social engagements. In such a coat she could cope with almost anything.

Christiane Bailly is a tall, bony woman with almond-shaped eyes the color of black olives, a husky voice and the distracted air of the heroine in a new-wave tragedy. Her black hair tumbles into her eyes and straggles down to her collar. Self-effacing and pensive, she lacks business sense and a partner who could thrust her onto the center of the stage and throw her cues. Her first husband was André Frenaud, an existentialist poet. She is currently married to Antonio Stinlo, an architect who was one of Paco Rabanne's classmates at the École des Beaux-Arts. They live in the Marais section of Paris in a garret which they have remodeled and decorated in powerfully contemporary terms with bleached wood beams, abstract paintings and a minimum of furniture. It is a gathering place for the Young Turks of French fashion, theater, and music.

She has been a painter and a writer. For a while, she modeled at Balenciaga and Chanel, and, like Emmanuelle Khanh, made her own clothes. Their original style caught the attention of the editors of *Elle* who put her in touch with Chloe, a manufacturer for whom she designed a few numbers in 1961. Since then, she has designed for half a dozen manufacturers, chiefly sportswear and daytime clothes. "Frenchwomen buy very classic evening dresses. It's hard to get an avant-garde idea across," she observed.

Her strongest affiliation has been with Nale Junior. "It interests me to have a young client, to see my clothes in the street," she has said. Once she accosted a young brunette in the street and asked her, "I designed the coat you are wearing. Do you like it?"

The limitations of the French ready-to-wear industry, which still operates with the mentality of a nation of small shopkeepers, hems in the creativity of a Christiane Bailly, who has not yet signed contracts with American manufacturers. "We are not industrialized enough. In America, the machines pay for the designer's experimentation."

The French consumer market, by itself, is not immense. "The French are very individualistic," she said. "One woman refuses to wear what the other wears, so how can we have great production? In the provinces, if one woman has a blue skirt, another doesn't want it. A big manufacturer can only sell five of a style in one city."

The designer who balances adroitly between the spectacular and the rational is Michèle Rosier, one of the best-known yé-yés on this side of the Atlantic. The blond Miss Rosier, who designs to the sound of yé-yé music, has been nicknamed "The Vinyl Girl" because of her arresting raincoats made out of shiny plastic that looks like old-fashioned kitchen tablecloths. The sensation that they give the wearer of being enclosed in a Turkish bath has not stopped them from becoming an international fad.

She carried the turnabout that Emilio Pucci started in skiwear to its next plateau with explosively colored, exhilaratingly feminine outfits. Some of them, like the ski mini-dress, are vaguely disturbing to ski purists. Miss Rosier designs for White Stag in America as well as for Pierre d'Alby and V. de V., her own company in France.

The daughter of Hélène Gordon Lazareff, the editor of *Elle,* she spent her teen-age years in New York during World War II and attended the Nightingale-Bamford School. She followed her mother into journalism but in 1960 when a French manufacturer countered her criticism of his line with the rejoinder, "See if you can do better," she turned to designing sportswear.

Miss Rosier, whose inventions are based on new utilizations of colors and man-made materials, she declared herself a permissivist in fashion. "Everything beautiful has the right to exist, the eccentric as well as the rational, provided it's cheap," she has said. "I prefer bad taste to good taste; it's gayer."

The most outlandish designs to emerge from Paris after André Courrèges had semi-retreated from the scene were the work of Paco Rabanne, who uses a tool kit instead of a sewing machine. His ideal woman is a technological spirit, clothed in plastic that clanks and jingles when she moves.

Paco Rabanne is a pseudonym for Francisco Rabaneda Cuervo. The son of a Spanish army officer, he was born in 1934 and went to France with the wave of political refugees five years later. Like Courrèges, Paco is a Basque but a jolly, gregarious Basque rather than a touchy loner. "Courrèges did something that had to be done when it had to be done," said Paco Rabanne, who sympathized with Courrèges' despair at having his ideas copied without remuneration for himself, but he disagrees with his withdrawal. "When you are in fashion, you do not have the right to stop." Although he applauded Chanel's comeback collection in 1954 because it provided an antidote to the swollen-topped, pinch-waisted look that had lingered long after Christian Dior introduced it in 1947, he said, "Chanel has no right to keep bringing out the same suit year after year."

A dashing figure with merry hazel eyes and a luxuriant brown moustache that quivers as he talks, Paco Rabanne studied architecture at the École des Beaux-Arts. He supported his studies for a dozen years by designing jewelry for haut couturiers like Balenciaga, Givenchy and Dior.

"Architecture and fashion have the same material function," he says. "Now I am an architect of women." His women are no old-fashioned Sybarites. They are tempted by modern gifts of aluminum and plastic.

Paco's ideal woman is not a nymphet, he says. "Girls of 18 bore me. I'm too adventurous, too eccentric and expensive. I need a woman who is sure of herself. A woman who will say, 'Paco, I have a need to be admired. I need décor.' At 18, she doesn't need décor. I prefer to attack the elegant woman. I like Veronica Lake, the beautiful femme fatale. I'm crazy about her. I've seen all her films," he said with a little shiver of pleasure. Paco Rabanne, a bachelor, brings a refreshingly masculine effervescence to French fashion.

He joined the yé-yé team in 1962 after he saw Emmanuelle Khanh's and Christiane Bailly's designs. Recognizing the promise of a new movement, he asked to work with them. They and Michèle Rosier began using his plastic embroidery and jewelry that year. The friendships forged then have endured. No one is more thrilled by his success than they.

He thanks America for boosting him, however. "The American buyers were coming to me all along," said Paco, who had been turning out bold, geometric jewelry and accessories made of thin, hard plastic for eight years before he became the toast of Paris in January 1966. *Elle* magazine had finally recognized him the previous June when Jean Shrimpton wore one of his plastic headbands in a photograph on its cover.

"The French fashion editors never paid much attention to me unless they happened to go to New York and there all the Americans asked them, 'What about Paco? What's up with Paco?' "

Paco Rabanne's enthusiasms about America range from the elegance of Henri Bendel to the beauty and taste of New York women to the deliciousness of the shrimp cocktails and sirloin steaks. He puts two fingers to his lips and blows a kiss of appreciation. As for American businessmen, they pay well and they act decisively.

"In America, they say yes even to bad ideas. In France, they say no first," he said.

Paco's clothes, which he introduced, appropriately, in the Faubourg St. Honoré gallery of Iris Clert, the most avant-garde art dealer in Paris, are not cheap. His dresses made of plastic disks held together with chains sold for $200 to $500 at Lord & Taylor in New York. But no sooner had they established a new industrial-society chic than Paco was making a coat of ostrich feathers glued to plastic tape.

He then designed a paper dress for the Scott Paper Company.

"Very cheap, and the woman will only wear it once or twice. For me, it's the future of fashion," said Paco Rabanne.

VII

THE PARIS MYTH

WHAT would Christmas be without Santa Claus?
What would fashion be without the myth of Paris?

Twice a year, in frigid January and damp July, the merchants and fashion editors of the world assemble to perpetuate the myth. It is a wearisome happening staged in the stifling salons of the haute couture houses, which, with a couple of exceptions, are situated in the 8th *arrondissement* of Paris, hard by the luxury tourist traps around the Champs-Élysées.

Someone invariably faints or threatens to. Someone is invariably offended by the protocol of seating or picks a fight over the loss of a place on one of the frail gilt chairs. A delicate artist suffers a case of the vapors. Writers panic, buyers fret, old editors doze and shy designers are smothered with kisses after the last repetitive numbers in their interminable collections have been shown. With each passing season, the flower arrangements—magnificent stereotypes fit for a marshal's funeral—surpass the content of many couturiers' creative output.

And when the ten days of monotonous pyrotechnics have ended, the audience disbands to repeat for global consumption the semi-annual fiction that fashion has just been conceived. Most of them were brainwashed before they saw the performances for the first time long ago, so they won't say anything. A few newcomers comprehend the deception. They are appalled by the scraggly hemlines and the loving-hands finish on what they had been repeatedly told are masterpieces. They gasp at the effrontery of a designer who passes off someone else's hackneyed idea as his inspired invention. But they hold their tongues. Agnostics are not welcome in the fashion business. Rather than be excommunicated, they permit themselves to be mesmerized the next time. And they, too, conspire to preserve the legend.

Why shouldn't they? Most women have never respected a style until it is authorized by the Paris couturiers. In the Sixties, the couturiers have continuously ratified ideas taken from across the Channel, across the Atlantic or from their own backyards. The source of whatever fashion novelty Paris has had to offer moved from the 8th *arrondissement* on the Right Bank to the 6th and the 14th on the Left Bank. In these unsnobbish districts, little shops spawned the relevant fashions of the decade—ready-made, reasonably priced and catchy.

Like most legends, the myth of Paris is rooted in fact. Once upon a time, fashion was created by the haut couturiers. One reason that the middle-aged public—men as well as women—succumb so easily to the myth is that they remember the autocracy of the great designers. 1947 is engraved in their memories. One day there were broad shoulders and short, straight skirts. Then on February 12, Christian Dior decreed a New Look. Hemlines fell. Waistlines were pinched. Skirts billowed. There was nothing a woman could do with her wardrobe except throw it away. It was a costly experience and they remember it.

What they forget is that it had to happen. The New Look was the inevitable reaction to wartime austerity. The restrictions on the use of fabric had been lifted in the United States a few months before. Seventh Avenue manufacturers—Norman Norell being the first— were lengthening the skirt. But Dior did it with the authority of the Paris couturier. The spotlight was on him and besides, he gave the lengthened skirt meaning with a nostalgically feminine silhouette.

The next radical change came 11 years later with the chemise. Balenciaga had been loosening the silhouette since the early Fifties, as had Hubert de Givenchy, an aristocratic young giant who made his presence known starting in 1951 with plucky ideas. The waistline had been wandering all over the lot for some time, a sure sign that designers were restless and perplexed. By the summer of 1958, the waistline was banished, but the essentially sensible silhouette decreed by Paris was copied too quickly and too cheaply.

The revulsion to the sack, particularly the version with the bow stuck right under the haunches, prompted a resistance movement from American husbands. But the sack or the chemise refused to die because it was right for its time. The absence of a waistline in a dress signified the new freedom for women. It took until 1965 for it to be embraced across the board. The next year, designers were fiddling with belts, but women were reluctant to part with their liberty so soon.

Actually, nothing happened to the silhouette between the mid-Fifties and the mid-Sixties that was not an evolution or a consolidation of Balenciaga's original intention. The A-line, the H-line and the Trapeze of Dior and his disciple, Yves Saint Laurent, as well as the Chanel suit with the unbuttoned or loosely fastened jacket were variations on the theme of doing away with restrictions. Each season, another batch of gimmicks was released with the usual fanfare to fool women into believing that something was happening in the haute couture when, in fact, almost nothing was.

Even Courrèges, the only real shaker in the Paris couture during the Sixties, was improvising on the theme of Balenciaga, his former master. He shortened the hard shell that is Balenciaga's prescription for modern woman, but he realized that it required a new proportion. The white boot broke up the long expanse of leg. Nevertheless, other designers were harvesting the same vineyard and it was possible for a woman to ignore Courrèges and choose other alternatives without being condemned as tacky.

Like Balenciaga, André Courrèges is a Basque and a tailor rather than a dressmaker. He is similarly given to mystery and suspicion. Cristobal Balenciaga has made the couture business seem like divine revelation, and the tactic has brought him far richer rewards than if he had played hail fellow well met. Courrèges, a butler's son who studied engineering before taking up the needle, has not been quite as successful with the act. He alternately plays the prophet and the martyr with a touch of the megalomania that these roles demand.

André Courrèges is an olive-skinned man of medium build with dark brown hair receding from a high forehead. His alter ego, perhaps even his superego, is Jacqueline Barrière, a young Basque with cropped beige hair and the boyish figure requisite for the Courrèges pants she nearly always wears. Courrèges calls her Coqueline and keeps her constantly at his side.

On one of his secretive visits to New York in the spring of 1966, during which he stayed at the Pierre Hotel under an assumed name, he and Coqueline roamed through Seventh Avenue visiting workrooms and talking to manufacturers who were interested in backing him.

Coqueline was arrayed in the famous tattersall checked coat with hip-encircling belt and white boots. In gum-soled shoes and an olive tweed jacket with a bumpy hem and three inches of white shirt protruding from its sleeves, Courrèges looked like one of the Spanish workers who flock through the Gare d'Austerlitz looking for jobs in Paris. When recognized, Courrèges and Coqueline darted away like frightened gazelles. They are an inseparable pair who make their associates aware that three is a crowd. Red-haired Ariane Brenner, who serves Courrèges as spokesman and apologist, quit with hurt feelings. Emmanuel Ungaro, a tailor who left Balenciaga to join Courrèges, struck out on his own and is trying to prove that he can carry the ball and score the touchdown that Paris needs so badly.

Courrèges dropped the ball in the fall of 1965 at the peak of his fame. He had stepped out of the shadow of Balenciaga in 1961, when he was 38, opening a little salon on the Avenue Kléber. It seemed like an apartment on the moon to the buyers and the editors who were used to the gilded, 18th-century façade of the haute couture. In a room as white and stark as a monk's cell, faintly scented with hyacinths and resounding to the strains of the classic guitar, Courrèges offered clothes that were modern architecture. He hammered out a few ideas, but he was adamant about them. "At first people were shocked by the airplane; now everyone takes it. Women don't wear pants to the office yet, but they will," he said in February 1964. Norman Norell had suggested the same thing four years before with his far less militant, knee-length culotte.

Courrèges' preference for the colors of snow, steel and a few pastels originated as much in economy as in vision. He couldn't afford the costly embroideries of the established haute couture. The white goggles with the slits were a sudden improvisation not intended as a style. But like everything in his small crop, they were taken by the vultures. By the spring of 1965, white boots were stomping, out of context, all over the sidewalks of New York. His spartan coats with contrast piping (unfortunately translated with lumpy shoulders), his cowboy hats, and even Courrèges-inspired underwear were everywhere. Almost none of the revenues from the bonanza accrued to him. Courrèges was just what the fashion industry was looking for. His ideas were so simple and clear that they could be stolen without a blueprint or pattern. Only the superb tailoring of his trousers could not be repeated, although the concept of the pants suit could. Courrèges was shamelessly copied, but few of the copyists bothered to pay him. In bitter despair, he declined to present a fall collection for 1965. He declared that he was going to find a way to produce his own moderately priced ready-to-wear. In that way, he would be selling his ideas to the public, but with some profit to himself and without having them caricatured.

A French bank gave him some financial backing. L'Oréal, a French manufacturer of beauty-treatment supplies and hair coloring, signed an agreement to distribute a perfume bearing his name. Courrèges moved to a new salon on the third floor of a building at 40 Rue François Premier. It had the same pristine decor, white walls and white vinyl cubes for chairs. When a stranger rang, the doors creaked open automatically and from nowhere an aide materialized to put the caller out. Courrèges made clothes for a handful of private clients who could be trusted not to reveal his secrets to rapacious manufacturers or the press. But the whisper around Paris was that there was nothing to steal.

He visited America incognito and when his presence was detected and reported in *The New York Times,* a press conference was hastily called at the Fifth Avenue office of L'Oréal. Courrèges, who aspired to design for the modern woman, performed like the Delphic oracle in a Grade-B film. Photographers were barred from the meeting. Coqueline stood behind him like a silent phantom. The public relations director of L'Oréal announced, "He is here in America for the obvious reason that he likes American women."

Courrèges' remark, as interpreted by Ariane Brenner, who was then on the verge of leaving him, went something like this. "Before I can love American woman, she must love me. I know American woman like my work. I love her courage. I like the way she is built physically. I try to understand the American woman and I try to understand the market.

"If I am not a showman," Courrèges said apologetically, "it's because I am timid, and I can't change. If I'm not a star sometimes, it's because I want to be behind. I'm here to prove to you I don't hide. I thank you and you will see me each time you need me. *Au revoir.*" And then he vanished. The American manufacturers with whom he had conferred found him elusive and no accords resulted from the visit.

In February 1967, Courrèges staged a comeback. He continued to ban manufacturers and buyers, but admitted the press to his spring collection. In two years he had softened a little, rounding his austere shapes with curved seams and scallops. The boots were gone but white bobby socks and round-toed, Mary Jane slippers served their function.

His bid for the mass market was a group of 15 designs in 5 colors and 4 sizes that were sold as ready-to-wear in his showroom one flight below his haute couture salon. The price of a coat was $200, as against $800 in his haute couture collection. Courrèges, it would seem, had turned his back on Everywoman.

Odd as Courrèges' behavior may have been, it served to spotlight the malady of the Paris haute couture. All through the Sixties, the haute couture has been deteriorating. Rising costs, disappearing customers and the economic and social turnabout that has occurred in France, just as in all the other developed nations of the world, have sapped it of vitality and leadership.

For 300 years before this decade, except in times of war and siege, the dressmakers of Paris decreed fashion. Nowhere else in the world was elegance taken so seriously or supported by such a reservoir of talent, skilled craftsmen and cooperative clients. The Paris couturiers, from Charles Frederick Worth to Christian Dior, were benevolent dictators whose fantasies amused the moneyed aristocrats and the socially ambitious tycoons' wives while simultaneously fueling the French fabric mills and the fashion industries of other countries. British fashion, Scandinavian fashion, American fashion (despite its native supply of design talent) were mirrors held up to the Paris haute couture.

For most of the 20th century, the couturiers served two mistresses. The one they loved was the private customer who wanted elegant clothes made to her whim and specifications and who respected the painstaking detail and the technologically wasteful ritual of perfection stitched up by humble hands behind the scenes. The other was the commercial customer, the manufacturer or the merchant, who purchased the dressmaker's design in order to reproduce it. That customer paid more than the private client, was hemmed in by regulations and tolerated as an unlovable patron. Through the commercial customer, fashion filtered down from the clouds where it was created for a small elite to the masses.

Creative dressmaking, which the haute couture is supposed to be, was essentially a dialogue between the designer and a small clientele. The designer provided the costumes for their elaborate and rigidly prescribed social life—the rituals of tea, theatergoing and balls—enacted behind the walls of great mansions and villas. They, in turn, gave the designer inspiration and criticism. The pivot of such women's existence was their sessions at the dressmaker. The choice of a dress or hat took days. The color of a lining was pondered for hours. In the fitting rooms, they were tyrants. Before one dress was finished, it had been sat in, stretched in, tugged at and scrutinized from a thousand angles. The suspicion of a wrinkle or of surplus fabric meant that little hands would rip and start all over again. Every time the client went on a diet or drank too much at lunch before a fitting, the labor costs rose. When women had no reason for being other than decorative objects, when life was stratified and slow-moving and when labor was cheap, the haute couture was feasible.

In the spring of 1957, half a year before his death, Christian Dior described such fashion muses as being rich, Parisienne, and between the ages of 35 and 40. There were, he guessed, no more than 7,000 to 10,000 of them. A decade later, their ranks had diminished and the dialogue was interrupted. It was not that the rich were fewer. If anything, they were more numerous and the vintage of their money no longer mattered as much. But they had become unfaithful. Some of them were finding other uses for their money. Prestige for some lay in goals other than the attainment of elegance. The minuet-pace of their lives had quickened to jet speed. The international scale of social activity had broadened their vistas. When status comes from having the latest fad from London or New York, the snob appeal of the dress that takes three fittings before it will be delivered in four to six weeks lessens.

Furthermore, many of these women of 35 and 40 were taking fashion lessons from their teen-age daughters and nieces. They were imitating their manner of dressing and dancing and even their insouciance. Elegance had ceased to be a virtue. The newer values were audacity, pragmatism and wit. The lady of the spotless glove, the coiffure with every hair in place, and the king's ransom in jewels had given way to the amoralist, the girl astronaut and the adorable clown.

The younger women who piped the tune of fashion did not patronize the haute couture. It wasn't only that they rejected the bastions of their elders, but that the haute couture had become too expensive.

The private client pays $500 or $600 for the simplest, least expensive dress at Pierre Cardin, $800 for a wool daytime dress at Yves Saint Laurent. Prices for evening clothes run into thousands of dollars. If the customer pays with American traveler's checks, she receives a 14 per cent discount. The majority of private clients at the house of Yves Saint Laurent are American. Jean Claude Taffin de Givenchy, business manager for his brother Hubert, has estimated the American portion of their customers at 70 per cent. Considering the prices, no wonder.

The typical, well-to-do Frenchwoman has always been prudent about money. With her innate fashion sense, she avoided the styles that manufacturers bought to copy and stuck to those with dateless elegance. Often, she bought her haute couture clothes when the models were marked down at the end of the season. Or she patronized a little dressmaker who obtained the toiles or muslin patterns of the best designs through contraband sources immediately after the collections were shown. In the last decade, as rising textile and labor costs forced the couturiers to raise their prices, the typical bourgeoise has abdicated from the haute couture, leaving the field to reckless foreigners. And as her little dressmaker has disappeared, she started buying clothes ready-made. According to one estimate, 70 per cent of French women's clothing now comes from a factory. Fifteen years ago, it was sewn by someone's hand.

Custom dressmaking is failing in France for the same reasons that it has become nearly extinct in America. Women think they have better uses for their time than standing for fittings, and, with their figures slimmed by diet and exercise, they don't have to be measured and pampered. Even in France, the social requirements of dress have become less formal and women can find more realistic clothing in the ready-to-wear shops than most couturiers seem capable of producing.

The couturier finds it increasingly difficult to operate in the black.

"No couture house makes money on its private clients," Yvonne de Peyerimhoff, the *directrice* of Yves Saint Laurent, has said. "If there is a good response from buyers, we break even. If we do less, we can't break even." In 1965, the House of Dior told the Reuters News Agency that it netted no more than a $70 profit on the sale of a $1,400 evening dress to a private client. Each Dior collection costs a minimum of $200,000 to produce. Pierre Cardin said that his collection, which is smaller than the Dior spectacular, costs between $120,000 and $180,000.

Except for a few couturiers who have been able to maintain the dialogue with the private customer—Mme. Alix Grès and Pierre Balmain, the hero of European women and what remains of international royalty, were notable examples—the great dressmakers have become dependent on the commercial customers. In 1957, American buyers were spending $1.5 million a year in the Paris haute couture. A decade later, indications were that the amount had not increased and in some years had declined.

The couturiers make commercial customers pay 25 to 30 per cent more than the private clients and they must deposit cautions or admission fees to see the collections against which their purchases are charged. The cautions and the terms vary with each house. Balenciaga and Givenchy, of course, are the most demanding, particularly of the American merchants who are still under their spell. One season, Givenchy set a $1,500 caution and a minimum purchase of two models per buyer. This meant that a store that sent its coat and dress buyers could not escape without spending at least $6,000. With such heavy commitments involved, buyers have grown increasingly nervous about Paris, and many of them wait for the reports of the press or their associates before visiting a house. Bad reviews from the press for his fall 1964 collection, when he essayed a mid-calf hemline, cost Yves Saint Laurent $100,000 in cancellations from buyers. As a result, he decided to bar the press until a month after the buyers had seen and ordered. Balenciaga and Givenchy have succeeded with this stratagem for years and until recently it enhanced their glamour. Under gentle pressure from Richard Salomon, head of Lanvin-Charles of the Ritz, who bought control of Yves Saint Laurent in 1965 from the previous backer, Mack Robinson (a finance company operator from Atlanta, Georgia), Saint Laurent relented and admitted the press four days after the buyers.

Although he did not react as drastically as Courrèges by withdrawing, Saint Laurent, like most couturiers, felt that he was abused and cheated not only by the press, but by the world-wide fashion industry. It is the designer's age-old complaint about piracy. In the case of Saint Laurent, it is undeniable that many have traded on his name without paying him. Every season, mileage is gained from his collection by manufacturers and buyers who do not see it. The first Mondrian-look copies to hit the American market came from a Seventh Avenue manufacturer who did not buy the original design from Saint Laurent. Ohrbach's generated tons of publicity by being the only New York store to sell copies of his famous transparent dress in the spring of 1966. The store is one of Saint Laurent's best customers, but the buyers didn't dare to invest a substantial portion of their budget in a dress that would appeal to a few exhibitionists. Saint Laurent had only put the dress in his show as a publicity gag, anyway, never expecting it to be taken seriously.

So Ohrbach's obtained its copies in New York from a manufacturer who had it made in Hong Kong, sold some to pop fashion celebrities, like Mrs. S. Carter Burden, Jr., Susan Stein, and Mrs. Robert Scull, and took markdowns on the rest. Mme. de Peyerimhoff rebuked the store's fashion director, but all had to be forgiven. Saint Laurent can't afford to lose good customers.

The couturiers know that paper patterns of their designs are peddled in Italy two days after their showings. Some American manufacturers get their French inspiration through that avenue. Saint Laurent stopped selling to Italian manufacturers whom he suspected of guilt. But as soon as one hole is plugged, another leak springs.

Private customers are presumed to be one source. The couturiers check the credentials of women who come to buy. At run-of-the-mill houses, a telephone call from a hotel hall porter will suffice, but at the others admission is a more elaborate farce, like that of gaining entry to Regine's New Jimmy's discothèque in Montparnasse or one of the gaming clubs of London. Still, the couturier cannot prove that a social luminary lends her purchase to a manufacturer or dressmaker and is reimbursed her cost, which is less than the manufacturer would have paid. At least one New York custom dressmaker, who provides a society clientele with Paris styles, will not disclose (and the couturiers cannot figure out) where he gets them.

The Paris haute couture has always supported two leading French industries, textiles and perfume. Until the summer of 1961, the government subsidized the couturiers for agreeing to use at least 90 per cent French textiles in their collections. For an important house that attracted customers from abroad, the subsidy came to about $25,000 a year. When President de Gaulle decided to end this aid, many houses cut down the number of their styles by as much as a third. In 1965, the 75-year-old house of Lanvin closed nearly half of its workrooms. In recent years, Lanvin has been known more for its perfume Arpège than for style innovation.

Despite all the roadblocks they erect in the path of the press (such as prohibiting photographs to be released before the date when the clothes are to be delivered to stores and manufacturers), the haut couturiers desperately need the publicity fallout from the semi-annual showings to sell their perfumes throughout the world. A major reason for Gabrielle Chanel's return to the couture after a 15-year retirement in 1954 was to bolster the sales of Chanel Number Five, the world's most famous perfume. American sales of the scent run to about $9 million a year.

As the actual influence of the haute couture in creating styles declines, the importance of its perfumes and other sidelines, like neckties and hosiery bearing the couturiers' names, increases. The couturier licenses a manufacturer or perfume distributor to use his name in return for royalties or percentages of sales. The licenses are negotiated with different companies in various countries. In the case of fragrances sold in the United States, the custom is for the American distributor to import the bottled perfumes and the essential oils to be used in the toilet waters and bath powders. The latter are packaged here.

The ineluctable glamour of the French dressmaker washes off on the perfume that carries his label. When a man buys a one-ounce bottle of Marcel Rochas' Madame Rochas for $27.50, he fantasizes that he is giving the object of his affections a $2,000 dress. Marcel Rochas died in 1955, and his couture house was closed after his death; but his widow, Hélène, does a magnificent job of keeping the magic of his name alive with her own go-go personality.

It's so much easier, though, to sell a perfume with a live couturier in the background. The House of Fragrance is the American distributor for the fragrances of Hubert de Givenchy and of Millot, a French firm whose most popular scent is Crêpe de Chine. In 1960, Millot came out with a new perfume, Insolent. It was intended as competition for Patou's Joy, then the most expensive perfume. Insolent had a sexy luxuriousness that made every woman who had a chance to dab herself with it immediately feel like Cleopatra wrapped in sable. But the difficulty of launching a new scent without the backing of a dressmaker's publicity defeated it. Helen Van Slyke, president of the House of Fragrance, decided to throw her advertising budget behind Givenchy's Le De, L'Interdit and his cosmetics line. Even though he is as aloof as a Bourbon pretender, the six-foot six-inch Marquis Hubert James Taffin de Givenchy, couturier to Audrey Hepburn and favorite of Jacqueline Kennedy in her White House days, is bound to shed a helpful glow over his perfume and lipstick eggs that sell for $80 a dozen. Besides, as a bachelor who was born in 1927 and takes excellent care of himself, Givenchy has a long way to go. Insolent became an underground perfume and died in infancy in America. In France, it was reissued at a lesser price and fainter strength. Its admirers mourn whenever they pass a perfume counter.

When Mack Robinson, Yves Saint Laurent's backer, put his interest in the couture house up for sale, Lanvin-Charles of the Ritz picked it up to safeguard the rights it had already acquired to Saint Laurent's new perfume, Y (pronounced ee-grec in French). The cosmetics house had the American distributorship for Arpège and the other Lanvin perfumes.

The House of Christian Dior has projected the licensing concept to its widest application. In 1966, the headquarters at 30 Avenue Montaigne was the "cradle of creativity" for a global trade of $42 million in perfumes and other products from women's shoes, gloves and lingerie to men's shirts and ties. Marc Bohan, the designer of the haute couture collection, visits the workrooms that manufacture Christian Dior ready-to-wear in London and New York one or more times a year. Each has its own designer who interprets Bohan's mood of the preceding season. The Paris studios supply licensees with sketches, colors and samples of whatever they are supposed to manufacture. Dior hosiery licensees (the American manufacturer is the Berkshire Knitting Mills) get together every two years to compare notes. Dior costume jewelry is designed in Paris and manufactured in Germany. With millinery, the British and American manufacturers may choose different hats to copy from the couture collection, because of different tastes in the respective countries.

Elsa Schiaparelli, the queen of Paris couturiers in the Thirties, creator of shocking pink and broad-shouldered suits, closed her couture house in the mid-Fifties, but still owns a perfume company. She visits the United States periodically to stir up publicity and to exercise what a spokesman for Schiaparelli, Inc., a division of Kayser-Roth, termed "slight supervision" over the handbag accessories, men's neckwear and dress shirts, furs, umbrellas, shoes, millinery, jewelry and wigs that it licenses to different manufacturers. "If she were to die, the stocking brand would continue unimpaired," Alfred Slaner, president of Kayser-Roth, once said. The company has, at various times, manufactured stockings under the name of Yves Saint Laurent, Mr. John, Ceil Chapman, John Frederics, Suzy Perette, Simonetta and Mollie Parnis.

Sham relationships have given licensing a black eye through the years. The Federal Trade Commission, which considers it an unfair and deceptive act, misleading to the consumer, to advertise a product as having been designed by someone when, in fact, it was not, has stopped American manufacturers from selling lingerie under the label of Jacques Heim and hosiery ascribed to Jeanne Lanvin.

The fashion industry is rife with gossip about designers who cannot recognize their own so-called work. One tale involves a Paris designer who passed a glove counter in a New York department store heaped with cotton gloves bearing the couturier's name, and announced, "Everyone knows I can't abide cotton gloves."

If the couturiers need the twice-a-year showings to glamorize their names and publicize their more profitable franchise enterprises, the American fashion industry is equally loath to give up Paris for its own reasons. First, there is the status built into the trip. The prestige of a job in many businesses today is equated with travel. As soon as a buyer or an editor starts going to Paris, his or her status rises. As soon as he stops, the industry interprets it as a signal of oblivion. Paris is only seven hours by jet from New York, but the American fashion businessmen consider it a heavenly planet. In Paris, fashion people are esteemed. And they are wined and dined. Even if one doesn't attend many collections, there is so much side action. Where else but on the French fashion circuit could a lowly manufacturer or writer encounter such international celestial bodies as the Duchess of Windsor, the Vicomtesse de Ribes and former Queen Soraya?

But American fashion needs Paris for more profound reasons. In a decade when nothing significant has been happening to the silhouette, when there are so many other temptations than clothes, merchants must constantly find ways and means of pulling customers into their stores. Paris is a sure-fire way for many kinds of stores.

The low-margin operators, like Ohrbach's and Alexander's, estopped by Seventh Avenue designers from using their names, find in the cooperative haute couture of Paris, whose designs they copy at reasonable prices, a semi-annual opportunity to assert a high-class affiliation.

The luxury emporiums use the Paris haute couture as a bit of one-upmanship on their competitors and as a convenience for the wealthy, usually not-too-young customer who doesn't want to be bothered with the siege of ordering and fitting in Paris. Bergdorf Goodman, which has maintained its consistently money-losing custom salon for the sake of prestige, buys about 50 designs a season in the Paris haute couture.

A woman can order any of them, made to her measure and with any changes she wishes or exactly as Paris decreed them down to the identical linings, hooks and eyes. Bergdorf's prices are higher than the Paris couturiers'. New York custom tailors and dressmakers are paid more than their Paris counterparts for one thing. But what's a few hundred dollars more or less to a Mellon, a Ford or a Kennedy?

In Chicago, Marshall Field promotes Paris on the strength of saving its customers the trans-Atlantic fare. The store spends about $100,000 a year at each of four couture houses—Balenciaga, Givenchy, Saint Laurent and Dior—for models in sizes 8 to 16, which it sells at approximately the same prices as they would cost in Paris, plus alterations. Fresh shipments are received each month during 10 months of the year. Who buys them? Women from Denver, Omaha, Cleveland, New Orleans and points west and southwest who fly into Chicago for the day with their husbands in their company airplanes. Or tag along for a convention. Some of them order by telephone. A woman in Colorado Springs called up for a $1,650 eyelet cotton dress by Balenciaga. In Allentown, Pa., Hess's Department Store imports $100,000 worth of European couturier clothes in order to bring fashion news and excitement to steel-mill and coal-mining territory. They are rarely sold. The expenses are chalked up to promotion.

Neiman-Marcus, the store that tries to keep oil producers' and ranchers' wives from straying out of Texas for their wardrobes, frequently makes a hullabaloo about Paris, either by conferring one of its annual awards on a French designer or by staging a French promotion. When Gabrielle Chanel was honored, Neiman's gave a barbecue on a ranch. The ageless couturière, whose licorice eyes had presumably seen everything, was bowled over by the added dividend of a fashion show in which a top-hatted bull and a cow with a tulle veil played groom and bride.

Two of the world's biggest retailers of women's clothes keep their eyes peeled on Paris. Sears Roebuck has a resident buyer scout the couture and the boutiques for ideas, but prefers not to mention specific designer names. Montgomery Ward, which sells $500,000 worth of clothes a year in its 502 retail stores and 1,151 catalogue stores and agencies, is a loyal customer of the haute couture, as well as of the young ready-to-wear designers of France, Italy and England.

Ward's buys designs in the Paris couture to be adapted by American manufacturers to sell from $12 to $100. Sometimes, as in the case of Paco Rabanne's first exhilarating showing of plastic disk dresses, the purchases are solely for the edification of Ward's merchandising executives.

Twice a year, Rita Perna, the fashion coordinator, leads a herd of American and European designers on a tour to half a dozen large and medium-sized cities. Nearly 10,000 persons see and hear such lesser lights of the Paris couture as Simonetta or Philippe Heim, son of the founder of the House of Jacques Heim.

Seventh Avenue manufacturers look to Paris for the shape of clothes and no one is more distressed by mounting caution prices and the dearth of news than they. Among the couture's best customers have been Adele Simpson, Jerry Silverman and Kimberly Knits. Mollie Parnis gets inspiration in Paris, too, but being a wise woman, as well as a strenuous socializer, she uses up her caution on something she can wear herself. In 1961, Givenchy kindled the renaissance of the ornately beaded and embroidered evening dress. Although she denied that there was a direct connection between her designs and his, Miss Parnis' jewel-embroidered evening shift dresses, at nearly $1,000 apiece, became the American socialites' uniform of 1965 and 1966.

Few on Seventh Avenue are as candid as Victor Joris, one of the most adventurous American designers, who regularly attends the showings with his employer, Justin Lipman, president of Cuddlecoat. Mr. Joris explained:

We buy one model for the body and another for the fabric. We got the idea of bold fabric from Ungaro. We try to buy the first coat. You see, the French designer runs one body silhouette through his line. No matter how many variations he shows, basically he started with one coat. The master coat is never as exciting as the others. It's sort of like a game to figure which body he started with.

I can take that coat, make my pattern and then change it any way I want. We buy the master coat and the retailers buy the others. The stores buy for this season. We buy for several seasons.

In 1960, Ricci did a green coat with an X collar. In 1966, we still had a version of it on our line. We never go to Balenciaga because he's too old. Givenchy is getting old now, too. In 1961, Givenchy had a short, pink cotton coat. It had a beautiful bustline. We bought it and put it in wool and one store sold 1,000 of our coat.

Said Justin Lipman, "Victor and I go to the showings in Paris and the main thing we go for is to give Victor confidence that we're on the right track." Victor Joris' mid-calf-length coat over a short skirt appeared in *Glamour* magazine a year before Marc Bohan showed longer coats over knee-high dresses for fall 1966. But he credits *Glamour*'s editors with the inspiration and says that anyhow, Philippe Guibourgé, Marc Bohan's assistant at Dior, had sent up a trial balloon for the new length in an earlier sportswear collection.

What the manufacturers don't pick up directly from the haute couture, the fashion magazines supply. "You can suggest an idea to an American manufacturer, but unless he can see it, he doesn't understand it," a fashion editor said. *Vogue* tries to stimulate Seventh Avenue manufacturers with its twice-yearly seminars held in the Green Room, so called because Billy Baldwin endowed it with a carpet the color of grass and green-and-white printed wallpaper and matching draperies. The impressionable manufacturers are wooed by *Vogue* editors (they are there to be inspired not only about design, but about advertising in the magazine as well), served culinary triumphs on white china and Georgian silver, and instructed by being shown sketches that represent looks the fashion editors believe in.

If those hints are not sufficient, the editors can be more helpful. In the spring of 1966, Diana Vreeland felt in her bones that the suit and the coat with the martingale belt would be right for fall. Sketches were prepared for the seminar and when Seventh Avenue failed to fall into a martingale mood, an editor was dispatched to Mrs. Vreeland's apartment, where she plucked a Paris couturier's coat with a martingale belt out of the closet and gave it to a manufacturer, who whipped up such a coat for *Vogue*'s August issue.

The editors of *Mademoiselle* introduced the French yé-yé designers to America by shopping the Paris boutiques and passing their purchases to Seventh Avenue manufacturers. In 1964, Sandra Horvitz, then 25 and one of the youngest fashion editors on the college-girl-oriented magazine, bought a tight, ribbed sweater (a fad that had sneaked up from St. Tropez in 1960 to the Paris boutiques) and gave it to a manufacturer whom she also persuaded to make a hipster skirt. "The manufacturers all said that no one would ever wear a tight sweater," Mrs. Horvitz recalled three years later, when the poor boy sweater had become an international epidemic.

In 1964, she also detected in the Paris boutiques a kittenish dress that looked like an A-shaped, elongated sweater with a tight armhole. She fed several of these to American manufacturers, who made their versions coincide with a feature in the August 1966 college issue. By then, Paris was saturated with shapely knits. In early 1967, the body-hugging sweater dress was news in New York.

The invaluable shapes of Paris come to America through other sources, too. The ready-to-wear manufacturers of England, Ireland, Germany, the Netherlands and Italy, all of whom have stepped up their sales to American stores, get their patterns in Paris. So do the furriers. Finn Birger Christensen of Copenhagen, the fun-loving Dane who has put Scandinavian mink on the map but who gets his kicks out of turning the pelts of lions, buffaloes, wolves, antelopes and even horses into inexpensively snappy coats for younger women, goes shopping in Paris.

Mr. Birger Christensen, who has a congenial association with Henri Chombert, the avant-garde furrier of the Rue St. Honoré, doesn't bother with Balenciaga and Givenchy. They're too expensive and evolutionary, a fashion euphemism for static. It means that they move a seam, change a collar or take a sliver off the skirt from one season to the next. Birger Christensen wants action and he gets it in the muslin patterns of Courrèges (when he was still selling to commercial customers) and small couturiers, like Philippe Venet and Louis

Feraud. Such customers also dig in the boutiques, like Dorothée Bis and Laura, where they will buy a coat or a suit off the rack and milk it for what it's worth in cut or some obscure detail.

Fashion, then, is no longer a French monopoly, but rather an international association. Paris is not the style capital of the world that it once was. It is, simply, the most convenient mine for the clothing-makers, the merchants and the publicists of fashion. There is no denying, of course, that the French have a knack for fashion just as they do for cooking, just as Americans do for industrial technology and the English for acting and parliamentary government. Given an egg, a few bits of ham and cheese, some flour and milk, a French cook will perform a miracle. Given some old ideas of their own or someone else's, see what French designers will accomplish. Almost as if in comic defiance of De Gaulle's policies, French fashion designers lived on inspiration from the United States and Britain in the Sixties. Take the Scottish kilt, the tweed sweaters and coats worn with knee socks and moccasins that took Paris by storm in 1966. These were the fashions of the American college girl, eastern seaboard division, circa World War II, when the Ivy League and the Seven Sisters believed in the rule of Britannia.

The obsession of the young French ready-to-wear designers with American industrial technology and pop culture was fed back into the haute couture. When Yves Saint Laurent labored and came forth with pea jackets, pop-art dresses, nailheads and vinyl, neckties and gangster suits, when Pierre Cardin used industrial zippers and girlish jumpers for shockers, even the true believers in the Paris myth were sorely tried. Those ideas were spawned seasons before on Seventh Avenue or in French ready-to-wear. Why should anyone want to pay $1,000 or more to own or to copy a rehash of a $60 fashion? Only a diminishing number of merchants and wealthy exhibitionists who need assurance from the old gods. But they are not enough to maintain the myth.

By the middle of the Sixties, it was obvious that the wave of the future was in mass-produced, relatively inexpensive clothes. What vitality there was in French fashion came from the young free-lance designers of ready-to-wear that was sold in the boutiques, those small shops that had sprouted like wild daisies in the most unpredictable districts during the decade.

The ready-to-wear designers, often women, were a different breed from the haut couturier. Intelligent (even intellectual), artistically gifted, they were attuned to their generation and to the modern era. They addressed themselves to an anonymous clientele, composed chiefly of young girls and women newly emancipated from the tight, social taboos of the French social system. The buying power of such customers as individuals was a fraction of the couturiers' customers, but in the aggregate (and especially after their influence spread), it was enormous. Their needs and their convictions, their insatiable appetite for fashion had almost nothing in common with those of the haut couturiers' inspirational woman. The *prêt-à-porter* designer's dialogue was conducted with the working girls of the fashion industry —the models and the editors of *Elle*—and their sisters in advertising, public relations and the arts. They compete to be the first to wear fashion novelties and to parade them before a mass audience in the streets of Paris and in the casual restaurants and cafés of Montparnasse and St.-Germain-des-Prés.

In the second half of the Sixties, the haute couture tried to adjust to the realities of the mass-fashion era. When the decade opened, the influential houses were those of Balenciaga, Givenchy, Chanel and Dior. Five years later, Balenciaga and Givenchy had become academicians. The Chanel suit was a badge of conservatism. André Courrèges, Yves Saint Laurent and Pierre Cardin, considered the radicals a few years before, were aggressively trying to marry themselves to ready-to-wear, as was the House of Dior. The rest of the houses struggled with the greatest identity crisis in the history of dressmaking. Their survival depends on how they resolve the dilemma, whether to be private dressmakers or mass marketeers.

The couturiers who explored the latter course preferred to describe their houses as "laboratories of ideas." It sounded less commercial and it preserved the mystique that fashion could only be nurtured in a hothouse before being transplanted to common soil. In the fashion upheaval of the Sixties, however, the laboratory had moved from the salons, fitting rooms and design studios of the haute couture to the sidewalks, the shopwindows and the ready-to-wear manufacturers' workrooms.

Nevertheless, the realists among the couturiers tried different methods of establishing profitable contact with masses of younger, less affluent customers. Artistic designers recast themselves as mass-production executives.

In 1967, the House of Christian Dior started manufacturing ready-to-wear to sell for about $60 to $120 in a Miss Dior boutique on the Rue François Premier, next to the couture house, and in stores throughout France. Backed by Marcel Boussac, the textile magnate, and run by Jacques Rouet, its tough-minded business director, the House of Dior is as profit-conscious an enterprise as any international machine-tool company. Marc Bohan, its chief designer, typifies the new haut couturier. A slight, bashful man with soft brown eyes and hair, he could easily be mistaken for the youthful French financiers and industrialists who scramble over the globe scouting for business. He cuts an anonymous figure in dark blue suits of medium-weight fabric tailored in London. His neckties are sober. Bohan always seems on the verge of a blush. When a question is posed, he hesitates, breaks into a dimpled smile, and gives a cautious, brief reply.

Marc Bohan is the gifted designer turned loyal corporation man. He doesn't appear to mind if the women of the world are grateful to phantom Dior instead of live Bohan or if *Women's Wear Daily* gives credit to his assistant and friend, Philippe Guibourgé, for some of his most captivating designs. Guibourgé has designed two *colifichets* (French for knickknacks or fantasies) collections a year including sportswear, after-ski and at-home clothes, and some of his trifles, like the longer coat, have been trumpeted later in Bohan's couture collections. Bohan gives the House that Christian Dior built what it needs, a comprehensive collection containing a few explosives that will keep the name of Dior in the headlines and lots of adorable clothes that will make the salesbooks sizzle. A Bohan suit can start a romance; one of his ball dresses can break up a marriage.

A widower whose wife was killed in an automobile crash and father of a teen-age daughter, Marc Bohan understands women and never lets them down. "Women want something new, but they don't want a big change," he said in 1963. "I try to make changes in many things but not spectacular. People get bored with the sack one minute, the A-line the next. And then you know what happens? They wear sweaters and skirts and it's hard to get them back to wearing clothes."

Marc Bohan has worked hard for his place in the sun. A milliner's son, he began his apprenticeship in the haute couture in the mid-Forties in the houses of Robert Piguet, Edward Molyneux and Madeleine de Rauch. His attempt to open a house with Raphael failed for lack of capital. He was hired by Jean Patou, but his name was not put on the credit list. Bohan did a stint of free-lance designing in New

York, including a group of coats for Originala. In 1958 when he was 32, he signed on at Dior to design its clothes for the English market. He was dismissed in the summer of 1960, presumably after friction with Dior's successor, Yves Saint Laurent. By fall, Saint Laurent was in the army and Bohan was summoned back.

Marc Bohan was the quiet, steady fellow whom the management of the House of Dior called to replace the prodigy they no longer wanted. When Christian Dior died in the fall of 1957, Yves Mathieu Saint Laurent was hustled from the backrooms, where he had been a promising assistant, into the spotlight of the executive office. He was an immature, gangling 21-year-old with nearsighted blue eyes encircled by horn-rimmed glasses. His father is a prosperous insurance broker from Oran who left Algeria with his family after the country was granted its independence from France and resettled in Paris.

Yves Saint Laurent performed like an obediently precocious youth in 1958 when he came up with the Trapeze line that ensured the dominance of Dior. But his next collections, though fertile with ideas, did not please his masters and their clients. In 1960, he was drafted into the army, an obviously poor specimen for military service. He suffered a nervous breakdown, was discharged and sued the House of Dior for not reinstating him.

In 1962, Yves Saint Laurent opened his own house at 30 bis Rue Spontini in the elegant residential quarter of Passy in the 16th *arrondissement,* some distance from the congregation of couturiers in the 8th. Pierre Bergé became his business manager. Yvonne de Peyerimhoff, the short, blond and infinitely charming *directrice* of the House of Dior who had worked on Seventh Avenue 30 years before, agreed to run his salon. He attracted one American backer and then another.

Saint Laurent is one of the most engaging and prolific designers in Paris, but it is his personal misfortune never to have grown up. Now in his early 30's, he is a classic case of the aging wonderchild who longs for the youth he never had. Shy, nervous and capricious, he almost goes to pieces before producing a collection. He is strongly attached to Mr. Bergé; to his two younger sisters, who have married and made him a fond uncle; and to his youthful, pretty mother, who is credited with sparking his Mondrian look of 1965 when she gave him a book of reproductions of the Dutch artist's paintings.

Actually, the use of bold blocks of color had already been essayed on Seventh Avenue. *Glamour* hit the newsstands in America with a photograph of a kind of Mondrian treatment in dresses a few days before he presented his collection.

Saint Laurent explained the connection between his mother's present and his dresses, which were the sensation of that season. "One day I was in a discothèque, very happy, feeling good and there I got the whole inspiration. It wasn't Mondrian exactly, but the feeling. It was not in opening my book that I got the idea of copying Mondrian. I got the feeling of gaiety and I added a little something. The most important thing is not the details, it's the feeling. The Mondrian is a detail. The important thing is the feeling."

"The inspiration is in the atmosphere," said Saint Laurent in the fall of 1965 when he was brought to the United States on a whirlwind tour to launch his new fragrance, Y. He behaved delightfully during a general press conference in New York, to the surprise of his traveling companions, who never knew if he would lapse into speechlessness or call for more tranquilizers.

Like most visiting French couturiers, Saint Laurent was enthusiastic about the "gorgeous architecture" of the city. "When you look at that mass of buildings, it's something like the pyramids in Egypt or the statues in Rome," he said. And he didn't doubt that it would affect his designing, he added in half-English, half-French.

But, he went on, nothing could touch the atmosphere of Paris. "It's the main reason why France is so important today. The United States and Spain have good designers. The thing that seems to be lacking for them is the atmosphere. Maybe it's the old roofs, the little girls in the street, the artisans, the 10,000 people who make a little design for the buckle of a shoe. Paris," he concluded in a torrent of French, *"est comme une vieille grandmère qui a beaucoup de recettes dans son sac* [Paris is like an old grandmother who has many recipes in her pocketbook]."

Judging from his output of pea jackets, football helmets and pop-art dresses, Yves Saint Laurent profited from his American trip, but he didn't enjoy it very much. He wanted to meet Barbra Streisand and to go about unrecognized with people of his own age. Instead, he was trotted around like a trained seal for interviews, personal appearances and big parties tendered by the big guns of American fashion.

The older he gets, the more haunted he is by youth. His most successful designs are his youngest. Saint Laurent is the begetter of the gamine look that belongs to the cute kid with swinging hair. Every time he tried to turn on the spout of ladylike elegance, his commercial customers were disappointed. So he turned around and produced Lolita clothes, driving home his point by showing them on models with totally undeveloped bodies and the faces of sleepwalking children who are poor eaters.

And who flocked to his salon? Some not exactly decrepit types, like Leslie Caron, Princess Stanislas Radziwill (her sister, Jacqueline Kennedy, has ordered by mail a few times), Catherine Deneuve and Françoise Hardy, but also many of what the French call women of a certain age, like Margot Fonteyn, the ballet dancer; Jacqueline de Ribes, the banker's wife who epitomizes the old school of hard French elegance; the Duchess of Windsor; and a number of American million-airesses with starved figures, Dorian Gray faces and chunky diamonds flashing from their wrinkled hands.

Saint Laurent has one of the levelest business heads in Paris. Fore-seeing a day when the private clients will have deserted the haute cou-ture, Saint Laurent, who buys his own clothes ready-made in the Eng-lish and Ivy League-accented shops of Passy, opened a ready-to-wear boutique on the Left Bank in the fall of 1966. It was for young women, he said evasively, "from 15 to while still young in heart," and the prices were supposed to match.

They didn't. The cheapest little knit dress was $50; a vinyl raincoat with crocheted sleeves, just like one of his styles of two seasons past, was nearly $90. And, of course, they were snapped up by middle-aged Americans. The youngsters could content themselves with $6 chain belts for the hips or bright wool stockings at $4 a pair, the same prices they were fetching in New York, where working girl salaries are two and three times higher than in France. "We need fun," Saint Laurent had said. "Fun is more important than luxury." Like the goose that lays golden eggs, Saint Laurent has pretty expensive notions of fun.

Saint Laurent Rive Gauche, as the boutique is called, is housed in a former bakery shop at 21 Rue de Tournon near the French Senate and on the edge of the student quarter. It is orange from ceiling and lacquered walls to carpeting. A larger than life painting of the designer by the Spanish painter Eduardo Arroyo greets shoppers at the door.

The clothes are manufactured by C. Mendès, a firm owned by the family of the former Premier of France Pierre Mendès-France, that also makes ready-to-wear with the labels of Venet, Castillo and Carven. In the first collection, Saint Laurent was not embarrassed about issuing the same nailhead jersey dresses, black velvet pants suits and little shifts with pop-arty red lips above the bosom that he had in his couture collection two months before at ten times the price. He promised to lower prices as business increased. A few weeks later, another Yves Saint Laurent boutique opened in Marseilles. Still more were planned for other cities in France, Europe and America. The Left Bank boutique is a "pilot boutique" owned by the couture house. The branches are franchise arrangements on which the couturier makes no investment, but collects a percentage of wholesale volume.

Pierre Cardin, the other live wire of the Paris haute couture, was to follow Saint Laurent to the St.-Germain-des-Prés section of the Left Bank in 1967 with two boutiques, one for teenagers, the other for older youngsters. Cardin boutiques had already opened in London and Tokyo. When Cardin says inexpensive, he means it. In the London boutique, a green velvet-walled bower in Selfridge's department store, the dresses, coats and suits were in the $25 to $60 range. They were made by an English manufacturer who used Cardin toiles (the patterns made out of tailor's muslin).

In 1966, he rearranged his couture house at 118 Faubourg St. Honoré as a feminine fashion center with a made-to-order department and a slightly less expensive boutique department. Across the street, he opened a six-floor building for men's fashion.

For nearly a decade, Pierre Cardin had been the idea man of the Paris haute couture, shooting off inventive notions like fireworks on the 14th of July. But success eluded him until the mid-Sixties, when his shaped silhouette for men's clothes shook up that dormant industry. By then, the rest of the women's fashion designers had caught up with his avant-garde pace. His collections, which pioneered cutouts and neo-vulgarity, had formerly been labeled kooky, unwearable and gimmicky.

Pierre Cardin is the son of a well-to-do wine merchant from St.-Étienne, a bleak city in the coal-mining region of central France. "I don't like good wine, I like *vin ordinaire*," he once said. When he was 17 he slipped into unoccupied France and found work as a tailor. Later, he served as an administrator with the Red Cross. After the liberation of Paris, he joined the House of Paquin. The extravagant costumes he created for Jean Cocteau's film *Beauty and the Beast,* based on sketches by Christian Bérard, won him acclaim and an introduction to Christian Dior, who hired him. Cardin was a member of the team that produced the New Look. He spent three years with Dior before he struck out for himself, principally as a designer of costumes for the theater and films and for the fancy-dress balls that are so dear to fashionable Parisian hearts. In 1957, he presented his first haute couture collection.

The House of Cardin has always been smaller, less stuffy and formal than the other couture palaces. The *vendeuses* are young and agreeable, unlike the black-frocked nannies who stare the new customer into place in houses like Balenciaga and Givenchy. Cardin showings are more like comedy revues than papal processions. The models are not afraid to ham it up.

When Nicole Alphand, the most formidable charmer on the diplomatic circuit, joined his team in 1965, Cardin's became a powerhouse of the forward-looking haute couture.

"I am his right arm," explained Mme. Alphand, a golden girl in her late 40's who can wash and set her hair into a flip coiffure and who alternately sprays herself with Cardin's spicy scent for women Singulier and his robust fragrance for men Bleu Marine. "Now he has two right hands in different ways." The other is André Oliver, Cardin's long-time associate and friend, a clever designer who could have scored on his own. In public, Oliver plays the smily, curly-haired fop out of Molière to Cardin's haggard hero by Stendhal.

Pierre Cardin is a slightly built man of sallow complexion, gray-blue eyes sunken in lofty cheekbones and thinning brown hair that slips across a high forehead. He makes it a habit to drive himself until he collapses. "I'm 43," he told a woman seated next to him at lunch during his visit to New York in 1966. "I look more old and little if I have not this suit," he asserted, promoting the Edwardian silhouette he was wearing in brown herringbone with a pale green shirt and olive foulard necktie.

Jeanne Moreau, the French film star with the melancholy smile and well-publicized tendency of falling in love with her directors, has been the woman in bachelor Cardin's life. The personal relationships of Paris couturiers have never been easily translatable into American suburbanese, but it is apparent that Moreau and Cardin have exchanged affection and inspiration. He has dressed her in the bias-cut crepes with pastel fox borders that suit her image of a woman who cares more for passion than for fashion. Some of those styles keep cropping up in his most space-agey collections.

"I don't like women to look like men. I definitely don't like pants for women except in the country or for sport. They're not feminine," said Cardin, whose mannequins have small, round but honest-to-goodness bosoms. His favorite is Hiroko Matsumoto, an exquisite Japanese who prances around the salon arching her insteps like a circus pony. "Oriental women are very exciting," Cardin said, "but they are always covered up." He was getting around to his theory of showing more of men's bodies with his shaped suits and less of women's with his unfitted silhouette. He commented:

> My clothes for women are sexy but loose. It's stupid if you need to see everything that a woman is. You must use your imagination. If you see immediately, the charm is finished, you know. It's like a book. If you know everything immediately, it is not exciting.

Getting down to practicalities, though, Cardin said that the loose dress was mandatory as long as skirts are short. "Imagine with so short a skirt if you have a lot of breasts and waists, it's impossible. And the large woman looks more elegant in something loose."

Cardin has made no secret of his boredom with the outdated role of ladies' dressmaker. He would rather spout ideas, get them into the wardrobes of the masses and be paid for his efforts than have them publicly criticized and privately stolen by other designers, as was his sad fate for many years. Cardin has designed almost everything and for everybody from children and teenagers to women and men. He has had his ups and downs, but now his course seems set in the direction of a Paris-based Cardin empire. Through a number of franchise contracts with manufacturers in France and other countries, his styles are reproduced and sold at various price levels. Cardin receives royalties on the wholesale volume. He is not obliged to invest capital in the manufacture of his designs, but he retains the right to approve the distribution.

In 1966, Cardin resigned from the Chambre Syndicale de la Haute Couture, the trade association of the Paris couturiers which regulates the semi-annual showings with only slightly less red tape than a Soviet party congress. Originally, the rules forbidding publication of sketches or photographs of the styles until the models are delivered to the buyers a month later were reasonable safeguards against piracy that protected the commercial customer as well as the creative designer. But as the couturiers increasingly became imitators rather than innovators, and as most of the houses resorted to cute tricks for circumventing the rules, like immediately showing a few of their designs on television, the regulations were shown to be hypocritical nonsense. Cardin acknowledged this on a television broadcast a few weeks before the January 1967 showings:

> The couturier who has elected to dress millions of women instead of 5,000 privileged ones scattered across the globe needs to have his collection talked about in order to support the distribution of his ready-to-wear. And that, as quickly as possible. When he presents his haute couture models to the press, his ready-to-wear models are ready to appear in the street. They await the kick-off. The sooner the better.

Rather than cling stubbornly to the myth of the haute couture and risk drowning, Cardin prefers to swim with the tide.

In the phenomenon of the boutique, the Sixties saw the emergence of new hatcheries for fashion. The word means shop or studio as distinct from large store. In 1935, Elsa Schiaparelli had opened the first boutique as an adjunct to an haute couture salon on the Place Vendôme and filled it with madly elegant frivolities in clothes and accessories. Slowly, the other couturiers borrowed the notion of displaying their perfumes, costume jewelry and scarves in small departments on the main floor of their houses. As the prices of their made-to-order collections soared to discouraging heights, many of the couturiers expanded the variety of items in their boutiques to include a smattering of less expensive, ready-made clothes. The impetus for the couturiers' venture into ready-made fashion and menswear grew out of their boutiques. But the really significant styles and fads of the decade originated in the independent boutiques of Paris, London, New York, Rome and Dublin. Melbourne sprouted boutiques. So did Copenhagen and Lagos.

Eventually, boutique became a cliché that covered everything from the sublime to the salacious. But the essential meaning of boutique, however grand or depraved, is a place where a woman can find self-expression in wearing apparel. In the inexorable, world-wide drive toward mass anonymity, the boutique is an oasis of identity. By the boutique in which she shops, a woman describes her life style.

The first to apply the boutique concept to a large and dignified institution was Geraldine Stutz. In 1958, at the age of 33, the hazel-eyed brunette was handed the presidency of Henri Bendel by W. Maxey Jarman, the chairman of Genesco. He had acquired the 61-year-old New York specialty store with a glorious past as fashion caterer to the carriage trade at a time when it was reportedly suffering a financial hemorrhage.

Mr. Jarman, a corporate prestidigitator from Nashville, Tenn., who is not afraid to entrust big jobs to women, tried tinkering with the property himself for six months, then passed it to Miss Stutz with a long tether. She gave herself five years to succeed. Almost on the dot, she announced that the red ink had turned to black. Bendel's became the fashion bellwether of the Genesco empire.

Miss Stutz, a Phi Beta Kappa from Mundelein College, had been shoe editor of *Glamour* and then a vice president of the I. Miller retail shoe stores. She sensed "the beginning of the era of woman as an individual" in fashion and the need for a new kind of personal store.

She began by smashing the rules. First, she scared away the fat ladies. "We picked a customer to concentrate on," she said candidly. Mostly, she was a small woman who wore size 4 to 14 and gauzy underthings with A or B cups and bikini panties. "She's 20 to 60, depending on her point of view, but she's hip. And she is not going to grow old with me," said Miss Stutz.

In an action also calculated to frighten off mobs of impulse shoppers, she cut up the street floor into an arcade of tiny shops in which the browser usually found herself stranded in an oasis of formidable chic with a solicitous but not unfriendly saleswoman.

These shops were the first of the boutiques within a store, although Miss Stutz avoided the name. She prefers to call the shoe department The Bottier, the cosmetic department The Gilded Cage. She divided the upper floors as well into nooks named The Fancy and Cachet and The Jean Muir Shop. Miss Stutz transformed Bendel's into a mirror of her uncompromising fashion-editor taste. A daring retailer, she was one of the first to buy from the French yé-yés, the young British designers, as well as Americans like John Kloss and George Stavropoulos before the public and her competitors were educated to their ideas. The small orders she placed were gratefully received in return for her ability to generate yards of magazine and newspaper publicity and to attract a clientele that is seen in all of the right places. Geraldine Stutz created a superboutique for the woman who uses fashion to proclaim her definite, contemporary style. In so doing, she inspired a host of imitators.

The mid-Sixties saw the onset of the boutique mystique. From then on, most of the high and mighty fashion leaders wanted it known that their clothes came from the small shops with the low prices. It was the latest form of inverse snobbery in fashion that had started when Chanel took the humble jersey of the stableboy and made it more chic than satin and velvet for duchesses.

Shopping in boutiques was like altering the birthdate on a passport. It certified that a woman was a swinger. Press agents who had trained their clients to drop the names of the Paris haute couture or the Seventh Avenue galaxy had to re-educate them to murmur Biba (the London boutique, owned by Barbara Julanicki, where Brigitte Bardot, Julie Christie, Geraldine Chaplin and Françoise Hardy bought the $10 dresses and $25 coats by the half dozen) or Laura, the boutique that Sam and Sonia Rykiel had put on the fashion map of Paris despite its plebeian address, 104 Avenue Général Leclerc, near the penultimate stop on the Porte d'Orléans Métro line. Audrey Hepburn did a blitz-krieg at Laura after preliminary raids in the boutiques of St.-Tropez and the Rue de Sèvres. *Elle* and the rest of the fashion press treated her boutique conversion as gravely as if she had been filing for divorce from Mel Ferrer.

Suddenly, it wasn't only the middle-aged mothers who were following their daughters into the boutiques but even the lively grandmothers. The Duchess of Windsor bought an Emmanuelle Khanh coat at Dorothée Bis, the legendary Paris boutique where Petula Clark, the pop singer, found her silver kilt. Elie Jacobson, the proprietor of the shop, was less than ecstatic about the patronage of the older elegantes. "The bourgeoises, they are difficult customers. They need saleswomen and fitting rooms, the things that the young will skip if the clothes are cheap enough," said the father of the French boutique movement and godfather of the yé-yé designers whose clothes he was among the first to promote.

Dorothée Bis looks like a warehouse gussied up with red velveteen-covered walls and aluminum ceilings. The racks and the banisters for the catwalks inserted between the crowded rows of merchandise are made of aluminum pipe. The dressing rooms amount to slabs of full-length mirrors around which curtains can be whisked along an arc of pipe just big enough to accommodate one doll-sized customer. The phonograph music is loud, lively and constant.

"Rich women try to buy here but they want muslin fittings. I say to them, go to the couture," says Elie Jacobson. "I can't make alterations. All we can do here is sleeves and a hem and nothing is returnable. A girl in her teens comes here because she wants to be dressed by us. A woman of 40 or 45 comes, we ask $4 for alterations and she screams it's a scandal. Even though the pants only cost $10.

"At 45, 46, 48—it's hard to say this—but a woman's bosom isn't where it should be or her hips either. A woman that age needs an haute boutique."

Elie Jacobson, who aims to be the industrialist of modern French fashion, operates from an office as big as a double telephone booth on the second floor of his Rue de Sèvres shop, the only one in the Dorothée Bis network that he actually owns. The cell is choked with papers, boxes and samples of merchandise. Designers, manufacturers, seamstresses, peddlers, employees and his wife, 4-foot 9-inch Jacqueline of the jet hair and kohl-rimmed eyes, keep poking their heads through the door. Mr. Jacobson, who can gaze into his wife's eyes without stooping hardly at all, is a rotund man with curly brown hair and near-sighted eyes rimmed by round, steel-framed spectacles. He resembles a Talmudic scholar earning his keep in a vaudeville show. His attitude toward fashion, business and life is passionate, decisive, whirlwind and semi-comic.

"I was a wholesale furrier, making rabbit coats, very sporty and young," he recalled in the fall of 1966, as he sat on top of the hottest fad of the moment, coats of rabbit dyed in sparkling colors, plaids and stripes or with braid-like bindings. "And I wasn't selling them."

That was in 1959. To help make ends meet, his wife opened a little hole in the wall at 35 Rue de Sèvres, near the Sèvres-Babylone Métro stop on the Left Bank, on the sleepier fringe of the intellectual and artistic quarter, an easy stroll from the Sorbonne. They called it Dorothée because that was their favorite female appellation (although they named their three daughters Corinne, Laure Anne and Carole) and expected to do $10,000 business a year. Sales multiplied tenfold. Mrs. Jacobson called for help. Her husband, a third-generation furrier, jettisoned his sinking business and came running. In 1962, they opened Dorothée Bis for sportier, more casual clothes next door at No. 39.

By the end of 1966, the Left Bank was a mushroom patch of imitative boutiques and Dorothée Bis and its chain of six franchised shops grossed more than $1.5 million a year in sales. The proprietors of the boutiques, on the Rue Marbeuf across the Seine, in Lille, Marseilles, Perpignan, Brussels and Milan pay 8 per cent commission on their wholesale purchases of merchandise that Elie Jacobson has bought for them. Frantic inquiries were coming in from other prospective boutique owners on three continents. It was through mass purchasing that Elie Jacobson was able to launch the new wave of inexpensive, far-ahead fashions, such as the little-girl look, knee socks and peaked caps, cutout dresses, pants suits and crazy stockings. "I buy in quantities, maybe 1,000 of a good number," he said. "My wife and I see 5 collections a day, maybe 30,000 dresses a year. We pick 100 of these styles and perhaps 10 of these will be best-sellers.I put a coat in one fabric, but several colors, and only 5 sizes, from 8 to 16. I treated dresses like washing machines," said Jacobson the entrepreneur. "I lowered the prices and the big stores had to follow me.

"My wife and I are like this," he said, drawing an X on a piece of paper. "She's more dressy, I'm crazy about sportswear. But we buy together. By majority vote." Jacqueline Jacobson started designing knitwear when she couldn't find anything but classic twin sets. Her first sweaters, ribbed poor boys, were knitted by students. Then she inaugurated crocheted sweaters. By 1966, her dresses that looked like elongated homemade sweaters were a French fever. In 1967, Albert Alfus, a Seventh Avenue manufacturer, was reproducing them in Italy to sell for $50 to $80 in stores in the United States.

"I'll define modern fashion," Elie Jacobson offered. "The greatest success is the jean. Even the Rothschilds are wearing it. It's the outfit for the whole world. Now for me, the problem is to find a way of personalizing it. In the last few years, fashion has become more than what's on a model or a new style. It's the spirit of life, ideas, movement. People don't talk about construction anymore. The era of serious fashion is over. Today you can laugh at fashion. Or at least smile."

By the mid-Sixties, the boutique had become the panacea for the big business with tired blood. Every department store in America that thought shucking off a stick-in-the-mud image would boost sales clutched at the boutique formula. Set aside half an aisle or a whole department, call it a boutique, clutter it with irreverent merchandise, decorate it with lead pipes or mock Tiffany lamps, staff it with inexperienced salesgirls, play rock 'n' roll music and import a homosexual to run it. Chicatiques, Carnaby Street shops, Places Élégantes, whatever they were called, the intent was the same. The boutique is everybody's dish of tea.

Fashion is ready for a new incubator.

VIII

FROM THE CRADLE
TO THE BEST-DRESSED
LIST AND BACK

"Youth is a wonderful thing. What a crime to waste it on children."
—*George Bernard Shaw.*

"Adolescence . . . a social process, whose fundamental task is clear and stable self-identification. . . . Adolescence, as a developmental process, is becoming obsolete."
—*Edgar Z. Friedenberg,* The Vanishing Adolescent, *1959.*

"The principle of multiple determination operates here. Anything like the mini-skirt has many reasons for it."
—*Dr. Edwin Z. Levy, child psychiatrist,*
The Menninger Clinic, Topeka, Kansas.

IN the Sixties, the fashion industry has converted Shaw's epigram into action. Designers, their associates in hairdressing and cosmetics and most of the women who lead the erratic parade of fashion have arrogated the property of youth, and erased the boundaries between childhood and maturity. As recently as the Fifties, there were at least three groups—those who voted, teenagers (a repulsive mutation that Americans had developed through gross materialism, or so Europeans said) and children. In the Pop Decade, the United States is becoming one big, anxious play group. And teenagers have erupted all over the world, but particularly in England and France where they are referred to as buying power or *pouvoir d'achat.*

Fashion, a principal perpetrator of pop culture, exploits the young through an unholy alliance of merchandisers and misguided parents. But the victim is also a tyrant to the same degree that the manipulator is a puppet. The fashionable child is a prop and a consumer, a means of distraction for adults as well as of social and economic gain, an authority and a wanderer on a road without signposts.

Sixties fashion marched backwards from the college campus to the nursery. It started with blue jeans and babushkas, two fads that students had appropriated from the lower orders of society, proceeded to the Sunday-school girl's reefer and the Alice-in-Wonderland hairdo. In the spring of 1964, Norman Norell designed an Eton suit with a pleated skirt for mature women. He admitted that inspiration struck him as he passed a Madison Avenue shopwindow and saw a Merry Mites suit for boys who take sizes 3 to 6x. After that came skirts that exposed the knee and part of the thigh, flat-heeled shoes, and the ruffled dress snatched from the newly christened infant. Courrèges picked up its bonnet and added a Martian touch.

According to the laws of nature and reason, no adult female (unless she was gravely ill in body or mind) would be able to or want to fit into children's clothes. And so the fashion industry started brainwashing. It toppled the old idols, the sophisticated mannequins who looked as though they dined on bird seed but had lived a lot. The paragon of the Sixties became the nymphet, heretofore the playmate (imaginary or real) of old lechers and genius authors.

Lolita, the heroine of Vladimir Nabokov's novel of the preceding decade, was 12 years old and stood 4 feet 10 inches tall. Twiggy, the British model girl of late 1966, was 17 and 5 feet 6½ inches tall, but she weighed no more than 90 pounds and measured 31 inches in the bust, 22 in the waist and 32 in the hips. She even made childish sounds when pressed.

By early 1967, Twiggy was a valuable property. Her manager tied her into an opportunistic promotion of Twiggy-tagged merchandise and her asking price for her modeling services shot to $120 an hour. Significantly, she made simultaneous appearances in the pages of *Seventeen* and *Vogue*.

Vogue had been recruiting juvenile goddesses ever since the beginning of the Vreeland regime in 1962. Mrs. Exeter, the protagonist of the magazine's recurrent feature about a chic and charming grandmother, wasn't even accorded a decent obituary. She just vanished along with elegance to be replaced by chicerinos, youthquakers and breakaways like Chér, the feminine half of a pop singing team; Mia Farrow, the boyish-bobbed girl bride of Frank Sinatra, and Romina Power, the late Tyrone Power's daughter, whom *Vogue* exalted at 14.

The editors of *Vogue,* who almost always practice what they preach, grew younger, too. While the editors of *Mademoiselle,* which is edited for the "adult young woman" who has graduated from *Seventeen,* went on looking like campus post-postgraduates, the *Vogue* ladies of the same vintage and older regressed still further. They and their followers like Mrs. Charles Revson, the wife of the cosmetics manufacturer, paled their lips and let their hair grow down their backs. They put on shoes without heels and dresses without waistlines and bust darts. They also restyled their facial expressions, erasing any vestige of emotion, experience or thought. Some managed to speak in the girlish voice of Jacqueline Kennedy who was looking more and more like Caroline with her streaming locks and rising hemlines.

"We used to dress like Jackie Kennedy; now we're dressing like Caroline," Bess Meyerson, Miss America of 1945, told a fashion-show audience in August 1966.

Out there in the real world, to which fashion magazines and high-fashion designers seldom relate, there is some suspicion that Americans are turning into a race of giants, what with orange juice, vitamins, beef and strenuous exercise. Brassiere manufacturers assert that the classic average size is ascending from 34B to 34C and 36B and that demands for the D cup, formerly bought by lower-U matrons and inelegant cinema sexpots, are coming from younger women. Nevertheless, when Marc Bohan and the British film *Tom Jones* restored the bosom in 1963 after half a decade of exile, it turned out to be a 15-year-old bosom rather than the voluptuous one of yore.

High fashion thinks small. To be chic is to buy from the Smaller Than Small department at Henri Bendel. "I take an 8," strapping lasses tell saleswomen, who can hardly restrain their guffaws. As a result, many manufacturers have renumbered their sizes, although few will admit it. "My 10 is an American 8," said Jean Muir, the British designer who is a favorite of Bendel's, but her confession was made in London.

Being à la mode, then, poses a problem of reconciling opposites. *Vogue*'s solution is to accommodate the human to the merchandise. Sound philosophy in a consumer society, come to think of it. *Vogue* not only exhorts its readers to narrow their knees and shrink themselves into their skimp dresses with diet and exercise, including a champagne diet to satisfy alcoholic readers and advertisers of wine and spirits, but to do everything possible to remain young forever. It has publicized a schedule of hormones to be taken from the ages of 17 to 85; a Human Chorion Gonadotropin Injection Series, devised by a Roman doctor to supplement a 500-calorie diet; animal transplants given by the Niehans Clinic in Switzerland, and the removal of facial lines with electric needles and plastic surgery. There's no doubt where *Vogue* editors stand—shoulder to shoulder with Dorian Gray.

Of all the cuts that females have endured in the name of fashion, the youth kick is the cruelest. It magnifies flaws by exposing them. Suddenly, the most invulnerable woman, the fashion model, has been revealed to have not only feet of clay but bowed legs, pudgy knees, a touch of varicose, pigeon toes and curvature of the spine.

Jawlines slack over turtle necks, false eyelashes fail to adhere to receding eyelids and even with David Webb animal bracelets at the wrists, a woman's hands refuse to lie.

Maybe this punishment fits the crime. But think what it inflicts on the innocent. "I don't want to be 12 so soon again," protested a 20-year-old as she gazed at the models in brief skirts, calf-high socks and Mary Jane slippers in the January 1966 issue of *Glamour*. "The styles are made for teenagers and old women take them. I look at an old lady in white stockings and I think, 'Will I ever come to that?' " a 13-year-old eighth-grader in a New York public school for the intellectually gifted wondered in May 1966.

When mama essays the little-girl look, it follows that her little girl must resemble a wicked midget. In the spring of 1965, American moppets were uniformed in spare Courrèges tunics and coats. The next winter, little feet stamped in little white boots. In 1966, dotted vinyl jumpers and matching tights for toddlers, Pucci-type printed Caprilan shifts for size 7 girls, op-art stockings, epauletted pea jackets and military overcoats cascaded into the children's departments. As soon as floor-length hostess skirts and shifts struck the adult fashion scene back in 1963, children's designers mimicked the trend. "If the mother invites people for drinks at 7, the child can wear this to say hello in," a children's buyer explained about a $70 velveteen number. The next season, a buyer in another store admitted that she had taken what the trade calls a bath on her children's at-home collection. Foolish grandmothers and childless friends had bought them for Christmas gifts, which mothers had returned on January 2.

Nevertheless, two and a half years later, velvet culottes in Pucci-type prints (yes, Pucci again but this time in the 3 to 6x range) and a fur-trimmed lace robe were modeled in the children's fashion show put on in New York by The Fashion Group, an organization of women executives in the fashion industry. The commentator identified the robe as "grandma's *robe de soir,* a bauble for a rich child." Obviously she meant the same grandmother who orders mink coats for her grand-daughter and if the store demurs, as Bergdorf Goodman has, settles for a $350 vicuña coat. The commentator covered herself by citing statistics. According to *Variety,* the entertainment industry newspaper, "pre-schoolers have extended their television viewing." Ten thousand 2- to 5-year-olds preferred the news and weather on NBC at 11 P.M. Then some of them switched to the CBS movie, but 3,000 were catching *The Johnny Carson Show* until midnight.

The speaker was Jane Trahey, advertising whiz (she coined the slogan "It's not fake anything, it's Dynel") and humorist. She disclaimed expertise about children ("Since the only children I have been exposed to in the last few years have been the ones I make up for the Florence Eiseman advertising campaign, and the Rob Roy campaign, and the Danskin campaign . . .") but as a communications specialist and mass educator, Miss Trahey could speak with confidence.

She gave a rousing statement of the principles which have come to motivate much of the juvenile fashion industry. Unfortunately, her speech was not published outside the trade press.

"Today's child can talk to an adult (if he cares to) as an adult," she told her audience. "Why? Because he has been trained and house-broken by the best daddy in imitation alive today; the TV daddy. The child of today is completely audio-visual. And if there is a key to him at all, it's one big lovely key that I call the ECONO-KEY, for this is indeed the era of the AFFLUENT child, not the many-faceted child, But the MONEY-faceted child. . . .

"Today, two thousand million dollars—that's two billion bucks—are ladled out by parents, fond relatives and arriving houseguests, each and every year, to some forty million little darlings, for that hour or two of screaming 'Look what I got!' pleasure," said Miss Trahey, referring to what long, long ago was the sacred day of Christmas. "Now who gets this billion dollars each year? Well, 20 per cent of it goes to little old Barbie and her dynasty of friends. Eighteen per cent goes to the baby car industry for anything on wheels, 5 per cent goes to the shoot-em-up world, and 5 per cent for trains and 9 per cent for games. . . .

"Well, from what I gathered at the various committee meetings I attended, some of your market has too many preconceived notions about the children's ready-to-wear world. Some of you, I gathered, still live for the peaks and valleys. Back-to-School, Christmas, Easter. All worth living for, but doesn't it seem like you are being short-sighted and short-changing yourselves when the kids have dollars jingling in their pockets, and mamas have dollars tucked in their Gucci bags all year long? Some of you I heard don't respond to the quick reorder for the hot dress. Many of you have never felt the pull or tug of a good TV commercial, and it seems to me that someone in your world just ought to be able to tap this big TV market—even if it's only market by market. The toy people do, the kids food market does, and the encyclopedia world gets in there. How about you?

"It would seem an obvious place to get at the child who is at home in this visual world. By the time a child is two years old, he can distinguish, from the bottom of his playpen, three faces: mama, daddy, and Johnny Carson. He knows by age three which detergent is which detergent and with a little coaxing can imitate Mary Miles. . . ."

There were no children listening to Miss Trahey that afternoon in May 1966 except for the fashion show mannequins and it's rather a shame since her message was so clear and forthright. Children never hear their duty to consume explicitly defined any more than they are told that they are coordinated accessories to upwardly mobile parents. They just learn by osmosis which is probably the most effective and least painful way. The trouble is that they often receive conflicting signals. The two roles are not always compatible because the standards of commerce and society differ sometimes. And if the fashion industry seems confused, it's because not all merchants and fashion editors have Miss Trahey's single vision. Some of them are social aspirants and/or parents as well as mass merchandisers.

A designer named Rachel Lent has charged herself with giving a "new look" to little boys. "Such a staple, basic market," said Mrs. Lent critically when she journeyed from Birmingham, Mich., in 1964 with designs inspired by her 4-year-old son, Kevin. The Lents, including daddy Franklin, an art director with the Ford Motor Company, installed themselves at the Plaza Hotel and called up buyers and fashion editors. They came, looked at the clothes, which were to sell from $10 to $35 in sizes 3 to 6x, approved of Mrs. Lent's theories, placed orders and wrote feature stories.

"Everything has been Eton or terribly appliquéd, and no color," said Mrs. Lent, listing what was wrong with boys' clothes. "Little boys are all bones and beautiful little necks. They should have clean lines and nice colors, without looking like little girls, of course. I also love white on little boys." But don't little boys have an affinity for dirt? someone asked. "I change my son two times a day. I want him to have pride in himself," Mrs. Lent replied.

She took the Eton jacket and made it into a cutaway. "It's an 18th-century look," she said. She did away with collars and sleeve buttons. Short pants buttoned onto shirts instead of being held up with straps. "They're always falling and driving little boys crazy," she said. She also omitted the fly from the pants, seemingly unconcerned about what this would do to a newly toilet-trained size 3. Nevertheless, Rachel Lent struck a responsive chord in the fashion industry. Said *Women's Wear Daily* on September 19, 1966:

> RACHEL LENT ALWAYS DOES EVERYTHING RIGHT. Mrs. Lent's Holiday clothes for little boys are paragons of fashion rectitude and propriety. Her attention to just the right fashion details makes all the difference.
>
> LITTLE MR. RIGHT wears Mrs. Lent's blue worsted playsuit with white stitching trim and white pearl buttons. Mrs. Lent never heard of plastic buttons.

Two months later, *Women's Wear* reported again on Rachel Lent:

> RACHEL DOESN'T APPROVE of the way most parents dress their boys. "Mothers do everything for their little girls except buy them fur coats, and the boys walk into school in T-shirts and jeans. A child's appearance has an awful lot to do with his behavior. Put a girl in a pretty dress and she behaves like a lady. If you put a boy in something he really likes he will behave like a well-mannered child—and I don't mean like Little Lord Fauntleroy."

Until recently, little boys had been the last of the free souls. They were let alone between the time they graduated from diapers until they felt compelled to become teen-age pests. No one bothered about their fashion quotient. Then jealous mothers, whose friends were having such fun coordinating themselves to their daughters, started lobbying. Designers heard them. Now they and wishful writers like those who work for *Women's Wear Daily* refuse to believe that boys are made of snips and snails and puppy dog tails. As far as they and other progressive elements in the fashion industry are concerned, boys are coordinated sugar and spice. They can be coordinated to their mothers, sisters or their fathers. "Dressed like twin brothers, a father and a son," reads a caption in *L'Express,* the French weekly news magazine, beside a photograph of a three-foot pygmy with sideburns descending to the bottom of his earlobes, his hands jammed into the pockets of his tweed trousers. "We've already had the mother-daughter look. Thanks to the lightning progress of baby ready-to-wear, it's been extended to boys. Junior may, like papa, wear a crinkled cotton shirt, coordinated shetland pullover and trousers and buckskin jacket. Provided, alas, that papa can afford them. Striped crinkled cotton shirt, 39 francs. Shetland, open at the neck, 69 francs. Trousers, 59 francs. Buckskin jacket, 220 francs. O'Kennedy, 50 Champs-Élysées." Figure roughly 5 francs to the dollar.

Boy or girl, the child who performs his duty as an accessory to his mother and father must have a look, a carefully coordinated look. The ideal family has a total look consisting, for example, of a child tailored by Rowes of Bond Street, a father with the unmistakable seal of Huntsman of Savile Row and a mother stitched together by Mainbocher. Or a fillette in a Dorothée Bis Bis mini-knit with a *maman* in a Christiane Bailly jersey from Dorothée Bis and a *papa* with a suit from the *prêt-à-porter* department at Pierre Cardin. In the absence of suitable parents, the child may be coordinated to the family that his would like to be. Would anyone ask a 4-year-old with a blue Y on his sweater if his father really went to Yale?

Even if their parents are inept about style, the Sixties generation of kids has its own idols. Caroline and John F. Kennedy, Jr., are perennial leaders of the Best-Dressed Children's List, an unofficial register that has never been formally published because there is no need to. There are more than enough Kennedy cousins to fill the places. The three children of John Vliet Lindsay are their potential rivals. "We've got another little John," exulted a press photographer after Lindsay's election in 1965. He was referring to the mayor's son, then 5, the same age as John Kennedy. What with their skiing, horseback riding and private school attendance, the Lindsays are just the sort of children who enrapture socially conscious editors. Their parents, however, have an old-fashioned reluctance to use them as props, except in the dire need of a campaign.

The Kennedys, then, have to bear the brunt of the mass media's attention. *Women's Wear Daily* photographers have caught young John leaving the Colony Restaurant after lunch with his mother and snapped Caroline en route from her Fifth Avenue apartment to the Convent of the Sacred Heart. Unfazed by Caroline's uniform, *Women's Wear* managed to run up a trend in her monogrammed schoolbag.

"We are all people who like to identify," says Joseph Miller, president of the Miller Harness Company, an emporium for horse and rider that hasn't been hurt one bit by the Kennedys' patronage and by the widespread dissemination of photographs of Caroline and her mother in the saddle. "When you see those pictures, they look so nice. They look as though they were the chosen people. Naturally, mothers feel that whatever people like that want for their children, they want it too."

John Kennedy lacks his sister's enthusiasm for horses, but he shows every sign of being a regular guy, according to the Central Park playground benchwarmers who have observed him in chinos and turtle neck. Nevertheless, he is piling up negative points from his peers because of the sissy styles his mother foists upon him for state occasions when the photographers are on hand. He managed to come undone from the white silk shirt with ruffled front, blue satin cummerbund, white shorts and black patent slippers that he wore as a page in a Newport wedding. But the harm that just such outfits and his hairdo have done to other boys his age is incalculable. "Young John Kennedy, in his red shoes and the way his mother keeps him so impeccably dressed have had a lot of influence on children's fashion," said Bill Blass as he started designing for little boys.

John's haircut may have brought adverse criticism from around the country into the White House when he lived there, but since then it has become epidemic. The impact of his sister's blond hair drawn to the side with a barrette when she was his age was minor by comparison. Before John was born, the mophead coiffure was called the "English cut" or the "Prince Charles" and it was a struggle for a mother to refuse it for her son if she patronized chic children's barbershops like Michael's or Paul Molé's on Manhattan's Upper East Side. In those neighborhoods, England has always been the mother country and the crew cut the mark of the American peasant. When Prince Charles was a small boy, his hair was worn parted to one side with moderate bangs that left half the forehead bare, high sideburns and a clean-shaven neck. But then the heir to the British throne faded away to Gordonstoun, America gained its own royal family and little John Kennedy became the trend setter in young male fashion. Under his leadership, the coiffure thickened into a thatch with a pronounced bulge at the back. The bangs grew into the eyes. The "John-John cut," as it came to be known, was conferred even on boys who go to public or private progressive schools rather than traditional, English-accented institutions. They liked it, though, because it reminded them of the Beatles.

In 1966, Mrs. Kennedy directed the barbers at the Carlyle Hotel, where her son had his hair tended, to lengthen the sideburns and to shorten the bangs over the eyebrows so that at least the width of an adult finger was visible. In back, the hair was shaped to hang straight and long from the crown almost to the collar. These subtle changes, which were almost identical to tonsorial developments in such jet-set barbershops as Jerry's on Madison Avenue and Alexandre's men's salon in Paris, had their repercussions on the kiddie circuit. Sideburns descended to the tragus—the fleshy, cartilaginous protrusion at the front and mid-point of the ear—unless a mother was terribly stubborn or stylishly obtuse.

John Kennedy succeeded not only to the Prince of Wales' hairdo but to his childhood tailor as well. Rowes of Bond Street, "the custom tailor for boys and girls," which has been clothing the children of the British Royal Family for 100 years—it invented the sailor suit for Queen Victoria's offspring—has been sending its man, Kenneth Barnett, to the United States twice a year for 30 years. On these expeditions Mr. Barnett encamps at the Plaza Hotel in New York with brief forays to Boston and Philadelphia. In their younger days, Caroline and John wore the Rowes brother-sister, double-breasted French blue Harris tweed coats with the stitched velvet collars and the inverted back pleats and half belts. (At seven, a boy announces his departure from childhood by being measured for an open-necked style in a more solemn color.) The Kennedys own other styles from the Rowes wardrobe, which runs the gamut from duffle coats and kilts to Liberty lawn dresses with genuine smocking, Eton suits in navy serge or barathea with short pants (that American parents have given up trying to keep boys in past the age of seven), little Buster suits with velvet pants and silk tops and the black patent-leather shoes with large silver buckles that hark back to Oliver Cromwell.

But the Harris tweed coat with the stitched velvet collar is the one that the *cognoscenti* recognize in Royal photographs. It costs about $75, plus 25 per cent United States customs duty, a bargain, the faithful believe, because the large seams and four-inch hems give it an indefinite life span. Three years, Mr. Barnett says, but that does not include handing the coat down to a relative. The price also embraces the bespoke-tailor sales treatment, that trenchant mixture of understatement and overpoliteness that some Americans find so satisfying, even if it does make them ashamed of their accents and conscious that they talk too loudly.

The Rowes Harris tweed coat has been the backbone of the classic children's market for decades but in 1967 the British manufacturers who copy it for the popular-priced juvenile market were suddenly referring to it as the John-John coat. So were the American manufacturers and so was the French magazine *Elle,* which headlined a version of the coat and a shetland sweater and flannel shorts as THE JOHN-JOHN LOOK.

The Kennedy children's look is, unquestionably, a form of Anglophilic fashion with a touch of the *ancien régime* as practiced by the international set. It's a look of gentility and security, of knowing one's place right at the top in a world where children were not heard, but, when they were seen, they looked exquisite. It presupposes a British nanny up to the age of six or thereabouts when, as the avid Kennedy-watchers noted, one changes to a Swiss-French governess.

"People who are fortunate enough to have nannies would still like neat little shirts and that well-cared-for look," said the merchandise manager for the children's departments of Harrod's of London when she came to New York in the fall of 1964 to buy infants' stretchwear, blue jeans, T-shirts and those "lovely plaid boys' shirts." The average child, she asserted, "spends a lot of time out of doors." Miss Bell was putting her finger on the crux of the matter, something that middle-class women in many nations found out after they started taking care of their own children and doing their own housework. The old English look is predicated on someone else coping with the child on a steady basis, and trotting him out, immaculate and chic, for brief contact with adults.

Why are children toilet-trained later in New York than in Colombo, Ceylon? Because in New York there are diaper services and washing machines, as well as psychiatrists. Why did the number of children between 2 and 12 departing for foreign parts from airports in the New York area jump 120 per cent from 1956 to 1965? Partly because there was no one to leave them with at home when their parents wanted to travel.

The realities of childhood are stimulating the captains of the new French ready-to-wear industry to venture into the kiddie field. "The problem with children is that they should always be in sports clothes, but in France they are always dressing them up. That's going to change, I hope," said Elie Jacobson, who has added a children's section to his boutique. Even now, the chances are that the child in dungarees and sneakers leaning into the boat basin of the Tuileries is Parisian while the one in the sweet knitted short pants suit is a tourist from New York.

The basic philosophy of the old British school of children's fashion was sound inasmuch as it allowed a leisurely childhood. The silhouettes were honest about the shape of a child's body, the fabrics and colors soft and undistracting. American designers like Helen Lee adopted and modified it for mass consumption. Miss Lee once put it this way:

> I am saying, little girl, I think you are a real human being. I want to dress you with dignity. In other words, I want to give the child presence without gimmicks or gadgets. I think back to the time I was a child, and how I felt when I wore my pretty dresses. Designers should do this for adult fashions, too.

That was in 1964, the watershed of the pop Sixties, and Miss Lee, a grandmother, was already sounding quaint.

British mass manufacturers are updating the classics by translating them into machine-washable fabrics and livelier colors. Unfortunately, some of them feel obliged to inject something of Carnaby Street and the Kings Road and when they come up with blinding prints and hip-hugger belts for toddlers (don't they know that toddlers don't have hips?) the consequences are depressing. Restraint, one of the most admirable British characteristics, is, however, the enemy of forced obsolescence, as the English merchants who are trying to memorize their American mass merchandising lessons have caught onto.

American fashion editors are even more ambivalent and that's why the world of children as depicted in a fashion magazine is such a slick, sick fantasy. Trying to perpetuate the dying life style of the British aristocracy and attempting to whet consumer appetites under the pretense of disseminating news are irreconcilable objectives. The biggest advertisers in their publications are the producers of Kodel, Orlon, Fortrel and other fibers that go into mass-produced, mass-priced clothes by manufacturers whose taste often affronts the editors' refined sensibilities.

And so the fashion editor takes the $6 synthetic knit suit she despises and sticks it on a child model whose hair is brushed into his eyes, and whose sausagy thighs will protrude from the short pants. Heavy English knee socks and sturdy brogues provide the subliminal message. Depending on the publication that employs her, she may put him in a group photograph with a Eurasian boy (straight black hair completely obscuring his forehead), a Negro girl and a child of either sex who has the map of Lodz on its face. But all of them are English from the knees down with identical heavy cuffed socks and brogues. That's fashion's melting pot.

Fashion editors have a stubborn sense of mission about lifting the taste level of the masses that survives any amount of commercial compromise they are obliged to make. And so, in the same issue in which they "take care of the musts" (feature merchandise by big advertisers) they try to garner some space for the crusade.

The editorial pages that are the *quid pro quo* for the advertisements have captions that carefully enunciate the name of the manufacturer and the fiber that makes the fabric in the garment so attractive to nanny-less, laundress-less mothers, as well as the price of the garment, which is usually sensible, too. The advertiser is supposed to be kept happy by seeing his name in print and by the flood of orders that will result. Unless, of course, the readers are baffled by the presentation.

Take the December 1966 issue of *Harper's Bazaar,* which contains two pages of advertising in the front of the magazine for Kate Greenaway dresses in Kodel and cotton, and Dacron and cotton fabric. Toward the back of the magazine are four pages of photographs of Kate Greenaway dresses in Dacron and cotton, size 7 to 12 (usually worn by girls from 6 to 10 years old). The model is a ballet dancer of indeterminate age and melancholy mien. She stands barefoot amid deep grass and leafy trees, clad in a simple lace-banded shift that would have ended in a proper length for a child, halfway up the thigh, were it not for a lace ruffle under the hemline. The caption reads:

> Lace-trimmed pantalets peeping from under the refreshing simplicity of a pale chocolate brown shift with encirclings of lace— a perfect treat to wear on a visit to the Palace of Sweetmeats in the Forest of Christmas. The pantalets, our concoction. Dress by Kate Greenaway, in Dacron and cotton. About $11. At Bonwit Teller; Wanamaker's, Philadelphia; Frost Brothers, San Antonio. . . .

Translation: The pantalets are not for sale because the manufacturer didn't make them, but the fashion editor believes in them. Could it be because Pierre Cardin and Jacques Tiffeau were making them for mini-skirted adults?

So much for expediency. Now onward to the articles of faith.

In the same issue are four pages of color photographs, entitled "Rhymes in an English Nursery," depicting what might as well be dear Queen Victoria's children making merry while mama confers with Disraeli in another part of the palace:

> TWINKLE, TWINKLE, LITTLE STAR? HOW I WONDER WHAT YOU ARE! Peeping out between the curtains of the night nursery, Edwina Hicks questions the Little Star while Master Ashley rides carelessly by on an antique toy-horse tricycle. Edwina wears a turquoise poplin pinafore tucked over a bright green poplin dress. Master Ashley companions her in a poplin shirt, a jerkin, knee breeches of corduroy. The children are the son and daughter of Mr. David Hicks and Lady Pamela Hicks. Mr. Hicks is the prominent interior decorator; Lady Pamela, the daughter of Lord Louis Mountbatten and a cousin of the Queen. Their home, decorated by Mr. Hicks, is the brick, early Georgian, Britwell Salome, in Oxford.

> LITTLE POLLY FLINDERS? SAT AMONG THE CINDERS. Nestled in her nursery fireplace at Hampstead, 4-year-old Lady Cosina Vane Tempest-Stewart, daughter of the Marquis and Marchioness of Londonderry. Locks tucked in a mob cap, Lady Cosina wears pink corduroy. The fashions on these pages were designed by Jinnie Spencer for Mary-Louise of London.

No, the sun never sets on the British Empire, as far as the American fashion industry knows. While Debrett's peeresses are in the editorial offices, the Mods are in the counting house. Many American children's manufacturers went to Carnaby Street in 1965 and 1966. They seized the flowered shirt, low-slung pants and Dutch caps, and reproduced them in sizes 2 and up, advertised them and unloaded them on the same customers to whom they sold bow ties, racetrack tout jackets and Tyrolean hats the years before.

Another group of manufacturers, more nostalgic perhaps, tries annually to fob off on the same audience Norfolk jackets and knickers, tweed shooting suits and cricket-match suits just like that which the Duke of Windsor sported when he was Prince of Wales. Epauletted navy blazers just like those the male couples wear to the movies on Third Avenue were the latest version.

The fashion editors deplore their greed and insensibility and when no one is looking, they uphold the old order. Manufacturers advertise to parents who live in places like Minneapolis and Queens, a crowded borough of New York that fashion editors never see except when en route to the airport or to their week-end bungalows on Long Island, just a few miles away from the villas of Southampton. Fashion editors address themselves to parents like themselves. That leaves a great many parents out in the cold.

Fashion editors and, for that matter, most of the senior editors of the mass media live in Manhattan and, if they have children, send them to private schools, preferably the kind that almost never admits dress manufacturers' children. These are the schools that stress superficial manners and upper-class diction and an academic program that used to lead straight to the Big Three and the Seven Sisters via Hotchkiss and Miss Porter's School. Now, of course, some of the most distinguished families are sending their sons and daughters to be educated in Florida and the Midwest.

In the private grammar schools, however, the fashion editors' children can still hobnob with the right sort. Little boys with long hair and short pants, and little girls with long hair and navy, gray or green uniforms. And their parents can get a foot up on the social ladder by working on the committee for the school benefit which is usually a rather chic supper dance or theater party. If the boy attends St. David's or the girl the Convent of the Sacred Heart, there's always the hope (slim, but enough of a hope to sell tickets) that Jacqueline Kennedy will come to the party.

The children learn very early about status by association when their classmates invite them to go trick-or-treating down Park Avenue in a chauffeur-driven car or to come to private movie screenings on their birthdays. The children see the significant looks that their mothers and fathers exchange when they read the invitations and say to each other, "Do you know whose child that is?" When the mothers R.S.V.P., they may be disappointed to find themselves talking to a governess or an answering service, but sometimes when they drop off their children at the party they catch a glimpse of a very important parent.

And they know what children wear in Fifth Avenue apartments and East Side town houses where the servants' uniforms are coordinated to the color of the walls and the children are served individual jelly omelets and shaped sandwiches from a caterer and slices of $25 birthday cakes. They are entertained by professional puppeteers, clowns and magicians, and when the parties are over, the guests ask their mothers, "Why can't I have a clown at my party?" And as the years go by, they ask, "Why can't we go skiing at St. Moritz for the spring vacation?" and "Why can't we spend the summer in Europe?"

Fashion editors usually can't afford it, that's why, but they can arrange to have a daughter's hair cut at Kenneth's or Vidal Sassoon so that she can attend a teen-age charity dance like the Goddard Gaieties. That's one of those events for 13- and 14-year-olds who live on the East Side of Manhattan and go to private schools. Proceeds benefit a community center on the West Side.

Yes, it's a rarefied atmosphere for children that fashion editors are tuned into and that they try to convey to their readers. The conviction that prevails in the offices of fashion magazines and increasingly in the offices of mass-circulation magazines and newspapers is that Americans are upwardly mobile people and that they want and need all the assistance possible so that they will know how to behave when they get where they are going. And a well-dressed child shall lead them.

While the fashion editorialists promote the standards of taste and conspicuous pleasure of the Old Guard, the crassly commercial elements cut out the folderol and use saturation bombing. The tactics are not new. It's just that the targets are getting younger. As a brassiere manufacturer who specializes in the 10- to 15-year-old market told

Women's Wear Daily in July 1966, "Considering the fact girls reach maturity a year earlier every 10 years—we expect this range to broaden substantially. More 9- and 10-year-olds wear a bra today, whether they need it or not."

It all adds up to money and the kids get the idea. The people whom grown-ups look up to these days are not only rich but luxuriously packaged. Youngsters' idols, from Bobby Kennedy to the Beatles and their proliferating imitators, are well endowed with coin of the realm and call attention to themselves with distinctive clothes and hair styles. Money is power, children learn by observing adults and putting what they learn to practice. "Parents wangle pretty well," said a ninth-grader, coolly stating her generation's success in extracting money from their elders. And if they don't succeed, the kids go out and earn it themselves.

American teenagers have long been accustomed to being regarded as a financial statistic. In 1965, they spent $3.6 billion on clothes, $1.5 billion on entertainment, $570 million on toiletries. And for a dozen years before that, market researchers were polling them on the preferences that account for those figures. But teenagers as a recognized power elite did not exist outside the United States before this decade. They made up for their tardy arrival with a vengeance. It took the British teenager, as manifested in the Mods and their pop entertainers, to formulate the new equation. Money plus appearance equals power. Thanks to them, adolescents the world over have been able to infuriate their elders and then bring them to heel, with outrageous clothes and the length of their hair.

> We wanna be different and clothes are one way to differentiate. We want to stand out in the crowd, we want to show the world we don't like the way it is, all the time. We want a change. Mini-skirts give you this young, free feeling that makes you proud to be a teen.

Thus spake a 15-year-old participant in a panel discussion on "The Mod Look—Its Effect on Teenagers" at a meeting of the Catholic Youth Organization's New York Archdiocesan Teen-Age Federation held at the New York Hilton Hotel in November 1966. A male panelist of the same age added, "Long hair makes the boy stand out. Striped pants make the boy look taller."

The technique to which he alluded had been refined five years before in Britain by the Mods, the modern youth of the Sixties. Fastidious, cheerful peacocks, the Mods had replaced the Rockers, the sullen rebels of the Fifties for whom John Osborne had spoken with *Look Back in Anger*. The Rockers were the leather-jacketed motorcyclists, the British counterparts of the romantic ritualistic gangs of *West Side Story*. The Mods were polite and temperate. They poured as much as two-thirds of their earnings into splendid clothing, of a style distilled from American cowboys, French musketeers, English Edwardians and whatever struck their fancies at a sudden moment. Mod boys and girls sometimes matched each other's flaring trousers and flowing hair. At other times, they switched the old symbols of the sexes, the girls razoring their hair close to the skull. One day they dressed as Victorian grannies, another day as space-age maidens flaunting 10 inches of tempting thighs.

The Mods were just as contemptuous of adults as the Rockers but with their clothing and their hair they succeeded, where the Rockers failed, in getting the better of them. At home and abroad, the immediate repercussions were felt in the school and the home, centering on the girls' fractional skirts or enveloping pants and, most heated of all, on the boys' hair.

"The hair is the most important thing," explained a student in a New York public junior high school where the extroverts asserted themselves with anti-Vietnam war buttons and boots. "Long hair looks much more attractive to youth. It's a symbol. Even if you have to wear a suit and tie, you'd still be all right, but if your hair's cut short, the boots and buttons don't mean anything."

Dr. Edwin Z. Levy, a father of three as well as a psychiatrist specializing in adolescent problems at the Menninger Clinic, comments:

> Fashion comes late to Topeka. The fads are extreme in Kansas City and by the time they reach Topeka, there's something new in New York. But boys' hair got here faster than anything. The schools here, as elsewhere, are reacting strongly, as if hair were more important than what is inside the head. Hair now occupies the same position as smoking. They are both symbols. How families go round on smoking or hair is indicative of the whole relationship between the parents and the kids. Hair is tied in with rebellion. One kid, when his parents are after him, comes home with a shaved head. Another lets it grow.

The kids maintain that hair has nothing to do with sex. The heroes of the Middle Ages all had long hair and for centuries a beautiful mane was a symbol of masculinity. Many adults say long hair makes boys look like girls. But, in a way, I think that's too simple-minded.

The hair—like the bare feet, the cut-off sweatshirts and all of the fashion that makes it difficult to tell a boy and a girl apart—serves two functions. To enhance and also to disguise. Extreme hair and clothing put a gap between the kids and the rest of the world, and bring the kids closer together. Partly, it's a tremendous spoof. There's a natural tendency for people to bug other people. Kids against grownups most of all.

But the kids do it with such frightening aplomb. Born into the era of mass communications, raised on pop culture, they speak its language—an international tongue—more fluently than any adult. The manipulated astound their manipulators. Listen to Odette Papier, 17, a fourth-year student in a private girls' school in The Hague. The Dutch candidate for International Teen Princess of 1966, a competition sponsored by women's magazines in 15 countries, she has just arrived in New York on her first flight across the Atlantic. Her chestnut hair is cut to shoulder length with a fringe over the forehead, her brown eyes skillfully ringed with eyeliner. The hem of her dress ends two inches above her knees. On the plane, she wore a pants suit and changed when she reached her hotel. She wishes her school permitted the girls to wear pants. She has all kinds in her closet, bell bottoms, low-slung hipsters.

She speaks English easily, pronouncing "total look" without a trace of accent. She believes in it. She likes to shake at the Beat Clubs (beat like the Beatles, she explains patiently, and they don't do the twist anymore) where she drinks Coke or Seven-Up. Yes, she has seen *Hullaballoo, Shindig* and *Hollywood A Go-Go* on television. Yes, Dutch television. Her favorite performers? Sammy Davis, Barbra Streisand, Charles Aznavour, Frank Sinatra, the Beatles of course, Ella Fitzgerald.

London is the fashion center of the world now, not Paris anymore. The United States? "I like jeans, of course, Wranglers, Levi's. I have them in white, black and blue. My sister, Yvette, is 12 going on 13. She wears very short skirts, bobby socks and Courrèges boots. The boots are finished now, of course."

To win the Dutch portion of the contest, she had to answer many questions about fashion and entertainers and also write in 100 words what she would say if she could make a speech before the United Nations. She answered that she would propose the end of racial discrimination and the outlawing of the atom except for peaceful purposes. She takes a pair of giant, square-framed sunglasses out of her Chanel pocketbook and sticks them on top of her head. And off she goes to Chicago to be pitted against the other finalists in the contest, which is also sponsored by the Hilton Hotels, Kiwanis and Sears Roebuck. For the winner, a trip around the world seeing the sights and plugging the sponsors.

There are oodles of such prizes for the fashion-conscious teenager. A two-week expense-paid trip to Paris in a contest sponsored by Neiman-Marcus and *Elle* magazine for the girl who writes the best answer to what young fashion means in her life. An overnight stay in Nassau for the members of the teen fashion board of the Richards department store of Miami.

An advertising campaign pitched to teenagers too young to drive ties in a Pontiac car and a Thom McAn shoe "with bucket seat heel pads." Two million entry blanks for prize cars are filled out. Car sales jump. Shoe sales leap. Explanation: Teenagers brought their parents to display rooms to see the car.

"We're constantly trying to figure out what we can do to make teenagers predisposed to our brands before they actually come into the market," says the research director for a major advertising agency. One product promotion expert supplies high school home-economics teachers with teaching aids that carry a built-in plug for a client who manufactures men's shirts. "When these girls grow up, they'll be buying 65 to 75 per cent of the men's shirts sold," she said.

Nothing is too good for kids. "Mother and I go shopping together. If she doesn't like something I do, chances are I'll get it," says a ninth-grader in a private school in New York where clothing allowances run as high as $40 a month. One girl is endowed with $500 a season.

Paris-Match, the French weekly, investigates youth (17 million or a third of the French population are under 20), "a formidable buying power." The owner of a boutique across the street from an elite high school in the fashionable Passy section of Paris puts a jacket, hand-painted in screaming colors, in the window to attract attention. It costs $70. A boy buys it. The proprietor is not surprised. His clientele is the *jeunesse dorée,* the gilded youth of Paris. Their clothing budgets average $600 a year. They shop without their parents, half of them equipped with blank checks signed by their fathers.

"Surprising fact: the gilded youth is not the only one to waste its money," the magazine notes. A sociologist reports on a working-class suburb. The poorer the family, the more likely the kids are to keep all of their wages for pocket money. The poorest homes are the ones with the best stocked record collections, the best turned out sons who change their outfits every two months and keep up with the latest styles.

If the parents are permissive, reluctant to deny their children anything, one can hardly expect the merchants to hold back.

Two out of five American teenagers have charge accounts. As set up by a department store in Arkansas, the teen-age charge-account plan requires a parent's signature, credit of $60 a month, 12 months to pay.

Stores woo youth with the music it loves. The Dayton Company in Minneapolis mounts a Super Youthquake for 3,500 teenagers, a spectacular featuring folk rockers like Simon & Garfunkel and, of course, fashion designers like Luba of Elite Juniors, who puts on the standard youthquaking fashion show consisting of models who jerk, frug and gyrate down the runway and strip down to a bit of a dance dress. This is fashion? This is retailing? It's show biz.

Bergdorf Goodman pipes rock 'n' roll into its spotlit, pipe-racked Bigi department for girls from 12 to 17. On Saturdays, teen-age packs swarm into the paneled elevators, jostling the Rolls-Royce trade. Henceforth, management reserves a special elevator for the kids and hires young, inexperienced salesgirls from 16 to 29 to communicate with them. What's happened to Bergdorf's, the old customers demand? Why, Bergdorf's is keeping young friends loyal, between the time they outgrow the sane and charming children's department and the day someone offers them an Emeric Partos sable coat. In its first year, Bigi did a million dollars' worth of business.

Department stores employ full-time youth coordinators to keep teen-age girls up to their false eyelashes (over 13 per cent of teen girls own a pair, according to one survey) in fashion advisory boards, fashion shows, bowling clinics, good grooming and make-up courses and charity work.

Some stores extended the idea to teen boys just as a spate of male teen-age fashion magazines erupted. "We want to talk to teen-age boys on their own level about their own activities," said Bernard J. Miller, publisher of *Scene,* a teen-age quarterly offshoot of *Esquire.* The first issue contained articles on sports, grooming, clothes and music, backed up by advertisements of clothes, musical instruments, records and eczema preparations.

Addressed to boys 13 to 18 years old, *Scene* was intended to do for teen-age boys and advertisers of teen male products what *Seventeen* has accomplished for the female of the species. Consistently shattering its own advertising records, *Seventeen* (median age of readers is 16 years, 7 months) has pioneered the girl teen fashion market, creating demand and finding manufacturers to fill it.

"We help teen-age girls to spend money happily and wisely," said Kay Corinth, *Seventeen*'s merchandising director, who was instrumental in organizing 500 teen boards in department stores. She crisscrosses the country talking to teenagers. "They look cuter out of New York," she said. "They love new things. Kids won't buy markdowns." And they're right up to the minute on the trends, even if they can't pronounce them. "On the West Coast, Mod was Maud and Courrèges was Courage, but they knew about them," Miss Corinth reported.

Thousands turn out for the fashion shows in stores where she has arranged promotions. Like *Seventeen*'s London Look of March 1965, which capitalized on the British fever the magazine had induced during the past four years. The London Look sold 100,000 pieces of merchandise in stores throughout the United States.

A promotion is a sleight of hand by which a magazine persuades one or more manufacturers to produce merchandise geared to a theme, when and where to advertise it (the magazine, of course) and acts as a marriage broker between them and the stores (usually one in a city) that will carry the merchandise. The marriage is a multiple affair, in these days of high advertising rates, and the participants may include, besides the manufacturer, a fiber manufacturer, an airline that picked up the transportation tab and a foreign national tourist bureau.

In June, in connection with its bulging August back-to-school issue, *Seventeen* mounts an extravaganza in the grand ballroom of the Waldorf-Astoria for 1,750 merchants, who pay $15 apiece to be educated to fall fashion trends and incidental intelligence that will enable them to understand the 12,417,000 teen-age girls between 13 and 19, who constitute 12 per cent of the total female population of America, and have $7.1 billion a year of their own. (These are *Seventeen*'s 1966 figures and although they differ from other pitchmen's figures, as figures always do, they agree that teenagers come in millions and spend billions.) The show, billed as a service to advertisers, costs about $50,000 to put on, what with 34 mannequins and 120 behind-the-scenes helpers whipped into shape by Broadway producers. Besides the fashions, the attentive retailers are entertained by several rock 'n' roll groups, dancers and other teen-age heart throbs.

Girls just into their teens are the nation's most avant-garde fashion cultists. The shortest skirts, the most impudent pants suits, the most bizarre jewelry, the most literal acceptance of whatever the current fad is are displayed by girls from 13 to 15. After 16, the symptoms of collegiate conservatism appear.

"When you're older (17 and 18), you want to dress more conservatively," explained a 14-year-old in the ninth grade at the Fieldston School, "because by then you've been as sophisticated as you want at 14, 15 and 16 and you realize how ridiculous it is. And besides, you'll be going to college where everybody is the same and you don't want to give them the wrong impression about yourself." A classmate interjected, "This year the seventh grade is much farther out than we were."

The reason that the fashion industry's bombardment falls on more receptive ground at tenderer ages is plausible to a psychiatrist. "If you take the man-woman pair as one of the aims of life, there is a great deal of tension in early adolescence because the girl is incomplete in terms of this pair," Dr. Levy says. "As she gets older, she's had some pairing and the possibility she'll get left, or that something is wrong with her, is less of a fear. As she experiences more boy-girl relationships, she has an opportunity to become more satisfied with herself as she is."

But even boy-girl relationships are developing earlier. "Status has to do with sex," explained a 13-year-old eighth-grader in an upper-middle-class Chicago suburb where it's almost impossible for one girl to have more Villager coordinated outfits than the next. The best cliques consist of all the people who neck at parties, said this miss, who had already been to the Near East, the Far East and Europe, and dined at 21 and the Four Seasons in New York by her tenth birthday.

Everything is occurring sooner. The race to Harvard starts in nursery school. So it follows, as the release from the Boys Apparel Buyers Association says, that boys of 7 have a say in what they wear.

If the pre-schooler has been readied for reading by the television set, can climb into Santa's lap and ask for the Cheerful Tearful, the Suzie Homemaker kitchen equipment, the new Barbie doll who is 15 and carries her own eyelash brush, and a Batmobile for her brother, why shouldn't she be retrained to ask for a Rudi Gernreich-Alyssa dress or a coat by F. W. Fischer, the Ben Zuckerman of Lilliput?

Why not? From the cradle to the Best-Dressed List and back is just a vicious cycle.

In spite of all the sophistication, communication and education, no matter how world-wise kids seem, we tend to forget their innocence. We forget how long they remain innocent. Though they may be knowledgeable in one area, they still may be bewilderingly naïve in another. Lots of parents assume kids are not naïve.—Dr. Edwin Z. Levy.

IX

BEAUTY MARKS

I N the Pop Decade, the man who came to dinner was the hairdresser. When dinner was over, he stayed for the dancing.

In June of 1966, *The New York Times* published a photograph of Mrs. John R. Drexel III, an Anglo-American aristocrat who is positive that one of her ancestors was at the Battle of Agincourt, frugging with a Manhattan hair stylist in Newport, R.I. A comparative unknown in the coiffing hierarchy who was identified only as Mario, he had been invited to the stateliest of American summer resorts to minister to the tresses of one of Mrs. Drexel's friends.

Three months before, Kenneth Battelle, the nation's No. 1 coiffeur, was spotted by the same newspaper's chief society scribe being warmly greeted at the 25th anniversary celebration of the National Gallery in Washington, D.C., by Mrs. Paul Mellon, daughter-in-law of the founder. The following summer, *Women's Wear Daily* reported the presence of Mr. Battelle on a superselect list of movers and shakers attending a party that Mrs. Mellon gave on Cape Cod in honor of Jacqueline Kennedy's birthday.

Vidal Sassoon, a crimper (hairdresser in the argot of London's East End slums), became a peer of the English pop meritocracy of artists, writers and dress designers. Alexandre of the golden shears moved with *le tout Paris,* the French branch of jet society.

The hairdresser has always been a combination servant-confidant-

psychotherapist not unlike the nurse to Juliet Capulet. His social elevation in the Sixties merely reflects the fact that he has become the most
important man in a fashionable woman's life.

In the era of disappearing clothes, a woman must claim attention,
more than ever before, with her face and hair. "I defy a woman to
wear a Courrèges without a really great make-up and hairdo," said
Kenneth.

No major change of silhouette occurred in the first six years of the
decade. Crazy legs, assertive hair and the painted face compensated
for insignificant garments. Fashion happened below the hips and above
the shoulder.

A new and respected professional, the make-up man emerged from
the movie studio and the backstage dressing room to gild the partygoing housewife who could afford his services. The most skilled
amateurs were girls just over the threshold of the teens who mastered
eyeliners before logarithms. Their mothers and grandmothers, even
their maiden great-aunts, felt compelled toward adult education. A
$15 make-up lesson, at least, seemed necessary in order to present a
contemporary façade in professional and social competition.

To dye or not to dye was no longer a question deliberated in the
secrecy of the beauty salon booth. For one thing, hairdressers had
taken down the partitions. For another, home coloring preparations
were as foolproof as ready-mixes for cakes and rolls. If appetite, emotion and the aging process could be regulated by pills and injections,
where was the rationale for letting nature have the last word on hair?

It seemed quite fitting in August 1966 that the televised account of
the wedding of Luci Johnson, the flip-coiffured, White House teenager, was sponsored by Clairol, a leading hair-dye producer. Luci's
older sister, Lynda Bird, did not suffer the fate of the unmarried sister
with a bookish reputation for long. George Masters, the Hollywood
hair stylist whose income was reported to be nudging the $100,000-
a-year mark, transformed her into a swinging glamour girl. His tricks,
as confided in an article in the *Ladies Home Journal,* included arching
her eyebrows and giving her a fuller hairdo.

The Sixties may well go down as the age of mass narcissism.
Women (and, increasingly, men and children, too) became preoccupied with their appearances and addicted to the products and
services for the embellishment of face, hair and body. Into the spotlight of fashion stepped a new group of stars, no lesser celebrities of

pop culture than the designers of dresses and the women who exhibited them. They were the hairdressers of the three main fashion centers.

Hair styling challenged the suzerainty of fashion design. For the first time, women worried more about their hair, spent more time and money on tresses than on their clothing. A working girl who earned $75 a week might well allot $8 of her salary to a session at a hairdresser.

The milliner, that age-old rival of the hairdresser, was finally driven to the mat. "I don't like hats," said Brigitte Bardot. "I prefer my hair. It is part of my personality, undisciplined like me." Her rumpled tresses, doll-blond with the brown roots visible on occasion, were the result of a lot of work, her hairdresser once disclosed. "You can't imagine," sighed Jean-Pierre Berroyer. The secret was very little water, dry shampoos every two days, lots of brushing, the least teasing possible and shearing "one centimeter every two weeks."

Many women less flamboyant than B.B. also decided that they would rather express themselves through their hair and most such coiffures defied the wearing of a hat. The most astute millinery designers, like Halston Frowick of Bergdorf Goodman and Adolfo Sardiñas, did not fight reality. They designed point d'esprit pompoms, feathery headdresses, pigtails that looked like anything from show hunters' tails to strings of onion and garlic, masks, goggles, hoods and sun visors. They legitimized the babushka and thought of a dozen scarf tricks. By the furthest stretch of the imagination were their concoctions hats, although the price tags read as though they were.

Much of the money that once might have been allotted to hats was diverted to wigs, switches, falls and endless varieties of false hairpieces. In 1958, Hubert de Givenchy figured out that his starkly simple sack dress called for an uncomplicated but substantial hairdo. Carita created bouffant wigs for his mannequins. Once the dread secret of the bald, or the custom of extreme Orthodox Jewish matrons, the wig became a fashion and an industry. According to one estimate, 30 million hairpieces were sold in the United States in 1966. The best were made of hair shorn from Italian village women. They cost from $300 to $500, were given tender, loving care by the owner's hair stylist and saved the day when she traveled or impetuously took a swim.

The less expensive wigs were made of Oriental hair or synthetics.

Red Chinese hair was embargoed by the United States, of course, and when federal agents suspected that Communist locks were being mixed with European shipments, the hairdressers and the wig merchants feared the worst.

The new rank of the hairdresser was indicated by the opulent décor of his salon. Elegant decorators were retained to make these beauty parlors look like anything else. In 1961, the Revlon salon opened on Fifth Avenue with an atmosphere alleged to be that of a Pompeian palace. Michel Kazan held court in 18th-century France.

In 1965, the mood turned expensively casual. Geraldine Stutz installed a hairdressing salon in Henri Bendel done up in "glowy" peach and green with trellises and wicker furniture and flower-printed wallpaper. When David Crespin, "the underground swinging hairdresser" whom she asked to run the salon, departed a year later to open his own, he hit upon the yellow print and rustic furniture suggestive of a sunny country house.

The expense of establishing and maintaining these luxurious premises were usually borne by the hairdresser's backers. Either a group of grateful clients who were related by blood or marriage to the nation's great fortunes footed the bill, or else the benefactor was a mammoth beauty corporation that needed help with its image. In either case, the relationship made the hairdresser a business executive. To make these salons break even, they had to attract a large clientele and a considerable staff to render them service.

The most talented hairdressers are artists of the scissors and comb. In the affluent Sixties, painters and sculptors moved out of their garrets and were reckoned men of property. The artists of hair changed in like manner. They have impressive apartments and week-end country places. They drive fast, expensive automobiles, and their homosexuality is no longer taken for granted. Some of them, like Alexandre and Vidal Sassoon, write books. With the help of a ghost, of course.

Good hairdressing is not confined within certain national boundaries, but creative styling may be. The newest coiffures are invented to accessorize the newest clothes when they are presented to buyers and the press by the leading designers. The bubble came out of Paris, the geometric cut out of London with the Mod clothes. Some secondary fads have blossomed in New York. The straight fall of hair that Michel Kazan attached to the heads of the models in the Galanos showing of January 1966 precipitated a rush to Alice-in-Wonderland manes among fashion editors and socialites. A year later, it was in the subway.

The haute coiffures of the last decade, however, originated in Italy, France and England. The tool and technique that revolutionized hairdressing, the fat roller and back-combing or teasing, came to America from Europe. The Italian cut (short, curly and casual) infected the world in the mid-Fifties. It was succeeded by the bubble, a straightened and inflated coiffure that balanced the chemise. It evolved into the bouffant of longer hair set on huge rollers, brushed out and teased until it rose like a soufflé, then was sprayed to stay in place.

The excesses of any fashion, no matter how flattering in its initial concept, bring it to ridicule and eventual disgrace. The swollen hairdo gave women, particularly those with nondescript features, a feeling of confidence. The teasing and the hairspray kept locks from straying and that bred assurance, too. But the teasing and the spray were relied on too heavily by unskilled hairdressers who used them to correct their mistakes. The stylist who cannot perform magic with his scissors is the overzealous back-comber.

The large roller eased the hairdresser's task by providing him with pliable hair. The vogue for artificially straightened hair was fueled by the schoolgirl look in fashion and the influence of the Oriental mannequins who captivated the Paris couturiers and prompted outbursts of Eastern styles. The frizzy permanent was like the dress with a waistline and a belt. It announced that the wearer was behind the times.

Teenagers ironed their hair. Luxury hairdressers wielded the electric comb or simultaneously brushed and applied the hand dryer. Women who had been admired in childhood for their wavy hair underwent straightening treatments. In the first half of the Sixties, curls went the way of bosoms, hips, shapely legs and tiny feet. Ugly ducklings had their day.

Late in 1966, when designers were tampering with belts again, Vidal Sassoon came up with a short, permanented style modeled after the head of an ancient Greek god. Elrhodes, the two brothers whose salon on the Faubourg St. Honoré looked like a space ship, followed with a curly, windblown style for the Paris couture collections of January 1967.

Despite the efforts of hairdressers to promote cleverly cropped hair, most women preferred an abundance of tresses. Only Sassoon had really succeeded in selling short, but then his hairdo became a way of life and badge for a certain kind of contemporary woman.

The consummate master of the complicated coiffure, as well as the most prolific creator of current hair styles, is Alexandre of Paris. Author of such mass passions as the beehive, the artichoke and the Marienbad, Alexandre specializes in custom hair sculptures that would have made him a darling at the court of Versailles when Marie Antoinette was in residence.

During Jacqueline Kennedy's triumphal visit to Paris in May 1961, Alexandre transformed her into a Gothic Madonna with bangs and waves surging onto her cheeks. That was for a reception at the Élysée Palace. For a ball at Versailles the next evening, he crowned her with a hairpiece shaped like a tambourine and studded with five diamond pins. The jewels were modest in comparison with the $2.8 million in gems with which he once finished off a hairdo for the Vicomtesse Jacqueline de Ribes, a Parisian banker's wife who is a walking advertisement for the haute couture.

The king of the haute coiffure, as Alexandre likes to think of himself, also serves as his own court jester. "I didn't come to America to sleep," he interrupted a solicitous aide who met him at the airport in New York in 1962. "I came to make a revolution." The rebel was resplendent in a sage-green suede suit and matching necktie punctuated with a gold and ruby bug, a blue shirt with a pleated front, a gold cardigan sweater and tan shoes.

In 1966, when he went to Rome to do the hair styles for Elizabeth Taylor and Richard Burton, two of his most ardent patrons, Alexandre was induced to take a small part for himself in their film *The Taming of the Shrew*. He played the Ambassador of Spain, costumed in black and gold with a thin ribbon of beard following his jawline from ear to ear and digressing up the middle of his chin. He kept the beard for several months after he returned to Paris. Although he frequently works for the theater and the opera—he came to New York in 1966 to do Leontyne Price's wigs for *Antony and Cleopatra,* the first opera given in the new Metropolitan Opera House in Lincoln Center—the Taylor-Burton film offered Alexandre his first professional acting role.

Actually, he never stops performing. A genial ham, Alexandre prances through life like an ebullient character in the copious literature of the French farce. His first tour de force before an international audience occurred in 1955 at the wedding of Princess Ira von Furstenberg and Prince Alfonso Hohenlohe-Langenburg in Venice. As he bent to finalize the bride's coiffure, Alexandre tumbled into the Grand Canal.

Nowadays, he executes his capers in a setting worthy of the national Opéra-Comique. His salon at 120 Faubourg St. Honoré, next door to the House of Pierre Cardin, is a grand endeavor reminiscent of the Second and other Empires. The walls of the high-ceilinged rooms are covered with pastel silks and hung with gold-framed portraits of 18th-century royalty and signed photographs of more recent celebrities either regal or rich. Drawings by Jean Cocteau encrust the green-tiled washing room.

Although a friendly democrat in his manner, Alexandre acts suspiciously like a monarchist sympathizer. His lackeys and his press releases stress his titled clientele. On a steady basis or only when they pass through Paris, Alexandre has coiffed such crowned and un-crowned heads as Queens Frederika of Greece and Sirikit of Thailand, the Queen Mother of Rumania, Empress Zita of Austria, Grand Duchess Charlotte of Luxembourg, as well as Princess Margaret of Britain and Princess Grace of Monaco. Wives of heads of state, like Mrs. Kennedy and Mrs. David Ben-Gurion, have submitted to his comb, as well as such sovereigns of the silver screen as Audrey Hepburn and Greta Garbo, and singers like Juliette Greco and Maria Callas. At the last tally, it was 5 queens, 40 princesses and 10 presidents' wives.

Alexandre is prepared to cloister them in private rooms, if they wish. Usually, however, he performs in the main salon, a large bullpen dominated in the center by a leopard-printed plush hassock. Here, clients in pink smocks—some clutching tiny French poodles—languish between washings, sets and comb-outs. Chez Alexandre, as at most of the great beauty salons, the utmost patience is required of the customer. Waiting is as much a part of the ritual as it is in the dining room of an Intourist hotel restaurant in the Soviet Union. The nervous woman is advised to bring tranquilizers or stay away.

A short brunet with eyes the color of *café filtré* and pearly teeth gleaming beneath his moustache, Alexandre is custom-tailored by Cardin. His scissors are gold. He "creates" in a setting as frenzied as Times Square at theater time. The chair and table at which his client is seated differ from the surrounding ones of his black-suited stylists only in the detail of his portrait that hangs above. A shampoo with cut by Alexandre and a set cost $20 as against $11 if one of his assistants does the cutting.

"Fashion is created by the eye, by the theater, by a pretty woman," he once said. "To adapt it, and adopt it, one must act with prudence. You should not destroy a woman's style but, instead, accent it."

Alexandre slashes away at the client's hair. As it falls in a blizzard to the beige and red parquet floor, an aide whispers intelligence into his ear. Alexandre leaves his victim one-third shorn and rushes over to comb out another woman. "That was Bettina," he says upon his return 15 minutes later. Bettina, as every one knows, was the companion of the late Aly Khan.

Click, click go the scissors until the aide reappears with additional information. This time, Alexandre might be gone for 20 minutes and, if the client has not fainted from staring at her pathetic reflection in the mirror, she discovers upon this return that Alexandre had been conferring with any one of a number of Baronesses de Rothschild.

Eventually, Alexandre signifies with a click that the act of creation is over and directs a stylist in the setting of it. Aeons later, he will complete the confection by combing, teasing, festooning with false hairpieces or whatever the client and the occasion demand. Alexandre's basic cuts are masterpieces of enduring simplicity. His fame rests, however, on the intricate coiffure. Looped, beribboned or bejeweled, it gives the wearer all the breathtaking artifice of a suckling pig dressed by a master chef and laid on a banquet table.

Alexandre is, as a matter of fact, something of a gourmet although his heart belongs to the *ratatouille* and *ailloli* of his Mediterranean boyhood. He was born Alexandre Raimondi on September 6, 1922, in St.-Tropez. In those pre-jet-set days, it was a quiet fishing village on the French Riviera. His mother ran a grocery store. According to his press release—a document that reveals as much about the inner core of a hairdresser as a Rorschach test—he is of Florentine descent with an ancestor, one General Pavone, who fought against Napoleon during the Italian campaign. Alexandre treasures the general's sword and other military relics.

Despite the example of the heroic general, Alexandre has a peaceful nature. "While still very young and under his grandmother's influence," the release states, "he was already strongly attracted by things pertaining to fashion, and preferred dolls to tin soldiers just for the pleasure of curling and dressing their hair."

At 15, he went to work in the salon of Antoine at Cannes, where he soon won his first royal title. He was dubbed King of the Egg Shampoo. "Then came his military service, in the course of which he became orderly to an army chief medical officer with a passion for music, who made him ride a bicycle beside him with his scores while he himself, on horseback, blew a horn. Then came the 'maquis' during World War II and the liberation of France."

Alexandre made it back to Cannes in time to be discovered by Yvette Labrousse, winner of the Miss France beauty contest of 1930, for her wedding to the Aga Khan in October 1944. Alexandre created the Begum's nuptial hairdo. In due course, she presented him to the Duchess of Windsor who invited him to come to Paris and, once, to accompany her to the United States to arrange her hair for a ball.

"Everything I have done is thanks to the Duchess of Windsor. I owe her my career," Alexandre says. With growing fame and a nucleus of customers acquired through the duchess, Alexandre teamed up with the Carita sisters, Maria and Rosie, a pair of Spanish siblings whose salon on the Faubourg St. Honoré is also a clubhouse for international society. In 1957, he entered into an association with Harriet Hubbard Ayer, a cosmetics company started in 1887 by a New York society woman that now is part of the Unilever soap and food products complex, the world's sixth biggest company.

The Alexandre salon occupies the second floor of the Harriet Hubbard Ayer Building. Entrance to the salon is through the Ayer cosmetics shop and into a small, green-walled elevator. Alexandre creates new make-up styles for the company which sells beauty products in 65 countries. He also draws royalties from salons in Beirut, Milan, Brussels, Antwerp, Lille, London, and the Marbella Club in Spain which are licensed to use his name and his hair styles and to send their hairdressers to be trained at his salon in Paris.

Alexandre has come a long way from St.-Tropez to the pinnacle of fashion. Married and the father of a son and daughter in their early 20's he lives grandly in an apartment in the 16th *arrondissement*. It has been decorated by Jansen, the elegant interior decorating firm. There and in a country house at Coulommiers outside Paris, Alexandre serves a lordly table.

"Wines? I serve only Château Lafite-Rothschild," he told Ninette Lyon, *Vogue*'s culinary writer. He has entertained the peers of fashion and the arts—couturiers Yves Saint Laurent, Marc Bohan and Pierre Balmain, painters like Marie Laure and writers like Françoise Sagan. Jean Cocteau was one of his chums.

Alexandre earns his pleasures. On an average day, he works from 9:30 A.M. to 7 P.M. Tuesdays and Fridays are busy days; Saturdays are frantic. During the semi-annual haute couture showings, he creates coiffures for many of the leading collections, then repeats them for photographs to be published in the fashion magazines. At those periods, he keeps going into the early hours of the morning.

Early in 1965, he opened a salon for the pampering of tired businessmen and playboys, on the Rue Marbeuf, just off the Champs-Élysées. Its atmosphere is no less florid than in his Faubourg St. Honoré headquarters, but the theme is that of an English club as filtered through a Latin sensibility. An old English clubman would be distinctly uncomfortable amidst the gold-plated washbasins set in marble counters, the brown buckskin and mahogany furniture, the quantitative touches of buffalo horn (one of Alexandre's passions) that are not damped by the 19th-century regimental prints, the portraits of English royalty and the Highlanders' brass seals on counters. The pair of gold-leaf candelabra that stand in the main hall was a gift from the Duke and Duchess of Windsor.

Not only financiers but monarchs like Prince Rainier and King Hussein of Jordan and actors like Richard Burton and Frank Sinatra have patronized the salon. Alexandre makes himself felt in the men's salon chiefly through his portrait, which hangs in the main styling room. When he visits, he does so as an overseer or a client. He does not wield his golden shears. The styling is entrusted to six male hairdressers who are promoters of longer hair for men. The Alexandre coiffure is relatively short on top of the head, but it grows purposefully into the shirt collar in back. If the hair is naturally curly, so much the better. Sideburns descend almost to the jaw in puffs. It's a romantic, *belle époque* look that goes with the Edwardian suit silhouette of Pierre Cardin. If a client is bald, effort is concentrated on the sideburns and on hiding the bare spot. Polite but firm pressure is applied to dissuade men who demand a crew cut.

At opposite ends of the London hairdressing pole are René and Vidal Sassoon. A woman who knows and admires them both explained the difference: "A *lady* would go to René but not to Vidal."

The stress and pronunciation she gave to the noun were pregnant with British meaning.

René Moulard coifs the ladies (with capital and lower-case els) of the realm, starting with Princess Margaret, whom he accompanied on her trip to the United States in the fall of 1965, and Princess Marina, and working down to Blandfords and Bedfords and the uncoroneted wives of Guinness and Onassis. One expects to find a duchess under the dryer at René's salon at 66 South Audley Street in Mayfair, but it is also expected that her presence will be unheralded. René does not capitalize on his pedigreed clients by talking about them to the press.

Occasionally, he is caught within the press cameras' rangefinders, as when photographers at the British wedding of the year 1961 recorded René in gray topper and tails arranging the hair of Miss Henrietta Tiarks before she went down the aisle to marry the Marquess of Tavistock.

"I respect advertising," said René one day as he was observing his midday ritual of taking lunch and a glass of wine at Massey's Chop House next door to his salon, which closes down from 12:15 P.M. to 2 P.M. "But as soon as I advertise and get too much publicity, I would lose some of my clients. When you have the persons, what could help?"

René's skirmishes with the English language contribute to his Gallic charm, which is of a unique degree of virility in hairdressing circles. As one proper English lady put it, "He's the most adorable, sexy one of them all. He's absolutely irresistible."

She was not exaggerating. René is tall, broad-shouldered and lean with blond hair and matching eyebrows straggling over merry blue eyes. The presence of his wife, Huguette, who tends to business matters and is addressed as Madame René, and two daughters on the verge of the 20's undoubtedly discourages more forthright declarations from his clients.

René came to London in 1950 after a dozen years in the employ of Antonio, then a leading Paris coiffeur. His clients had been on the order of Lady Mendl, Marlene Dietrich, the Gabor sisters and ambassadors' wives. They reported to him when he came to London. After several professional and personal vicissitudes, he opened his present salon in 1955. He prospered "just by relationships and a social clientele, a bit of luck and a bit of talent, a nice connection, don't you think?" asked René, who doesn't overcharge for prestige. Although he is part of the social hairdressing axis which also includes Alexandre in Paris and Kenneth in New York, René's prices are the lowest. He charges 6 guineas or $18 for a shampoo, cut and set. With one of his stylists, the price is $7.

His salon is the least pretentious of the three. It consists of a spacious room with chairs and styling tables against the walls, a rear gallery for shampooing and a rotunda in the center where the customers, fitted out with orange smocks, sit under the dryers on orange and black chairs. The carpeting is a subdued green that harmonizes with the tranquil hum of activity.

Court work, meaning the styling of a Royal head, is done in a room to the left of the entrance decorated with yellow silk-covered walls and an Oriental rug. Her Highness sits before a marble-topped table on a chair upholstered in royal blue.

Everything, in short, is ordinary *chez* René, including his scissors. "To go with my plain and dreadful character," he says with a grin that is just the jolly side of wicked. On a visit to New York, he dropped in at Kenneth's mansion. "He was very nice," said Kenneth's London counterpart. "But when I saw his establishment, I said to myself, 'How can he sleep with this big thing on his shoulders? I would be scared.' "

Like Kenneth, René has a mixed blessing in his most famous patron. Princess Margaret, like Jacqueline Kennedy, has recalcitrant locks that the press photographers' cameras seldom fail to catch. The princess spends a great deal of time in the country and once she took a year to let her hair grow out. Under such conditions, the public tends to blame her hairdresser.

And René, after all, stands for something. A romantic, soft style compounded of tendrils and puffs, all femininity and rounded lines and "a bit of fashion." With it, says René, "a lady can put on a gown from any one [of the great couturiers preferably] and go to a ball and know she will be noticed enough. Not too much.

"I think there is great mystery in women and one must preserve it. Fashion must be a mystery. The reserve, the great elegance of life, of the woman who has been dressed at the great dressmakers, who has been passing at the great jewelers, who has been passing at Maximilian in New York. This is perfection, this is elegance, which I like to see lasting."

In the fashion of hair, as in the fashion of clothes, ideas hover in the air, but it usually takes one person to draft them into an explosive statement. Vidal Sassoon, the Courrèges of coiffeurs, applied modern geometry to hair.

But he also personified the take-over of fashion by youth, the bloodless rebellion of the English underdogs and the fact that fashion is no longer run from Paris, but by an international network. It is no coincidence that Sassoon has styled the mannequins' hairdos for Rudi Gernreich and Emmanuel Ungaro, the disciple of Courrèges. Or that sunglasses by Oliver Goldsmith, the pop artist of opticians, are sold in Sassoon salons.

A Sassoon hairdo discloses more than a conversation about the woman who wears it. "Homely girls have personality with my cut," Vidal Sassoon has acknowledged. "With curls they were nothing. The healthy, sexy, chunky look of the hair gives them a new attitude. Within six months, these girls have new clothes, new shoes." They do the newest dances.

"People keep trying to bring back curls and romance. It's not the age," he said in the fall of 1966. A couple of months later, he brought back curls but in a style for a young Apollo that did not give the lie to what he had said before. The hair was still cut in a geometric shape, leaving the ends as thick as the root. Then it was permanent-waved, leaving an even curl through the hair from the root to the ends. The hair was then rippled through with the fingers. No setting was needed.

"Nowadays women have to do things and they have to have something they can really throw about," he had declared. "Many women are still wearing hair like their grandmothers, but their grandmothers were more elegant because their hair styles fitted into the picture then. Nobody is designing airplanes, ships or cars for 1935, so why ask me to make women look like they did in 1935?"

Vidal Sassoon has no reason for nostalgia about his grandmother's day. His breed of Englishman only came alive in the present. He is not a renegade of the family of English financiers or a cousin of the poet with the same surname. Not unless you trace cousins to the umpteenth degree. "Sure, we come from the same place. We're all the same Sephardic Jews," said Vidal Sassoon in a voice that still echoes the East End. When he first tried to get a job in a Mayfair salon, he was advised to take elocution lessons. He did for a year and it sandpapered the Cockney accent down to the minimum. Now he advises his apprentices to preserve theirs as an inverse snob asset.

Technically, Sassoon is not a born Cockney. His birth certificate says that he came upon the scene in 1928 in Shepherd's Bush, an undistinguished neighborhood in the west of London, a sixpence Underground ride from Mayfair. His father, now dead, was a carpet dealer. The family moved to the East End when Vidal was three. He remembers being evacuated during World War II. "They handed us gas masks and sent us to the country." At 14, his mother took him to a crimper to have him apprenticed.

> I loved football and sports, that's what I was interested in. But I had to work and my mother said why not take hairdressing.
>
> Professor Adolph Cohen, that was the name of the place, on Whitechapel Road in the East End, the ghetto of London. Professor, that's what they called the old master hairdressers. He was a beautiful old man. He said it will cost 100 guineas for the three-year apprenticeship. We didn't have 100 shillings. We were living hand to mouth. And so we started to leave and as we did, I opened the door for my mother. He called us back. "It's a long time since I saw a young man as well-mannered as you," he said. "Start Monday."
>
> I wasn't well-mannered. I couldn't wait to get out, that's all. But it was my first lucky break. I started as a shampoo boy. It was during the war and they had no cleaners so I had to clean the place out first. But I learned finger waving, stand-up curls, reverse curling, effilating, and spiral permanent waving. In any field, before one can really be artistic, one must first be a technician.

Later, Sassoon was to rebel against these techniques, particularly the business of subdividing the hair into strips, pinning them with screw clips and cutting it in layers. The essence of the Sassoon cut is a sculptured shaping of the head achieved with blunt cutting by a smaller than average, four-inch scissors. The hairdresser uses the crown of the head as his guide.

From East End apprentice to lord of the new British meritocracy took 21 years, with a year out when he was 20 to live in the Negev. He worked in several Mayfair salons for about 10 years until a client gave him $8,500 in 1954 to open a salon with another stylist on the third floor of a building in Bond Street. The loan was repaid with interest, but when Sassoon needed $110,000 to move to the street level at 171 New Bond Street, he turned to an international financier for a silent partner. The tycoon gives free rein to the hairdresser, with whom he deals through his attorney.

The New Bond Street salon, the seed of the Sassoon chain, is the most prestigious. It has all the serenity of a Mod mob caught in an oversized telephone booth, but this is where a swinging duchess sits on the staircase and some of the most exquisite "birds" in London press themselves against the corner of a wall, reading magazines and waiting to be set or combed. More than 1,000 clients are tended to each week and sometimes they queue up in the street.

Here, after hours, have come Christopher Plummer, Terence Stamp and some of Vidal's other "mates" in the acting fraternity to have their hair cut. Peter O'Toole's hair was bleached for his role as Lawrence of Arabia at Sassoon's.

Sassoon himself is barbered by one of his staff. His dark brown hair is medium long, parted on the left and brushed softly to the right. His unobtrusive sideburns and his jazz classic tailoring by Doug Hayward and Bobby Valentine, the tailors of London pop society, contrast with the definite Mod appearance of his employees.

Sassoon's boys are, for the most part, longhairs. "You can't," one of them told a client who expressed a desire to let her hair grow, "because you'll look like a boy." These Carnaby Street aficionados give his salons the mesmerizing appeal that warms the modern décor of glass, chrome, stainless steel and black terrazzo.

For all their sleek exterior, Sassoon salons are the friendliest in the haute coiffure. The open space and cheek-by-jowl proximity bring to hairdressing the camaraderie of the Chelsea boutique. The language is swinging London (in 1966, supers and *ciaos* were flung through the air) with footnotes of crimp slang, the argot of the East End hairdresser. Most of the staff is Cockney or provincial. They are remarkably young. Roger Thompson was 22 when he became director of the salon in the Grosvenor House at its opening in 1963. "Our thing is youth; it's not a gimmick," he said. Many come as rosy-cheeked apprentices at 15, paying $600 for a three-year apprenticeship which may be shortened if they learn quickly. They receive $7 a week plus tips, starting as shampoo boys and grasping the scissors after three weeks. They practice during the three "school nights" a week when courageous young women offer themselves as guinea pigs in exchange for free hair styling. Ultimately, they may earn as much as $350 a week and, like Roger, drive an Alfa Romeo. Vidal owned a Lancia at one time. In New York, the apprentice system does not obtain, but a few American hairdressers who were earning as much as $250 a week laid down their scissors to follow Sassoon at $65. A cut by Vidal Sassoon costs $25. A shampoo, set, and cut by a salon director is $12.50.

Another thing that sets Sassoon staff apart from previous hairdressing tradition is their masculinity.

"The hairdressing business here," said Vidal Sassoon during one of his month-long visits to New York, "is all mixed up with the fag thing. It's the wrong attitude. That's the way it was in London until René came over from Paris. Even a hairdresser who had been a wrestler thought he had to get all gussied up like Liberace. I don't care about my people's personal life as long as they are pros. But it just so happens that they are mostly men and they go around New York proving it."

The Sassoon cut, startling as it may seem at first to the woman about to receive it, is a matter of evolution, not revolution, its creator maintains. "I did conventional things for 15 years, soft perms and the like," says Vidal Sassoon. "In 1961, I began experimenting. When you work with designers who are doing something, like Rudi Gernreich and those fabulous birds, Mary Quant and Emmanuelle Khanh, you need to do hair to go with what they are doing. It happened to be me that did it. I worked very hard developing a line. First I took the back and made it short, then gradually longer in front." That year, Mary Quant asked him to fix the hair of her mannequins so as not to interfere with the high collars she was showing in her collection. "All I really did was take the pageboy and reverse it, giving an elegance to the neck. Where most men choose legs or eyes or some other part of the anatomy, I am fascinated by necks. The back of the neck remains good even when a woman gets older. It doesn't wrinkle too much."

Sassoon insists that his look is not only for the young. Fortyish and fiftyish women have tried it. "It's all the bones and the personality," he said, adding a wish that he could put his scissors to Jacqueline Kennedy's mane. "She has the bones," he said with a reverential sigh.

Next, Sassoon tried the one-sided look, long on one side, square on the other. Then he started cutting points. His five-point haircut made him the rebel leader of the haute coiffure. It brought him an offer from Charles of the Ritz, then in search of a youth image, to back him in the United States. In June 1965, the Charles of the Ritz-Vidal Sassoon salon opened in New York at 803 Madison Avenue. Another Sassoon salon is in the Woodward & Lothrop department store in Washington, D.C.

Whatever Sassoon does is based on his theory of perfect cut. He makes the customer stand up and shake her head back and forth until he is satisfied that her hair swings back into proper shape. "She can shake from now until Sunday and it won't fail," he said with pride. "Only thing is she'll get a headache." The hair is set on huge rollers, dried and brushed out while the stylist moves a hand dryer over it for a straightening effect.

Sassoon has continued to evolve his look. He added a heavy fringe over the forehead and down to the eyes. "It opened the eyes and threw out the cheekbones. I must say it worked a charm and suited people who thought they couldn't have worn it," he said. He amplified his geometry with square curls and squared, Veronica Lake wigs for evening. "I must say the girls we worked on had a lot of pluck. They were out on a limb," he admitted. So was Vidal Sassoon. For a while, some of the hairdressing fraternity, as well as the critics of British pop fashion, tried to saw off the limb. But they failed.

"Fashion is very much a young thing," he added. Pushing close to 40, Vidal Sassoon tries rather anxiously to stay young. He keeps fit swimming in indoor pools almost daily and he has the health faddist's implicit faith in wheat germ, honey, vegetable juices, fruit and vitamins. His narrow frame remains as wiry as a 17-year-old's. Vidal Sassoon has no problem about wearing hip-hugger trousers.

In London, he inhabits a flat in Curzon Place in Mayfair. Eugene Howe, who designed his Bond Street salon, decorated it for him in bold, modern style while Sassoon was away on one of his New York visits. "It's a convenient pad," said Sassoon, then a divorcé who didn't stay home much. In February 1967, he married Beverly Adams, an American actress.

A pad, as he once defined it, is "a small place where you deposit yourself and your suitcases and sojourn for a while. Flats are large and people live in them."

Houses are still larger and some people work in them.

Kenneth, America's No. 1 hairdresser as reckoned by fame and influence, installed his salon in one of the most magnificent Edwardian piles in New York. The five-story stone mansion at 19 East 54th Street was valued at $1,000,000 when he leased it in 1962. To turn it into a beauty factory, he selected Billy Baldwin, a decorator who had previously accepted no more commercial assignment than the Round Hill Club in Greenwich, Conn., or some of the offices of Condé Nast Publications. Mr. Baldwin, a pet of the millionaire housewife with multiple residences, has labored in behalf of Jacqueline Kennedy, Mrs William S. Paley, Mrs. Thomas Bancroft, Jr., Diana Vreeland and Mollie Parnis. All of them have been Kenneth's clients.

"But this is like a home," admirers gasped upon seeing for the first time what Baldwin had wrought for Kenneth. "That's right, it's mine," replied Kenneth who had acquired some rather splendid tastes since leaving Syracuse, N.Y., a decade and a half before.

His partners, the Glemby Company, operators of a nation-wide chain of beauty salons, had given him carte blanche with his salon, which was intended as a prestige generator for an eventual line of beauty products, as well as of a luxury salon network. In 1968, a Kenneth salon will open in Chicago in the Bergdorf Goodman branch.

When Baldwin asked him how he visualized his dream headquarters, Kenneth said, "I think the most amusing and pretty place I've ever been is the Brighton Pavilion. However, I remember it being pink and blue and white and gold. I want more character. My favorite color is red and yellow." In his apartment in the East 50's at that time, Kenneth had a red bedroom and bath. Baldwin gave Kenneth exactly what he asked for. And if some fashion outsiders thought that it looked like a bordello, that's because in April 1963, when the salon opened, Susan Sontag had not yet synthesized her "Notes on Camp." That third stream of taste, neither good nor bad, but stylized to the point of excess, was still held exclusively by *Vogue* editors, homosexuals and other pioneers of pop culture.

Nine hundred yards of Indian jungle flower carpeting woven in Scotland, 500 yards of paisley fabric for the tent room in which the hair dryers are placed, the smaller amounts of various printed fabrics for the individual styling rooms, the *chinoiserie,* bamboo wallpaper, rattan and flower-printed Porthault towels added up to a riot of color and pattern. It seems plausible now that fashion has been transfused on all fronts with camp taste. The salon set a trend for the boutiques that subsequently sprang up all over Manhattan's Upper East Side.

The opulence of the décor corresponds to the prices. A shampoo and set are $9, to which is added $25 for a haircut by Kenneth or $8 by a member of his staff. Kenneth's fee for performing outside the salon is $100 an hour or $500 a day plus transportation, a figure that just about quintuples the honorarium that the federal government pays consultants on national policy. He carries his equipment in a black attaché case from Hermès of Paris.

Although working girls who want to splurge are not turned away, Kenneth's is the game preserve of fashion society. Style notes may be cribbed from a glance at the coat rack in the flower-printed cloakroom where clients divest themselves of their spare, horizontally worked mink coats (or their Originala architectural wools or their linen smock dresses or whatever *Vogue* says The Beautiful People are wearing at the moment). The gossip is always the freshest out of the oven in which Eugenia Sheppard's, Carol Bjorkman's and Suzy Knickerbocker's columns are baked, which is to say that the news at Kenneth's has to deal slightly more with the comings and goings, the make-up tricks and the potpourri of conspicuous consumption rather than with passionate romances. It is always possible to glean a crumb or two of information about Jacqueline Kennedy, the establishment's most famous client. But not from Kenneth, who sidesteps inquiries with chilly adroitness. Mrs. Kennedy was resident in the White House when the salon opened and her imprimatur was manifest in the numerous photographs of herself and the President, signed in her finishing school backhand with sentiments such as "For Kenneth, with good wishes always, Jacqueline Kennedy" that adorned the antique tables in Kenneth's sunny, yellow-paisley styling room.

They have since been removed. But Kenneth once admitted, "Mrs. Kennedy hasn't hurt." He added, "Because it's given me a new dimension as a person. The pride in doing her and resisting saying anything about her. To be able to do her without wearing a Jacqueline Kennedy button." Kenneth had been doing Mrs. Kennedy's hair for five years before she became First Lady. He went to Washington to style it for the inauguration and for innumerable occasions afterward. Her bouffant coiffure that swept the nation was his contribution, as was the girlish mane she cultivated after she moved to New York.

Kenneth tends to discount the value of a celebrity clientele. "If we had more celebrities, it wouldn't matter if their hair didn't look better," he said. "Publicity may bring them in, but if they're not happy, they won't come back and bring their friends. Eighty-five per cent of the clients don't come here because of the celebrities.

"I must say it's exciting to have the names and meet the people who are celebrities and to make them look better. Marilyn Monroe had curly hair," said Kenneth, who is one of the proselytizers of straight hair via the roller or de-kinking lotion if need be. What pleased him most about Marilyn, he said, is that "she loved her hair" when he got through with it. So do most women who have been styled by Kenneth. Their gratitude tends to be effusive. Kenneth accepts praise with an expression of almost Oriental inscrutability. He is the Mr. Cool of the haute coiffure. The only thing that ruffles the calm, he says, "are people who don't know their job; then I feel myself becoming violent."

Toward the client, however, Kenneth behaves with the impersonal punctiliousness of a Park Avenue diagnostician. "Are there things you love or hate about your hair?" he asks. "Is there a way you always wanted to wear it and never did?" Often as not, the reply is, "You're the doctor."

When Kenneth starts cutting, the impression of the skillful physician heightens. He is a careful, methodical cutter. He wields the scissors and razor with his left hand and interrupts his silences only for professional queries such as, "Is this your own wave?"

The client sits in a brown leather chair studded with nailheads that can be raised or lowered like a dentist's chair. Her feet touch a needlepoint footstool monogrammed with a K. It takes Kenneth at least 20 minutes, more likely 30, to do a haircut. The set requires another 15.

One reason that women submit with such confidence is that he does nothing radical or contrived. His forte is a soft coiffure with a natural swing. A woman invariably feels pretty after a Kenneth hairdo and some man invariably confirms her feeling with a compliment.

Kenneth is one of the cleverest stylists of short, flattering coiffures. His shell cut was a masterpiece of brevity. In 1967, he predicted a gamine haircut like Mia Farrow's. Nevertheless, his reputation is pegged to an abundance of tresses, usually achieved with the contents of his wig room. Undoubtedly, this is because the fashion editors and the clients with whom he is in closest touch have steadfastly refused to be bobbed. Diana Vreeland has always believed in lots of hair. It takes a certain kind of woman to feel female with a Sassoon haircut and the women who go to Kenneth are not that kind. Some of them went from being debutantes to society matrons without changing the length of their hair. Others simply realized that a mane is a safer way to arrest attention than a small, neat head. A good listener, Kenneth gives women what they want. "Nothing is for everybody," is his verdict on hair styles.

The soft sell characterizes Kenneth's technique as a businessman. A low-key actor in a showy setting, he dispenses personal skill with authoritative precision. Kenneth may be one of the foremost artists of the shears, but he is also the president of Kenneth Beauty Salons & Products, Inc., as well as vice president of the Glemby Company. In the latter capacity, he gives demonstrations and trains stylists. Kenneth is the Picasso of coiffure, comporting himself like Robert S. McNamara.

"The hairdresser is certainly an artist to an extent," he said shortly after the salon opened. "But he is a servant. That word doesn't scare me at all."

Kenneth employs a publicity girl, as do most leading hairdressers, but her job is to arrange for photography and to deal with fashion and beauty editors. Kenneth's publicist is not expected to grind out myths about her employer. He does his own talking and it is straight from the shoulder. Kenneth, the all-American hairdresser who always thought the title "Mr. Kenneth" too arty, has an all-American biography.

Kenneth Battelle, born April 19, 1927, comes out of Syracuse, N.Y., a university and industrial city in the northern part of the state. He has made no effort to excise the flat, almost Midwestern twang of his native habitat from his speech.

His was a considerable family of females consisting of a divorced mother and four younger sisters. He served in the United States Navy for 18 months, "mostly as a war-bond salesman," he recalled. "I used to play a portable piano. It was so small I was continually running off the keyboard."

After his discharge, he enrolled as a liberal arts student at Syracuse University but financial pressure soon obliged him to leave. "Since I had six months left on my G.I. benefit, I looked around for a well-paid vocation I could master in that time. Hairdressing seemed to suit me. I'm not exactly the construction-gang type. I had enough of piano playing by that time and I'm not a painter. But I wanted to get into a creative job so I signed up for a hairdressing course." He had written to *Vogue* to advise him on the selection of a school. "I got a list of schools three miles long from them and finally chose the Wanamaker Academy of Beauty Culture in New York because I liked the sound of the name."

Kenneth augmented his $65-a-month allotment by playing the piano in supper clubs. He also had a bit part in a Broadway show that folded in two months. With his hairdressing diploma in hand, he returned to Syracuse where he worked for four years in a local beauty shop learning and practicing everything there was to know about the trade from manicures to hair coloring.

As soon as his sisters were out of school and able to fend for themselves, he set out for Miami to seek his fortune. He didn't find it and within the year was in New York trying out at Helena Rubinstein's salon, which was then directed by Michel Kazan. Kenneth stayed for five years and acquired not only a knowledge of haute coiffure but friendships with the fashion press. Working on assistant beauty and fashion editors and setting hair for photographic sessions brings nothing lucrative in the way of tips, but it does afford an opportunity to invent styles and to make contacts. As Kenneth went up in the world, so did many of his customers.

His next way station before striking out for himself was the beauty salon that Lilly Daché had added to her millinery establishment. In the six years that he tarried there as chief hairdresser and salon director, Kenneth coiffed the wife of Senator John F. Kennedy and a bevy of stars like Marilyn Monroe, Judy Garland and June Allyson. By then, he had become something of a connoisseur of the arts— one of his favorite hangouts is the Parke-Bernet auction gallery —and a confidant of the distaff power elite. He can chitchat knowledgeably with them about their special interests like Antigua, the latest museum acquisition and the real nature of Bobby Kennedy.

Kenneth is a man of average height and girth and a round face with even features and gray-blue eyes. His thinning sandy hair, just the least bit flecked with gray, is styled by Jerry, who also ministers to William S. Paley, the chairman of CBS. A snappy dresser, Kenneth was wearing shaped suits and chicly noisy haberdashery long before dandyism was recognized by the American men's fashion industry. The double-vented jacket with the flaring skirt, the wide tie fixed with a jeweled stickpin, the vividly colored shirt and the pinky ring have been in his wardrobe for years. The only discordant note in his peacock elegance are his wedge and rubber-soled oxfords. They testify to the fact that Kenneth's luxuries are acquired by hard work standing on his feet.

What with photography sessions, sorties to the homes of super-celebrity clients for sets and comb-outs on grand occasions, traveling, lecturing and the normal details of running a large enterprise, a 14-hour day is no more unusual for Kenneth than for any corporate executive. Lunch forgone or gobbled at 3 P.M. between client appointments is not exceptional either. He turns up at a number of fashion society happenings just to keep current on how hair is being worn. Kenneth is an authentic pop-fashion celebrity but, although a bachelor, he does not function as an escort service.

He has put a great deal of his money and his soul into a week-end summer retreat on Fire Island, a resort off the Long Island coast that has a diverse population of beatniks and settled families. Kenneth's house is at a narrow point of the island overlooking the bay and a dune's throw from the ocean. It is an elegant beach house in an eclectic style of West Indian, Japanese, modern and period. There is no electricity and no nearby places to shop. Just seclusion and only an odds-out chance of encountering the beautiful butterflies who dominate the public life of Kenneth Battelle.

X

THE MALE OF THE SPECIES

IN the Sixties, men and women discovered they had something else in common besides the game of seduction and the institution of the family. The new subject of mutual interest was fashion. The haut couturiers, led by Pierre Cardin of Paris and Hardy Amies of London and John Weitz, an American sportswear designer, took to designing clothes for both genders. They found masculine fashion infinitely more rewarding.

Toiletries, cosmetics and hair-dye producers followed suit. By the mid-Sixties, annual sales of scent and beauty preparations for men had reached the half-a-billion-dollar zone. Among teen-age couples, the trend was to smell alike, as well as dress and coif alike.

Newspaper and magazine writers compiled and published Best-Dressed Lists for men. *Vogue* and *Harper's Bazaar* appointed men's fashion editors. Among the new pop fashion celebrities were men, not necessarily of the arts or the clothing industry, who were perfectly willing to disclose the secrets of their wardrobes and even pose for fashion photographs. The His-'n'-Her fashion show sparked a boom in what had been a splinter vocation, professional male modeling. In particular demand were Mod models with Byronic hairdos and pencil-slim hips who could jerk to the Mersey beat, and broad-shouldered mannequins with tame haircuts and thrust-out jaws who could feign the virility of a Quai d'Orsay diplomat or a Wall Street banker.

What caused this outburst of togetherness, this renaissance of the dandy in an era of technology? Pessimists attributed it to male decline. As women became more aggressive, invaded masculine professions and usurped male prerogatives, men fell back on being peacocks, they reasoned. With clothes, men were reconstructing their diminished manhood.

Undeniably, women were rethinking their place in society and the respective roles of men and women were being revised. Concurrently, as feminine clothes became less intricately made, less interesting (even to the point of disappearing), masculine raiment took on shape, color and provocative detail. On a more positive note, however, the male fashion explosion could be attributed to the shorter work week and longer periods of leisure, the liberalizing effect of travel, affluence, and the influence and preponderance of the young.

Finally, it was a matter of harmony. "When a woman gives a party so that she can wear her Ken Scott pajamas, she won't have her husband in gray Dacron. She wants her family to keep up," observed Jack Daniel "Danny" Zarem, an executive of Bonwit Teller, the Fifth Avenue women's specialty shop that installed a Pierre Cardin men's boutique in the fall of 1966.

Mr. Scott, the Hoosier who found fame and fortune in Milan designing ebulliently printed outfits for women to wear in their own and other people's homes, did his best to be helpful. In January 1967, at the semi-annual fashion showings at the Pitti Palace in Florence, he sent 25 male Milanese university students out on the runway in wide-legged host pajamas, flowered jackets with zippers and no lapels, and evening sweaters with embroidery on the collars. Each model was accompanied by a girl mannequin in a Ken Scott dress. Most of the American buyers smiled and paid no heed. But the point of Ken Scott's presentation was completely logical. After Eve ate the apple, and gave one to Adam, didn't they both sew themselves fig leaf aprons? Once women learned the psychological, social and economic uses of fashion, could men stay ignorant for long? Could a Rudi Gernreich-Vidal Sassoon kind of girl find lasting happiness with a man in a Hickey-Freeman suit who had his hair clipped at the corner barbershop? Obviously not. Fashion coordination of the sexes was the solution of the Sixties.

In this decade, women and the fashion industry have ganged up on the American man to rid him of his inhibitions about dress. Actually, the assault was world-wide but the potential return was greater and the going rougher in the United States. Outside of the Ivy League collegian and the western cowboy, there had been no deep-seated tradition of masculine currying. Englishmen hallowed their tailors and Italians their barbers, but the American man aspired to look clean, neat and undistinguishable from the next suburban commuter. Furthermore, he was terribly sensitive about his masculinity. It took constant travel and observation that abundant hair and the scent of perfume did not seem to hamper the feats of the Latin lover to make him buy fragrances and hair sprays. Clairol tied its advertising of Great Day men's hair coloring to the economic asset of youth and such two-fisted users as longshoremen, farmers and policemen. Furriers who realized that their salvation lay in the temptation of the male customer stressed the he-man angle.

"I analyzed the situation and decided that two things were holding men back from wearing furs," said Ernest Bogen, a Seventh Avenue furrier. "One is the questionable masculinity of the wearer. But if you go back far enough, you can associate fur with the caveman, Tarzan and the Huns. There's that feeling of overcoming the beast and taking his coat for yourself. Then there is the matter of price," Mr. Bogen continued. "A man who spends $5,000 for a mink coat for his wife will not spend $1,000 on himself, even the kind of man who would buy himself a $500 vicuña coat."

He and other furriers who explored the heretofore virgin territory of men's fur fashions scored their biggest breakthroughs with ski parkas and car coats made of hair seal, wolf, raccoon, wolverine and calfskin that cost no more than several hundred dollars. The furrier who thought up a double-breasted ranch mink coat (hair up, no less) to sell for $4,500 had to take it apart and restyle it for a woman.

It took the advent of pop culture with its exhibitionism, its mass media bombardment, its externalizing of the search for identity and its conspicuous consumption to turn the tide. The watershed of male fashion history was 1966, just as 1964 had been for women. In 1966 the shaped suit passed into the men's clothing manufacturer's line, the foulard pocket handkerchief into the middle-class husband's and father's Christmas stocking. The crew-cut man in the shapeless gray flannel suit was a grocery clerk or an unregenerate electronics corporation executive. Jerry Spallina, the Madison Avenue hair stylist (as the jet set calls its barbers), described the effect he was striving for in these terms. "When I get through, the customer should look like he needed a haircut three or four weeks ago."

The length and luxuriousness of a man's sideburns were the barometer of his cosmopolitanism. At chic men's salons like Jerry's, the sideburns were sprayed with hair setting lotion, brushed and dried with a hand-held appliance to make them fluffy. The technique was comparable to what went on in women's hairdressing parlors under the name of teasing.

All of these symptoms portended a drastic change in male fashion that had been gathering momentum through the decade. James Laver, the costume historian, suspected in 1964 that it might be as severe as the one that had occurred at the border of the 18th and 19th centuries. At that time, he pointed out, Beau Brummell and his confreres among the Regency dandies started wearing dressed-up versions of hunting clothes in town. These sporting outfits of plain cloth signified, wrote Laver in an article in *The New York Times Magazine,* "that the day of aristocracy was over and that the day of gentility had arrived. There were to be no more peers wearing their orders proudly on their embroidered coats. There were to be only gentlemen in plain cloth and immaculate linen . . . no more beplumed and gold-laced tricornes, but only well-brushed top hats."

Gentility became formalized monotony as the 19th century progressed. Male fashion evolved through the periodic adoption of other sporting fabrics or styles for ordinary wear. But gentlemen did everything possible to avoid being noticed by their clothes except through the discreet sign language of cut and tailoring.

"The long reign of gentility is over," Laver concluded in 1964. "What kept men's clothes formal for over a century was the idea that there was something 'caddish' in any departure (at least in town) from a very rigid norm. This restriction seems to have been overcome. A man no longer feels it necessary to show his social caste by his clothes. . . ."

In the last sentence, Laver must have been thinking about England, where the class system seemed to be breaking up although even there the Mods had used fashion as a form of social protest. In the United States, the curious phenomenon of increasing social snobbery, evidenced in the proliferation of debutante cotillions and the growth of the fashion-society columnist, found a tool in men's fashion. Male seekers after social status, as well as rich men's sons who chose the dilettante path, set themselves apart from other Americans by their clothes. Their reward was the equivocal distinction of becoming fashion leaders.

The designer who went to work tie-less and socks-less, aping the millionaire sportsman-playboy, was light years ahead of the Ph.D. economist who always wore a white shirt and discreet cravat to his office in the computer corporation. "Leisure is becoming status," Danny Zarem observed. Could a fashion trend that seems to deny the need or desirability of work be prescience in the age of automation?

The dandies of the technological epoch are a motley segment of the population. Homosexuals, teenagers and an increasing group of men such as actors, communications specialists, fashion industrialists and others who have a commercial interest in their appearance set the pace of the new sartorial excitement.

Without the homosexual network in retailing and editing and the adolescents waving their easy-come, easy-go dollars, it is unlikely that the archconservatives of the menswear manufacturing industry would have come around to the shaped, double-breasted suit for another half decade.

On the burning issue of the decade, hair length, such diverse types as John F. Kennedy, Jr., the Beatles, Marc Bohan of Christian Dior and the salesmen in Splendiferous boutiques stood shoulder to shoulder against such reactionaries as school principals and the United States military.

Male fashion leaders were goaded by wives, playmates and other female associates. If some day, as John M. Willig, the men's fashion expert of *The New York Times* Sunday department suggested, men will be "discussing their clothes like horseplayers discussing bloodlines ('You like this suit? It's called Executive Suite—by Esterel out of Lord & Taylor')," it's only because the Courrèges by Kimberly out of Saks Fifth Avenue practitioners will have taught them how.

The male of the species is more of an individualist than the female fashion plate although his idiosyncrasies are more complex and subtle. A fashion ignoramus could detect Courrèges boots or a Saint Laurent Mondrian dress, but it takes almost as much effort as a senior college thesis on Persian art to discourse knowledgeably on the merits of Turnbull & Asser haberdashery, Lobb footwear or the comparative tailoring philosophies of Bernard Weatherill, a New York Englishman, and Charles Harmaniantz of Paris.

"I'm concerned with fit and look," explained Danny Zarem, a shoe manufacturer's son from Savannah who acquired the habit of elegance at Yale University right after World War II. He was a fashion whip for the men's retail division of Genesco before he transferred to co-educational merchandising at Bonwit Teller.

"I go through as much as Mrs. Paley," he said. "I drive the tailor out of his mind with the shoulders and armholes but I do it so that once the suit is in my closet I never think about it again."

Generally, American male fashion leaders incline toward the custom-made suit. In clothes well tailored to his measure, a man's shoulders stay straighter and the incipient paunch fades from sight, they agree.

Price is not the factor it is in women's fashion where made-to-order clothes cost as much as school tuition. The best ready-made suits for men are in the $95 to $200 range in New York, where custom tailors ask $245 and up. London tailors charge $185 and up. The custom department of Pierre Cardin in Paris, where prices hover at the $400 mark, is the most expensive.

London tailors are the most status-fying for Americans but the game of instant fashion recognition is terribly tricky. Getting to London regularly for fittings puts a man one-up on the innocent pretender who deals with Savile Row tailors on their semi-annual prospecting trips to America. On the other hand, the incipient snob who boasts offhandedly that he can always spot a coat by H. Huntsman of Savile Row by the way the shoulders look in back is in danger of being put down by a patron of Blades of Dover Street, one of the swingier custom establishments. The smuggest smiles were worn by those who possessed the telephone number of Doug (for Douglas) Hayward, the underground tailor to London's most distinguished Mods and other notably successful internationalists in the popular arts and finance.

Just into his 30's, tall and compellingly attractive by virtue of his searching blue eyes and a nose shaped like a blackthorn stick, Hayward has outfitted several lords and one Beatle (Paul McCartney), Cockney screen stars like Terence Stamp and Michael Caine, and Americans like Kirk Douglas, as well as John Osborne, the writer, who would be accused of betraying the angry young men if he turned up in a Savile Row suit. A range of superbly tailored corduroys answered his needs.

Until he surfaced and settled into a shop on Mount Street in the spring of 1967, Doug Hayward called upon his clients in their homes or hotel rooms and accepted new accounts only upon personal recommendation. "Hullo," he answered the telephone suspiciously in his workroom in Fulham, a rundown section of Southwest London that his clients never saw. If a newcomer's credentials passed muster, Hayward drove over to see him in his blue Alfa Romeo and spent an hour over a drink discussing anything but suits.

"I get an idea of the image he wants to project," Hayward said. "A suit should be an extension of one's own personality. What *they* are wearing means nothing. When I see a man in his own environment, he can't be pompous. When a man goes into Savile Row, he's either aggressive or submissive. Both are bad attitudes."

Hayward is one of those vigorous new talents from humble backgrounds who brought vitality and ambitious standards of achievement to British arts and crafts in the Sixties. A native of Hayes, a small town near London, he started as an apprentice tailor at 15. In 1963, he struck out for himself in a small basement room in Pall Mall. His first client was an international film producer, who ordered 10 suits. In less than three years, Hayward was pledged to the pop celebrity fraternity. "I get invited where no tailors ever were before," he admits. His wife is a television film production manager, his friends are on the order of Sassoon and Stamp and his club is the latest Chelsea trattoria in which they assemble.

Thus far, Hayward has put no distinctive style into fashion currency. "What's the point of everyone walking around with the same back or the same sleeves, the same lapel?" he asks. "If that's the case, you might as well turn them out by the ten thousands. Everyone wants to feel very personal and you don't have to wear purple suits to do it. I'd like to line up 10 people for whom I've made suits and no one would know they were made by the same tailor.

"Oh, if I get a young man with an undeveloped personality, I suggest something loosely based on Cardin. Slim but it looks tight. What I do mostly is based on a classic line with a modern look. It's the same all over the world now. A slim line with high vents in the jacket, width at the bottom of the trousers. If I do a modern film, I may do something Mod but I'm not a Mod tailor."

Hayward designed the clothes for the actors in *Modesty Blaise* and *Casino Royale* as well as for several European television films. In 1966, he flew to Hollywood to produce four suits for Tony Curtis to wear in *Don't Make Waves*. He has a growing list of customers who await his periodic visits to Rome, Paris, Berlin and Munich.

No male fashion leader is likely to have less than two dozen suits and several dinner jackets in his closet. Nor will he have to rent a tailcoat for white-tie occasions. If he patronizes a custom tailor, he surely has his shirts made to order as well. Custom-made underwear, on the other hand, as one authority said disapprovingly, is "the ultimate ostentation."

Cummerbunds and frilly shirts with dinner jackets—or referring to the latter as tuxedos—draw the gentlemanly shudders of the New York leaders. For them, black tie means black jacket even in subtropical resorts.

"Blue jackets are for the frilly-shirt people," proclaimed S. Joseph Tankoos, Jr., an international real estate investor who owns two socially approved hostelries, Delmonico's in New York and the Colony in Palm Beach. His wife, Ruth, belongs to the Norman Norell, Paris haute couture and coordinated real jewelry clique of fashion leadership.

White dinner jackets are unspeakable as far as Mr. Tankoos is concerned but Pierre Cardin would disagree. A white piqué dinner jacket (double-breasted and priced at $150) to be worn over a zippered, white piqué evening shirt for $40 was one of the introductory bonbons in the Pierre Cardin boutique at Bonwit Teller.

Mr. Tankoos, a regular on Best-Dressed Men's Lists, is a split fashion personality. "I dress for the environment," he said. In Palm Beach, Southampton and Monte Carlo, he blossoms forth in emphatic shades of pink and green. "But all solid colors, none of that plaidshirt business for me."

In New York and London, where he goes on business "every 8 or 10 weeks for about 48 hours" (and nips in to "keep another suit going in the pipeline" at Hogg Sons & J. B. Johnstone, Ltd.), he is a study in dark blues and grays. "I like to go out a lot and I'm very busy," said Mr. Tankoos, an activist in fashion society. "I often don't have time to go home to change from a gray check to a dark suit. So I start out in the morning ready for anything that turns up." The transition from day to evening is marked by administering the electric razor that he keeps in his office cupboard.

Mr. Tankoos cuts down on the number of vital decisions he must make by wearing tasseled loafers with everything. His midnight-blue Chesterfield overcoat, with which he sports a matching or light-gray homburg, go beautifully with his blue and silver Rolls-Royce.

In the Sixties, the ferment in men's fashion occurred in London, the traditional capital of male elegance for almost two centuries, and in Paris, the feminine stronghold. To a certain extent, the cities switched sexual roles. London became a fascinating aviary (the Mod synonym for a girl is a bird) and consequently a center of young female fashion. Paris yielded a bumper crop of dandies dancing to the tune of Pierre Cardin. But London did not lack a masculine revolution. The gorgeous birds paired themselves with male Mods, those working-class boys of 15 to the early 20's who wielded economic power by preening themselves.

The barricades of the male Mod rebellion were on Carnaby Street, an obscure alley behind the grand shopping thoroughfare of Regent Street. On Carnaby Street, England's new cocks of the walk found their plumage. In its informal boutiques, the youngsters from the provincial towns and the city slums bought their boisterous finery—shirts that screamed in print or pattern; trousers that delineated their slim, boyish hips and flared toward boots; peaked caps to clap on flowing heads of hair. Keeping step with the fickle tastes of its adolescent clientele, Carnaby Street fashions provided an alternating current of shocks. Up vinyl vests, down Norfolk jackets; stringbean ties one week, five-inch flowered cravats the next.

Along with the Beatles, Carnaby Street became an international symbol of youth's new assertiveness. Like the pop musical entertainers, it was adored, deplored and exploited. By the mid-Sixties, it had made poor men rich, suckers out of the unknowing.

John Stephen, a grocer's son from Glasgow, was the tycoon of Carnaby Street. Before he was 30, he owned 10 of the shops on the grubby lane and another 14 in the London area. He drove about in a Rolls-Royce and was hailed as a savior by American merchants seeking instant fashion bait for young spenders. John Stephen boutiques, characterized by eardrum-piercing pop music and striped plastic tents for fitting rooms, broke out across the United States and Canada. The Dayton Company of Minneapolis led the way in 1965. Stern's, a New

York department store that was anxiously rejuvenating itself, called its department John Stephen of Carnaby Street to make sure that no one missed the point.

By the time that Carnaby Street had become a sacred name in the New World, the original had degenerated into a shameless tourist trap. The unkempt, unwashed representatives of the international dropout cultures in filthy jeans and World War II officers' jackets jostled the German, Japanese and American sightseers on the narrow sidewalks. French couturiers came to buy dishtowels made out of the Union Jack, to giggle at the mural of the naked man in one of the shops' fitting rooms and to inspect the sleazy satin mini-dresses and frilly G-strings in the all-girl boutique on Carnaby's offshoot, Ganton Street.

Diners' Club and American Express credit cards were pasted in the windows of the Carnaby Street shops, which indicated how much they had lost their spontaneity and their economical prices. A pair of checked hipster pants in one of John Stephen's emporiums was $16, one of the ubiquitous turtle necks, $11.75. Hardly bargains in any medium of exchange.

Early in 1967, the American menswear industry admitted that Carnaby Street had been mined with booby traps. Mod stood for "mark ours down," according to one melancholy joke in the trade. Young males had shown themselves to be as fickle as females in their attachment to clothing styles, the merchants said. The industry had also neglected to do its sociological homework. If it had, it might have comprehended that the American teenager did not have to prove the same point of social injustice by overspending on outrageous garb that English lower-class youth did.

But although Carnaby Street had become the nadir of pop fashion, its constructive influence cannot be dismissed. It had even infiltrated Savile Row. A generation of wealthy, young and cosmopolitan Englishmen, like Princess Margaret's husband, Lord Snowdon, and the peers' sons who were experiencing the exhilaration of making money in once despised, now booming occupations like communications and international sales, still respected the luxurious quality of custom tailoring, but they also wanted some of the liveliness of Mod styling. The tailors of Savile Row and Sackville Street, heretofore the most uncompromising of snobs, flinched, but they narrowed the trousers and dispensed with the cuffs if the customer insisted.

"I don't like Carnaby Street, but I must be grateful to it," Doug

Hayward said. "If not for them, I wouldn't be here. Ten years ago, no one would have trusted a tailor under 50."

And if the Mods had not publicized fashion togetherness, would the haut couturiers have found it so easy to hurtle into male territory? Hardy Amies, the archetype of the haughty dressmaker, Anglo-Saxon breed, has proved that in fashion it is possible to be all things to both sexes. Dressmaker to the Queen, designer of expensive, ready-made women's clothes, and style catalyst for the international common man —Hardy Amies is all of these, at least. From an authentic Georgian mansion on Savile Row, he keeps a foot in two opposite worlds, one of the tight, privileged past, the other of the democratically expanding present, while joyously raking in hard currencies with both hands. In 1966, Hardy Amies estimated that he was drawing royalties on $70 million in world-wide wholesale volume of men's clothing and accessories bearing his name. His women's fashion activities accounted for sales of $3 million.

The location of his empire's headquarters is fraught with strategic significance. His neighbors to one side are the bespoke firms like Huntsman that know how to put a customer in his place and whose notion of sales promotion is to permit passersby a view of their tailors sewing behind the glass windows of their basement. On the other side, toward the top of Savile Row, at No. 18, is one of the John Michael men's shops with those American credit cards prominently displayed in the windows and merchandise hung on chrome-faced mannequins and ticketed with plausible prices. The clothes here have a slightly American accent with an overtone of Italian. They aren't really Mod but neither are they furled-umbrella and black-bowler fashion. The shop and a score of similar ones belong to a manufacturer, John Michael Ingram, who claims Lord Snowdon, Rudolf Nureyev and the Aga Khan on his list of customers.

Ingram is Ingram and Huntsman is Huntsman and never the twain shall meet except that they do in a way at Hardy Amies. The Scottish doorman who helps the ladies out of their Rolls-Royces, ushers them up the steps and over the threshold of No. 14 is a radiant fellow done up like a musical-comedy master sergeant in a navy-blue uniform festooned with quantities of gold braid and rows of campaign ribbons. Sergeant Murie is part of the Hardy Amies family, an aide explains, even though he is rented property. He is a member of the corps of commissionaires, veteran noncommissioned officers who hire themselves out to commercial enterprises like Amies' that want a touch of pomp and circumstance.

Inside, the House of Hardy Amies exudes the aura of haute couture with taupe carpeting, crystal chandeliers, gauzy curtains, fragile chairs for customers to perch on while taking in the collections, and saleswomen in slate-blue wool and pearls. When business is sluggish, they sit behind an interior bay window that overlooks the staircase from the first landing. The House of Hardy Amies was once the dwelling of Richard Brinsley Sheridan, the dramatist and parliamentarian. He died there in 1816. Before that, he had suffered financial ruin and, they will tell you at Amies, he used to peek out the window to see whether his callers were creditors.

That is not Hardy Amies' problem these days. He receives his visitors, who must huff and puff up to the top of the house and through cramped passages (18th-century mansions were not built for commerce) before they attain his office, a book-lined room pointedly furnished with a rosewood and stainless steel desk that is pure second half of the 20th century.

"What the hell are they going to wear in Australia?" cried Hardy Amies in a booming, upper-class voice to a caller on a sunny morning in the fall of 1966. The day before, buyers from three continents had jammed into one of the ballrooms of the Savoy Hotel to see the annual collection of menswear he designs for Hepworths Ltd. "These are young-at-heart, good clothes in good taste which we dare to hope leads to good manners," the commentator told the assembly in confident, British broadcasting diction. He implied that taste levels would rise in their respective countries, and so would profit margins, if they placed orders for Hardy Amies-Hepworths clothes, which are cut along tapered lines with slender trousers and meager lapels and here and there a suppressed waist.

The press had seized upon one of the styles in the collection, a suit with a pair of shorts in place of trousers. Since London was earning world renown with its mini-skirted girls, the outfit had been dubbed the mini-suit, to no one's surprise.

The collection had an international theme calculated to demonstrate that Hardy Amies can prescribe for the well-dressed man around the globe. When he reached the end of the collection and Sydney, he had asked himself the question and supplied the answer most likely to put the name of Amies in headlines.

Hardy Amies has a definite flair for dramatics, a talent which first manifested itself in school theatricals. He made his debut as Jessica in *The Merchant of Venice*. Nowadays he plays the witty, urbane, impeccably attired British bachelor as written by Noel Coward. Six-foot-one and lean, with navy-blue eyes, brown hair and a fine nose, he once moved Gloria Emerson of *The New York Times* to pronounce him the world's most handsome royal dressmaker.

Amies will not be restrained behind his desk. He doesn't chat, he declaims, turning his noble profile to be admired by his caller. One hand slips easily into a pocket; the other grasps his folded tortoise-rimmed spectacles. He is John Gielgud posing for Yousuf Karsh.

A descendant of an old Kentish family, Edwin Hardy Amies was born in London in 1909. His father was an architect, his mother a saleswoman at Miss Gray of Bond Street, a court dressmaking establishment. He attended Brentwood, a public (or as Americans would say, private) school in Essex, tried for an open scholarship to Cambridge University and when he failed was sent to the Continent to learn French and German. His father thought those languages might equip him to be a journalist. Instead, he became a salesman for a weighing-machine company, then a business analyst for the House of Lachasse, a London couturier. In 1937, having become managing designer, he jumped into the limelight that was shining on London for the coronation of George VI, with a tweed suit called Panic.

In 1939, he joined the army as a private and was assigned to the intelligence corps. Later, he volunteered for parachute training but never put it to use. In 1944, by then a lieutenant colonel, he was assigned to head the Special Forces Mission to Belgium. The Belgian government decorated him for his service after the war. In 1946, following demobilization, Amies secured financial backing from British and American friends and opened his own couture house in its present site, later adding the house next door to his property.

He and Norman Hartnell, with whom he shares the title of Dressmaker to the Queen, founded the Incorporated Society of London Designers. Nicknamed the "Big Twelve," it was the world's most exclusive if hardly the most adventurous fashion organization. As a spokesman once explained, "Our members must be able to design evening gowns that can be worn with tiara and casual tweeds that look right in a Tudor castle. Paris sells fashion; we sell clothes."

The honor of holding a royal warrant of appointment has its drawbacks. Amies' creative instincts are held in check by such considerations as the fact that Queen Elizabeth is most often photographed exiting from an automobile and her dressmaker must provide her with clothes that enable her to do so with maximum grace.

"Headed by the Queen herself, a list of customers reads like *Debrett,*" discloses the typewritten biography that Amies gives to the press and prospective licensees. It goes on to drop the names of a few viscountesses, countesses and duchesses. "Mr. Amies is particularly pleased to record the fact that a number of his customers are distinguished ladies of American birth such as Lady Brownlow and the Countess of Sefton."

The trouble with this upper-crusty background, as Amies was not the only couturier to perceive, is that it is atrophying. "The handwriting was on the wall," is the way Hardy Amies put it. "Although someone else wrote it. It had always been permitted in couture to do sidelines, preferably of a steady nature apart from the bubble and squeak of couture. In Paris, they have the scent business which exploits the name of the dressmaker. We've never been able to do it in England largely because we don't have the fields of Grasse.

"The couture here, we make a modest profit, but it's not very exciting in modern terms or for the energy expended. So we started the boutique in 1950." Installed on the street floor just inside the front door, as couturiers' boutiques usually are, the Hardy Amies boutique sold ready-made clothes. In 1961, the production of the clothes was undertaken by one of a large group of manufacturers using the Hardy Amies label. Other manufacturers are licensed to make Hardy Amies blouses, scarves and knitwear.

"I put some ties in the boutique and then a firm came along and said, 'Will you design men's shirts for us?' This was a gimmick, I think, although they weren't a gimmicky firm at all. Then tie people came along and said, "Look. In Paris couture they are doing ties; you should do it, too.' "

That was in 1957. "It went rather like a bomb," said Amies, understating the case with a slang expression that has opposite meanings on different sides of the Atlantic. "Next thing I was invited to do things for Hepworths. That was in 1961. I didn't know very much about mass-produced men's clothing but luckily, I'd acquired a financial adviser and he looked into the company."

Hepworths Ltd. is a vertically integrated company of multiple tailors that manufactures moderately priced men's clothing at the rate of half a million suits a year for its 380 retail stores in Great Britain. The multiple tailor is a British institution that accommodates the Englishman's desire to make a statement about himself with his clothing.

Aristocrats and British gentlemen have always gone to custom tailors. Starting in the 19th century, companies like Hepworths (which was founded in 1864) catered to the new industrial middle class by offering its members a choice of silhouette, shape of trouser and fabric. Through mass production, the prices were kept low. A Hepworths suit designed by Hardy Amies costs between $54 and $90, depending on the fabric. The customer is measured, receives a try-on of the suit and delivery within five weeks.

"I don't think that they or we knew what we'd got hold of," said Hardy Amies after his sixth collection for Hepworths had been presented. "Then we said, 'Hell, we've got to have hats and shoes and gloves.' We found ourselves talking to these firms and they said, 'Hell, we need you.' A pajama firm said, 'Come and talk to us about pajamas.'" As one of his aides rejoiced, "Now we can produce a Hardy Amies man from top to toe."

Amies asserted, "Three per cent of the men in this country have been influenced by me in the important part of their wardrobe. I've shortened everybody's overcoat." The Hardy Amies mini-topcoat—whether in checked wool to match the suit, in fake fur to wear in a sports car or in waterproof cotton with colored wool lining to brave a storm in—terminates at mid-thigh.

> My gillie collar, on a high-fashioned suit jacket, has been copied all over the world. I'm influencing the taste of the country. Or at least I hope so.
>
> This men's explosion, why it's absolutely dotty. It came about because there are no professional gentlemen anymore. There are none. Where is the Prince of Wales, the king of men? Now style is classless. The only thing that isn't classless is quality.
>
> It's somewhat of a bore for me, though, because now everyone wants to talk about clothes to me. At least it used to be that when I was with the chaps, I didn't have to bother.

Men as well as women are always intensely interested in what Hardy Amies is wearing. Honor obliges him to confess that his personal wardrobe is custom-made in his workrooms.

> Two years ago, I decided I liked all the blue suits in my wardrobe best, so I went over completely to blue [said Amies, an azure vision in a sapphire-blue suit with a gold and black silk kerchief stuffed in its breast pocket, a robin's egg blue shirt and a nearly navy blue knit tie].

> I always wear bright navy blue now. "You're in blue again, I see," they say, and I say, "Yes," and then they shut up. When I go on a trip, I pack a couple of dozen shirts. I know they are going to be blue. A dozen ties. I know they will be blue. My dinner jackets are dark blue. My dinner shirts are still white and I think they are likely to remain so.

> At first, Hepworths resisted blue. We can't sell blue, they first said. For the first two or three years, they wanted browny olive greens. Then they had a frolic with burgundy. It absolutely swept the States. It was horrible. The fancier the color, the better quality is necessary to put it over.

> Then I realized why the masses were against blue. It was too near the old blue serge like daddy said they had to have. I've a tremendously unsophisticated audience, you know. Hepworths is strong in the provinces.

> I said, "I don't mean *that* blue." A women's designer has very helpful tricks. But I couldn't say to a chap, "Blue is becoming to you; it makes your skin look younger. Blue is one of the most becoming colors. It does things to your pigmentation."

> My staff is all wearing blue. I've just done it this season although the house colors were white, brown and black. One thing I'm envious of is Pierre Cardin's Bleu Marine [confessed Amies, looking downcast for the first time. The title of Cardin's male fragrance means navy blue in English].

He perked up as he contemplated his forthcoming trips to Melbourne, for a promotion of Hardy Amies menswear as manufactured by an Australian company, and to the United States and Germany where he hoped to make similar arrangements. In December 1966, he signed a five-year contract with Genesco as men's design consultant.

Genesco manufactures Hardy Amies suits and coats to sell for $100 to $150. His task was to do for the upwardly mobile males of Newark and Nashville ("the Mr. Everyman of discrimination," he said) what he had done for those of Manchester and Bradford. As he had explained in his *ABC of Men's Fashion,* a slim volume published in 1964, "I feel that some of the success I have achieved in designing clothes for men, in a very wide market, is because I have been able to become a bridge between men of the established classes and those who shop in the High Street."

The *ABC* gives helpful advice for such emergencies as what to wear in the enclosures or the boxes at the Royal Ascot Meeting ("It is not necessary to wear a silver-gray tie") or to funerals ("Friends are happy to lend you things"). It also contains many kernels which reveal more about the author than the subject. The bowler hat should be worn "either square on top of the head or tilted forward on to the nose. It should never be worn abroad, never by foreigners, and Americans who attempt to do so should be fined."

As for shorts, wrote Mr. Amies before he was faced with the problem of Australia, that "inelegant" style should never be worn except on the beach or a walking tour.

"A clean pair of pyjamas each night is a luxury which makes riches worthwhile," he philosophized. "Many men give up and wear nothing."

Pants. "We mean the things we wear under what the Americans call pants."

Buttonhole. "Unless you are Mr. Gulbenkian or a stationmaster, you should never wear anything but a dark red carnation, or possibly a white one for a wedding."

British style. "No one will now disagree that the well-dressed Englishman is the international beau ideal."

Hardy Amies, who had packaged British snob fashion for the masses, might have to make a few adjustments for the American Colonies.

The most influential voice in high fashion for men during the Sixties was raised by another women's designer, Pierre Cardin of Paris. In 1961, Cardin, whose ideas had always been considered just a little farfetched, opened a pair of boutiques on the street floor of his house at 118 Faubourg St. Honoré. He called them Adam and Eve and filled them with the usual repertoire of accessories and relatively inexpensive ready-to-wear to divert his regular clients and attract the American tourists who like to impress their friends back home with a couturier's label, even if it is on something minor like a scarf, sweater or a necktie. But Cardin didn't stop there. In 1962, he presented a collection of men's fashions with his regular haute couture showing and from then on, the Adam boutique with the bottle-green velvet walls became the mecca for the new French dandies.

Cardin had been personally dissatisfied with men's fashion. French tailors had been stuffing their clients into suits of woolen armor with heavily padded shoulders and foreshortened jackets. The young people of Paris, on the other hand, had made their mark after World War II with the beatnik look.

Cardin proposed a slender, supple silhouette that was an obvious imitation of the Edwardian English gentleman. It was a lean look based on a hacking jacket with a natural shoulder, slim sleeves set in a high armhole, a nipped-in waist and a pronounced flare below the waistline. The trousers were essentially Levi's with a modified bell shape. Like Carnaby Street, Pierre Cardin owed something to the American cowboy.

The fabrics in which the suits and matching coats were made were sober enough. District checks and plaids and earth-colored tweeds were again the passion of the English country gentleman. Forceful colors, arresting stripes and checks were applied to shirts and neckties, which expanded to four inches in width. Hats had heightened crowns and a rakish curl to the brims.

Anglomania raged among French youth, who wanted instant fashion packaging from the English landed gentry. One of the foremost sartorial heroes of youngsters who weren't even born when he abdicated his throne and embarked on a career of pointless leisure was the Duke of Windsor, exemplar of the audacious cravat and clashing patterns in tweeds and shirts.

The double-breasted navy blazer, shetland pullover and regimental striped necktie became the French equivalent of the American gray flannel suit of the Fifties. "Shetland smells of security," said Danny Zarem of Bonwit Teller. Not by chance were two of the boutiques that catered to the rich kids of the 16th *arrondissement* named Mayfair and Harvard. They dispensed a full range of shetland and other English classics.

Cardin knew how to Gallicize Anglomania better than anyone else. Frenchmen—and others, like Cecil Beaton, who look to Paris for divine fashion revelation and can afford to patronize the Adam boutique—paid him from $360 to $400 for a suit made to measure. Those who could not gave him the compliment of copying him. The couturier saw to it that he benefited from the flattery. Forty manufacturers were licensed to produce Cardin's men's clothing and furnishings, on which he reaps royalties. (A ready-made Cardin suit sells for $80 to $90 in France.) To maintain the standards of quality without which chic becomes caricature, he concerted their activities and reserved rights of approval on several matters, including distribution. The name and the styling of Cardin were disseminated throughout the world via Cardin men's boutiques or departments in leading stores. In 1966, the global trade in Cardin men's merchandise was estimated at $12 million a year, probably 15 times what his women's activities yielded.

On the other side of the Faubourg St. Honoré, he opened a six-story, modern palace where a man could be completely outfitted by Cardin in either custom or ready-to-wear. The house at 118 reverted to a strictly feminine domain.

One of the most perceptive and farsighted men in French fashion, Cardin was not content to stick with Edwardian England. In 1966, he contemplated the future and apparently decided that men will be too busy for gentility. It also seemed a little ridiculous for girls in flat shoes and short skirts to be seen with men dressed as their great-grandfathers. He made his point by showing masculine and feminine fashions together in his fall collection, in the first half of which he introduced his cosmo-corps silhouette. The distaff version was based on a jumper worn over a contrasting turtle-neck jersey and matching miner's helmet. The glowering male mannequins who accompanied the girl models into the salon wore similar headgear. Their trousers were straight and seamless and tucked into gaucho boots. Turtle-neck sweaters were topped by sleeveless, roll-collared vests that fastened up one side with industrial zippers.

This space-age fashion decree, which did away with jackets and neckties, was a little too much for the average male citizen to countenance. Even intrepid souls faced the wrath of restaurant headwaiters. Some of the women who saw the collection were disturbed by an ancient Grecian note: the meaningful glances that one of the slim-hipped mannequins in the avant-garde garb exchanged with the homosexuals in the audience.

When the Pierre Cardin boutique opened at Bonwit Teller a few months later, little of the cosmo-corps styles were stocked. Even so, the updated Edwardianism struck most American males as daringly extreme. "I bought the hat," said David Evins, the shoe manufacturer who, despite his constant exposure to high fashion, is a representative of the solid citizenry. "Eventually, I'll work down to the jacket. If I were younger, I'd wear those trousers."

While Hardy Amies of London and Pierre Cardin of Paris were invading America, John Weitz of New York had captured London. John Weitz-designed menswear was selling at the Austin Reed shops, one of the more spirited and Americanized retail operations with its own manufacturing setup. Weitz' manly face and form, modeling John Weitz clothes, of course, appeared frequently in British newspapers and magazines.

Weitz's British press splash was engineered by one of the most effective London publicists, John Addey, who also saw to it that Vidal Sassoon did not keep his light under a bushel. Weitz, author of an unpublished novel and columnist for a London magazine, has never been a slouch at self-promotion either. But the fact remained that he had something valid to say to a powerful male audience in Britain and the United States, for whom his approach to fashion was the sanest and the most useful. For this reason, more than his drumbeating exercises, John Weitz was at last winning the recognition he had sought for 20 years as a major force in fashion design.

"I'm the modern man's designer," he said late one afternoon in the fall of 1966 in his studio at 110 West 40th Street, a two-minute sprint from the jungle of Seventh Avenue. He was preparing for one of his trans-Atlantic hops.

"The modern man should be able to pack in the tiniest of suitcases and travel at the drop of a hat." He removed his beige worsted jacket lined in white and gold houndstooth check and rolled it into a ball. He wasn't risking much because the jacket had neither shoulder padding nor canvas backing through the body. "He should depend on no servants. When he gets to a hotel and has to change into dinner clothes and the valet service is closed as it always is, he shouldn't be bothered."

He unrolled the jacket, shook it out and held it up, uncreased, for inspection. "People are deluded by polka dots, put in a tizzy by the houndstooth lining. They don't see the truth of clothes," he declared in a British-tinged baritone. He slid back into the jacket.

"Slant pockets. Why? Because I spent years of my 43 trying to find my pockets here." He jammed his hands into imaginary horizontal slits.

"I'm building modern clothes for modern men," Weitz repeated, doffing his jacket again. "The modern man should be able to wear the identical shirt on business or on a boat." He unknotted his wine-red necktie, slipped it off, unbuttoned his pink shirt and pulled it out of his trousers. Weitz stood there, in his modern office 23 stories above the sidewalks of New York, all six foot two inches of rugged, brunet, strong-jawed, hairy-chested self. Here was Tarzan about to call Jane out of her penthouse, or maybe James Bond poised to jump into bed or a swimming pool. The purpose of his striptease accomplished—Weitz wanted to show that his shirt was squared off at the hem—he pulled himself together again.

"Dinner shirts. Mine have instant cufflinks." He produced a white broadcloth shirt with small brass buttons. "So the modern man has no worry about losing the box of studs and wrinkling his shirt getting into them. I know the jewelers won't like me but I always lost those damn little cases with the studs. And I've sacrificed all the pleats. I don't expect to be Errol Flynn at night," said John Weitz, who enjoyed one of the best swashbuckling reputations in American fashion. Now, just beginning to go gray at the temples, he has closed the daredevil chapter of his life and settled down with his third wife, former actress Susan Kohner, and their toddler son into a kind of dashing, haut bourgeois existence.

Take the John Weitz shoes, they're gloves for the feet [said he, wriggling a foot out of a golden brown suede moccasin buckled at the side and folding it like a bedroom slipper]. But what will you do in the winter, they ask me. In the winter, I go from my office to lunch at the Colony, then to a meeting. Between the Colony and the meeting, it's a slush race. I want light shoes because they'll go inside rubber boots.

I've aimed at tomorrow's man. Not the astronaut but merely tomorrow's businessman. The interesting men are the increasing group of young, middle-aged people. I'm not really concerned with kids. I'm concerned with the terribly young, 40- and 50-year-olds like myself. The men who run the businesses and the men behind the groups who make the noise on TV. The *nouveau* young.

Fashion is only the instrument through which people belong to a group. All I do is follow my own taste. That's style. In Europe, they are great on styling but they do nothing on construction or to change the design of clothes.

Cardin's suits are based on the 1910 cavalry officer's stance, the *gentle*man's stance. [Weitz struck a pose with his left foot thrust forward, his chest thrown out and his nose turned up toward the ceiling.] Carnaby Street has taken the Edwardian look and dandified it.

I'm concerned with the man of 1970. I started with Brooks Brothers, the Chanel of menswear, the first to make natural clothes. I'm merely going several steps beyond Brooks Brothers.

I call it contour clothing. I like a waistline [possibly because he still has one]. Because I like the nipped, one-button jacket and I make it soft so that the button can do the work instead of that old-fashioned darting.

I discarded two buttons at the waist but not the two at the sleeve. Why? Because I didn't want to go into a business meeting and have someone say something was missing. I keep the notched lapel because right now I would be dreadfully embarrassed with a shawl collar in a business meeting.

Men are more vain than women. Because of their fearfulness and conservatism, it takes more effort for men to look chic than women. The negative is also effort, you know. I'm not willing to say I want to be disbelieved because of the length of my hair or the color of my shirt. I would never wear brown suede shoes in a business meeting in Detroit.

My appearance must suit my security. My clothes must be so styled that they don't need courage to wear them.

The only place a man looks elegant is at the thigh [he gave a profile view of his trouser leg]. You see, slim thighs and straight down to the shoe. Contour pants.

Weitz trousers are stovepipes that start just above the hipbone. He did away with the waistband in order to bypass the spare tire that he noticed develops when a male waistline is encircled by a straight leather belt.

Weitz put his hat on. A modified brown Stetson, it had a floppy brim and a wide, red and white paisley band.

> Once a month, I wear it and if at the end of the day I feel I've been through an obstacle course of smiles, I put it away. The day I can go through a whole day without a single person giving me a look or pushing his elbows into his friend's ribs, I will have a manufacturer make it. I'm through trying to prove a point. Now I'm suggesting this hat as a field hat to wear with corduroy pants and leather jackets in the country.

John Weitz men's clothes reach the public through a variety of manufacturers with whom he has design contracts and who pay him a fee for each collection. At $135 to $185 for a suit, $30 for pants, John Weitz is top-bracket ready-to-wear. He is a one-third owner of a company that manufactures in small quantities the suits that are sold in the John Weitz Shop at Lord & Taylor, the Fifth Avenue store that provided the first showcase for his designs. That department serves as a pilot boutique for his newest ideas. The next stop is the John Weitz Shop in the Austin Reed store on Regent Street in London. A season later, many of the designs are mass-produced by the Austin Reed wholesale division on a world-wide basis.

A number of John Weitz Clubs—he prefers the word "club" to boutique, just as he chose the word "aroma" instead of scent or fragrance for the cologne in his International Club line of toiletries—have opened in prestige stores throughout the country.

John Weitz was one of the first Americans to recast himself as a wide-ranging free-lance designer in the manner of Emilio Pucci or Emmanuelle Khanh. Today, he designs children's clothes for Weather Winky, girdles for Perma-Lift, and a compact collection of women's sportswear for the Season One boutiques at Abercrombie & Fitch.

> Isn't it peculiar to do men's clothes in a women's store [like Lord & Taylor] and women's in a men's store [like Abercrombie & Fitch]? I don't think the sexes are moving together but the clothes certainly are.

Weitz has been retained by industrial companies for advice on a variety of subjects from the use of plastics in playpens to safety in motor cars, the design of airplane interiors and the directing of fire-arms to the female market. During the Kennedy years, he told Quaker Oats to raise its status by offering mother-and-daughter outfits "with the Jackie and Caroline look" as box-top premiums. In those days, he did not consider such activities remote from his basic business as a women's fashion designer.

> I'm like the original dressmaker. He was the man who understood women, told them to change their hairdos, told their husbands what to get them for Christmas. I'm an adviser on the subject of dames.

In 1964, he entered the menswear arena. It has become the most important part of his business.

Weitz had been one of the most intelligent, straight-talking and capable women's designers on Seventh Avenue. Fashion editors re-acted to him as college girls to a victorious halfback, and the women who wore his designs were grateful for their functional verve. Yet John Weitz, who was always mentioned as one of the brighter young American designers, in the same breath but not as kooky as Rudi Gernreich, never quite seized the brass ring on the fashion merry-go-round.

Weitz refers to Rudi Gernreich and himself as Central Europeans. Rudi was born in Vienna, John in Berlin. His father was a clothing manufacturer. For the same reasons that the Gernreichs left Austria for Los Angeles, the Weitzes went to England.

John attended St. Paul's, a public school in London. He used to recall it as the place where he played varsity rugby. These days, he is too caught up with enjoying and multiplying his success to dwell on distant school days or the feats of derring-do which colored the earlier Weitz legend.

At 16, he became an apprentice to one of the great dressmakers. This decision to work with his hands instead of studying for a uni-versity degree was at the core of Weitz's personal dissatisfaction during the next 20 years. But he has come to terms with himself. Now he can say with some pride, "Sports are my hobby. My craft is dressmaking and tailoring. I can stand and drape all day." He would have to be caught in the act to be believed. He looks too much like a sportsman, an actor, an advertising executive, anything, in short, but what Americans imagine fashion designers to be. The avocation of journalism is a soothing outlet for Weitz, the sidetracked scholar.

He spent a year in Shanghai waiting for his visa to the United States and playing more rugby. Three days after his arrival in New York, he went into the army as a private and emerged as a captain at the end of World War II.

Weitz' mother had gone into business manufacturing housecoats and hostess lingerie. He joined her for a while until he had the chance to show some of his sketches to Dorothy Shaver, the president of Lord & Taylor, who had encouraged other young American designers like Bonnie Cashin, Claire McCardell and Gernreich.

Miss Shaver put Weitz in touch with a manufacturer and his career as a sportswear designer began. He achieved more than modest fame for his clean-cut clothes that, unlike most designers' efforts, really could be worn sailing or shooting or skiing and therefore won the respect, as well as the gleam in the eye, of the skilled sportsman. He appeared in the sports columns as often as on the fashion pages. An excellent swimmer, a snow- and water-skier, bobsledder and water-polo player, he also competed in sports-car races and was a member of the British Morgan team at Sebring.

> I was like a lot of Central European boys [he says now]. "Motor racing was my baseball. It was my heroic thing to do. A lot of us went into it in America because there were no professionals. As soon as we developed our breed, we dropped out. I was like the San Marino tennis champion who finds himself at Forest Hills among the Aussies. There are not many tennis players in San Marino.

> I keep the list of the 1957 entries at Sebring so that I will never be tempted. [He extracted the list from his desk drawer. His name is at the bottom of the list on which 15 names were circled.] They're all dead now. [He pointed to the circles.]

> I stopped racing in 1958. The last time I raced I did it because *Life* wanted me to do it for a story. My partner was killed and I said to myself, "What am I doing this for, just because a magazine wants me to?"

> I like racing car drivers. They were the first group of internationalists who invaded this country. The only way to find out

what was happening in London or Rome yesterday was through them. They pretended death wasn't there. When someone dies they say, "That cannot be because I have an appointment with him tomorrow to go to Monte Carlo." I wasn't like that. When I saw a crack-up, I couldn't keep up speed for the next four laps.

But Weitz wasn't just a sporting designer. He did some of the best maternity clothes of the century, neat, cheerful and not too expensive. As the father of three children from two of his three marriages, Weitz could be presumed to be cognizant of the architecture and whims of the pregnant woman.

"I was a flop in maternity, except for the 300 women or so who adored the clothes," he said. "There are so many factors. You can have a marvelous, willing manufacturer but the wrong retail outlets. Or the right retail outlets and no facilities to sew the clothes." Weitz went through all of the wrong combinations. He also resented the myth of Paris:

Paris is where the greatest attention is paid in women's fashion. A burp there is worth an aria.

Anyway, with me, in women's wear design I was never quite believable outside of sportswear. I'd be showing evening dresses and they'd be damn nice evening dresses and someone would say, "When are you bringing out the pants?"

And so finally I said to myself, "If I can't make it in women's wear world-wide, I'm going to make it in menswear." I feel natural in menswear because for the first time I'm wearing my own clothes. I'm working out all my bugaboos, all the things I'd say to a tailor and he would say they can't work. And I'd say, "I know they can because I'm a trained tailor." Once at Henry Poole in London, they said to me, "We suggest you do your own, sir."

Weitz does a gratifying imitation of a Savile Row tailor talking down his nose. "Then they took me off their list."

Now Weitz is in a position to call the shots and to pick and choose. It's a comfortable position to be in. "When I was young and small, I got stuck with licensees. Now I'm a big boy and they have to listen to me," he says, not vindictively.

I hope by the time I'm 60 or 65, I'll have made my dent and can sit back on my rear side. I don't expect to be more important than a clothes designer deserves to be, which is not very important. A designer is nothing more than a visual, social columnist. Clothes may be part of a time and if they say, "Oh, yes, that was the time of the Beatles and the John Weitz contoured suit . . ."

No, if they just say the contoured suit, I'll be satisfied.

INDEX